Among the Jasmine Trees

Among the Jasmine Trees

MUSIC AND MODERNITY IN CONTEMPORARY SYRIA

Jonathan Holt Shannon

Wesleyan University Press MIDDLETOWN, CONNECTICUT

Published by Wesleyan University Press,
Middletown, CT 06459
www.wesleyan.edu/wespress

First Wesleyan paperback 2009
Printed in the United States of America
5 4 3 2

ISBN for the paperback edition: 978–0–8195–6944–8

Library of Congress Cataloging-in-Publication Data

Shannon, Jonathan Holt.
Among the jasmine trees : music and modernity in
contemporary Syria / Jonathan Holt Shannon.
p. cm. — (Music/culture)
Includes bibliographical references (p.), discography (p.),
and index.
ISBN-13: 978-0-8195-6798-7 (cloth : alk. paper)
ISBN-10: 0-8195-6798-1 (cloth : alk. paper)
1. Music—Social aspects—Syria.
2. Music—Syria—21st century—Philosophy and aesthetics.
3. Syria—Social life and customs—21st century.
I. Title. II. Series.
ML3795.S415 2006
780.95691—dc22 2005028912

The publisher gratefully acknowledges assistance from the
Manfred Bukofzer Publication Endowment Fund of the
American Musicological Society.

Wesleyan University Press is member of the Green Press Initiative. The paper
used in this book meets their minimum requirement for recycled paper.

In Memoriam

FATEH MOUDARRES

(1924–1999)

Dedication

To my mother,

LINDA KAY SHANNON

Damascene jasmine
Has white claws
That pierce the walls of memory . . .

—Nizār Qabbānī,
Lā Ghāliba ilā Allāh

CONTENTS

FIGURES

A NOTE ON TRANSLITERATION

In this work I use a transliteration system adapted from that of the International Journal of Middle East Studies (*IJMES*). For Arabic text in the modern standard variety (*al-fuṣḥā*), I closely follow the IJMES usage with the exception of initial al-, which appears only in proper names and Qurʾānic verses. The transliteration of the different varieties of colloquial Arabic spoken in Syria presents numerous problems. I have aimed for clarity and in most cases have brought the transliteration in line with the standard variety so that readers unfamiliar with Syrian colloquial may identify the standard equivalents, if they exist. I use the standard Arabic plural forms, although in many cases I utilize colloquial plurals when the standard plural forms are seldom or never used (*nās muḥtaramīn,* not *muḥtaramūn*). When Arabic plurals would prove awkward or unnecessary I have used the English -s (e.g., *dhikr,* pl. *dhikr*-s, and not *adhkār*). Speech is transliterated in the closest approximation to the variety used. Qurʾānic text citations refer to the Arabic original and translations are adapted from N. J. Dawood's translation (1991). I give proper names full articulation and use European spellings for commonly used proper names (George and not Jūrj) and non-IJMES transliterations when individual artists use them in their own publications or recordings (Moudallal and not Mudallal).

The transcription of Arab music presents unique challenges of its own. I have again aimed for simplicity, using capital letters to indicate all pitches. The neutral second interval ("half-flat" or "quarter-tone" interval) is indicated by 𝄳 and the "half-sharp" by 𝄲.

PREFACE

Now in the final act,
disaster tows our history
toward us on its face.
What is our past
but memories pierced like deserts
prickled with cactus?
What streams can wash it?
It reeks with the musk
of spinsters and widows
back from pilgrimage.
The sweat of dervishes
begrimes it as they twirl
their blurring trousers into miracles.

—Adonis, from
"Elegy for the Time at Hand"

Maṭlaʿ: An Elegy for the Time at Hand

In his "Elegy for the Time at Hand," the Syrian-born poet Adonis evokes a sense of the modern condition in the Arab world.[1] With lines echoing T. S. Eliot's *The Waste Land,* he conjures a bleak vision of a society mired in decay and grief for a withered past. Later in the poem, images of decay and waywardness mix with an almost apocalyptic violence as the Arabs approach what the poet calls "the final act" of their contemporary drama. Facing an eternal "sea" of exile and impotent to shed tears, they utter bootless cries while the salt spray stings their wounds. According to Adonis, "the time at hand" has come, the here and now of the struggle for the future; and yet, in this vision the Arabs respond to impending disaster by escaping to the banality of nostalgia and the solipsistic comforts of mysticism.

Adonis presents a bleak vision of contemporary Arab society, and a deeply cynical view of current responses to the crisis of modernity in the Arab lands.

Indeed, the Arabs find themselves living through a period of marked crisis, their aspirations for cultural and social modernity thwarted by lengthy periods of colonialism, postcolonial instabilities, persistent economic stagnation, and crises of political legitimacy. From the struggle for Palestine and the devastation and bloodshed in Iraq, to internal struggles for self-determination from the Maghreb to the Mashriq, Arabs still face numerous challenges in meeting the needs of the present and in articulating visions for the future—one that looms as increasingly uncertain.[2]

Among the Jasmine Trees investigates how music in Syria shapes debates about Arab society and culture, and how discourses of decline and crisis have shaped music. In doing so I attempt to show how, contrary to Adonis's bleak vision, many Syrians recover a source of strength and vitality in their cultural heritage in an effort to negotiate a pathway to modernity. In the context of the search for modernity, aesthetic practices such as performing and listening to music come to play an essential role in the elaboration of concepts of personhood, community, and nation. They do so through accessing rich domains of sentiment and affect, which, I argue, play an important role in defining modern subjectivities in Syria today.

In Syria, as around the Arab world, the arts are an important arena for the struggle for the future. These visions increasingly evoke the past, often through discourses of a return to the Arab heritage—a response that Adonis decries in the poem yet that remains powerful in Syria today. The turn to heritage in the quest for an authentically Arab modernity produces in contemporary Syrian art what I call "the aesthetics of authenticity"—practices of cultural creation and consumption that promote the formation of social worlds based on a dichotomy of the authentic, perceived as true and good, and the inauthentic, perceived as false and bad. In aesthetic realms ranging from music and poetry to painting, architecture, and narrative, among others, Syrians find either remembrances of lost glories—of the literary and scientific achievements of ʿAbbasid Baghdad, medieval Cordoba, or early Arabia—or reminders of present failures—of imitation of the West, the loss of traditions, and shattered hopes for the future.

From the early twentieth century through the 1950s, Syrians, like their counterparts in other Arab nations, drew inspiration from the West and embraced many elements of European culture, just as Europe drew enormous inspiration from the Orient, as Edward Said (1978, 1994) has demonstrated. Yet, from the 1960s onward, many intellectuals, politicians, and artists sensed that Westernization simply had gone too far and had led to a loss of local cultural specificity.

As one Syrian film critic told me, "In the fifties we used to say '*kull shī faranjī baranjī*' [Everything from the West is Best], but now things are different. There's a lot more interest in heritage and old things." The category of "heritage and old things" does not consist simply in a catalogue of cultural traits and artifacts, such as what one might find in a museum. Understandings of heritage are fluid and contested, and many factors play a role in determining what particular individuals consider to be heritage in the first place. For this reason, heritage might best be understood as a tradition involving collective memories of the past, conceptions of selfhood and social identity, and attitudes toward the future (MacIntyre 1984; see also Kirshenblatt-Gimblett 1995, 1998). In a similar manner, the Moroccan critic Muḥammad ʿĀbid al-Jābrī (1991) suggests that heritage is to Arab society what the autobiography is to the individual. That is, like the individual's attempt through autobiography to create order from the chaos of a life's events and experiences, heritage represents Arab society's attempts to make sense of itself, to find or impose order, and often to round off the rougher edges of what is commonly understood as history.

Different cultural agents use heritage in different ways to support their interests. Self-styled defenders of tradition, for example, tend to emphasize the Islamic aspects of heritage, while cultural modernizers often see these same elements as sources of backwardness and instead emphasize more secular intellectual and artistic domains. Some Syrians reject heritage altogether as an impediment to modernity. For their part, politicians utilize the discourses of heritage and authenticity to promote claims to authority and legitimacy. This often occurs through specific channels of patronage, for example in organizing heritage arts festivals, as well as through forms of censorship that restrict the public sphere.

Yet, Arab fascination with heritage and history, suggests Adonis, has resulted not in its valorization so much as its debasement; now reified as "heritage," Arab history is being dragged, the poet writes, "on its face" by the disastrous circumstances of the contemporary world. Echoing Adonis, one Aleppine poet remarked, "We walk on our *turāth* (heritage) as if it were *turāb* (soil); here there is little respect for the past, and little understanding of it." According to these poets and others, an overriding interest in the Arab past and the numerous discourses of authenticity and heritage that accompany it have not led to a sought-for reawakening—instead, it merely has produced another form of cultural slumbering (see Mbembe 1992, 2001).

Another way of understanding cultural "slumbering" is as a crisis of cultural confidence—what Adonis has described as a "double dependency" on the Arab past and on the Euro-American present for cultural models because of a lack of Arab creativity in the present (1992: 80). Evidence for this abounds in contemporary Syrian culture. From modern poetry to architecture, painting, and music, the glories of Arab civilization are considered by many Syrian commentators to be long faded as novel genres, many inspired by European cultural forms, dominate the cultural scene today. Decay, if not decadence, tends to be a prominent theme in discussions of Syrian culture, and music has come to occupy a prominent position in current debates about the present course of Arab society and its future prospects. Six centuries ago, the Andalusian scholar Ibn Khaldūn argued that music serves as a barometer of social-cultural change—prophesying cultural upswings and declines.[3] How can the crisis of contemporary Arab culture be heard in its musical forms? What might the turn to heritage in all its aspects, including the musical, indicate? Can it bring forth new currents of thought and give new directions to Arab society in the twenty-first century?

Poetry is the supreme art of the Arab peoples, with a rich history and vibrant contemporary presence. Indeed, modern Arab poets are somewhat akin to American rock stars and it is not uncommon for a reading by such well-known poets as Adonis or Mahmoud Darwīsh to draw crowds in the thousands. Music has been closely allied with poetry from pre-Islamic times to the present, with shared oral aesthetics of performance and listening, and shared roles in the construction of modern subjectivities around the Arab world (see Racy 2003). For that reason, the twentieth-century Egyptian diva Umm Kulthūm could rise to prominence not only as the "voice of Egypt," as Virginia Danielson (1997) shows in her important study, but in many ways the voice of the Arab people more generally, and of their aspirations. Both because it has a distinguished place in Arab cultural heritage and because it is the most popular, accessible, and portable of artistic media, music engages and orients debates about culture and society in Syria and is an essential player in how the past is used to authenticate and thereby legitimate various contemporary cultural practices. Popular music in its many varieties is easily the most widely listened to music in Syria as elsewhere in the Arabic-speaking Middle East. The music associated with high culture and the classical Arabic language—what some might call "classical Arab music"—has more limited popular appeal, though many Syrians would acknowledge its symbolic weight and importance. Yet, because of its associations with tradition and heritage, the music offers a rich cultural space in which performers and listeners mutually construct "authentic" aesthetic experience, and at the same time mutually construct what it can mean to be modern in Syria today.

Aesthetic practices such as music need to be understood not only as art forms but as mediating practices that promote modern conceptions of self and society. While these conceptions are related on some levels to European ideologies, Syrian artists and cultural brokers deploy them as critical alternatives to European modernity in what some scholars are calling a quest for alternative or counter modernities.[4] The construction and evaluation of authenticity in musical performance engage with much broader and deeper debates about culture and the nation that are at the heart of postcolonial aesthetics in a variety of contexts.[5] For many Syrian musicians and music lovers, modernity consists not so much in European techno-rationality, but rather in a cultural realm animated with spirit and sentiment, and expressed through a discourse of the emotions. "Oriental spirit" (*rūḥ sharqiyya*), "emotional sincerity" (*ṣidq*), and "musical rapture" (*ṭarab*), among other terms, not only describe musical aesthetics but also promote conceptions of personhood, community, and nation that need to be thought of as posing a counter-narrative to European Enlightenment ideologies that stress the autonomous, rational self. As Kathryn Geurts (2002) has shown, sensory aesthetic terms often index deeper affective and moral states. My aim is to uncover these associations in Syrian musical worlds and to show how affective and moral states associated with musical aesthetics participate in the construction of modern subjectivities in ways more subtle and perhaps more powerful and deeply seated than more overt intellectual discussions and debates.

For many Syrian artists, intellectuals, and critics, debates over the present and future course of Syrian and Arab culture and society often revolve around the question of how to achieve authenticity within modernity, not against it. In their formulations—expressed in diverse performance situations from listening to cassette tapes, to participating in Muslim ritual, to performing on stage—authenticity, as embodied in the diverse practices and ideologies understood to comprise heritage, is what will carry them into the future on solid footing. Far from being atavistic, in many ways heritage is connected intimately to how these Syrian artists and thinkers envision their future, their modernity.

Unlike discourses of modernity in the West, which tend to emphasize the role of rationality and its public (and published) constructions (Berman 1982; Giddens 1991; Habermas 1987; Taylor 1989, 1999; cf. Reddy 2001), in Syria, I argue, it is the aesthetics of sentiment and emotionality that constitute the basis for creating an alternative modernity. In Syria, as elsewhere in the Arab world, music often bore the brunt of modern cultural criticism, as many intellectuals blamed Arab weakness, emotionality, and "backwardness" on the music's heavy emotional appeal; some critics even called for the banning of traditional music, especially the *ṭarab*-style associated with emotional rapture or ecstasy.[6] Yet, in a more positive evaluation of musical heritage and sentiment, the question of emotionality has played an important role. Like their counterparts in other Arab nations, many Syrian artists and intellectuals have embraced emotionality as a positively valued aspect of their search (usually implicit) for models for a national culture. Against those who may disparage emotional expression and interest in heritage as hindrances to progress and change, these culture brokers find in the sentimentality of heritage points of resistance not only against the more general cultural drift toward the West, but also against the corruption and desuetude of the modern Syrian state. Indeed, the valuation of heritage and emotionality sometimes has come into conflict with the interests of the modernizing state, which promotes secularism and rationality. Yet, just as often, the state has recognized the appeal of these domains in articulating a vision of a progressive and modern Syrian nation with a unique spiritual-cultural heritage.[7]

What is it about contemporary Syria that allows for discourses of authenticity to flourish there perhaps more than in other Arab contexts? The turn to heritage in contemporary Syrian art does not occur in a vacuum, isolated from the social and cultural contexts in which artists and audiences engage in aesthetic experiences. Syrian artistic production and reception occur within the context of Syria's relationship to the other Arab lands, and especially to Egypt. Moreover, many contemporary Syrian artists have studied at European academies, sometimes those of Paris, Rome, and Madrid, but more often institutes and universities in the former Soviet Union and Eastern Europe. Syria's connections to Eastern Europe have been stronger as a result of military and economic cooperation. New York and Los Angeles, for their part, historically have drawn few Syrian artists and intellectuals. Thus, the work of postcolonial Syrian artists and intellectuals needs to be understood in these large circuits and orientations, both regional and global.[8]

Among the Jasmine Trees seeks to identify and explore some of the discourses, assumptions, theories, and ideologies of contemporary Syrian artists for whom the question of authenticity is an important determinant of their artistic practices. Many but certainly not all Syrian artists are concerned with heritage and authenticity, and even for those who are, conceptions of cultural heritage and authenticity vary and there is little consensus on what constitutes authenticity. In fact, there is more consensus on what is inauthentic culture, the most often mentioned example being the contemporary popular song. For that reason, the aesthetics of authenticity is constituted largely in cultural performances as a negative aesthetics. In addition, for many artists, the urge to work with heritage derives from its potential financial benefits as well as (or in lieu of) any innate dedication to heritage preservation or authenticity. Heritage pays, both in terms of local and foreign consumption of heritage commodities (especially so-called "traditional" handicrafts) and in terms of official sponsorship and patronage of heritage-related arts: paintings of the Old Cities, the "classical" Arab musical repertoire, folkloric dances, and festivals, for example.[9]

My analysis of the turn to heritage focuses on musical performance, though I refer to a range of cultural practices that constitute the contemporary Syrian art world (Danto 1964), including painting, poetry, and certain spiritual practices. With respect to music, I focus not primarily on popular music but on the performance and reception of the *waṣla,* a suite of instrumental pieces and songs in both classical and colloquial Arabic arranged according to melodic mode (*maqām*). Syrians of all walks of life associate this music with Arab-Ottoman high culture, the Andalusian heritage, and earlier Arab-Islamic civilizations, and across the Arab world it is heard as one type of Arab classical music.[10] The genres of the *waṣla* include instrumental preludes (*samāʿī, bashraf*), instrumental improvisation (*taqsīm*), classical poems set to music (*muwashshaḥ, qaṣīda*), and colloquial songs (*mawwāl, qudūd ḥalabiyya*). Yet, the notion of a "classical" Arab musical heritage is a modern one with a specific genealogy of developments in twentieth-century Egypt, Syria, and Lebanon. In many ways, the quest to define the outlines of a modern Arab classical musical tradition parallels the rise of Arab nationalism and the search for an Arab modernity, so analysis of the musical domain implies analysis of these others as well.

In Syria, the *waṣla* is associated closely with the city of Aleppo, the traditional seat of music in the pre-modern Levant and still a rich source for contemporary musical performance and the birthplace of many important Syrian artists, including Ṣabāḥ Fakhrī, perhaps the greatest living Arab vocalist. For this reason, I conducted much of my research on musical aesthetics in Aleppo and with Aleppine artists, both instrumentalists and vocalists. Yet much of what they say about the music applies to musical communities and discursive practices in Damascus and elsewhere in Syria, as well as across the Levant. Readers familiar with the high-culture musical traditions of Egypt and Palestine, for example, will find similarities in my discussions of Aleppine practices and ideologies.

Although I do not focus on the performance of popular music—in the sense of Arab pop music and transnational and World Music styles—I refer to a variety of pop songs and the contexts in which they are produced and consumed in Syria because the contemporary pop song in its different guises features strongly in debates about contemporary cultural trends. In many ways, the popular songs are more "authentic" than the songs of the *waṣla* in that they more accurately and authentically convey the concerns and stylistic choices of

Arab youth today. Given that approximately half of the overall population of the Arab world is age fifteen or younger (UNDP 2002), their consumption habits are not insignificant for understanding Arab aesthetics today. Although most Syrian youth today do not actively listen to heritage music, many of those I interviewed argued that the music of the *waṣla* is the most "authentic" expression of Syrian musical tradition; this was echoed in interviews with pop music artists, music producers, and recording engineers, suggesting the symbolic importance of the music for Syrian and Arab understandings of self.[11]

I focus my analysis on musical performance and aesthetics—ways of music making, discourse about music, and habits of listening (what Christopher Small (1998) has termed "musicking"). These aesthetic practices are not unique to Aleppo or to Syria, but parallel region-wide musical aesthetics and performance practices in other urban Arab and Mediterranean environments. Nonetheless, both because the context of my research was Syria and because musical performance in Syria has been little studied, I devote most of the following pages to a discussion of the particularities of musical aesthetics in Syria, with a special emphasis on Aleppo. Scholars of other regions of the Arab East, and especially Egypt, will find in my analysis many similarities as well as important differences between conceptions of tonality, rhythm, emotional responses to music, and the overall social significance of musical performance in Aleppo and other urban centers in the Levant. In fact, given the very different trajectories of Syria, Lebanon, and Egypt in the twentieth century, the social and cultural contexts of musical performance can vary significantly in these countries, even when artists borrow from a shared vocabulary of terminology and aesthetics discourse about music making (see Racy 1986, 2003). The musical performance practices of North Africa, while often claiming similar origins in Andalusian Spain, are for the most part distinct from those of the Arab East (see Guettat 2000; Touma 1996).

Any study of aesthetics necessarily implies a study of the relationships among power, authority, legitimacy, and ideology—not the least being ideologies of art and aesthetics. Aesthetics has never been merely or primarily about conceptions of beauty abstracted from its social context and reified as an ideal (Eagleton 1990). Rather, like standards and judgments of authenticity and inauthenticity, aesthetic valuations are socially constructed. All aesthetic judgments are what Kant termed "dependent"—that is, grounded in certain contextual conditions; there is then no free beauty, in Kant's sense of the term, nor can aesthetic experience be disinterested (Kant 1952).[12] In Syria, judgments of musical authenticity are relative to the cultural context in which they are made and subject to changing tastes over time. No single standard suffices for determining any musical work's or musician's quality or authenticity.

Furthermore, the study of aesthetics and aesthetic judgments necessarily implies an ethics, for labeling an art form or cultural practice "beautiful" or "authentic" often is to associate it with ethically proper behavior, if not virtue. Just as importantly, to call something "ugly" or "inauthentic" is to equate it with the dangerous and morally suspect. In many ways, the aesthetics of authenticity constitutes a moral discourse. In a similar manner, a given aesthetics also implicates a politics, since all artistic productions and cultural practices occur within the context of relations of power and authority that, through systems of patronage and censorship, condition or limit forms of production and consumption. As Robert Plant Armstrong has noted, "it is more useful . . . to think of the nature of the aesthetic as being more rewardingly approached in terms of relating to power than to beauty, for example" (Armstrong 1981: 6; see also Armstrong 1971). Following Armstrong's insight, it is perhaps more fruitful in this context to examine what a particular work of art (whether oral or visual) does and not how it looks or sounds.

The ethical and political dimensions of aesthetic sensibilities are especially relevant in discussions of authenticity in Syria. Syrian officials seek to cultivate a sense of a national culture that they project not only as ethically, politically, and culturally authentic, but also beautiful, that is, aesthetically pleasing—even if only to the state. Since the 1960s, the Arab Socialist Reawakening (Baʿth) party—at the time of my research under the leadership of the late President Ḥāfiẓ al-Asad and now under the leadership of his son, President Bashār al-Asad—has played a dominant role in national and local political and cultural life.[13] It is not uncommon, for example, for an artist to invite local party bosses to an exhibition or recital. Moreover, most major artistic productions are sponsored or patronized by the local branch of the Baʿth party or by the Ministries of Culture or Information, usually led by Baʾthist ministers. Through these avenues of official patronage (as well as via the darker alleyways of censorship), the Syrian state aims both to promote certain visions of Syrian and Arab society and culture and to frame or limit allowable discourse on culture and society. What gets promoted as "beautiful" is often what certain cultural and political authorities consider to be "authentic." As a result, in a heavily politicized cycle of authentication and legitimization, the "authentic" then becomes construed as the "beautiful" and vice versa.[14]

A study of the aesthetics of authenticity in Syria thus necessarily seeks to uncover aspects of these relations of power and authority and the ideologies of authenticity that frame the very conception of artistic beauty as well as the production and consumption of art and forms of cultural practice. I address such issues as they arise in specific ethnographic contexts—arguments about the origins of Arab music, forms of patronage of musical concerts, and so on—

and argue that the aesthetics of authenticity is, on the one hand, a discourse of culture and tradition, and, on the other, a discourse of power and privilege.

My research explores the question of how musical heritage promotes modern subjectivities, and how it helps Syrians navigate heavily politicized and policed terrains of the self and nation. But I do not do so by focusing entirely or even primarily on politics. This may come as a surprise (or relief) to those familiar with research on modern Syria, most of which has favored political and economic over cultural analysis. While being sensitive to the placement of my study in the wider context of American and European scholarship on the Arab world, in writing this study my aim has been to portray the human dimensions of contemporary Syria, what the majority of scholarship has neglected. Of the works written on contemporary Syria, most deal with politics, political history, the French Mandate period, Syrian authoritarianism, the Arab-Israeli conflict, and similar topics.[15] While these issues are important, they certainly are not the only things that can be studied within Syria, and, as I suggest above, they also can be explored productively through analysis of aesthetic practices such as music making. In fact, I believe that focusing primarily on politics leaves us blind (and deaf) to the richness of Syrian culture in its many forms. It may also make it even easier to demonize a country and its people when we do not recognize that it is home to wonderfully creative artists, a centuries-old poetic and musical tradition, and ordinary people who strive to bring order and meaning to their lives in ways that are often far from the so-called "political realities" of the day, which are often more relevant to Western analysts than to "natives."

Some readers may argue that by focusing on musical aesthetics I ignore authoritarianism and oppression in Syria, that I have not attended closely enough to forms of institutional power, or that I have been blind to the very real suffering of the Syrian people. Nothing could be farther from the truth. My Syrian friends and colleagues include many who have borne and continue to bear the weight of an oppressive regime. Yet, despite all of this, Syrians in a wide range of lifestyles continue to raise children, work, seek pleasure, solace, and meaning in their daily lives . . . and to listen to music. And they often do so with grace, humor, and charm to boot.

Acknowledgments

This work would not have seen the light of day without the support and encouragement of numerous individuals and institutions. The research on which this work is based was funded through the generosity of fellowships from the Near and Middle East Research and Training Program of the Social Science Research Council (1994, 1996) and the Fulbright-Hays Dissertation Research Abroad Program (1996–1998) and Middle East, North Africa, and South Asia Regional Research Program (2004). At the City University of New York Graduate Center, I benefited greatly from the guidance and comments of Vincent Crapanzano, Talal Asad, Jane Schneider, Stephen Blum, and Louise Lennihan. Julia Butterfield, Alcira Forero-Peña, Alfredo Gonzales, Murphy Halliburton, F. Trenholme Junghans, and Carmen Medeiros helped get the project on solid footing. Martin Stokes of the University of Chicago provided encouragement on the project and helpful comments on an early draft of the work. Ali Jihad Racy's generous and insightful comments made the final text stronger and clearer. Suzanna Tamminen and the editorial staff at Wesleyan University Press and University Press of New England made the birthing of this project enjoyable through their efficiency, patience, and good cheer.

I extend my deep appreciation to Ibrāhīm Ḥamad of Cairo, Egypt, my first oud teacher, and to his family for introducing me to the art of listening to and performing Arab music. Mustafa al-Kurd of Jerusalem, Palestine, offered important lessons on the oud and Arab musical aesthetics and politics. In New York City, Najib "The Oud Man" Shaheen and Simon Shaheen helped keep me close to the music when I was away from Syria through their good friendship and inspiring performances. Alexandre Tannous and A. P. Joseph always had good questions and abundant enthusiasm for the music and my research.

In Syria, I thank the many friends, acquaintances, teachers, and officials who made my research possible. I acknowledge the Syrian Ministry of Culture for permission to undertake my project and the staff at the Asad National Library for their generous assistance in finding materials. The staff at the American Cultural Center in Damascus, and especially ʿAbd al-Raouf ʿAdwān, facilitated my work in every way. Husain Nāzik first welcomed me to Syrian music, and ʿAdnān Abū al-Shāmāt was a generous teacher in Arab music history and theory. Hussein Sabsaby has been a close friend and inspiring performer, and ʿAli Sabsaby provided me with excellent ouds, fine repair work, and friendship. ʿĀdil al-Zakī and his son Ayman of the Shām Dān music store in Damascus provided friendship and hundreds of quality recordings of Syrian and Arab artists, which allowed me to form an essential sound archive and begin to learn the secrets of *ṭarab*.

Special thanks are due to Muḥammad Qadrī Dalāl, my friend and teacher, and to his family in Aleppo. Without Mr. Dalāl's encyclopedic knowledge of Arab music and culture and his warm guidance and friendship, this project would have suffered greatly. I thank Sabri Moudallal for his inspiring voice and warmth, and Muḥammad Hamādiyeh, director of the al-Turath Ensemble, for his great friendship and assistance in my research. I also wish to extend thanks to Mr. and Mrs. Wasil al-Faisal and family of Homs and Damascus, Syria, and to Hala al-Faisal, for assisting in much of the research on which this work is based. The late Fateh Moudarres was an inspiration and provocateur throughout the period of my research, and I fondly remember the hours spent in his Damascus studio listening to music and talking about aesthetics.

Last but not least, I wish to thank my family, without whose support I never would have finished this work. Linda Shannon-Rugel and Herman Rugel offered unconditional love, respect, and support. To my brother, Chris, and sister, Pam, I offer thanks and gratitude for always asking how things were going. Extra special thanks are due to Deborah Kapchan for her patient encouragement, intellectual stimulation, and untiring love and support. May our son, Nathaniel "Nadim" Kapchan Shannon, grow to appreciate and love the music and the people who create it as much as I have.

Portions of Adonis's "Elegy for the Time at Hand" are reproduced courtesy of Northwestern University Press. Earlier versions of chapters 4 and 6 were previously published as "The Aesthetics of Spiritual Practice and the Creation of Moral and Musical Subjectivities in Aleppo, Syria," *Ethnology* 43, no. 4 (2004): 381–391, and "Emotion, Performance, and Temporality in Arab Music: Reflections on *Tarab*." *Cultural Anthropology* 18, no. 1 (2003): 72–98, respectively.

It is with sadness that I note with the publication of the paperback version of this book the passing of two of my great friends and teachers in Syria. Mr. ʿĀdil al-Zakī, one of the last of the great *sammīʿa* and a connoisseur of all things related to *ṭarab* died in August 2005, a year after we last shared together our love for Arab music in his famous shop, now closed. August 2006 marked the loss of Ṣabrī Moudallal, and with him one of the great voices of the twentieth century. His deep, hearty voice always reminded me of the purr of a gentle lion. Our world was made better by their modesty, humor, great spirits, and enduring humanity. May this book remain a small testament to the beauty and love they shared with so many. *raḥimahuma Allah.*

Among the Jasmine Trees

INTRODUCTION

The Aesthetics of Musical Authenticity in Contemporary Syria

> The craft of singing is the last of the crafts attained to in civilization, because it constitutes (the last development toward) luxury with regard to no occupation in particular save that of leisure and gaiety. It also is the first to disappear from a given civilization when it disintegrates and retrogresses.
>
> —Ibn Khaldūn, *The Muqaddima*

Maṭlaʿ: The *Muṭriba* and the Restaurant

Arriving in Damascus one cool November evening in 1996, I found Syria awash in banners celebrating the twenty-sixth anniversary of the "Great Corrective Movement," a national holiday marking the coming to power of Ḥāfiẓ al-Asad on November 16, 1970.[1] Every plaza in the city center was strung with banners, every fountain was alight with colored lights, and at every major intersection nationalist jingles could be heard crackling from battered speakers dangling from light posts or the facades of buildings. No one seemed to be in a festive mood, however. When I asked my taxi driver what was going on, he turned down his radio, glanced at me in the rearview mirror, then turned the radio back up and continued driving to the hotel.

Later in the evening, as I settled into bed, a young woman vocalist (called, somewhat grandiosely, a *muṭriba*[2]) began to sing from the roof-top garden of a nearby luxury hotel, filling the night air with the latest Arab pop hits. Her performance included a rendition of what was easily the most popular song in Syria that year: the Egyptian superstar ʿAmru Diab's "*Ḥabībī yā nūr al-ʿayn*" [Beloved, O light of my eye]—perhaps the most popular Arab song of the 1990s. Her throaty and to my ears melodramatic vocals were enhanced by their

Yusef al-ʿAzmeh Square, Damascus, 1996.

passage through an enormous PA system with heavy reverb—I was to learn throughout my stay in Syria that high volume is an important feature of the aesthetics of most live music, the implicit principle seemingly being, "If you can't feel the sound reverberating through your body, then it isn't loud enough." The so-called *muṭriba* was accompanied by the sound of what has become the standard pan-Arab pop orchestra: the *org* or synthesizer; the *ṭabla* (goblet drum) beating out the fast and repetitive *baladī* beat (sometimes replaced by or even in conjunction with a drum machine)[3]; and there may have been an electric guitar and bass to round out the ensemble, as is common in hotel lounge bands in Syria, Lebanon, and Egypt. Such groups rarely include the oud (*ʿūd,* Arabian short-necked lute) or *nāy* (end-blown reed flute), instruments more often associated with the classical music traditions of the Arab East. I found the music grating and had a hard time falling asleep, despite my jet lag.

After a mostly sleepless night, I decided the following evening to avoid the well-microphoned *muṭriba* and head to the Old City of Damascus for some "authentic" Arab music. I also was keen to dine on the justly celebrated Syrian cuisine. My guide book to Syria described the Omayyad Palace restaurant as offering "delicious Syrian food in an authentic atmosphere," adding that the restaurant featured a live band playing "traditional" music, so I decided to go. Located just steps from the seventh-century Umayyad Mosque, one of the glories of Islamic architecture, the Omayyad Palace takes its name from the Umayyad Dynasty that ruled the early Islamic empire (661–750 A.D.) from its seat of power in Damascus. The restaurant is said be located on the site of the grand palace of the first Umayyad prince, Muʿāwiyya Ibn Abī Sufyān. All that remains of the palace is its large cellar, occupied by the present restaurant.

Descending the narrow staircase to the restaurant, I find it to be the very picture of authenticity. Stepping through a beaded curtain, I am greeted by a waiter dressed in a fancifully embroidered vest and billowy black pants reminiscent of the folksy *shirwāl* that peasants wear. As he leads me across the main room to a table, I take in the scene. The walls are constructed of thick black and white blocks of marble reminiscent of the local *ablaq* ("striped") style. Various items of "authentic heritage" adorn the walls—large engraved brass saucers, Damascene swords in their bejeweled scabbards, small inlaid wooden frames and mirrors, black-and-white photographs of the Old City. A number of shelves and display cases also exhibit old-style coffee pots, *nargīla*-s (water pipes), and assorted items such as old glass perfume bottles, ancient oil lamps, miscellaneous old ceramic bowls, and odd trinkets. A sign in English and Arabic reads, "For Display Only"—suggesting that it is a "truly" authentic place, like someone's home. You can't buy the décor; in a sense it isn't even décor.

My table is a low wooden stand inlaid with mother of pearl supporting a brass saucer much like those hanging on the walls. The paper napkins stuffed in a faux inlaid box labeled in English "Damascus" seem to detract from the scene, but I am soon enough distracted from any thoughts of inauthenticity by the waiter's invitation to go ahead and fill my plate at the expansive buffet. I rise to get my food and notice a dwarf-like man going from table to table with a pot of unsweetened coffee served in small ceramic cups, like that served on special occasions such as weddings and funerals. Returning to my table with a plate piled high with *kibbeh* (ground lamb and cracked wheat), tabbuleh salad, *fatteh* (a Damascene dish made of chickpeas and bread), a stack of olives, hummus, pita bread, and a bowl of lentil soup balanced precariously in my hands, I sit and contemplate this culinary paradise. Looking around me, I find a number of families and a small group of tourists who are also eating, their guide books jutting out of their jacket pockets (mine is hidden safely in my bag), and, like me, ogling the place. However, most of the clientele do not seem to me to be tourists, or at least not in the usual sense of foreign visitors. Some seem to be locals, and many in fact are carrying on in Arabic. Over the course of the evening, I learn that the patrons consist largely of Lebanese and

Musicians at Omayyad Palace restaurant, Damascus, 1996.

elite Damascenes and their friends coming to eat good food and experience an "authentic" atmosphere—just as the guide book says.

But I am there for two things: the food and the music. Having cleaned my plate and gone back to the buffet for seconds, I return to my table and settle in to hear the music to which I will be devoting my research. My notepad and pen feel itchy in my jacket pocket, but I decide to set anthropology aside and try to just absorb the experience. A group of five young musicians are seated along the back wall before an enormous and gorgeous inlaid wooden chest, a number of swords, and a large golden tapestry depicting a scene of Arab horsemen hanging from the wall behind them. The musicians are dressed in traditional clothing, each wearing an embroidered white *ʿabāya* or woolen robe, and playing the instruments of the traditional Middle Eastern ensemble (or *takht*): *qānūn* (lap zither), oud, *nāy, ṭabla,* in addition to a vocalist. Not withstanding the garish banner hanging to one side announcing in red and yellow letters "Happy New Year and Marry Christmas" [*sic*], the scene is entirely "authentic." To the other side of the ensemble sit two men dressed in flowing white robes with elongated conical brown turbans on their heads; they are the group's *mawlawī* or "whirling dervish" dancers, named after the Mawlawiyya Sufi order of the thirteenth-century Muslim mystic Jalal al-Din Rumi.

The musicians are performing a *samāʿī* , one of the basic instrumental genres of the traditional Ottoman-Arab repertoire.[4] I have already learned several and recognize that they are playing one of the "standards" composed by the famous nineteenth-century Ottoman composer Tatyus Effendi. However, I am a little dismayed at the somnambulant performance. The musicians look as if they are asleep and their playing seems mechanical to me, but still it beats hearing the loud hotel singer and her synthesizer accompanist. After the *samā'ī*, the ensemble begins to perform a slow *muwashshaḥ*, a genre of classical poetry of Andalusian origin set to music. The *mawlawī* dancers rise and begin their unique dance: twirling slowly counterclockwise, their heads tilted to the right, their right arms raised and left lowered at an angle to their bodies. Their loose skirts billow as they spin, faster and faster, while the ensemble plays a steady beat behind them. Yet the dancers too seem tired—bored, even—and I, though fascinated, wonder what on earth Sufi dancers are doing in a Damascene restaurant.

The other patrons, soaking up the sounds like so much sonic décor, busily attend to their dishes and conversations. Every once in a while someone pauses to nod a head or shout a feeble *Aywa!* [Yes!] or Ah! in the direction of the ensemble. Some of them seem enraptured by the atmosphere, while others are apparently less moved. The gurgling of *nargīla*-s can be heard coming from the corner where a bunch of men sit and stare off into space.

"Whirling dervish," Omayyad Palace restaurant, Damascus, 1996.

Sitting alone watching this parody of "tradition," I feel depressed. Did I come all the way to Syria to conduct research in restaurants listening to this mechanical stuff?

Among the Jasmine Trees explores how musical performance offers a cultural space for the negotiation of modern subjectivities and the construction of modernity in Syria and the Arab world today. The modalities of performing and enjoying music in Syria, diverse and contested as they are, reveal some of the nodes of solidarity and fractures in a society coming to terms with itself and its place in the modern world. In Syria, the concept of "authenticity" (*aṣāla*) has come to play a particularly important role in precipitating debates, clarifying points of cultural cohesion and conflict, and motivating performances among intellectuals and cultural agents: writers, painters, poets, architects, journalists, playwrights, cinematographers, essayists, and, not least, musicians. What is "authentic" Syrian and Arab art? What is "inauthentic"? Who determines the shifting boundaries between authentic and inauthentic, between culture and vulgarity? In the diverse and overlapping art worlds of contemporary Syria—worlds not unto themselves but participating in a series of loosely defined regional and international art worlds and scenes—debate over cultural authenticity must be understood as an expression of the contradictions of the experience of modernity, contradictions felt across the Arab world today.

In Syria, as elsewhere in the postcolonial world, the arts are an important arena for the struggle over visions of the past, present, and future. These visions—always plural, sometimes incommensurate—have since the 1960s increasingly been articulated in the domain of the arts through discourses of authenticity and authentic culture, often articulated through the notion of a return to heritage (*turāth*) as the basis for creating a viable modern Arab culture; in this manner, authenticity becomes the marker of an Arab spirit distinct from Western modernities. A common feature of these discourses is their use of a specific language of sentiment and spirit to support claims to authenticity. Such terms as oriental spirit (*rūḥ sharqiyya*), emotional sincerity (*ṣidq*), and musical rapture (*ṭarab*) form part of a critical aesthetic lexicon for evaluating specific artists, works of art, and performances, often in terms of their putative authenticity. The discourses of authenticity and heritage, and the critical emotional lexicon employed to evaluate authenticity, constitute what I am calling the "aesthetics of authenticity" in contemporary Syrian art. Within the framework of this aesthetic sensibility, artists and cultural practices that are thought to be endowed with such emotional qualities as oriental spirit and sincerity, or that produce the experience of *ṭarab* in audiences—however these terms are understood—are considered to be authentic, whereas those that do not usually are dismissed as inauthentic. The distinction between authentic and inauthentic culture is often but not exclusively articulated in terms of the opposition of authenticity (*aṣāla*) and modernity (*ḥadātha*); other common binaries in Syrian critical discourse include Western and Eastern (*gharbī/sharqī*), modern and traditional (*muʿāṣir/taqlīdī*), and new and old (*jadīd/qadīm*). The fundamental assumption behind these oppositions is that traditional culture is authentic, and modern culture is inauthentic. As I endeavor to show in this work, both "tradition" and "modernity" and the binary oppositions they enable must be understood as products of the rise of modern sensibilities and subjectivities in Syria, as around the world.

Many Syrian intellectuals and artists assert their claims to cultural authenticity and legitimacy through an appeal to particular conceptions of the past—often the distant past (pre-Islamic, even prehistoric)—and heritage. Heritage evokes images of the collections of costumes, folk crafts, and customs that are found in so-called "heritage and folklore" museums throughout the Arab world. In a succinct critique of the notion of heritage in ethnomusicology, Barbara Kirshenblatt-Gimblett (1995: 169) suggests that the category of heritage usually encompasses "the obsolete, the mistaken, the outmoded, and dead, and the defunct" within a society. The designation of social practice or material culture as heritage, moreover, often "adds value to existing assets that have either ceased to be viable . . . or that were never very economically productive because the area is too hot, too cold, too wet, or too remote" (Kirshenblatt-Gimblett 1995: 370). My research has shown that in Syria, the broad category of heritage in many instances serves as little more than a catalogue of obsolete and dead cultural traits and artifacts—often those displayed in museums or in gift shops as traditional crafts or lifeways. Yet, in Syria "heritage" (in the form of discourses of *turāth*) at the same time plays a complex role in contemporary aesthetic and critical discourse, as well as in the constitution of modern Syrian national culture. Of course, not all Syrians would agree on what even counts as heritage. Does it include bodily habits and comportment as well as musical genres? Principles of creative engagement with the world as well as the material products of this engagement? Intellectual achievements in philosophy and science, as well as folkloric understandings of the world? Conceptions of heritage are fluid and frequently contested, and many factors (among them social class, religious and educational background, and gender) delimit how individual Syrians understand heritage and its relationship to national culture.[5]

In general, discourses of authenticity are most prevalent among members of what might be described as the modernizing middle class—those residing for the most part in urban centers and often among the first generation of Syrians having access to higher education. I have in mind "Amjad," the founder of a small publishing house in Damascus who hails from a peasant family from rural Aleppo and is proud of his strong voice and his ability to sing classical Arabic songs. There is "Nabīl," a documentary film maker of Palestinian origin who loves the older music, decries the new, and organizes musical appreciation sessions in his small home. "Khalīl," a dentist, is an avid art lover who plays the oud and gives frequent recitals in Damascus. I think of them in contrast to "Nawfal," scion of an elite Damascene family who once proudly showed me his collection of over two thousand classical European albums, and smugly pointed out that not one of them was by an Arab artist. Or "Bashīr," a French-trained architect who is obsessed with Bob Dylan and with what he likes to call "Bedouin blues," the music of the Syrian desert, but dislikes the traditional urban musics of Aleppo and Syria.

Certain religious elites also promote their notions of heritage, predominantly but not exclusively Islamic heritage, but these tend to have more modernist rather than Islamist leanings. In Aleppo, for example, some of the strongest supporters of the older musical genres come from traditional religious backgrounds; indeed, most prominent musicians have had strong religious training as well (see Danielson 1990/1991; Shannon 2003b). Members of established elite families often have little interest in heritage: they more often engaged me in debates about the merits of Mozart than, say, the Egyptian diva Umm Kulthūm or the great Aleppine composer ʿUmar al-Baṭsh, though, as mentioned, some members of elite religious and other "notable" families do show interest in heritage arts through patronage and attendance at musical performances.[6] The new political and military elite, many but not all of the now ruling ʿAlawite minority, do not have any generalizable relationship to the "classical" heritage, but many of them utilize discourses of authenticity and heritage in the context of official practices of legitimization and authentication of state power, or to claim a space in urban elite genealogies.[7] In this way, musical tastes can be understood as indexing social class and status within Syria in complex and contradictory ways.

In the context of what Syria's cultural and political elite deem to be inauthentic and vulgar aspects of contemporary culture—what critics in the West usually refer to as mass or popular culture[8]—cultural heritage constitutes a discourse of privilege. Syrian culture brokers usually do not categorize popular Arab cultural practices such as story telling and popular medicine as "heritage"; rather, they tend to relegate these and similar practices to the categories of folklore (*fūlklūr*), popular arts (*funūn shaʿbiyya*), or the catch-all category "customs and habits" (*ʿādāt wa taqālīd*). In Syria, heritage usually is construed as the preserve of high culture, "the best that is thought and known," in the way that Matthew Arnold defined "culture" (Arnold 1994).

In addition to being a discourse of privilege, heritage also constitutes a privileged discourse, lying at the intersection of aesthetic practices and state ideologies of culture and the arts in Syria, especially in the context of what Syria's cultural and political elite deem to be inauthentic aspects of contemporary culture (usually what critics in the West refer to as mass or popular culture).[9] Through state patronage of heritage arts (in festivals and national heritage orchestras sponsored by the Ministry of Culture, for instance), and through less auspicious means of cultural fashioning such as censorship and official cultural review boards, selected cultural practices are projected as valued aspects of Syrian national culture that need to be preserved and defended, while others are prevented from thriving in the restricted public sphere. Many of the Syrian artists I know attempt to negotiate the boundaries between these two arenas of struggle, between the imagined community promoted by the state, and the everyday practices of artistic creation and reception that are often at odds with such imaginings (Anderson 1991).

Competing understandings of heritage and such metaphors as Oriental spirit, emotional sincerity, and musical rapture (*ṭarab*) articulate a broader concern with formulating the outlines of a modern Syrian national culture engaged with Western discourses of modernity but at the same time asserting cultural difference from if not superiority to the West. Syrian aesthetic discourse articulates notions of modernity and national culture that, while derived to some extent from European ideologies of modernity and the nation, serve as critical alternatives to them—what some scholars are calling a quest for alternative or counter modernities.[10] Musical aesthetics thus comes to engage with broader debates over culture and the nation. Syrian artists and intellectuals construct and promote a sense of difference from the West through a discourse and particular critical aesthetic lexicon of the emotions. Such concepts as *ṭarab,* for example, express and enact conceptions of the self, community, and nation that pose a counter-narrative to European Enlightenment ideologies that stress the autonomous rational self. Instead, Syrian artists promote forms of modern subjectivity that are anchored in a domain of authentic spirit and sentiment, though for many it is not so much a matter of emotionality versus rationality, but of rationality tempered with sentiment—indeed, made more humane by it.

In many ways, Syrian and other Arab discourses of emotionality also can be read as responses to if not reappropriations of Orientalist depictions of the Arab peoples as hopelessly mired in their emotions, irrational, and childlike. As has been argued in the context of modern Arabic poetry (DeYoung 1998), the appropriation of colonial and Orientalist discourses of the emotional Arab by such Arab poets as Badr Shākir al-Sayyāb, for example, can be understood as a strategy for transcending colonial and Orientalist discourses to assert an emotionality that, far from being an impediment to social and cultural progress and modernity, can be a strong foundation for an Arab modernity and modernism.

As Partha Chatterjee has argued (1993), the construction and indeed investment in the distinction of two separate realms—the material and political versus the spiritual and cultural—is a common feature of anti-colonial and postcolonial nationalisms in a variety of contexts. Unlike Chatterjee, I want to emphasize that in the context of modern Syria, the features of the so-called "spiritual" or "cultural" domain and indeed the separation of material from spiritual realms is highly contested, subject to changing dynamics, and is not always the brain child of the indigenous elites (such as the Tagores in the case of India). Rather, in the case of Syria it is defended chiefly by new entrants to Syria's precarious middle class, by conservative elements of the traditional elite (the "notable" families in particular), and by some political elites disaffected by what they perceive to be the failures of modern Arab society. The Syrian state, for its part, co-opts many of the discourses of authenticity among middle-class intellectuals, artists, and others for use in its own ideologies of modernization and modernity—in the case of the present regime, ideologies that aim to construct Syria as the home for Arab secularism, pan-Arab socialism, and as the caretaker and promoter of Arab and Islamic cultural heritage; hence the value and importance for the state of promoting national folklore and classical traditions in the construction of an official Syrian national culture. Therefore we must strive to understand such practices as painting and music and related aesthetic discourses of emotionality and authenticity both in terms of how they express and enact competing conceptions of modernity and how they ultimately are situated within the context of ideologies of the postcolonial nation-state.

People and Places

My initial intention was to research the performance practices and aesthetic discourses of musicians in Aleppo and Damascus. "Musician" (*mūsīqī*) does not in any sense constitute a unified professional category, and in fact many musicians had other work, day jobs through which they earned a living and by which they referred to themselves: teachers, shop owners, in some cases engineers, dentists, economists. Some—usually the best—referred to themselves as "artists" (*fannānīn* sing. *fannān*) to avoid the social stigma associated with musicians in Syria as in many Arab and Islamic lands.

Most professional or full-time musicians in Syria are not members of elite families, and many do not have a university or even high-school education. Moreover, musicians, I found, are not always the most self-reflective artists and often have difficulty talking about their craft in the same way that poets, writers, and painters, for example, often discourse at length about their work. Only those with considerable formal training in music talk about their music and music making in a systematic way; others prefer to just perform and let the music speak for itself, which it usually does more clearly than words anyway. Therefore, in addition to my work with musicians I also worked with those who would consider themselves to be intellectuals and members of the artistic elite: writers, poets, dramatists, actors, architects, film and television directors, journalists, and art critics.

As I explore in chapter 1, music enjoys an ambiguous status in Muslim society, at once intimately involved in some spiritual practices and reviled by some as unorthodox or dangerous. Moreover, today musicians occupy a very low position on the status hierarchy in Syrian society as elsewhere in the Arab and Mediterranean world, and few professional musicians are from elite Syrian families, though many members of elite families have training in Arab music. This is especially true of more culturally conservative families, including those having strong ties to the religious establishment. Yet, these individuals maintain music as a hobby while pursuing careers in medicine, law, and business. If pursuing a professional career in Arab music might be an inappropriate if not scandalous choice for the elite, specialization in other artistic domains—theater, painting, cinema, for example—would carry fewer risks of opprobrium; many Syrian fine artists and authors (both men and women) hail from elite families.

For members of the modernizing middle class, those newcomers to the emerging Syrian public sphere of galleries, poetry readings, literary salons, and discussion circles, music and the arts are not only possible career choices (though with little financial remuneration), they are arenas of great debate about the current and future direction of Arab and Syrian art and society. Therefore my research sites, aside from lessons, recitals, concerts, and the homes of musicians, were the hangouts of the intellectuals: cafés in Damascus and Aleppo, the fine arts club in Damascus, intellectual and literary salons, public lectures, and private gatherings. In other words, this is by no means a study only of musicians or of working-class artists. Rather, I focus on how a certain set of intellectuals and artists and cultural agents of the middle and elite classes create works of art, attempt to understand their contemporary cultural and social significance, and articulate visions for the future. Hence I would not expect the aesthetics of authenticity that I describe here for these cultural agents—their "structures of feeling," to use Raymond Williams's phrase (1977)—necessarily to correspond to that of villagers, Bedouin, or the urban working classes, or others not engaged in these kinds of cultural practices and productions.

Moreover, my research was conducted almost entirely among men. I never met a single professional woman instrumentalist or composer, though there are several well-known female vocalists and many women study, compose, and teach music, and play instruments—with rare exception they do not play them professionally or publicly (an all-female Arab music ensemble from Syria's premier conservatory performs at international festivals, and women instrumentalists specializing in European art music are much more common). The absence of female musical artists is in contrast to much of the history of Arab music, in which women instrumental performers and especially vocalists were not only common but highly valued (see Danielson 1991, 1997, 1999; Van Nieuwkerk 1995). I did have numerous conversations and interviews with women journalists, writers, researchers, music teachers, and others interested in and knowledgeable about Arab music and Arab heritage in general, but all of my lessons and the majority of my research contacts were with men. This research bias reflects conceptions of gender relations and appropriate conduct prevalent within Arab and Muslim society, which often strictly enforces gender segregation. As a man, I was unable to attend all-women's performances and celebrations, many of which feature musical performance and song (I describe some based on written sources below). This is not to deny the centrality of prominent Syrian women intellectuals, painters, authors, theater directors, and actors in the shaping of the course of modern Syria, and in the articulation of modern subjectivities; yet the dominant discourses of modernity in Syria tend to be patriarchal. Needless to say, other researchers might make fruitful studies of female artists and of how women listen to and engage with Arab music. Not only does this relative absence of women in the musical sphere reflect the dominance of men in nearly all forms of public discourse in Syria, it also reveals how music making and discourses of sentiment and emotion in Syrian music are vehicles for the construction of masculinity.[11]

Furthermore, my interaction with non-musicians often led to debates about my research project on Arab music in Syria and the question of authenticity. As I explore later, many asked if there indeed is such a thing as "Arab" music? Is there a "Syrian" music? If so, how is it different from "Arab" music? What is authenticity? These questions and others upset many of my assumptions about authenticity and culture in Syria, and trying to answer them enriched my research. Often my interlocutors compelled me to choose sides in the debates I was addressing in my research about authenticity and vulgarity. As I relate in the following chapter, one prominent artist challenged me to choose which of two worlds I would move in as a researcher, referring not so much to two social classes or two musical genres but to two visions of culture and modernity: a vision of a spirit-infused authentic and modern culture, versus a nostalgic vision of a traditional culture overrun with the excesses of vulgarity and banality. I chose the former, as will become clear throughout this work. Certainly, many of my own biases against much of what is produced in the contemporary musical market today were confirmed through my interaction with like-minded cultural agents, though some were nicely overturned as well. I fully recognize that my position put me at odds with the majority of Arab listeners, for whom the modern song is an integral and enjoyable part of daily life. Yet my views aligned nicely with those of many of my informants, for better or for worse, and allowed me to be accepted as serious (what "serious" person would devote years to studying the modern pop songs?). My position also prevented me from addressing certain questions or blinded me to certain ambiguities, though I hope at least some of these ambiguities will become apparent in this work.

Local, Regional, and Global Contexts

Because performing and listening to music do not occur in a vacuum, isolated from the social and cultural contexts in which artists and audiences engage in aesthetic experiences, I strive to situate debates and contradictions regarding authenticity and music in the context of the other arts in Syria, as well as in the general context of daily life in a changing and complex cultural landscape. My intention is as much to raise questions about what Steven Feld (1994b) calls "cross-modal homologies" of different aesthetic modes of attention as it is to provide an outline for examining how Syrian intellectuals and artists of diverse backgrounds articulate their understandings of modernity and authenticity (see also Feld 1990, 1996)

It is important to note that Syrian artistic production and reception simultaneously participate in local art worlds and regional aesthetic circuits. This is especially the case with the engagement of Syrian art and artists in artistic markets and circles that encompass Lebanon and Egypt. Beirut, a mere few hours drive from Damascus (including the inconvenient border crossing and numerous check-points), hosts a far more vibrant artistic and cultural life than Syria today, partly as a result of its self-constructed role as a cultural broker between East and West, and partly due to historical political-economic circumstances. Syria's best artists perform and exhibit in Beirut, while selected Lebanese artists will do the same in Damascus or Aleppo, though usually the orientation (not to mention aspirations) of Lebanese artists lies distinctly to the North and West:

Paris, London, and New York. But because of the historical ties of Lebanon and Syria (indeed, the official Syrian line is that Lebanon remains a province of Syria, and Syria exercises decisive influence in contemporary Lebanese politics), there has been and remains a great amount of cultural flow between the metropolitan centers of Syria and Lebanon.

Whereas Lebanon can be thought of as the dressier younger sister of Syria, Egypt dominates Syria and the other Arab countries in the total quantity—if not always the quality—of its artistic production.[12] Long considered to be the cultural capital of the Arab world, Egypt has been a source of inspiration for a number of Syrian artists, both in terms of providing subject matter (for instance, themes from ancient Egyptian art) and as a center for study at Egypt's fine arts academies and conservatories. While Egyptian performance halls and galleries do not regularly feature Syrian artists aside from superstars like vocalist Ṣabāḥ Fakhrī, Egyptian artists both well-known and emerging make the rounds of Syria's halls, clubs, and galleries. In the old days, as Syrian musicians often told me, Syria was the cultural standard, and the great Egyptian artists—Sayyid Darwīsh, Dāwūd Ḥusnī, Muḥammad ʿAbd al-Wahhāb, Umm Kulthūm, and others—not only would perform in Syria but would receive the critical acknowledgment from Syrian connoisseurs that would enable their rise to stardom in Egypt and regionally, if not internationally. Today the balance is reversed, and Syrian artists, like many from around the Arab world, yearn to move to Cairo to secure commercial success, or retune (literally and figuratively) their musical styles to fit those popular in the Egyptian market.[13]

However, for many artists and intellectuals, Egypt symbolizes vulgarity and decadence. Many consider Cairene cinema and television, while still the regional leader in production output, to be coarse, melodramatic, even vulgar (see Abu-Lughod 2000, 2004; Armbrust 1996). In terms of music, the Egyptian star ʿAmru Diab's "*Habībī yā nūr al-ʿayn*" is just one of a flood of Arab pop music hits coming from Egyptian (and, more recently, Gulf and Lebanese) studios that many Syrian artists and critics label cheap and vulgar.[14] A common criticism of these newer styles of song is that they are too Western, meaning that they utilize instruments, rhythms, melodies, and systems of intonation characteristic of Euro-American pop music and so-called World Music.[15] The synthesizer (*org*), while a vital component of nearly every club and lounge ensemble in Syria as in Egypt, Lebanon, Jordan, Palestine, and the Arab-American communities in the United States (Rasmussen 1996), is excoriated routinely by partisans of cultural purism and heritage as inauthentic, inappropriate, and unabashedly vulgar. One older Syrian musician and composer decried its usage in modern Syria as contributing to "auditory pollution."

Yet, a moment's reflection raises the question: If these songs are so vulgar, why do they remain so popular around the Arab world and in Syria? Critics are quick to point out the general "debasement" (*inḥiṭāṭ*) of contemporary Arab culture as the context for the production and reception of these "vulgar" songs. The overwhelming popularity of this music among the growing youth population in Syria—as mentioned, upwards of 50 percent of the population is fifteen or under—suggests that criticism of popular culture reflects an Arnoldian bias against "low-brow" culture from the standpoint of "high-brow" culture. As I noticed on many occasions, many critics of these so-called vulgar songs listen privately to what they may excoriate publicly (see Ghuṣūb 1992), indicating that these "vulgar" songs are popular not only with Syria's youth, but with a broader segment of society—including haughty cultural elites.

Adorno (1976: 69) writes that every genre bears the mark of the contradictions that exist in society as a whole. Contemporary Arab popular music bears clear marks of the many contradictions and ambiguities of contemporary Syrian society: its uncertain search for authenticity, the often banal admixture of old and new, local and foreign. Seen in the light of contemporary cinematic conventions, clothing styles, architecture, drama, and literature, which often borrow heavily from Western conventions even when cast in local idioms, it comes as no surprise that contemporary music too adopts freely from Western models. At the same time, much of the local pop music also manages to retain elements of local conventions, especially folk music and what in general terms is described as *shaʿbī* or *baladī* music and culture, the popular music and culture of peasants and urban poor.

Moreover, the notion that the pure Arab musical tradition has been sullied by the incursion of Western music and popular culture, a common sentiment among Syrian intellectuals, does not accurately describe the rise of the modern pop song and the dynamics of the interaction of Arab and Western musical cultures (see Frishkopf 2003). In light of these discourses of decline and corruption, it is instructive to read mid-twentieth-century criticism of artists who by today's standards are considered exemplars of valued musical aesthetics but who in their own time were criticized widely as vulgar. A prime example is ʿAbd al-Ḥalīm Ḥāfiẓ, decried in his early days as vulgar but later lionized as a valued propagator of the older musical aesthetics.

For example, in a 1954 editorial entitled "The Cheap Songs" [*al-aghānī al-rakhīṣa*] that hints at ʿAbd al-Ḥalīm and others, Rātib al-Ḥuṣāmī, then Director General of the Syrian Broadcast Authority, argued that the songs of his day were: "of the cheap variety that have no meaning and no content and that cultured people reject, but which are requested by a large portion of the general population . . . the majority are nothing more than debased words drowning in love, desire, ardor and passion!"[16]

He goes on to excoriate what he terms love songs that have no connection with Arabic literature, especially poetry, and are little more than "unacceptable and unreasonable prattle" (al-Ḥuṣāmī 1965:1).[17] Yet, fifty years later, many contemporary listeners consider these songs to represent "authentic" Arab music and "Oriental spirit"—especially when compared to what is heard on the airwaves today. The "prattle" of yesterday has become the cherished "heritage" of today.

Matters of taste aside, the centrality of Cairo (and to a lesser degree Beirut and the Arabian Gulf) for contemporary Syrian arts problematizes the commonly held assumption of the predominant influence of Western European and American culture on the Arab world. Moreover, while many of Syria's prominent older artists studied at European academies, more-recent generations of Syrian artists, writers, and musicians (not to mention engineers, doctors, and architects) are more likely to be graduates of institutes and universities in the former Soviet Union and Eastern Europe. Moscow, Budapest, Sofia, Prague, Kiev, and Dresden have been as important to the younger generation of Syrian artists and intellectuals as Rome and Paris were to an older generation. Of course, few would pass up the opportunity to study in Paris, Rome, Berlin, Florence, and Madrid, and many prominent Syrian and other Arab artists in fact can be found in these cities today. However, these opportunities have been relatively scarce. Connections with Eastern Europe have been stronger because of military and economic cooperation between Syria and these countries since the late 1950s. For this reason, Eastern European conceptions of folklore, nationalism, and authenticity have had important influences on the visions of authentic culture of contemporary Syrian artists who studied at academies in Prague, Budapest, Bucharest, Warsaw, Moscow, and Sofia (see Rice 1993).[18] New York and Los Angeles have drawn relatively few Syrian artists and intellectuals (though many doctors and engineers). For postcolonial Syrian artists and intellectuals, then, the international refers to a complex network of political, cultural, and intellectual centers ranging from the Levant and Arab world, to Eastern Europe, and South and East Asia. Western European cities, though they may figure prominently in rhetorics of the international, are for most Syrian artists of secondary importance, while New York and Los Angeles hardly figure at all, except as performance venues for singers.

Performance and the Performance of Authenticity

A commonplace in anthropology and performance studies is that aesthetic concepts and the discourses of society and self that they engage do not exist independent of their particular performative contexts; that is, they arise or emerge in the context of performance (Bauman 1977, 1986, 1992; Bauman and Briggs 1990; Hymes 1975; Kapchan 1995). Moreover, aesthetic concepts and discourses are themselves performative, that is, they participate in the constitution of the contexts and performance situations in which they emerge and do not merely reflect them. In linguistic terms, we can understand aesthetic discourse as a metalanguage that refers to the indexical and pragmatic processes of context marking, framing, and creation (Crapanzano 1992; Silverstein 1976). Performance serves as a central organizing motif in this work, and I strive to discuss aesthetic practices and discourses as they arise in specific performance situations. Yet, performance can mean a number of very different things: music making, poetry readings, colloquial speech acts and genres, and so on. Beyond the particular acts and events of performance, I address performance as a mode of being and as a strategy of framing and differentiating diverse modes of practice and being (Bateson 1972; Bell 1992, 1997; Erlmann 1996; Goffman 1959; Schechner 1985). Therefore performance, when understood as a particular strategy of acting, can include a much wider range of behaviors and contexts than what we normally understand to be "performance." This is especially the case in the performance of emotion and sentiment in discourse and in the gestural economy of Syria's music cultures in which the intersubjective and reflexive characteristics of performance as a strategy are most apparent (see Kapchan 1995). Indeed, emotion if not emotionality is in many ways the centerpiece of the aesthetics and kinesthetics of musical and other modes of performance in Syria, and this accounts for the centrality of sentiment in what I am arguing are the outlines of a Syrian alternative modernity.

In the Syrian aesthetics of authenticity, aesthetic judgments are based first and foremost on the degree to which any given cultural object is considered to be authentic (*aṣīl*). Criteria of authenticity (*aṣāla*) include an object's relationship first and foremost to the Arab cultural heritage—itself a manifold of conflicting terms and concepts. The criteria of authenticity are filtered through the dialectics of local and the international, the city and the country, center and periphery, the modern and the traditional; conceptions of the self, the emotions, creativity, and the imagination; discourses of religion, language, and identity; and the reality of politics and patronage. It is this complex web of interrelated discourses and practices that I explore through analysis and interpretation of important currents in contemporary Syrian music. Modeled in some ways on a musical mode, which allows modulation to related modes, this ethnography modulates to themes that elucidate the depth and potential of the primary theme of authenticity—modernity, emotion, memory, and temporality are among the collateral themes.

Borrowing from the conventional structure of the genre of instrumental improvisation called the *taqsīm*, I open each chapter with a *maṭlaʿ* or opening evocation of the main theme of the chapter. These evocations are meant to provide a sense of the place of research, my positionality with respect to my interlocutors, and some of the central questions of the research—and just as often the assumptions that my research overturned or qualified. I conclude each chapter with a *qafla* or closing statement, much as a musician will close an improvisation with a closing cadence. The *qafla* reflects on the themes explored in the body of the chapter and invites the reader to pursue related themes in the following chapters. In this fashion, the separate chapters are linked not so much by a single recurrent theme as by a montage of related themes linked through what Wittgenstein (1953) termed a "family resemblance" to the main problematic of authenticity and modernity in Syria.[19] By using the strategy of montage, I attempt to have the text reinterpret in words the sense of listening to the music, though of course any such attempt is limited by the incommensurability of language and music. Moreover, like the music, in which musical process reflects both the inherent potentiality of a given musical mode but also the artist's mood and motivations, this ethnography reflects my own personal experiences and moods and motivations as an enthusiast of the music and culture, and as an ethnographer.

In writing, I have adopted a number of narrative strategies that suggest some Syrian forms of cultural expression. These include a heavy reliance on anecdote, for much of what I learned about cultural life in Syria was taught to me by my friends and acquaintances through the medium of the well-phrased anecdote. "Let me tell you a story . . ." (*baḥkīlak ʾiṣṣa. . .*) was a common way for people to tell me about certain customs or practices, musical or otherwise.[20] I will have recourse throughout this work to tell a number of my own anecdotes as well as stories others told me in an attempt to capture this important mode of cultural transmission. Another strategy is the use of linguistic and etymological evidence for certain claims and interpretations. Etymological and linguistic evidence is certainly important in Arab-Islamic culture generally, since it goes to the heart of such matters as the interpretation of sacred texts and conceptualizations of pan-Arab nationalism based on linguistic unity (see Hourani 1983). Yet, Syrians also use such evidence in the context of play and humor, and also with a certain amount of irony—especially in non-sacred domains. The richness of the Arabic language, its combination of classical, standard, and colloquial dialects, allows for continuous invention, metaphor, and word play, despite or even in confrontation with more literalist (even "fundamentalist") interpretations and interpretive stances.[21]

It is also worth remembering that ethnography is the result of a largely collaborative process of research. I was in Syria not only to receive knowledge from informants but to engage in scholarly debate and research with them. Many of the musicians with whom I studied and performed also consider themselves to be scholars and researchers; some present papers at international conferences and write articles and books on their music. Acknowledging the mutual constitution of knowledge in fieldwork helps overcome the tendency in anthropological and ethnomusicological research to construe the informants as Others residing in some Other time, namely, "tradition," even when they are engaged in what we characterize (caricaturize?) as a "struggle for modernity" (Fabian 1983; see also Blum 1990: 417–19). My participation in this process was as a co-researcher, lover, and novice performer of the music, and certainly as a junior partner in the overall efforts of a certain group of artists and intellectuals to understand and document the richness of their music. Nevertheless, I participated as one who potentially might "discover" something, and so many of my interlocutors exposed this expectation—or ridiculed it—by asking me, "What have you discovered?" (*shū iktashaft*?). My simple performances and demonstrations on the *oud*, my interviews and public lectures, and my lessons and interactions with so many musicians all attest to the mutuality of this process. I mention this not to trumpet my own achievements—modest as they were—but rather to raise the question of how our complex and compound identities as researchers imply a different sort of practice of anthropology, one closer to the practices of artists and musicians themselves, who often stress "complementarity" (Blum 1990: 418; Turino 1990: 409–410) and not the subject-object division common in so much traditional ethnography.

Therefore I strive to keep the voices of my interlocutors in the foreground in order to emphasize the collaborative nature of the research. As I have written this manuscript, at each turn I asked myself, "What would so-and-so say?" "Is this in line with what I learned in Aleppo?" and so on. At the same time, we need to follow Vaclev Havel's advice (cited in Blum 1990: 418) to "distrust words," especially when they come from those occupying positions of power who construe themselves as centers of truth. Certain of my interlocutors occupied positions of authority and had strong connections to local centers of political power. Others less well-connected also occupied certain positions within Syrian society that conditioned their forms of discourse and practice. All of them articulated ideological stances that need to be taken into account. So it is not merely a matter of giving voice to a multiplicity of actors but of contextualizing these voices in the overall fabric of Syrian society in which musical and other cultural practices are made meaningful.

In the following chapters, I explore the question of modernity through analysis of discourse about authenticity in contemporary Syrian music. Chapter 1 provides an overview of debates over musical authenticity in Syria, and outlines the major genres of Arab music performed in Syria today as well as the primary performance venues. I discuss some of the contexts and strategies of learning music in Syria and show how the local "cassette culture" (Manuel 1993) plays an important role in defining conceptions of musical and cultural authenticity. In chapter 2, I trace a genealogy of some of the keywords in debates about modernity in the Arab world, namely modernity (*ḥadātha*), authenticity (*aṣāla*), and heritage (*turāth*), drawing on accounts from nineteenth-century Egypt and Syria, as well as more recent writings from Syria, Lebanon, and Morocco. I examine the complex ways in which these terms find expression in twentieth-century Syrian musical discourse and practice, and argue that these debates in music participate in the composition of different visions of a Syrian alternative modernity. In chapter 3, I discuss some of the temporal and spatial dimensions of the aesthetics of authenticity in contemporary Syrian art worlds and examine how the idea of origin operates in constructions of tradition, heritage, identity, and authenticity in four narratives of the origins of Arab music. In chapter 4, I continue the discussion of musical origins with an exploration of a domain that many Aleppine musicians asserted was an origin of both their musical traditions and their own involvement with the music: the Sufi *dhikr*, the ritual invocation of God. I analyze *dhikr* both as a ritual context and as an art world in which conceptions of authenticity and personhood are conceptualized, invoked, and enacted. Moreover, I examine the role of temporality and modes of body memory in structuring the experience of transformation and transcendence in the *dhikr* and suggest how this relates to the construction and social reproduction of embodied experiences of moral and musical selfhood in Aleppo.

In chapter 5, I explore the *waṣla* or musical suite as the paradigmatic authentic genre of secular Arab music in Aleppo. I discuss three key terms in the critical aesthetic lexicon of "authentic" Arab music—melody (*laḥn*), lyrics (*kalimāt*), and voice (*ṣawt*)—and show how these critical-musical terms gloss emotional states that play a defining role in the constitution of authentic aesthetic experience. In chapter 6, I further explore the concept of *ṭarab* and argue that, like other terms in Aleppine discourses of music and emotion, *ṭarab* serves as a metaphor for the social context of performance and is one strategy for the presentation of positively valued conceptions of the self in the context of performance. Finally, I end this work with an examination of the concept of "Oriental spirit" in Syrian aesthetics and of how spirit and emotion perform and improvise on visions for an alternative modernity in which emotionality and sentiment are seen not as impediments to progress, but as the very substance of modern Syrian subjectivity.

ONE

Among the Jasmine Trees

ʿMaṭlaʿ: Among the Jasmine Trees

Soon after arriving in Damascus, I met Fateh Moudarres (1924–1999), one of modern Syria's—indeed, the Arab world's—greatest artists. "Ustāz Fateh," as he was known to his students and friends, was famous for his powerful paintings that evoke the Syrian countryside with their rich colors and characters drawn from rural life.[1]

A native of Aleppo and graduate of academies in Rome and Paris in the 1950s and 1960s, Moudarres advocated both modernism and authenticity in his art, arguing that authentic Syrian art in any medium should evoke a strong sense of place, of local geography, the smells and sounds of the countryside, the animals and plants, the very soil. His works convey geographical specificity through the use of strong colors, natural pigments, abstractions of simple themes from folk life and mythology, and an acute awareness of temporality—that is, of timelessness. His paintings, which have hung beside the works of Miro and Picasso, won several international prizes. Yet, he claimed that Syrian artists had not yet managed to achieve an authentic modern vision despite a few individual efforts, his own included.

In addition to his painting, Moudarres also published several collections of stories and poetry and recorded some of his own compositions on the piano. Indeed, he claimed to me to be a musician at heart but to prefer painting because, as he put it, music is "too noisy" for his tastes. Yet, he playfully suggested that one could experience what he called "silent music" in his canvases. Some of his works include portraits of peasants playing on simple reed instruments or carry titles that suggest a relationship to music.

Fateh Moudarres in his studio, Damascus, 1981.
Katrina Thomas/*Saudi Aramco World*/PADIA.

Entering his studio for the first time, I find it dark, almost cave-like, its rooms cluttered with canvases, paint supplies, and shelf after shelf of books in several languages. Ustaz Fateh is seated in the main room at a table cluttered with small tea glasses, ashtrays, books, pens, and various papers. He is conversing with a young artist, who gives up the seat of honor across from Moudarres when I arrive so that I can sit and speak with him. Small of stature and frail with illness, Moudarres nonetheless is a powerfully charming and charismatic man—his bushy eyebrows arch as his eyes gleam with brilliance and mischief. His voice, soft and grave, commands attention, like that of an ancient sage: No matter what he says, you simply must listen.

He has just finished another of his aphorisms, written on a blank sheet of paper and signed, "Fateh." I look around me and find them hanging here and there around the main room of the studio like so many manifestos or Confucian analects. Some are obscure—"That brigand paints the mountains with his voice"—others profound—"with one painting a man is able to found an entire nation."

After I introduce myself, we begin to speak about my research on Arab music and I ask him his opinion of the music today. Leaning back in his chair, he replies, "The music today is mostly rubbish . . . there's a lot of rubbish out there. It is the music of the 'mob,' not serious. Oriental music (*mūsīqā sharqiyya*) is serious, thoughtful, meditative. But today it is mostly lost. If you want to study it you must go and search for it. You must go to Aleppo, to the old buildings and neighborhoods, to the orange and lemon trees. You must hear the birds. . . . Go to the old quarters of Damascus, listen in the courtyards of the old Arab homes. There, among the jasmine trees, you may find it. . . ." Then, sounding like an old Sufi master—his bushy brows raised and a wry smile traced on his mouth—he proclaims: "You must choose between them." Pausing to roll a cigarette, he turns to another artist friend who has just joined us and asks him, "How was your exhibition?" leaving me to ponder his remarks.

What choice must I make?

Fateh Moudarres was challenging me to make a choice, I believe, between two worlds, the first the world of the older music—in his view associated with authenticity and deeply seated geographical and cultural truths and memories—the second the world of the contemporary Arabic pop song—in his view one of inauthenticity, vulgarity, and superficiality. While music is by no means the only domain in which the tensions of modern life are expressed in the Arab world, and Fateh Moudarres had similar observations concerning contemporary literature and painting, it has become one of the most important in recent debates over the trajectory of contemporary culture in Syria, as throughout the Arab world.[2] Partly in response to the rise of new, so-called "inauthentic" forms of culture, many Syrians, like their counterparts elsewhere in the Arab world, call for the preservation of the old, "authentic" culture. The dialectic of the old and new, authentic and inauthentic, manifests deeper contradictions of modernization and cultural modernity that I explore in chapter 3. In this chapter, I explore why someone like Fateh Moudarres would advise me to seek authenticity "among the jasmine trees" in the old cities of Damascus and Aleppo. Why Aleppo in particular has come to serve as the premier metonymic site of musical authenticity in modern Syria requires an outline of the city's political and economic history, an exploration of the principle musical genres that are performed there, and an analysis of the practices through which Syrians cultivate habits of listening to and evaluating music as "authentic."

Walking the streets of Damascus soon after my arrival, I came across a most curious advertisement for a computer company. Computers are readily available in Syria, hardware and software surprisingly inexpensive (much of it bootleg), and computer advertisements widespread in the major cities. However, this particular ad stood out because of its direct appeal to tradition. It depicted a computer tower case, keyboard, and monitor sitting on a glossy table top, but reflected in the table top were images of two large cuneiform tablets mirroring the computer and monitor. Above the image read the words, "Building on the achievements of our forefathers . . ." and the name of the company. The advertisement implied that the computer—icon of technological development—is an extension of early (very early) developments in Levantine civilization. In fact, some Syrian scholars claim that the earliest "computer" was developed in Mesopotamia, meaning a variety of the abacus and the concept of the zero, allowing for the eventual development of binary numbers and, five thousand years later, the electronic computer.

Notwithstanding these fantasies, the cuneiform computer advertisement illustrates some of the ways in which Syrians assert claims to cultural authenticity and legitimacy through an appeal to particular conceptions of heritage and the past—often the distant past (pre-Islamic, even prehistoric). Other examples include the use of the names of famous Muslim scholars and luminaries in the names of contemporary businesses. One finds an "Ibn Haytham Pharmacy" in every city, named after the great Muslim pharmacist. Likewise, "al-Rāzī," graces many a Syrian hospital, referring to the great Muslim doctor, while "al-Kindī" movie theaters are found in Damascus and Aleppo, though what the relationship between the philosopher and the cinema might be is unclear. In earlier decades, many theaters and establishments in Damascus and Aleppo carried European names, such as the "Luna Park," the "Dolce Vita," and "Versailles." The heritage names reflect both a modern nationalist sentiment as well as adherence to a law that requires all Syrian businesses to have an "Arabic" name, though what qualifies as "Arabic" is flexible. For example, the proprietor of the "Shām Dān" music shop in Damascus asserted that the words of his shop's name could mean something in Arabic, Persian, or Turkish, the three sources of the Arab-Ottoman musical tradition that the store features. In Aleppo, musical ensembles carry such names as "The Heritage Ensemble," "Ensemble al-Kindi," and "Ensemble Urnīnā," referring to the famous singer and dancer at the Assyrian temple of Bal.[3] One shop in Aleppo combines two well-known Aleppine tastes: "Heritage Sweets."

These few examples illustrate some of the diverse domains in which Syrians assert claims to authenticity and cultural legitimacy through an appeal to particular conceptions of heritage. In addition to public culture such as advertisements, political discourse is full of references to the past as part of official practices of legitimization and authentication of state power (see Wedeen 1999). In the realm of the arts, concern with heritage, however it may be conceived, presented, and understood by artists and their audiences, reveals the contradictions of the aesthetics of authenticity in contemporary Syrian culture. In conjunction with systems of patronage and Syria's major cultural institutions, this aesthetic sensibility constitutes a Syrian "art world" (Becker 1982; Danto 1964) in which artists and intellectuals debate and construct the meanings of authentic culture, the past, and heritage. Of course, different artists and audiences have different notions of authentic culture, the past, and heritage; indeed some reject the conceptions of others as "inauthentic." Still others reject the discourse of authenticity as false and misleading, arguing for cultural and political forms distinct from—indeed, liberated from—heritage.

The contradictions of these views and discourses reverberate through the art worlds of contemporary Syria. Around the Arab world and Middle East region in general, the arts play an important role in discussions about the direction of contemporary society and culture.[4] Conferences from Cairo to Casablanca draw intellectuals to debate poetry, painting, architecture, and music, and how they either reflect an ongoing sense of crisis or provide a means of articulating alternative courses for the future. The concept of authenticity and discourses of a return to the Arab heritage often are deployed by Arab intellectuals as foils to promote or critique modernist projects and identity politics (see Jābrī 1999, 1991; Ṭarābīshī 1991, among others). Debates surrounding Syrian arts participate in these regional intellectual and critical currents.

Concern with authenticity might be understood as simply a clinging to tradition if not a rejection of modernity. Yet, the turn to heritage in Arab arts participates in a broader concern among intellectuals, artists, and politicians with articulating the contours of a society and culture at once authentically Arab and modern—and neither "Arab" nor "modern" constitutes an exclusive or well-defined essence. Rather, these terms are cultural and political constructions that serve different interests. In the Syrian case, the construction and evaluation of authenticity articulate with conceptions of culture, ethnicity, and the nation that inform debates over postcolonial subjectivities in a variety of contexts.[5]

By investigating how Syrian musicians conceptualize and articulate their music, my aim is not only to provide ethnomusicological detail, but also to offer an interpretation of Syrian culture through its music, using the music as a window or rather as an "ear" into contemporary Syrian society and culture, and by extension onto debates that echo around the Arab world today. In turn, the Syrian case provides comparative material for an understanding of the aesthetics and politics of musical performance in diverse postcolonial contexts and contributes to a growing awareness of the sonic dimensions of cultural modernity.[6]

Aleppo and Its Musical Legacies

What would account for Aleppo's importance both in discourses of authenticity and in the history of Arab music, past and present?[7] Although some Syrians questioned my interest in Arab music and even the existence of "Arab" music altogether, almost no one questioned my desire to study that music—of whatever origin it might be—in Aleppo. Many people I encountered in Aleppo and elsewhere in Syria mentioned Aleppo's status as an important musical capital and the great preserver of Arab musical traditions (Saadé 1993). For many residents of the city, Aleppo's strong and venerable musical traditions are a source of pride along with the city's fabled architectural, literary, and culinary legacies. Although Damascus, as a result of the traditional rivalry between the two ancient cities, might challenge Aleppo's claims to fame in architecture, literature, and cuisine—to name just a few domains—few would challenge Aleppo's role as a great center for music. Indeed, Damascenes and others from elsewhere in Syria commonly assert their musical identity by praising Aleppo's achievements, especially in contrast to the more often recognized achievements of Egyptian musicians. Aside from recognizing the "Big Three" of famous modern Arab musicians—the Egyptian artists Umm Kulthūm, Muḥammad ʿAbd al-Wahhāb, and ʿAbd al-Ḥalīm Ḥāfiẓ—many Syrians argue that "true" Arab music is found in Syria, not Egypt. Some even claim that Egyptian music is at best overrated, at worst the root of contemporary depravity and vulgarity in Arab culture.

Historically, the musicians of Syria have contributed significantly to the development of Arab music in terms of both theory and practice, with Aleppo enjoying a particularly prominent place (Shiloah 1995: 72; Touma 1996: xix).[8] Known in local discourse as "The Cradle of Arab Music" and "The Mother of *Ṭarab*," Aleppo has been home and host to many of the Arab world's greatest musicians, composers, and theorists.[9] The great tenth-century philosopher and music theorist al-Fārābī wrote much of his *Kitāb al-mūsīqā al-kabīr* (*The Great Treatise on Music*) while resident in Aleppo at the court of Sayf al-Dawla al-Ḥamdānī.[10] While resident in Aleppo in the same period, al-Iṣfahānī wrote sections of the monumental *Kitāb al-aghānī* (*Book of Songs*), the first great encyclopedic reference on Arab music and poetry (Shiloah 1995: 72). During my first residence in Aleppo (1997–1998), an enlarged copy of the index to this work could be found on the wall above the card catalogue in Aleppo's National Library, indexing not just the great work but also its importance in Aleppo's musical-cultural consciousness and memory. Aleppine artists also played a significant role in reviving and preserving the Andalusian *muwashshaḥ* genre in the eighteenth and nineteenth centuries (Touma 1996: 83); the *muwashshaḥ* remains the staple of the Aleppine musical suite (*waṣla*), the premier "authentic" performance genre.[11]

In the modern period, Aleppo has been home to a large percentage of the Arab world's leading vocalists, performers, and theorists. Perhaps Aleppo's most famous musical son in the modern era is ʿAlī al-Darwīsh (1872–1952), who is remembered today as a skilled composer, performer of the *nāy* flute, and an important musical theorist and teacher.[12] ʿAlī al-Darwīsh taught such Egyptian masters as the great Umm Kulthūm, ʿAbd al-Wahhāb, and Riyād al-Sunbāṭī while an instructor at the King Fuʾād Conservatory of Music in Cairo (Mahannā 1998: 124–28; Ibrāhīm al-Darwīsh, personal communication, 1997). In addition, al-Darwīsh worked with the French Orientalist and music scholar Baron Rodolfe d'Érlanger while resident in Tunis from 1931 to 1939, helping him compose his important treatise *La musique arabe* (d'Érlanger 1930–1959; Mahannā 1998: 128–29; al-Sharīf 1991: 105). ʿAlī al-Darwīsh was likewise an important presence at the first Congress of Arab Music (*Mu'tamar al-mūsīqā al-ʿarabiyya*), held in Cairo at the behest of King Fuʾād in 1932. His sons Ibrāhīm (1924–2003), Nadīm (1926–1987), and Muṣṭafā (1928–2003) were trained by their father and made important contributions to Arab music theory, composition, and pedagogy. For example, Nadīm al-Darwīsh compiled and notated *Min kunūzinā* (*From our treasures*), a standard source book containing twenty-three suites performed in Aleppo (Rajāʾī and al-Darwīsh 1956). It is also important to note that, like so many prominent artists of his era, ʿAlī al-Darwīsh was an active member of Aleppo's Sufi orders, including the *mawlawiyya* or "Whirling Dervish" order (Mahannā 1998: 124–25; al-Sharīf 1991: 105; Ibrahim al-Darwīsh, personal communication, 1997).

The Aleppine composer and musician Kamīl Shambīr (1892–1934) worked along side Sayyid Darwīsh (1892–1923), the great Egyptian composer and popularizer of the musical theater and Arabic operetta in the early twentieth century (Mahannā 1998: 150). Shambīr is thought to have notated some of Darwīsh's works and himself wrote some twenty-seven musicals while working for the theatrical troupes of Najīb al-Riḥānī and Amīn ʿAtaʾ Allāh in Cairo.[13] Shambīr also composed a number of light tunes and instrumental dances that are still performed today, such as "Dance of the Coquettes" (*Raqṣ al-hawānim*).

Zuhayr Minīnī, Damascus, 2004.

With respect to composers and performers of the *muwashshaḥ,* few names stand out as much as that of ʿUmar al-Baṭsh (1885–1950), the great Aleppine religious singer (*munshid*) and composer of *muwashshaḥāt* (*washshāḥ*). Like ʿAlī al-Darwīsh, al-Baṭsh was active in Aleppo's then-vibrant Sufi communities. According to a view presented by many Syrian music scholars, al-Baṭsh was almost solely responsible for reviving the *muwashshaḥ* genre in the Arab East and giving it renewed vitality (Mahannā 1998: 137–44; al-Sharīf 1991: 132–33). Certainly the *muwashshaḥ* was composed and performed elsewhere in the Arab East, but al-Baṭsh's output was prodigious. He is thought to have composed over 130, of which some 80 have been notated and survive today. ʿUmar al-Baṭsh moreover revived older songs and "completed" those that had been inherited with certain sections (*khānāt*) "missing," including many by Sayyid Darwīsh (Mahannā 1998: 140).[14] In addition, al-Baṭsh trained the majority of Aleppo's major singers of the last fifty years, including Sabri Moudallal, Mustafā Māhir, Zuhayr Minīnī, Hassan and Kāmil Bassāl, Muḥammad Khairī, and Ṣabāḥ Fakhrī. His stamp is still heard in Aleppine performances today, in terms of both compositional and vocal style.

Other important names from among Aleppo's musical progeny include the composer and vocalist Bakrī al-Kurdī (1909–1978); Sabri Moudallal (b. 1918);

Ḥassan Baṣṣal (center), with (from left to right) ʿAbd al-Ḥalīm Harīrī, Muḥammad Qadrī Dalāl, the author, and Ghassān ʿAmūri, Aleppo, 2004.

Ṣabāḥ Fakhrī (b. 1933), arguably the greatest living Arab vocalist; the late Muḥammad Khairī (1935–1981); Nouri Iskandar (b. 1938), former director of the Arab Music Institute in Aleppo, noted composer, musical modernizer, and researcher of Syriac and other ancient Levantine melodies; Muḥammad Qadrī Dalāl (b. 1946), a music researcher, current director of the Arab Music Institute in Aleppo, and among the finest contemporary oud performers in the Arab world (and my main teacher); Saad Allah Agha al-Qalʿah (b. 1950), currently Syrian Minister of Tourism, former Professor of Engineering at Damascus University, and a respected *qānūn* performer and music scholar; Mayāda al-Ḥinnāwī (b. 1958), among the Arab world's leading female vocalists; and many others.

Just as important as its reputation for distinguished scholars and performers has been Aleppo's reputation for its knowledgeable and cultivated listeners, the fabled *sammīʿa* or "connoisseur listeners" explored in depth by ethnomusicologist A. J. Racy (2003).[15] The *sammīʿa* are those who claim a "special talent for listening" (Racy 2003: 40; see also Elsner 1997) and a high degree of musical taste. Traditionally, they also functioned as arbiters of musical taste and aesthetics in urban center such as Cairo, Beirut, and Aleppo. Aleppine musicians often claim that no major Arab artist, including Umm Kulthūm and Muḥammad ʿAbd al-Wahhāb, achieved fame without having first earned the approval of the Aleppine *sammīʿa*. Numerous stories—nay, legends—abound of the importance of Aleppo's *sammīʿa* in determining the course of modern Arab music. One oft-told legend states that in the 1930s the then-rising Egyptian star Muḥammad ʿAbd al-Wahhāb came to perform in Aleppo. On the evening of his first concert, only a small number of Aleppines came to hear him—perhaps as few as seven in a theater that would hold two thousand (often said to have been the famed "Luna Park" theater, now long-since demolished). ʿAbd al-Wahhāb was stunned and disappointed but nevertheless gave a strong performance. On

Muḥammad Qadrī Dalāl, Aleppo, 2000.

the second night, the audience overflowed the theater onto the streets, with over two thousand people showing up to hear him inside the theater and some two thousand standing outside the theater. After this second show, ʿAbd al-Wahhāb asked the stage manager, "Why were there only a few people the first night and an overflow crowd tonight?" He was told, "Ah! Those who came the first night were our *sammīʿa*. No one in Aleppo will go to a concert unless the *sammīʿa* say the artist is good. You did well and therefore everyone came on the second night!" In other words, ʿAbd al-Wahhāb passed the test of Aleppo's *sammīʿa* and this allowed him, in the eyes of the Aleppines, not only to succeed in Aleppo but to succeed in the Arab world at large. He got their coveted "seal of approval."

Another legend involving ʿAbd al-Wahhāb and told in numerous versions, as most legends, says that the great artist wanted to meet with Aleppo's musicians and learn what he could from them. In an evening gathering with ʿUmar al-Baṭsh, ʿAlī al-Darwīsh, and others, ʿAbd al-Wahhāb asked if they had any *muwashshaḥāt* in the mode *sīkāh,* since none in this mode was known in Egypt at the time. ʿUmar al-Baṭsh replied that, of course, they had a full suite in that mode. When ʿAbd al-Wahhāb asked to hear it, al-Baṭsh replied that the time of day was not appropriate for singing that mode and that therefore he should come back the following morning when the stars would be more favorable, evoking the neo-Pythagorean theory of the correspondence between the different modes, the times of day, and particular moods. When ʿAbd al-Wahhāb departed, ʿAlī al-Darwīsh turned to al-Baṭsh and said in surprise, "We don't have any *muwashshaḥāt* in that mode! What are you going to do?!" ʿUmar al-Baṭsh replied, "Well, it's not appropriate for a city like Aleppo *not* to have any *muwashshaḥāt* in *sīkāh,* so I will compose some!" and that same evening he composed three and taught them to a chorus of singers. When ʿAbd al-Wahhāb returned the following morning, to his astonishment, and the astonishment of everyone else, al-Baṭsh and his chorus sang a complete suite in the mode (Mahannā 1998: 139–40; al-Sharīf 1991: 131–32).

What might account for Aleppo's famed musical importance? Many Aleppines attribute the city's musical and cultural strength to its historical importance as a center for commerce, learning, and industry. Located in northwestern Syria on the western end of the famous Silk Road, Aleppo served since the rise of the Ottoman Empire (in 1516) as the major center in the Levant for the overland textile and spice trade between Europe and Asia, via the port city of Alexandretta (Iskandarun) (Faroqhi 1987: 315; Inalçik 1997: 244; A. Marcus 1989: 146–48). Throughout the sixteenth, seventeenth, and eighteenth centuries, Aleppo had extensive and sustained contact with European powers, especially Venice, France, and England, whose merchants bought large quantities of raw

Aleppo's Citadel, 2004.

silk in exchange for gold, silver, and woolen and silk cloth, much of which was later redistributed to cities in the North and East (Faroqhi 1987: 337; Inalçik 1997: 244–45; A. Marcus 1989: 148). Trade with Europe was never stable, but Aleppo remained an important center until the late eighteenth and early nineteenth centuries, growing to be the third-largest city in the Ottoman Empire after Istanbul and Cairo, with a population topping one hundred thousand (A. Marcus 1989: 337–41). By the middle of the eighteenth century, European textile trade began to shift to Izmir and Istanbul (A. Marcus 1989: 152), and by the nineteenth century, Europe had come to dominate world textile trade, especially after British cotton "invaded" the region (Inalçik 1987: 381–83; Mitchell 1991: 15–16).

Like other cities in the Mediterranean Basin, Aleppo's commercial wealth spawned an active artistic and cultural life in the city. Aleppo developed strong traditions in music, literature, popular arts such as shadow plays and storytelling, and religious and other forms of intellectual scholarship (A. Marcus 1989: 227–37). Numerous scholars and local inhabitants refer to the Ottoman period as one of decline. Yet, Ottoman influence stimulated the culture of the Aleppine elites, some of whom did not even speak Arabic because of their Turkish provenance, and as a consequence the arts and culture of the city proliferated.

Aleppo's participation in pan-Ottoman culture still can be felt today in the city's architecture, cuisine, music, and even dialects, which use many Turkish words.[16]

Because of its commercial prominence, Aleppo was a magnet for traders from near and far, thus serving as a meeting point for people of diverse cultural traditions. Gathering in the numerous caravansaries after a day's labor, as locals like to narrate their history, these traders had no concern other than to sit back and relax, enjoy a fine meal, and listen to some music as a reward for their efforts. Soon Aleppo boasted a cosmopolitan mixture of musical and culinary styles—two areas of local culture of which many Aleppines are proud. The Aleppine genre of popular music known as the *qudūd ḥalabiyya* includes songs of Iraqi, Egyptian, Turkish, and Kurdish as well as Syrian origin (Qalʿajī 1988: 165–74).[17] Even today these songs, most of which probably date from the eighteenth through the early twentieth century, are sung in approximations of their original dialects: Aleppine, Iraqi, and Egyptian, for example. Aleppo's culinary traditions are also unique in Syria, especially the emphasis on grilled meats and zesty dishes. All of these factors grant the city and its cultural practices a special "*nakha,*" a particular scent or flavor that Aleppines argue distinguishes their traditions from those of Damascus or any other city.

Despite Europe's advances in world trade, Aleppo remained an important regional center for commerce and industry into the late nineteenth century, producing quantities of raw materials, textiles, soaps, agricultural products, and other commodities for regional and world markets. However, the opening of the Suez Canal in 1869 undermined Aleppo's position as European merchants took advantage of sea-based routes to India and the Far East. The shift from overland to sea-based trade coincided with a series of Ottoman reforms that had the effect of further marginalizing Aleppo from the growing global economy in textiles, its major export, while burdening the city with a flood of migrants from rural areas fleeing onerous taxation and seeking employment opportunities (McGowan 1988: 18).

The period of the French Mandate (1922–1944[18]) saw an expansion in Aleppo's economic position as new lands were claimed for agricultural development. At the same time, the center of commercial and administrative power began to shift to Damascus, site of French colonial authority. Syria's rapid economic growth lasted through the 1940s and 1950s because of a series of economic reforms that gave Syria one of the fastest-growing economies among developing countries at the time (Mason 1988). Yet, political instabilities and changing global patterns of trade in the postwar era challenged Syria economically and adversely affected Aleppo and its position as a commercial entrepôt. The city's economic position was undermined further by a prolonged drought in the late 1950s and by the nationalization of Aleppine textile and agricultural industries

Aleppine Courtyard: Bayt Wakīl, 1982.
Katrina Thomas/*Saudi Aramco World*/PADIA.

under the ill-fated union with Egypt (1958–1961), leading to major capital flight to nearby Lebanon, Europe, and the Americas, drastic declines in production, and the virtual decimation of Aleppo's merchant class. The decline of the city's merchants and urban bourgeoisie precipitated a decline in the context of much music making: the evening soirées (*sahra*-s) of song, food, and merriment held in the homes of the bourgeoisie, which epitomized early twentieth-century urban musical aesthetics in the Levant (see Racy 1998, 2003).

The city's economic fate was sealed with the rise of President Ḥāfiẓ al-Asad in 1970 and the centralization of political and commercial power in Damascus, especially after the "events" of 1982 (spoken of, if at all, simply as "*al-aḥdāth*"), when Islamist insurrections in Aleppo and Hama were violently repressed (Van Dam 1996: 89–94, 111–17). Compared to Damascus, Aleppo has nearly as large a population as the capital but has not received as much investment in infrastructure or its fair share of development programs, according to many Aleppine intellectual figures. They claim that this is a form of punishment for the earlier "events." Where the city has received attention, it has not always been benign: the destruction of an entire neighborhood for the purpose of building an ugly park featuring a statue of the president; the routing of major thoroughfares through older parts of the city, often bisecting entire neighborhoods and even individual buildings. Today, as Syria struggles to steer an economic course of development in the twenty-first century, increasing divisions between rich and poor, the evaporation of the middle class, and the increasingly Western cultural orientation of the elite means that the chances for the revival of the culture of music making characteristic of the era of the *sammīʿa* (the musical gatherings known as *sahra*-s) seem small.[19]

Music in Aleppo Today

Although its star has faded with the rise of Damascus as the political and economic center of Syria, Aleppo is still considered Syria's musical capital and retains an active group of musicians and numerous ensembles that perform the urban art music traditions that many refer to as "classical" (*klāsīkī*) Arab music.[20] Each of these groups is based on the so-called *takht* ensemble or some variation of it, consisting of the *qānūn,* oud, *nāy, riqq,* violin, and vocalist. Some add other instruments such as the frame drum (*daff*), and less often the synthesizer. So-called classical music today tends to be performed in restaurants and night clubs, venues considered less reputable—from the standpoint of the cultural elite and many musicians as well—than the private gatherings, which are fondly remembered by older musicians and even memorialized in television serials today.[21]

The "classical" tradition of urban art music in Aleppo consists of the genres of the musical suite (*waṣla*). More than any other city in the contemporary Arab world, Aleppo has made the *waṣla* the staple of the evening musical gathering (*sahra*). Aside from the *muwashshaḥ,* the *waṣla* includes instrumental pieces (*samāʿī, bashraf,* and *dūlāb*), instrumental improvisations (*taqāsīm*), the *layālī* (improvisation on the words *yā layl yā ʿayn,* "O night, O eye"), the *qaṣīda* (classical poetry sung to an improvised melody), the *mawwāl* (colloquial poetry sung to an improvised melody), and the *qudūd ḥalabiyya* (popular songs), and other light songs from the Arab urban repertoire. These genres share elements with a pan-Ottoman musical culture that arose in the important administrative and commercial centers of the Ottoman Empire in the eighteenth and nineteenth centuries, including Cairo, Damascus, Homs, Hama, Beirut, and other important Levantine cities.

The periodization of Arab-Ottoman music is not precise and it would be misleading to apply the categories of European music to Arab music (Danielson 1997: 14). In some ways, the use of the term *klāsīkī* reflects modernist concerns for classifying the music and culture and differentiating various genres: popular (*shaʿbī*), folkloric (*fūlklūrī*), bedouin (*badawī*), classical (*klāsīkī*), and the now ubiquitous contemporary pop song. "Classical" implies music commonly thought of as deriving from the Arab heritage and therefore of anonymous or very ancient composition; contemporary compositions by known artists in the same or similar styles might also be labeled "classical," such as the works of ʿUmar al-Baṭsh. Because this term arose in the modern period and in the context of nation building in the Arab world since the waning of colonialism, perhaps it is more accurate to refer to the music as "classicized."[22]

The "classical" repertoire derives most of its authority and authenticity from its opposition to the contemporary pop song, which is considered by defenders of tradition to symbolize inauthenticity. These songs, which borrow extensively from the instrumentation and style of Western music, commonly are heard on radios and in taxis and buses around Syria. As the new songs overwhelm the airwaves and cassette shops, they provoke strong emotional responses among critics (see also Danielson 1996). Antagonists refer to the contemporary songs variously as vulgar (*hābiṭa*), banal (*mubtadhala*), cheap (*rakhīṣa*), or—less judgmentally—youthful (*shabābiyya*). One publisher asserted that they are not only bad, they are dangerous to one's health (*qātila,* lit. killer); "they might cause you to have a heart attack due to their quick, repetitive tempos," he claimed. In many regards, the contemporary pop song has become the foremost symbol of cultural decline and decay for Syrian and other Arab intellectuals; it also has come to serve rhetorically as a negative pole in their aesthetic evaluations of authenticity as the prime exemplar of inauthentic culture—although in practice many intellectuals do in fact listen to and enjoy this music.

Closely related to the "classical" repertoire is that of sacred music. Aleppo has served as an important religious center for Sunni Islam as well as for a variety of Sufi brotherhoods (*ṭuruq,* sing. *ṭarīqa*), and it is home to number of Syria's leading religious singers (*munshid*-s), who perform varieties of religious song (*inshād*) at weddings and other celebrations in Aleppo. They also perform at weekly *dhikr* rituals at Aleppo's numerous Sufi lodges (*zāwiya*-s) and in private homes throughout the city.[23] The repertoire of the *waṣla* and *dhikr* overlap to an extent, and indeed many *munshid*-s perform "sacred" music in the *dhikr* as well as "secular" music in concerts of the *waṣla.* The close relationship between the two musical domains suggests that the distinction between "sacred" and "secular" is not clear-cut in Aleppo (see Shannon 2003b). Moreover, the majority of Aleppo's major vocalists and musicians have had strong training in religious song; it is commonly argued that training in the *dhikr* and other varieties of *inshād* is the best preparation for singing the "secular" repertoire (Danielson 1997: 21–27; Frishkopf 1999). This observation holds true for Aleppo's large Christian population as well, which has produced a number of fine vocalists and musicians who are skilled in the "classical" repertoire as well as the liturgies of their various congregations. Some Christian artists also have studied Islamic *inshād* to further their musical training (though I have found little evidence of Muslims attending Christian liturgies to learn their modal practices).

Aleppine musicians claim that the contemporary musical scene is far less active than it was even fifteen or twenty years ago. Yet, many are proud that at least some groups still preserve the tradition through performances and teaching of the older repertoires. Damascus has a far richer cultural scene in terms of overall numbers of concerts, shows, recitals, and exhibitions. Most of the major recording studios are located in Damascus, as well as numerous night clubs and performance venues. However, most musical activity in the capital tends not to be associated with the Arab tradition, as in Aleppo. Many of the concerts and recitals are of European music, for example the annual concerts of the Syrian National Symphony and the numerous recitals at foreign cultural centers, which draw large audiences. Much of the music produced, performed, and recorded in Damascus follows the modern pop styles. One is far more likely to hear a concert in Damascus by the pop icon George Wasoof than by Ṣabāḥ Fakhrī.[24]

However, Aleppo hosts far more concerts and recitals of the "classical" Arab repertoire. The city has its fair share of night clubs, the cabarets of old that were once respectable performance venues but have now declined into less desirable places, if not down right seedy; they tend to feature renditions of contemporary pop songs and favorite songs from the 1950s though 1970s. Many musicians who used to earn a good living performing in these cabarets attribute their decline to the influx of wealthy "Arab" tourists (usually wealthy Arabs from the Arabian Gulf). With rising conservatism in the 1970s and 1980s, many of Aleppo's mercantile and religious elite shied away from the once-famous cabarets and many musicians gave up performing in them. Now considered off-limits for "respectable" people—mostly meaning the middle classes and elite but also the pious in general—these establishments tend to attract denizens from the lower classes, migrant workers, and foreigners, though higher-class cabarets in Damascus are patronized by the wealthy.

Local musicians such as Muḥammad Qadrī Dalāl, the master oud player, give seasonal performances of "classical" music at some of Aleppo's ancient caravansaries and heritage buildings that date from between the thirteenth and sixteenth centuries. The annual Syrian Song Festival, although held in a dreary sports arena during the period of my research, is now held in the Citadel. In addition to the Citadel, Aleppo's numerous private clubs host summer evening concerts for local and regional artists. Concerts of European music also are held from time to time in Aleppo, though less frequently than in Damascus, and they garner only modest audiences. Occasionally, foreign cultural centers will sponsor jazz festivals or concerts of European and "World" music (non-European and non-Arab, in this context). More common are concerts of contemporary Arab pop music at Aleppo's clubs featuring pan-Arab superstars like Syrian George Wasoof, Lebanese Diana Haddad, and Egyptian ʿAmru Diab.

Despite the importance of Aleppo in modern Arab music, almost no research has been done on the contributions of Syrian artists to Arab music (see Belleface 1992; Saadé 1993). In contrast, studies abound of Arab music in Egypt (e.g., Danielson 1997; Frishkopf 1999; S. Marcus 1989; Racy 1981; Reynolds 1995; Van Nieuwkerk 1995), and to a lesser extent Iraq, Yemen, Tunisia, Morocco, and the countries of the Arabian Gulf (Lambert 1997; Schuyler 1990/1991; Touma 1996). The focus on Arab music in Egypt reflects both the common sentiment that Egypt is the cultural leader of the Arab world and the relatively greater openness of Egypt to foreign researchers.[25] In terms of Egypt's role, many Arabs and non-Arabs make the implicit identification of "Egyptian" music with "Arab" music. The Egyptian styles flood the contemporary markets and the past masters of Egypt have gained significant audiences outside of Egypt through the influence of the Egyptian mass media (Armbrust 1996; Danielson 1997; Racy 1977).

Syria, whose media and broadcast centers opened later than Egypt's and remained on a smaller scale, does not have the same pan-regional effect that Egypt enjoys. Non-Arabs as well as Arabs resident outside of the Arab lands perpetuate the identification of "Egyptian" with "Arab" music through concerts featuring Egyptian tunes and through their memories that draw on a time when Egyptian artists were ascendant.[26] Texts that treat "Arab music" as a whole often specialize in one region with only brief information about musical practices in others; this is the case, for example, with Touma's *The Music of the Arabs* (1996), which has rich information about music in Iraq, Morocco, and the Arabian Gulf (where the author had done research) but little information on music in Egypt and the Levant. Racy's *Making Music in the Arab World: The Culture and Artistry of Ṭarab* (2003) provides rich detail about music performance practices in the Levant, and especially the concept of *ṭarab*, but does not treat North African music cultures for whom the concept of *ṭarab* is also important, for example in the music known as *ṭarab andalusī* and *ṭarab gharnāṭī* (though North African understandings of *ṭarab* are distinct in many ways from those of the Levant). Moreover, his work does not address the wider concerns of music making in Arab society, for example broader issues of aesthetics that reach beyond music into the realm of politics and ethics. *Among the Jasmine Trees* thus aims to fill part of a gap in our knowledge of the diverse

Arab musical traditions by offering insights into music performance practice and ideologies of music and culture in contemporary Syria, as well as to establish an ethnographic framework for understanding them in Aleppo. In this sense it complements and extends the work of other scholars.

Music and Musicians in Syria: Ambivalences

According to one popular account, in early modern Syria musicians were grouped with thieves, dove trainers, and people who eat on the streets as those whose testimony was not permissible in court (Qaṣṣāb Ḥasan 1988: 85, passim). Dove trainers were suspect because they loiter on rooftops to train their birds, where they also have a view into the private domains of homes and thus are scandal-prone. People who eat in the streets were suspect (and remain so) because no one with a solid family and home would have to eat meals on the streets in the first place. As for musicians, their case is far more complex. As numerous scholars have indicated (for example, al-Faruqi 1985/1986), music and song have always occupied an ambiguous status in Islamic cultures, as in many other cultures. Despite the histories of celebrated court musicians of the Arab past, today musicians usually occupy a low position on the status hierarchy in the Arab lands, something clearly demonstrated by Karin Van Nieuwkerk in her research on dancers and musicians in Cairo (Van Nieuwkerk 1995). I found this to be the case in Syria, where muscians are looked upon by non-musicians with some distrust if not disdain, even among those who enjoy listening to music. Therefore the choice to be a musician or even to learn music is often a difficult one for Syrians, Muslim and non-Muslim alike.

For example, my main teacher, Muḥammad Qadrī Dalāl, hails from a prominent religious family in Aleppo, his father having served as the sheikh of a prominent mosque and his wife's father having been the city's chief religious authority (*muftī*). His desire to study music was met with resistance from his father, who only allowed him to study once he had demonstrated his serious intent in school and passed his preliminary school exams. Once he passed, his father hired the famous singer and composer Bakrī al-Kurdī to tutor him in music and song. Dalāl later went on to earn a degree in Arabic literature from Egypt's al-Azhar University, a prominent religious institution, and taught Arabic literature and language in Syrian and Moroccan schools for many years before devoting himself full-time to music performance and research. Music alone would not have been an appropriate career.

Many older musicians, especially those from more prominent families, claimed that they had to practice music in secret for fear of their parents' wrath.

One man, an employee at the Syrian Ministry of Pious Endowments (*awqāf*[27]), hid an oud in his closet and would only play when no one else was at home. He reminisced with me about the old days when he could "croon" (*yidandan*) with his oud. Even respected and established musicians from an earlier generation are said to have had others carry their instruments for them in the streets to avoid public censure. To be seen on the streets with an oud was considered shameful (*'ayb*), and this is still the case to some extent today. I was chided once by a gentleman for carrying my oud with me on the street. He argued that music was forbidden (*ḥarām*) and that no respectable person should perform it.

At the same time, music has gained some prestige as a diversionary hobby and as a finishing element of polite education among the elite. One way of avoiding the public censure of music making in recent years has been for families to allow their children to study European music and instruments, such as the Western-style violin, cello, flute, clarinet, and piano. Many elite families and those struggling to join their ranks associate European classical music with modernity, progress, and civilization, and consider Arab music to be backward. A Moscow-trained violinist and instructor at the High Institute for Music in Damascus, the son of a well-known Syrian family of musicians that includes prominent performers of Arab music, claimed that Arab music is irrational, leads to irrational behavior, and in general is an "insult" (*bahdalah*). At the time of my research, the Arab Music Institute in Aleppo had long waiting lists of students wanting to study piano and violin, yet only five students were studying the oud and six the *qānūn*—two quintessentially Arabic instruments. One day, during a conversation with the Institute's director, a woman came in to register her young son. When the director asked if the boy would like to study the oud, the woman proudly (and loudly) declaimed: "Oh no! My son would never play that kind of music. In fact he only listens to Beethoven and Mozart!" The director glanced over at me with a look in his eyes that said, "Not another one of those!"

Other families encourage the study of the "classical" repertoire as part of a heritage-based program of self-enrichment and study not dissimilar to classical notions of *adab*, polite education, which recommend study of the musical arts (Bonebakker 1988). One prominent Aleppine family includes members who, though all accomplished in music and the arts, earn their livings through more "respected" professions, such as medicine and engineering; for any one of them to become a professional musician would be unthinkable. I was often suspect because of my association with musicians and their domains, such as the Artists Syndicate, which conjures ignoble connotations of dancers and night clubs in the minds of elites ignorant of the syndicate's important role in Syrian arts. My position as a foreign researcher, though anomalous because of the subject matter, allowed me to retain some status in the eyes of suspicious elites;

my focus on the "classical" repertoire and not the contemporary pop song assuaged their concerns. Paradoxically, the great Arab musicians and especially singers are praised and enjoyed on a daily basis, but nevertheless the upper classes do not consider music to be a noble profession. Acting and to some extent even painting also are frowned upon. This is especially the case for women artists, whose activities are suspect in the eyes of conservative members of society, elites and others.

With respect to religious views on music, during my research I encountered individuals who told me that Islam prohibits music and that I might be better off leaving it alone. I recall attending a *mawlid* (a religious celebration, lit. "birthday") held for a young man who had successfully passed Syria's rigorous baccalaureate examination, a prerequisite for admission to university. A group of three *munshid*-s were invited to recite the Qurʾān and present some religious song. Afterward, I spoke with the main vocalist about his training and experience in religious song. He proudly stated that his golden voice was a gift of God so that he could better proclaim His praises. In fact, he claimed that while he was in London studying dentistry, many "unbelievers" (*kāfir*-s) had converted upon hearing his voice. He then took me aside and said, with some concern, that once I completed my study of music I should devote my life to something more "serious" and not let this interest lead me away from "the Straight Path" (that is, Islam). When I offered that many devout Muslims also have an interest in music and some in fact are performers, he stated that then they are headed for Hell because, according to Islam, only the human voice (*ṣawt*) and the frame drum (*daff*) are allowable, citing a well-worn Prophetic saying (*ḥadīth*) to support this claim. Musical instruments of all other varieties, he stated, are "forbidden" and should be broken.

A young hotel worker also claimed that I was endangering my soul by studying music and learning to play the oud. When I asked him about the fate of great Arab musicians such as Umm Kulthūm and Muḥammad ʿAbd al-Wahhāb, both of whom had strong religious training, he shook his head and said that they will pay a price for their music, that is, on Judgment Day. But many devout people, I offered, consider Umm Kulthūm to be a "*munshida*" (female religious singer) because of her religious training in Qurʾānic recitation (*tajwīd*) and religious song; there are even recordings of her reciting the holy text. "The female voice is an imperfection [*al-ṣawt al-unthawī aʿwar*]," he stated in a mechanical drone, as if reciting from memory, "and Umm Kulthūm will suffer for her singing and recitation of the Qurʾān."[28]

However, other Aleppine artists who consider themselves devout Muslims argue that the above views are excessive and that those who hold them are rigid extremists (*mutazammitīn*). For my teachers, all of whom were raised in religious families and served at different times in their lives as muezzins (those who give the Muslim call to prayer) and *munshid*-s, it is more the context of musical performance and less the music per se that determines its permissibility, though the type of music performed is also an important factor. If performed in a "respectable" venue—one defined tautologously as a place where "respectable" people would go—then music is something allowable (*masmūḥ*) in Islam. That is, it must be performed in a place where no alcohol is served, dancing is limited or non-existent, and where men and women do not mix in a socially unacceptable fashion. Examples of "respectable" venues include the Citadel's amphitheater, Aleppo's few public theaters and concert halls, the ancient caravansaries that are being renovated as performance spaces, and the private homes of "respectable people."

With few exceptions, those musicians and "respectable people" who denounce "vulgar" music decry Aleppo's night clubs as disreputable venues because they serve alcohol and cater to listeners' carnal rather than spiritual interests. One leader of a heritage-style ensemble, when I praised the voice of a promising young singer, told me that he would like to have that singer join his ensemble but since the young man performs in a cabaret he cannot allow him to join his group. Performing in the cabarets is definitely *ḥarām* from this musician's standpoint. Of course, from the perspective of the young singer and others who make a living performing in the cabarets, such work is permissible because it allows them to survive and provide for their families, especially in the absence of alternative "respectable" venues. One friend who performs in a cabaret claimed to earn approximately $800 a month performing six nights a week in a cabaret. By comparison, a university professor might earn $150 to $200 per month. Though they recognize that the atmosphere of the cabarets usually is not conducive to proper Islamic behavior nor very healthful, many of these performers claim to be at least as devout as those who spurn the cabarets.

However, repertoire is also an important factor in determining the permissibility of music. "Allowable" music usually means the classical repertoire, often including what some term folkloric or popular (*shaʿbī*) songs. The important criterion is whether the music feeds listeners' spiritual needs or rather leads to irreligious thoughts and motivations. Most contemporary pop songs are thought to fall in the latter category and therefore are decried by more conservative listeners as immoral, debased, and inappropriate. Yet, many contemporary listeners also take issue with certain songs performed within the context of the classical repertoire, such as songs that are overtly amorous (*ghazalī*). For example, some consider a well-known song performed by Ṣabāḥ Fakhrī to be inappropriate because it suggests the drinking of wine and irresponsibility.[29] While some listeners argue that such songs refer metaphorically to spiritual love or have deeper, Sufi meanings and therefore should be permissible, others argue that the style of the performance makes the difference in deciding whether or not a song is appropriate. For example, an amateur musician found Ṣabāḥ Fakhrī's performances "vulgar" (*shāriʿī*, "from the streets," or *sūqī*, "from the market") because he felt that Fakhrī emphasized the profane and not the spiritual aspects of the words.

Aside from ambiguous Qurʾānic verses and various examples from the *ḥadīth* literature concerning music, many of my teachers and friends cited the twelfth-century Muslim jurist al-Ghazzali's statements on song and dance in his *The Revival of the Religious Sciences* (al-Ghazzali 1901–1902, 1991) to support their advocacy of a "Golden Mean" or Middle Way between prohibition and unequivocal acceptance of music in Islam. In his writings, al-Ghazzali evaluates the evidence for a prohibition of song and dance and argues, in essence, that so long as song and dance lead the participant to serve Allah, then they are permitted; song and dance that excite only the carnal desires are clearly forbidden. He refers to song and dance with the term *samāʿ*,which literally means "listening" or "audition" and associated kinesthetic practices, and which in Sufi literature refers to a spiritual audition of sacred truths and not merely listening to music (al-Faruqi 1985/1986; see also Hirschkind 2001, 2004). According to al-Ghazzali and other Sufi thinkers, *samāʿ* leads one to Allah if done properly; otherwise it is dangerous and can excite desires and lead to sin.[30]

Learning Music in Syria

I conducted most of my research among intellectuals and artists, including many who consider themselves to occupy a middle-ground position in these debates: devout Muslims who are also practicing professional musicians. Although some Syrians might not have thought my studies to be serious enough, for one reason or another, one prerequisite of my engaging in debates in the field was learning the critical language used by Syrian intellectuals to discuss aesthetic issues. Regarding music, this required that I acquire numerous tapes for different artists, learn to follow the melodies and modulations, appreciate vocal qualities, and differentiate between strong and weak performances. Achieving this aesthetic awareness required intensive study and listening, often carried out in cassette shops over glasses of tea or small cups of coffee. It also meant taking music lessons and learning an instrument. Prior to my arrival in Syria, I had studied the oud for several months in Cairo with a private teacher.[31] This came about almost as an accident. While studying Arabic in Cairo, I had hoped to get acquainted with more Egyptians in order to learn the local dialect better. I also was pursuing a preliminary investigation into Islamic discourses in non-traditional domains and had decided that musicians might be an interesting group in which to study contemporary forms of Islamic practice and discourse, precisely because of music's ambiguous status in Islam.

In Egypt, I learned many of the basic modes and several popular Egyptian songs. I began to appreciate what numerous musicians told me are the three most important elements of a good song: the melody (*laḥn*), the lyrics (*kalimāt*), and the performer's voice (*ṣawt*). For a song to be good—and also "authentic"—it had to have a strong combination of all of these elements; lacking one of them is enough to make the song or the artist weak, if not "inauthentic." Despite my studies in Egypt, my understanding of the modes and technical skill on the oud remained limited, due in part to the complexity of the task, my own limitations, and my instructor's limitations as well.

Arriving in Syria in the late fall of 1996, I sought an oud teacher and found both a teacher and friend in the Aleppine virtuoso Muḥammad Qadrī Dalāl. Through our intensive sessions on the musical modes, the major genres and history of Arab music, and oud technique—over an hour a day almost every day for several months—I came to appreciate better the subtleties of the music and to become familiar with the terminology and critical discourse of music in contemporary Syria. Nonetheless, much of my fieldwork time in fact was spent convincing Syrians that I, as a foreigner, actually could understand their music and appreciate it. Many Syrian musicians and others expressed the common and not entirely unfounded belief that Arab music is too complex for Westerners and non-Arabs in general to understand; in fact, many Arabs do not understand it. Oftentimes I was told that a period of a year or two or three is insufficient for a non-Arab to understand the music and write anything intelligent about it. Quite accurately, one scholar suggested that I would probably be suspicious of him if he went to America and proposed to write a study of American jazz after only a year or so of study. One would need ten years in order to understand the music and its intricacies, not to mention the language, he suggested (and he had a valid point).

My position as a foreign music researcher meant that I was expected naturally to be ignorant of the music though praised for attempting to learn it. Yet, it also meant that I had to prove myself constantly before the suspicions of those who thought Arab music to be ineffable for non-Arabs. Whenever an oud was available, I generally was asked to play for people in order to demonstrate what I could do, and especially as a test for any manifestations of "oriental spirit"—that key yet elusive element of Arab musical aesthetics. Sometimes I was asked to sing songs, quizzed on specific modes, or enjoined to explain what I had "discovered" in their music. Only after many months of fieldwork was I able to convince people that I had at least a modicum of "oriental spirit." My public lectures (in Arabic) on musical topics and performances in public contexts convinced some of the doubters that I had entered, if only in a rudimentary way, the heart of their music and understood some of its secrets. In this fashion, my own performances as well as the recordings and performances of Syrian musicians became an integral part of my search for the keys to authenticity in Syrian music and culture.

Listening, Aesthetics, and Forming a Tape Collection

As much as knowledge of the genres and styles and skill on an instrument, it is one's skill as a listener that forms an essential component in announcing musical cultivation and taste. I constantly was asked, "To whom do you listen?" and given suggestions for tapes, specific recordings, and concerts. The question of what one listens to and what recordings are in one's collection are absolutely critical in marking and defending claims to authenticity. Among nonspecialists, a claim to listen to Umm Kulthūm, ʿAbd al-Ḥalīm Ḥāfiẓ, and Muḥammad ʿAbd al-Wahhāb is one common way to make a claim to being a cultured person and respecting cultural authenticity (especially to the foreign music researcher). Among the discriminating, however, to answer "Umm Kulthūm" is not sufficient. At a listening session organized by a dramatist friend at the home of a well-known woman music teacher, my discrimination as a listener was put to the test early. "To whom do you enjoy listening?" asked the teacher. I replied, "Umm Kulthūm," and, with a look of resignation that suggested to me, "Is that all there is?" she asked, "From which era [of her career]?" I had just listened to a harangue by a local cassette vendor about how beautiful and pure the early Umm Kulthūm was in comparison to her later work, so I replied, "Her early work, before she became well-known." This elicited a nod of approval and the remark, "Her best recordings are from the period of about 1928 to 1930. Afterwards she became too repetitive and emotionally less sincere (*muftaʿala*)," she remarked.[32]

Forming a collection of cassette tapes (and, recently, compact disks) is another component of determining and even performing one's musical taste as a symbol of wider "culture" (*thaqāfa*).[33] When I began my oud lessons, my teacher instructed me that the first thing I must do aside from obtaining a decent oud and practicing four hours every day was to begin collecting good tapes and listen to them regularly. Listening is considered a creative act among Syrians, and one's collection of recordings announces one's level of discrimination and culture. My teacher, for example, argued that he listens to "everything," and indeed he has recordings from numerous diverse musical cultures to prove it. Another musician friend went to great lengths to show me his "jazz" tapes that for him symbolized his cosmopolitanism.[34]

Most Syrians listen to music on cassettes, which form the backbone of a thriving "cassette culture" (Manuel 1993). Although first-run recordings are available in the market (the so-called "original" recordings or *aṣliyyāt*), most are bootlegged copies from original tapes, reels, and CDs, or copies of other copies. The quality of tapes hence varies tremendously, though a number of specialty stores have arisen that deal in high-quality cassettes, usually costing two or three times what a standard tape might cost (for example, SYP100 to 150 versus SYP50).[35] It is not uncommon to see audience members with rudimentary tape recorders at concerts, and not long after the concert bootleg versions of these tapes will appear in the market, now often in poor-quality MP3 format on CD. Yet, "bootleg" is hardly the appropriate term. Until 2001 and the enforcement of laws protecting intellectual property in Syria, "copyright" was not a word found in the colloquial dictionary; even with the new laws, Syrian artists rarely if ever receive any remuneration from the sale of recordings. As one musician and studio owner put it: "We have no rights in the market." In a way, the circulation of cassette tapes and MP3s has democratized the music market in Syria.[36]

The majority of music shops in Damascus and Aleppo carry the average run-of-the-mill recordings of the most recent pop stars as well as a handful of tapes of older masters. However, a few stores specialize in the "classical" repertoire and the great Arab artists of the twentieth century. I got most of my collection (almost entirely in the form of cassette tape) from these shops. I also would exchange recordings with my musician friends, with whom I would compare collections and ask advice about certain artists and recordings. Trading music became an important context for learning about musical aesthetics. Why was one performance of a given artist preferred over another? In which genres did a certain artist excel and, the converse, in which was he or she less skilled? What makes for a good voice, a good melody? Through engagement with local "cassette cultures," I was able to acquire certain habits of listening that allowed me to learn much about the music that I could not have learned from lessons alone. As one musician told me, "You have to learn how to listen before you can learn how to play the music."

Old and New

In the exchange of tapes and in the cassette culture in general, discourses of the old (*qadīm*) and the new (*jadīd*) are very important. I found that there is widespread agreement that earlier material by older artists is better than their recent material. For example, the owner of one cassette shop, a young man of perhaps twenty-two, argued that the older recordings of the popular singer George Wasoof are better than his new recordings, whereas anything by the late Egyptian singer ʿAbd al-Ḥalīm Ḥāfiẓ would be better than Wasoof's repertoire from any era. In discourses of authenticity, the old is almost always better than the new, which marks decay (*inḥiṭāṭ*). Indeed, the newer songs are blamed almost universally for lowering musical taste in Syria. Even many cassette vendors, whose livelihood depends on the sale of the "cheap" songs, argued that they prefer the older material. But closer examination of this discourse of debasement and the threat of the contemporary songs to the existence of the older ones reveals a somewhat different picture. First, not all is lost with respect to the "classical" songs and their conventions. Umm Kulthūm remains the single most popular artist not only on the airwaves but at cassette stands around Damascus and Aleppo. The owner of a stand in central Damascus that sells a variety of modern and "classical" songs, folk music, and even Western pop music claims that on any given day he sells about twenty-five Umm Kulthūm cassettes, whereas he might sell that amount of a contemporary singer only in the first few days after the cassette is released to the market. By comparison, he might sell five to ten George Wasoof tapes or a handful of ʿAmru Diab tapes—both very popular Arab artists who have large audiences in Syria. But the Egyptian diva still reigns as queen of the market with an average of twenty-five tapes a day, every day, for the several years this man has been selling them. Other vendors claimed similar sales proportions: the new singers might sell a lot when their tapes first hit the market, but Umm Kulthūm, ʿAbd al-Ḥalīm Ḥāfiẓ, and Muḥammad ʿAbd al-Wahhāb—the venerated Big Three—remain the top sellers. Syrian stars such as Ṣabāḥ Fakhrī also do well, especially in specialty shops that do not offer the "cheap" music. In such shops in Damascus and Aleppo, one finds aficionados, young and old, of older styles and artists such as Asmahān, Laylā Murād, Nūr al-Hudā, Bakrī al-Kurdī, and Zuhayr Minīnī.

The Stratigraphy of Musical Authenticity

The valuation of the old also is expressed visually in a stratigraphy of musical authenticity. In surveys of dozens of cassette shops in Damascus and Aleppo, and especially those in which cassettes were displayed in vertical cases rather than in storage boxes or drawers, I detected an interesting pattern among the cassettes. In almost all of these shops, Umm Kulthūm occupied the top row in the display cases. Only when the shop or stall also sold recordings of the Qurʾān was she displaced from the top rung, and in some instances she shared this honor with recordings of the holy text.[37] Even in those stalls in which tapes were arranged horizontally, Umm Kulthūm occupied the first row at what would be the top were the case to be righted vertically. In Aleppo, Umm Kulthūm often shared the high spot with other religious vocalists.

The association between Umm Kulthūm, musical authenticity, and her occupation of the highest strata in Syrian cassette shops was demonstrated graphically one afternoon at a small cassette shop near the Victoria Bridge and Hijaz Railway Station area of central Damascus. This particular stand consisted of a vertical display case standing upon a table that held another horizontal case as well as a large cassette player. Running the shop was a young man from Ḥasaka, a town in the Kurdish region of northeastern Syria, and he was accompanied on this particular day by two young men, one from Ḥamā in central Syria and the other from the Ḥawrān region in the south. I approached the stand and asked them if they had any tapes of Khiḍr Yā'ʾs, a well-known Iraqi singer who was scheduled to give a performance in Syria that month. The young man produced three tapes and placed one in the cassette player for me to listen to it. After a few minutes and the perfunctory questions (You speak Arabic!? Where are you from? Why did you learn Arabic? What are you doing here?), I spoke with them about their musical preferences and asked what they thought was the best music. I had been following up on Iraqi singers after discovering that many rural residents and the denizens of the microbus stations frequently listen to them. After debating the qualities of various Iraqi singers such as Khadr Yaʾs, ʿAlī al-ʿIssawī, and Kāzim al-Sāhir (the popular artist), the young man asked me if I wanted to hear something really good and authentic. When I said yes, he stood for a moment thinking, then grabbed a chair, stood on it rather precariously, and reached up to the top shelf of the display case to bring down a tape of Umm Kulthūm's "*Amal ḥayātī*" (Hope of my life). "This is the real thing," he seemed to be saying as he placed it in the cassette player; to me, his putting in the tape spoke better than any words to his understanding of authenticity. We stood there, the three of us, listening to the great voice, which for these young men, like so many others, was the voice of tradition, perhaps even of the Arab nation (Danielson 1997).

After Umm Kulthūm, I was surprised to find ʿAbd al-Ḥalīm Ḥāfiẓ occupying the second tier in the stratigraphy of musical authenticity in Syrian cassette shops. This Egyptian crooner, popular among youth and especially women but often considered a symbol of vulgarity by the cultural elite during his lifetime, has been resurrected as an icon second only to Umm Kulthūm (and the Qurʾān), at least in popular cultural displays. In almost all instances when Umm Kulthūm occupied the top rung, ʿAbd al-Ḥalīm Ḥāfiẓ would occupy the second. Only rarely was he displaced by others, and then usually by Muḥammad ʿAbd al-Wahhāb or religious singers.

To my initial surprise, however, ʿAbd al-Wahhāb did not always occupy the third place of pride in Syrian cassette-shop stratigraphy, though he almost always is mentioned among the Big Three. In fact, he often was exiled to a side display case or mixed indiscriminately with other artists having some relation to him or to musical heritage: Ṣafwān Bahlawān (a Syrian artist who studied with ʿAbd al-Wahhāb and adopted his style of singing), Ṣabāḥ Fakhrī, and so on. Often ʿAbd al-Wahhāb occupied his own corner. Instead, after ʿAbd al-Ḥalīm, a variety of contemporary popular singers jockey for third place: ʿAmru Diab, George Wasoof, Diana Haddad, Nawāl al-Zughbī, and other Egyptian, Lebanese, and Syrian singers. In fact, the majority of the shops and stalls feature a revolving collection of recent pop hits as well as the numerous "variety" collections and theme tapes, such as "'Variety 1998," "The Most Beautiful *Dabkāt* of 1997," "Best Songs," and "Love Songs 2002," produced by the shop owners themselves or, less often, by local studios. All of them, of course, are bootleg compilations.

This stratigraphy suggests that the older artists and hence older aesthetic values are not on the verge of extinction, as critics of the contemporary pop song claim. Yet, there is a strong sense among musicians and intellectuals that the older generations represent a Golden Age that never will be repeated. This is why the modern pop songs are considered to be such a threat; there appears to be no alternative. Unlike the West, where contemporary genres and styles have displaced but not entirely replaced the older, there is a fear in Syria that once the present "cultivated listeners" pass on, there will not be a generation capable of appreciating the older music and of promoting its aesthetic standards. This is confirmed in the music conservatories, where students are shunning the study of the Arab instruments, instead flocking to the piano, violin, clarinet, guitar, and other European instruments.

Qafla

This chapter has explored why Aleppo has come to occupy such an important position in Arab music as well as in discourses of authenticity in contemporary Syria. Its traditional commercial and political importance led to its growth as a regional center for Levantine culture, including a rich musical repertoire comprising a variety of genres and styles. In modern Aleppo, musicians and music lovers cultivate habits of listening through engagement in a local cassette culture: listening to, discussing, and trading recordings of favorite artists.

Examination of the cassette culture reveals the positive evaluation of older artists and even the earlier material of more recent performers, a phenomenon reflected to some degree in the layering of musical authenticity in local music shops. But this stratigraphy and statements about authenticity should not lead us to believe that there is consensus about authentic culture in contemporary Aleppo. Indeed, modern and modernizing Syria is rife with contradictions that can be heard in music: contradictions between advocates of modernism and defenders of tradition, between those who decry the contemporary pop song and those who adopt a more flexible position and listen to a variety of styles and genres. The next chapter explores the rise of the question of modernity and the concern with authenticity in Syria and sets the stage for further analysis of some of the contradictions of modernity in contemporary Aleppine music in the following chapters.

TWO

Sentiment and Authentic Spirit: Composing Syrian Modernity

Maṭlaʿ: Adorno at the Tourist Café

I set out by bus one winter morning for Aleppo from the new terminal on the outskirts of Damascus—the old one in the city center recently having been closed after a bomb planted by terrorists whom the Syrian press alleged were Israeli agents had ripped through a bus on New Year's Day, 1997, killing and wounding over fifty passengers. The bus ride was not too long—only about five hours—but it seemed longer due to the cacophony of pop songs and the shouts and screams of the on-board movie blaring from the overhead speakers. The new inter-city buses are a far cry from the colorful and venerable "Hob Hob" buses bouncing along with chickens on their tops, as depicted in so many tour guides; they are, in fact, far more comfortable than any American buses I've ridden. But there is the noise factor—the radio and television are almost always on, sometimes simultaneously, and usually at full volume. This trip was to be my initiation into life on buses, what I later would call "My Life with ʿAdel Imam," the famous Egyptian actor, since his movies are standard fare on the Damascus-Aleppo line. By the end of my fieldwork, I must have seen over a dozen of his movies.

I arrived in Aleppo on a cold, wet evening and made my way to Martyr's Square in the newer part of the city. Despite the large Martyr's Monument dominating the northern end of the square, locals refer to this area as "*Siyāḥī*," after the nearby *Siyāḥī* [Tourist] hotel. The hotel's café was to be the scene of many an afternoon's discussion for me and my Aleppine friends and in many ways was my virtual office in Aleppo. Not long after settling into Aleppo, where residential phone service was at the time still a luxury, I began to receive phone calls in the café, a privilege afforded by the head waiter, Abu ʿAli, only to "regulars." But on this first night I did not know what to expect, although I had made arrangements to meet a friend there who would put me up while I searched for an apartment.

By coincidence, a group of philosophy professors from Damascus University were seated in the café. They had come to Aleppo to give lectures at the university and were awaiting a midnight bus ride back to the capital. I settled in next to them and, after customary introductions, they asked about my research. One of the philosophers, a specialist in medieval Arab thought, immediately asked me, "What is your theoretical framework?" I was taken aback. Not only had no one in Syria asked me about theory, I actually had forgotten my theoretical framework, it had been so long since I had thought or talked about it. I muttered a few words about aesthetics and anthropology, about being eclectic, and so on, when my inquisitor—as I began to see him—stated, "Well, of course you must be using Adorno!" Adorno? I had rejected Adorno some years earlier for his statements on jazz (that it is not creative and promotes regressive listening, for example) and had only a passing knowledge of his aesthetic theory. I again muttered something about needing to look again at Adorno but also relying on Arab sources, when the professor thundered, "Adorno was a maestro! You must use him if you want to understand our music!"

Some Syrians had pointed me toward the works of such thinkers as al-Kindī, al-Fārābī, al-Ghazzali, and other great Muslim philosophers and musical theorists as important references for my research. In my mind, too, these were the paragons of authenticity and I spent many hours trying to acquire copies of their texts or poring over them in libraries searching for clues to the "genuine" Arab tradition. Ironically, it seemed to me, many also referred me to the British Orientalist and musicologist Henry George Farmer's history of Arab music (1929), now a standard reference for Arabs since its translation into Arabic, but I ignored it, preferring to read the "original" texts.

Within my first few minutes of arriving in Aleppo, I was confronting an unexpected challenge, and the message was clear: If I wanted to research and write something other than merely a documentary, self-celebratory study of Arab music in Syria, I would need to rise above my preconceived notions of authenticity and reach out, if not to Adorno then to some critical stance from which to understand the music that I had come to research. I had at once to be within the tradition, absorbing—osmosis-like—the sounds and spirit of the music and culture, and without it, finding my edge, my critical stance. This is one of the many paradoxes of fieldwork and this philosopher was among the first to introduce me to it. Much of my time in Aleppo and subsequently while writing was to be a tacking between these poles, a quest for what musicians said was the "heart" (*qalb*) of the music and a search for a critical perspective from which to understand it.

The suggestion that I look to Adorno for critical tools also indicated the international, trans-local nature of discourses on culture and authenticity in Syria. Most of the artists, intellectuals, and musicians with whom I studied and interacted had a far more sophisticated understanding than I of what it meant to be authentically Syrian and or Arab in the late twentieth century. For them, it was not a contradiction to read T. S. Eliot alongside Adonis—rather, it was part of their experience of modernity; one young writer even asserted that because *The Waste Land* evoked for him visions of the Arab world, Eliot was an "Arab" poet. I would at a minimum need to rethink many of my preconceptions, not the least being what I thought about authenticity and Arab music.

This chapter explores the conceptual terrain in which contemporary Syrian intellectuals and artists articulate notions of authenticity and cultural identity. To answer why it is that certain Syrian intellectuals and artists are concerned with authenticity requires an investigation into the historical conditions that have allowed the question of authenticity to be posed in the first place. The question of authenticity arose in the context of the question of modernity in Syria and around the Arab world, beginning in the late eighteenth century with the onset of European colonization of the region and continuing through the current struggles of Arab nations such as Syria to adapt to rapidly changing global political and economic conditions. Therefore, authenticity cannot be understood apart from its relationship to conceptions of modernity. In its turn, the experience of modernity in Syria cannot be understood as independent of the experience of modernity elsewhere, especially in Europe. Despite familiar tropes of civilizational clash and the differences between the Occident and the Orient with respect to cultural modernity and social modernization, in many ways modernity has been mutually constituted in the "West" and the "East," primarily through the mechanism of colonialism but also through post- and neo-colonial political, economic, and intellectual relationships.

I explore the conditions for the construction of modernity in Syria by way of the metaphor of musical improvisation. Understood as a form of composition in the moment, improvisation when applied to larger-scale processes of nation-building and socio-cultural development may help to settle debates about the nature of modernity, especially how to account for multiple variants of modern subjectivity and at the same time a seemingly singular logic. I argue that the conditions for the production of modernity—especially the colonial encounter—have allowed for the elaboration of multiple and sometimes contradictory constellations of characteristics that define modern subjectivity in different settings.

In Syria, the experience of the French mandate and the changing relationship of Syria to an evolving Euro-American–dominated global economy after World War II has meant that Syria shares numerous discourses of cultural modernity and social modernization with the West in its many guises. Today, nevertheless, Syrian intellectuals, like many of their counterparts around the Arab world, increasingly are striving to envision an alternative modernity at once Syrian, Arab, and modern.[1] A critical term in contemporary Syrian discourses of modernity and cultural authenticity has been that of heritage (*turāth*). In its myriad manifestations, heritage has come to embody numerous discourses of self and society in contemporary Syria, but especially those discourses that relate to the domain of affect and sentiment. In the context of debates about modernity, musical practices in particular become powerful agents for embodying affect and sentiment in ways that contribute to the definition of what it can mean to be modern in Syria today. This runs against the grain of most analyses of modernity, which have privileged techno-rationality and the political-economic trappings of the modern nation-state. Syrian modernity offers a way of understanding not only how Syrians and Arabs may differ from Europeans in the constitution of subjectivities, but also how such domains as the emotions and sentiment can become conscripted into national (if not nationalist) dialogues about modernity.

Keywords in the Aesthetics of Authenticity

What allows certain Syrian intellectuals and artists to question how they can be modern citizens of the world and at the same time retain a sense of cultural authenticity? To answer this question requires an examination of the historical constitution of some of the keywords in contemporary aesthetic discourse, primarily modernity, authenticity, and heritage. In what follows, I examine these terms as they emerged in four major periods in modern Syrian history: the late Ottoman Period (from the middle of the eighteenth century to the end of World War I); the period of France's occupation of Syria (1920–1946); the post-Independence period up to the June 1967 war with Israel; and finally, the period from the defeat of 1967 until the present.[2] In each of these periods, the concepts of modernity, authenticity, heritage, and cultural identity—always closely linked—assumed distinct forms and articulated with intellectual, political, and economic currents in the Arab lands and around the world.

Modernity (*Ḥadātha*)

In contemporary Syrian thought, the question of authenticity lies at the heart of debates over modernity. Indeed, in most textual discussions of the condition of modernity in Syria, the two terms form a binary pair; seldom is authenticity discussed in the absence of a discussion of modernity, and vice versa (Adonis 1986; Ṭarābīshī 1991; al-ʿAzmeh 1993; see Jābrī 1991, 1999 on Morocco). The Arabic term most commonly used to refer to modernity in these debates is *ḥadātha*. Literally meaning newness, novelty, or youthfulness, *ḥadātha* derives from the trilateral Arabic root ḥ-d-th, which also generates such words as *ḥadīth,* new, modern, but also speech, narrative, and Prophetic tradition; *ḥādith,* an occurrence, event, happening, or mishap; *iḥdāth,* production, creation, causation; and *taḥdīth,* modernization, renewal. The principle connotations of *ḥadātha* are thus newness, occurrence, and speech utterance.

A sense of newness also can be expressed by the word *jadīd* (new), though it is generally not used in Syria to connote modernity. Rather, *jadīd* generally is used in contradistinction to *qadīm,* meaning old. In some instances, *ḥadātha* describes the transformation from *qadīm* to *jadīd* (Barqāwī 1999: 50). In Egypt, as El-Shawan has demonstrated (1980; n.d.), *qadīm* and *jadīd* are used to refer to distinct types of musical heritage: *qadīm* refers to pre-WWI musical heritage, whereas *jadīd* refers to post-WWI styles, what in Syria are generally referred to as *ḥadīth* (al-Sharif 1991). When the connotation is newness, either term suffices. When the connotation is social or cultural modernity, usually the terms *ḥadātha* and *ḥadīth* are used. The eventfulness and the sense of occurrence implied by *ḥadātha* suggest some of the social and cultural implications of modernity that *jadīd* or the nominative *jidda* (newness) do not.

Finally, another word that arises in the context of discourses of modernity is *muʿāṣara* (contemporaneity). The connotations of *ḥadātha* and *muʿāṣira* are not identical; something can be contemporary without necessarily being modern or modernist. Yet, Syrian intellectuals tend to use them in very similar ways—that is, as a counterpoint to the concept of authenticity (*aṣāla*). Intellectual discourse on Syrian society almost exclusively uses *ḥadātha* to discuss social and cultural modernity, and hence I will use this term to refer to modernity with the understanding that Syrians sometimes use *muʿāṣira* to convey some of the same meanings.

It is important when considering the history of these terms and their relationship to discourses of art and aesthetics to distinguish between *ḥadātha* as cultural and intellectual modernity, and *ḥadātha* as social modernization (what is often referred to as *taḥdīth*). While modernity and modernization overlap to a certain extent, as in nineteenth-century calls for the reform and modernization of Arab society and culture, the latter term assumed greater importance in the post-Independence period as Syria embarked on an aggressive program of social modernization in order to create "modern Syria."[3] As scholars have shown for other areas of the world undergoing rapid social change in the period of decolonization (for example, Escobar 1995), Western modernization theories of the 1950s were advocated by both international agencies and modernizing elites as models for rational development and social modernization in the developing world. In many instances, these models replaced earlier models of cultural modernity or even modernism to the extent that for the generation coming of age in this period, the two terms were inseparable. This was the case in Syria.

Authenticity (*Aṣāla*)

The word *aṣāla* has come to mean the converse of *ḥadātha* in contemporary Syrian discourse. In the context of the dialectic of modernity and tradition, *aṣāla* signifies genuineness and therefore is translated commonly as authenticity.[4] However, the use of *aṣāla* to mean authenticity reflects a decidedly modern sensibility. Examination of Arabic and Arabic-English dictionaries and lexicons from the eighteenth and nineteenth centuries reveals that *aṣāla* did not refer to "authenticity" in the modern sense of the word. For example, in the late eighteenth-century Arabic dictionary *Tāj al-ʿarūs* (Murtaḍā al-Zabīdī 1966) and in Edward Lane's *Arabic-English Lexicon* (1978 [1863]), *aṣāla* does not carry the connotation of "authenticity" but rather refers to notions of rootedness, fixedness, permanence, and lineage.[5] The verb *aṣula-yaʾṣulu* means to be firmly rooted and established, or to be of noble descent, whereas the nominative *aṣl* refers to a root, a tree trunk, an origin point or foundation, a cause, a principle or fundamental, as well as noble descent and lineage. The adjectival forms *aṣīl* (having a root or foundation) and *aṣlī* (underived, original) often are used interchangeably to signify cultural practices and objects that are considered to be deeply rooted and therefore genuine (Lane 1978: 64–66).[6]

In contemporary Syria, *aṣāla* and *aṣl* retain the connotations of rootedness and pure descent. One commonly asks where a person is from "*aṣlan,*" that is, originally, referring to a particular geographical location and, implicitly, a specific genealogy. Those Syrians considered to be genuinely Arab tend to be those with an *aṣl* from the Arabian Peninsula. For example, a wealthy Aleppine merchant, when I asked him about his family's roots, brought out his family tree and graphically illustrated for me the ways in which the different meanings of *aṣl* as tree trunk and genuine and authentic descent may correspond. Held safely under lock and key in a special cabinet, the document—a parchment scroll measuring about six feet in length and a foot wide—depicts his ancestry (*naṣab*) literally as a family tree having a central trunk rising along the many pages of the scroll and numerous branches stretching off to the sides. The names of individual male members of his patrilineage are inscribed in leaves sprouting from each branch, arranged according to relationship to the founding line or trunk of the family tree. Newer pieces of parchment attached at the end of the scroll include the names of this man and his six sons. The oldest pieces of the scroll are very old and faded and hard to read. Yet one can discern the roots of the family tree planted firmly in the Hijaz, the region of the holy cities of Mecca and Medina in the Arabian Peninsula. According to the merchant, the scroll indicates that his ancestors first branched out of the Hijaz and migrated to Aleppo some five hundred years ago, thereby establishing himself as a member of one of the oldest Arab families in Aleppo. As further evidence of his authentic Aleppine roots, he showed me pictures of his family's expansive fifteenth-century home in the Old City; although the house remains in their possession to this day, they now choose to live in a modern quarter of the city.

The modern usage of *aṣāla* to refer to authenticity thus reflects an important shift in the meaning of the term that must be understood in the context of the dialectic of modernity and tradition characteristic of Arab thought since the nineteenth-century Arab Renaissance (*nahḍa*). Indeed, according to the Syrian historian ʿAzīz al-ʿAzmeh (1992: 13–14), "modernity is the root of authenticity" (*al-ḥadātha aṣl al-aṣāla*). Like Orientalism, modern discourses of authenticity—whether with regard to Islam, literature, or the nation—essentialize Arab culture and society as self-sufficient and unchanging (al-ʿAzmeh 1993: 42; 1992: 31–33). In this manner, *aṣāla,* like identity (*huwiyya*) and selfhood (*dhātiyya*), articulates implicit notions of political and cultural unity (al-ʿAzmeh 1992: 27). Thus, history is understood as consisting of the alternation of stages of internal purity and corruption by external agents, of ascendant authenticity and vulgar decline (al-ʿAzmeh 1993: 42; 1992: 17).

Napoleon's Invasion, The *Nahḍa,* and the "Shock" of Modernity

Historians of the Middle East commonly date the advent of modernity in the Arab World to Napoleon's invasion of Egypt in 1798 (Hourani 1983; Yapp 1987). When Napoleon's forces arrived, they not only brought with them superior arms and military training but also ideas of political, economic, and cultural organization, as well as scientific and cultural missions to advance these ideas. Faced with the superiority of European civilization and a pervasive sense of the decline of Arab culture under Ottoman rule, Arabs were provoked by the encounter into reexamining their own culture and society, according to these histories. Indeed, the Syrian-born poet and critic Adonis asserts that the encounter with modern European military and scientific technology produced what he terms the "shock of modernity" (*ṣadmat al-ḥadātha*) (Adonis 1986). The Arabic word *ṣadma* means not only a shock but a jolt, collision, or blow; it may also imply a psychic or psychological shock as well. According to this view, the shock of modernity moved many Arab intellectual and political leaders to attempt to reform Arab society and culture in a number of domains, including, of course, the military, but also politics, economics, education, language, literature, religion, gender relations, and the arts (Hourani 1983; Mitchell 1991; Barakat 1993). This was the beginning of what Albert Hourani termed the Liberal Age of Arabic thought, one characterized by curiosity about the West, great openness to new ideas, and simultaneously an increased interest in the past and in cultural authenticity, thought to reside in the past.

In the context of conceptions of history and change that presuppose an essential self, it comes as little surprise, notes al-ʿAzmeh (1993: 42), that the response to the engagement with (or shock of) European modernity is termed the *nahḍa*, or revival. Derived from the root n-h-ḍ, *nahḍa* literally means a rising up, a standing up, or a reawakening, and carries further connotations of revival, even renaissance. According to the prevailing historiography of this period, contact (or impact) with Europe inspired Arabs to reform their culture and society, to "retrieve an essence that the vicissitudes of time and the designs of enemies, rather than change of any intrinsic nature, had caused to atrophy" (al-ʿAzmeh 1993: 42). The "nahḍawist" visions of modernity were nevertheless plural and often incommensurate. As several scholars have noted, some secular reformers advocated a strict departure from the past and an acceptance if not zealous embracing of European culture and civilization (*ḥaḍāra*), while others advocated a more skeptical stance toward European society and culture (Barakat 1993: 239–65; Laroui 1976). Religious reformers also were diverse; some advocated a return to the envisioned purity of the earliest Muslim community (such as in the *salafiyya* movements), while others, usually termed by Western commentators as "liberal" or "progressive," advanced less radical visions (Barakat 1993: 242–43; Hourani 1983: 67–160). Finally, a variety of compromising trends emerged that advocated some eclectic mixture of borrowing from Europe what seemed most valuable while retaining certain practices from the repertoire of Arab customs and habits (Barakat 1993: 239–51). It is within these competing and contradictory approached to the question of modernity that I situate my discussion of modernity and Syrian music.

These contradictions are apparent in the Arab arts from the turn of the twentieth century. For example, this period witnessed a renewed interest in classical poetry—the *Dīwān al-ʿArab* or registry of Arab achievements and touchstone of Arab identity. Yet, with the revival of classical poetry came the rise of the novel as a genre of Arabic literature and a prodigious movement to translate works of European culture into Arabic. With respect to music, historians write of a musical *nahḍa* and the revival of classical "Arab" genres by such noted nineteenth- and early twentieth-century artists as Muḥammad ʿUthmān, ʿAbdū al-Ḥāmūlī, and Salāma Ḥijāzī (Lagrange 1996: 69–108).[7] This same period also saw the rise of new genres of light colloquial songs associated with the musical theater that developed in Cairo in the late nineteenth century and had roots in European and Arab-Ottoman theatrical and musical practices (Danielson 1997; Lagrange 1996: 109–11; al-Sharif 1991).

Indeed, in the period of the *nahḍa* we witness the rise of a modern conception of art (*fann*) as a mode of cultural expression independent of craft. Prior to the modern period, *fann* referred to techniques and technical abilities, such as chemistry and navigation in the technical sense, and not to painting and music per se, the latter of which was classified in classical texts as a branch of science and philosophy (Shiloah 1995: 45–47). Even today, remnants of the earlier association of *fann* with the technical professions remain in Syria. The "art" objects of glass blowing, wood working, and weaving are sold in the Ministry of Tourism's "Handicrafts Market" in Damascus. Of course, gathering these diverse practices under one roof and calling them "handicrafts" reflects more the Syrian Ministry of Tourism's classification than an indigenous one, but it serves as a reminder that the term "art," as in pre-modern Europe, referred primarily to crafts and techniques not associated with what we today consider to be a medium of personal expression. Therefore, when Arab intellectuals of the *nahḍa* and today express a desire to revive or preserve older artistic traditions, they may be imposing a decidedly modern conception of what art entails on an earlier association of art with craft and craft production.

Despite the diversity of intellectual and artistic trends in this period, a common assumption is that the *nahḍa* came as a response to a European impetus that indeed was felt by Arabs as a "shock." The idea that modernity shocked Arab society and culture suggests that the Arabic culture was somehow dormant and needed to be rejuvenated by the light of European modernity, understood in this view as an agent of change. Indeed, other terms used to describe this situation include *istifāqa, ṣaḥwa,* and *yaqẓa,* each of which means an awakening (Ṭarābīshī 1991: 18). These terms imply that the Arabs were asleep in what Rāshid al-Ghannūshī terms "the sleep of decay" (*nawmat al-inḥiṭaṭ;* cited in Ṭarābīshī 1991: 17). As the Syrian critic George Ṭarābīshī notes, shock has come to play a critical role in contemporary Arab discourse about the relationship of the Arabs with Europe and constitutes one of the central concepts with which

Arab intellectuals understand themselves (*waʿī al-waʿī al-ʿarabī li-dhātihi,* "the self-awareness of the Arab consciousness"; Ṭarābīshī 1991: 17). The state of shock, argues Ṭarābīshī, refers to the "shocked object" (*al-mafʿūl al-iyqāẓī al-tanbīhī,* "the awakened and stimulated object"), which passively reacts to the "shocking entity," which is Europe in its various roles as invader, colonizer, protector, and modernizer (Ṭarābīshī 1991: 18).

The metaphor of the shock of modernity suggests a physical and mechanical understanding of the relationship between Europe and the Arab world, namely the collision of one body in motion with another that is more or less stationary. This latter condition, according to the shock model, describes Arab society and culture in the late eighteenth century with the arrival of Napoleon's forces on the shores of Alexandria. Under the impact of the body in motion (the "West"), the motionless or inert body (the "East") was propelled into motion with a direction and velocity proportional to the energy and direction of impact. The resulting motion of the impacted body differs according to the ideology of the critic: forward along the linear track of modernity for optimistic secular modernists and their Western commentators, or, on the contrary, backwards toward the past in a search for authentic roots, or some variety of these two motions—the eclectic responses that Laroui outlines (Barakat 1993: 240; Laroui 1976). But in almost all cases, there was motion, and it describes the dominant European meta-history of modernity as linear progress.

Deconstructing the Term "Shock"

Few critics question the metaphor of the shock of modernity itself. Ṭarābīshī, although he acknowledges the physical metaphor of the term "shock," argues merely that the Arab response to its collision with Western civilization was not so much a shock, which implies a certain amount of resilience on the part of the struck body, but a trauma (*raḍḍa,* lit. bruise or contusion), by which the inert body is permanently damaged and incapable of proper forward motion. Adopting a psychoanalytic framework for the study of group behavior, Ṭarābīshī (1991) argues that the Arabs were traumatized by this encounter psychologically as well as physically, socially, politically, and culturally. Especially after the losses of 1948 and 1967, the formerly shocked entity has become, according to Ṭarābīshī, a "traumatized entity" (Ṭarābīshī 1991: 18).[8]

Adonis, Ṭarābīshī, and others subscribe to the notion that Napoleon's invasion represented a form of civilizational collision and that the Arabs were the inert body—subject to shock, from one perspective, or bruising, from the other (Barakat 1993: 239–42). Yet, can this picture be maintained? Pursuing the collision metaphor raises questions regarding the disproportional motion of the two bodies, their relationship to other bodies, in motion or inert, and the consequences of the impact for all parties. To what extent was the interaction of Europe and the Arab lands in the eighteenth century a collision or clash when, for example, French already were residing in Alexandria when Napoleon arrived (al-Jabartī 1993: 20), and, more significantly, when economic and cultural networks had linked the peoples of the Mediterranean basin for centuries by the time of Napoleon's adventures in the East (Abu-Lughod 1989)? While acknowledging the military and technological superiority of the French and Europe in general at the time, can we consider the Arabs to have been asleep and their encounter with Europe and European modernity to have been a collision (however shocking or traumatic it may have been)? Was the *nahḍa* merely a response to Europe, an attempt to return and revive a former state of purity?[9]

Moreover, while the notion of shock implies an effect solely on the body being impacted, the above-mentioned studies do not pause to reflect on the possible influences on Europe of the collision with the Arab world. Following Said (1978, 1994) and other critics of colonial and postcolonial European and Arab relations (Barakat 1993; Mitchell 1991), the encounter of "West" and "East" should be seen as having reciprocal if uneven consequences, among which was the mutual constitution or construction of modernity itself. First, the shock of modernity was felt in both "bodies" and was in a sense a product of the interaction of "East" and "West" and not merely an agent of the collision itself. That is, rather than being the outcome of a collision of the "East" with a modern "West," modernity was co-produced in the "West" and "East" as a result of their interaction. For example, Mitchell (1991) analyzes the role of colonialism not only in shaping European perceptions of colonial Egypt but of "enframing" European self-perceptions. Said's *Orientalism* (1978) and *Culture and Imperialism* (1994) discuss not only how Orientalist thought participated in colonial regimes of knowledge and power but also how Europe's experience with the Orient shaped the development of modern European art and letters. The "Orient" and the "Oriental" served as a mirror in which Europeans created their own self images to the extent that what we label "modern European culture" was a product of the interaction—and less so the collision—of Europe with its colonies.[10]

Arab discourses in the Liberal Age were not merely derivative of European enlightenment ideals, as the collision and shock metaphor would suggest. Rather, Arab intellectuals, while at times borrowing from European ideas of civilization and modernity,[11] at the same time proposed novel ideals and drew on an extensive Arab intellectual and political heritage in the quest to articulate their own visions of modernity; the diverse visions of such reformers as

Muḥammad ʿAbdū, Jamāl al-Dīn al-Afghānī, Rifaʿat al-Ṭaḥṭāwī, ʿAbd al-Raḥmān al-Kawākibī, Qāsim Amīn, and Shiblī Shumayyil, just to name a few, can hardly be thought of as merely derivative of European discourses (see Barakat 1993: 242–51). While the dynamics and consequences of this interaction were not identical for Arabs and Europeans and imbalances in power and influence often increased under colonial rule, yet neither were the relationships so one-sided as the shock of modernity metaphor and its associated discourses of cultural purity and authenticity imply.

Colonialism and Alternative Modernities

The mutual construction of modernity in the Arab world and Europe produced not a unified vision of modernity in both regions but rather different and historically constituted and dynamic visions of alternative modernities (Gaonkar 1999, 2000; Mitchell 2000, 2003; Taylor 1999: 162). What is meant by an "alternative" modernity? As used by Gaonkar and Taylor, "alternative" implies the existence of a "standard" or normative experience of modernity, which in their arguments is "Western" modernity in its many guises. Both authors argue for a "cultural" theory of modernity that privileges the contributions of "local cultures" to the eventual form that modernity assumes in different societies; their cultural models of modernity seek to counteract "acultural" or universalizing theories and models that stipulate a universal paradigm of the gradual banishment of tradition with the rise of techno-rational secular society. Yet, at the same time, the cultural model of modernity accepts the notion that modernity began in Europe and then spread to other lands as a result of European colonialism. This perspective gauges "alternative" modernities in comparison to an implied "normative" modernity: European cultural modernity.

In this work, I also adopt a cultural model of modernity and argue for the existence of particular varieties of Syrian modernities. Yet it is misleading to privilege European modernities as prior to non-European modernities and in that sense normative, even if aspects of social modernization began in Europe sooner than in Europe's colonies. The narrative chronology of colonialism—the dates of arrival and conquest, of specific economic and political reforms, and the like—draws attention away from the long-standing interactions of European and non-European peoples over several centuries and the mutual production of concepts and practices that we commonly associate with modernity: ideas about the individual and society, military and economic reorganization, pedagogical reforms, science education, the rise of mass media, the arts, and literature, for example (see Mitchell 1991; Viswanathan 1989). We therefore need to strive to understand "modernity" as a condition co-produced by Europe and its colonies, even before they were colonies, enacted through specific policies and practices, and differentially experienced in different cultures and eras.

Moreover, we must not assume that "Syria," "Arab," and "modernity" (let alone "music") refer to fixed entities and essences. As Talal Asad notes (1993: 16), narrative accounts of modernity within modern nation-states tend to assume the teleological development of fixed entities, even when they are not "making their own histories" but rather evolving or changing in response to outside agents (as in the shock of modernity metaphor). By advancing an analysis of possible alternative modernities in Syrian music, I do not wish to advance a notion of Syria as a fixed and eternal geographical and historical-political unity that developed an alternative modernity to that found in Europe, but rather as a rhetorical figure ("Syria") constructed in the context of competing visions of modernity in relation to those constructed in and as "Europe."

Recognizing the co-production of modernity in the colonial encounter between Europe and its possessions undermines the collision/shock metaphor of modernity and its experience in the colonial peripheries. At the same time, by arguing that contemporary Syrian intellectuals and artists seek to formulate some sort of alternative to Western modernity is to assume that European modernity somehow serves as a standard upon which other variations are alternatives. In this view, modernity may have been co-produced historically in the encounter between Europe and Europe's colonies—that is, it is singular in origin—but its development over the past two centuries has allowed for the evolution of multiple formulations—that is, it is plural in nature. Such a distinction allows for the formulation of more precise histories of political-economic and cultural developments around the globe and at the same time stands as a corrective to ethnocentric models of modernity and the rise of the nation-state.

Yet, as Timothy Mitchell suggests (2000: 11; 2003), adopting a multiple or alternative modernity perspective leads to a dilemma: How, given the seemingly endless possible configurations of multiple modernities, do we account for the overwhelming power and success of the European imperial and now American neo-imperial models of modernity? It would seem that not all alternative modernities are equally alternative; few Syrians strive to construct a South Asian, Latin-American, Chinese, or African model of modernity, for example.[12] The primary political-economic and cultural referents in Syria are (officially) Eastern Europe and the former Soviet Union, and (popularly) Western Europe and North America.

As a social and cultural condition, modernity was born of and in the colonial encounter between Europe and its colonies, including, and especially, the Middle East. It was not, in this view, a product of autochthonous European developments. Social modernization in Europe preceeded that in the Arab, Ottoman, and other colonized lands partly due to historical political-economic reasons, especially the conquest of the New World and the advantages this brought to European centers of power (see Wallerstein 1975; Wolf 1982). Europe's development, based on the extraction of resources from the lands it colonized and their systematic underdevelopment,[13] led the experiences of modernity to diverge so that Europe's modes of social, cultural, and economic-industrial production came to be understood as a standard by which to judge others, who in the Eurocentric model developed alternative (read "inferior") modernities.

Yet, the discourse of alternative or multiple modernities needs to be understood as a product of this process of standardizing Europe's experiences of modernity—not only its overt political and economic structures, but more importantly its modes of representation, organization of space and time, and regimes of politics and economy (Mitchell 1991, 2003). That is, the unequal power relations on which European colonial modernity was built remain masked in the alternative modernities model, so that "modernity" serves as a sort of socio-cultural fetish. Put another way, the concept of "cultural modernity" itself masks the unequal power relations that are the true basis for the comparison of "standard" and "alternative" modernities. In this regard, the quest for alternative cultural modernities (in West Bengal, Syria, Kenya, and elsewhere) is in fact a recognition of the unequal political-economic foundations of modern and modernist society, and not a response to European modernity, as Chatterjee (1993), Gaonkar (1999), Taylor (1999), and others would have it. The desire to construct a cultural or spiritual sphere of postcolonial difference marks at once the recognition of these unequal relations, and at the same time the misrecognition of their origins in colonialism.

In the case of Syria, the search for a cultural alternative to Western modernity (or the mimicry of Europe's experiences) has unfolded in the absence of a sustained progress toward modernization in the public, political, and material spheres, an absence due in part though not wholly to the underdevelopment of Syria under Ottoman and French rule. Hence, the only spheres in effect available for modernization are the cultural and spiritual, which offer a patina of (often socialist-inspired) ideologies of socioeconomic and gender equality, civilization and development, and technological progress, but nonetheless rest on continued patterns of cronyism, corruption, and dictatorial leadership.

Tracing the historical constitution of modernity in Syria—and by "in" I refer to this rhetorical time-space in which transnational processes of social modernization and cultural modernity are understood as developing in alternative forms—reveals its evolution in relation to French and other visions of modernity in the diverse "West," including those of the United States in the era immediately following Independence (1946) and, later, of Eastern Europe and the former Soviet Union from the 1960s until the late 1980s. The evolution of these different visions of modernity can be traced in the arts and music, which not only expressed or reflected these visions but played an active role in constructing them, especially through the contested notions of cultural authenticity and heritage, which came to assume greater prominence in discourses of modernity after the 1967 defeat (*hazīma*) in the war with Israel.

Moreover, authenticity came to be defined dialectically with respect to variously imagined "authentic" elements of Arab culture and "inauthentic" elements derived from the West. The most important of these, which I explore in the coming chapters, is the realm of the emotions and sentiment, understood by many Syrians and other Arabs as a defining element of their authentic selves. Techno-rationality, identified strongly with the West, is also often understood implicitly to be the opposite of Arab emotionality and sentiment; in fact, many Syrians argue that technology and hyper-rationality are the primary means for corrupting and debasing the authentic Arab spirit and for creating the inauthentic practices and beliefs that partisans of tradition claim dominate cultural life in the Arab world today. While it would be tempting to read rationality as a characteristic of modernity and emotionality as a characteristic of tradition, the discourses of techno-rationality and sentiment need to be understood not as antitheses but rather as two aspects of larger processes of the historical differentiation and unequal development between Syria, the Arab world, and Europe. Understood from a dialectical perspective, an authentic Arab modernity would be one in which the emotionality and true sentiment associated with tradition are combined with the technical sophistication and social civilization (*ḥaḍāra*) of First World modernity. The dynamic of this dialectic produces the aesthetics of authenticity in contemporary Syrian art worlds.

Improvising Modernity

Borrowing the concept of improvisation from music, I understand modernity as a process of self-composition within specific historical political-economic conditions, an approach suggested by the work of Pierre Bourdieu (1977) on the habitus and forms of agency within larger social structures (see also Bourdieu 1984; Calhoun 1993; Göle 2002). Musically understood, improvisation is not the ad hoc, spontaneous invention of music but rather a form of composition in the course of performance (Nettl 1998; see also Berliner 1994; Lord 1965; Monson 1996; and Reynolds 1995, among others). Artists draw on stock phrases, cultural conventions, and other of what Kant would call "conditioning concepts" in the composition of musical ideas and their actualization in a given performance. Neither fully pre-composed nor entirely invented on the spot, quality improvisations have the best qualities of pre-composed musics with an air of ingenuity and spontaneity. This is not to deny the mastery involved; indeed, for Arab music, master performers and astute critics differentiate between routine improvisations and "true" improvisation, when an artist draws on standard performance practices to create something that transcends tradition (see Racy 1998; see also al-Qalʿah 1997a).

In a similar manner, modernity is an act of composition (of selves, of nations, of economies and polities) in specific historical moments and specific spaces. Each "alternative" that we identify—South Asian, Arab, Melanesian, North American—refers back to a basic set of struggles, contradictions, and indeterminacies. National communities compose modern subjectivities through the selection of common, standard traits infused with culturally specific sets of meanings. Among the common traits are political and economic institutions based in the nation-state but having transnational connections and globalized networks with respect to the flows of people, media, technologies, finance, and ideologies (Appadurai 1990). At the same time, the orientations of different communities to these basic structural conditions are not identical but plural. Each can be thought of as an improvisation—a composition in the historical moment—that has recognizable relations to other performances as well as unique traits. For South Asia, Chatterjee (1993) identified spirituality as a distinct realm that marked Indian modernity as separate from (alternative to) European modernity. For Arab modernity, especially as I understand its unfolding in the Syrian case, sentiment and economies of affect and emotion constitute a basis of difference in the production and composition of modernity in the conditions of late capitalism.

This is not simply a matter of "theme and variation," with Europe setting the theme and other nations providing colorful local variations; such an approach would merely reiterate in musical terms the idea that European modernity is a standard upon which other, alternative modernities are based. European modernity is not the main theme upon which other nations improvise in their quest for alternative modernities. Rather, the improvisation metaphor suggests that all varieties and experiences of modernity, including Europe's, are improvisations on a related set of principles, representational practices, and political economic processes. Europe's differential power historically has meant that the texture and pitch of the European variation are echoed though never wholly reproduced in those of other nations. The reverse is certainly true, and we can hear elements of other nations' modern experiences in European improvisations: Orientalism in European literature, for example, is one result of this echoing (Said 1978, 1994). I like to think of the situation as akin to a jam session, with Europe currently laying down the major beat and melodic structures, but other nations and regions providing diverse melodic and rhythmic materials. In some ways, the phenomenon of World Music is a sonic example of this relationship. As Andre Gunder Frank has argued recently (1998), until the eighteenth century it was a Chinese model that organized a growing world system; there are signs today that an Asian-based modernity may return as the dominant model in the twenty-first century.

Another way to talk about the relationships among European and non-European experiences and structures of modernity is via the metaphor of "family resemblance" (Wittgenstein 1953). Different configurations of modernity, including ways of understanding the self and defining community, may not relate to one another on the basis of specific features, but rather in terms of likely or characteristic features of a family of related social and cultural constellations. In this regard, they can be said to have a family resemblance, even when the direct genealogical links among them are complex. The family resemblance metaphor for modernity allows for indeterminacies and disjunctures as well as shared challenges in the experiences of modern subjectivity in places as diverse as urban South Asia (Chakrabarty 2001) and rural Egypt (see Mitchell 2003). In a similar manner, Rodney Needham (1975), drawing on information science, advances the term "polythetic classification" to categorize strategies and behaviors characteristic of whole classes of entities—modern nations, for example—that cannot be well defined in terms of specific traits such as economic organization, cultural characteristics, and social dynamics (traits that in Needham's framework would fall under the rubric of "monothetic" classification). The wide array of social and cultural constellations that we call the modern (or even postmodern) condition share sets of likely dispositions, structures, and dynamics, but we cannot define in a precise manner what these characteristics must be in order for them to constitute modernity, alternative or otherwise. Moreover, precise definition risks over-asserting continuities and ignoring indeterminacies. A polythetic approach to modernity allows for such indeterminacies without ignoring the underlying structural conditions that unite diverse experiences of the modern condition.

A genealogical approach to modernity can be productive when understood in light of recent theories of kinship. Traditional anthropological understandings of genealogy and models of lineal descent may hinder our ability to understand the complex webs of ties between cultural phenomena that may have similar origins but unique histories of development and change, or divergent origins and convergent developments. Indeed, recently elaborated developments in molecular genetics and population biology have problematized the very concept of origin and models of the unilineal descent of biological traits (see Helmreich 2003). Newer models posit an "agenealogical" principle of lateral gene transfer that undermines teleological classifications of life forms. We might argue likewise that such a model accurately describes the origins of modern thought and modernity—multisited, complex, interpolated networks of ties at once political, economic, aesthetic, and imaginary. The origins of modernity cannot be traced back to an ur-modern Europe but rather must be located in a complex network of relationships, ideologies, practices, and political-economic processes driven at least in part by colonialism, and crystallized with the rise of nation-states. The farther back we reach in our quest for the origins of modernity, the muddier the lineage: for example, early-modern Europe's reliance on translations of texts from Muslim Spain's great libraries, themselves modeled on translations from the Greek and Latin from ninth-century Baghdad, problematizes unilineal Enlightenment intellectual histories (see Menocal 2002). And the earlier texts were already palimpsests of intricate intellectual heritages and inheritances. A "polythetic" perspective does more than merely obfuscate the origins of "Western" philosophy and history in a jumble of past influences; it undermines any attempt to base a history of the present on cumulative teleologies of progress and rationalization deriving from an essentially European trajectory. If there can be no standard model of modernity, if there is no essentially European modernity, how can there be "alternatives"? The improvisation metaphor, I suggest, offers a possible solution to the dilemma of how to account for the diverse "family resemblances" in the evolution of modern subjectivities, while acknowledging Europe's dominance on the world stage in the last three centuries.

Composing Syrian Modernity: An Historical Overview

With this in mind, the following question presents itself: How has modernity been composed and improvised in Syria? Tracing the development of modernist discourses and practices in Syria necessitates an excavation into the history of Syria's relations with Europe to complement the geneaologies of the terms used to promote and contest modernity in Syria delineated above. In what follows, I address these issues, focusing on debates within the realm of the arts and especially musical performance and music theory that reveal some of the contradictions in the quest to compose a Syrian-Arab modernity in the twentieth century. Since these debates took place in the context of Europe's colonial domination of the Middle East, it is not surprising that the West serves as a point of orientation (often as a straw man) for many early twentieth-century Syrian writers. The following genealogy is not meant to suggest a lineal history of cause and event but instead aims to excavate some of the ideologies and discursive strategies that were important in setting up the contemporary composition of modernity in Syria, which were similar to those in operation in other Arab lands experiencing the contradictions of colonial rule.

Following World War I and after some maneuvering among the European powers, France was granted a mandate over "Syria," which at the time included what is now Lebanon and parts of Turkey and Iraq.[14] The French mandate over Syria lasted from 1922 to 1944 and saw in addition to the fixing of the national boundaries of Syria—with the creation of an independent state of Lebanon, the granting of the Hatay Province to Turkey, and the ceding of the region of Mosul to Iraq, for example—the fixing of a national spirit in Syria, indeed the notion of a distinct historical-geographical entity called "Syria." Nationalism in Syria has taken many forms since the days of the mandate, from the "Greater Syria" ideologies of the 1930s to the pan-Arab sentiments of the Arab Socialist Baʿth (or Awakening) Party of the late 1940s and since (Hinnebusch 1991: 30–33; Hourani 1983; Khoury 1987). These ideologies articulated conceptions of modernity, both cultural and social, as well as distinct if implicit conceptions of Syrian culture and cultural authenticity to support these ideological claims.[15]

A focus on debates surrounding the modernization of Arab music can help shed some light both on the interaction of European and Syrian conceptualizations of modernity and culture, and on how this interaction produced distinct visions of cultural and social modernity in Syria in the 1930s and 1940s. I focus my remarks on the first Congress on Arab Music, held in Cairo in 1932, which had as one of its aims the scientific study of Arab music and its modernization, and then on Syrian reactions to the Congress and its proposals, which indicate a somewhat different understanding both of the music and of modernity. These sources reveal some of the contradictions concerning modernity and the relationships among social and cultural modernization, modernity, and Westernization. Also, they show that what is "authentic" Syrian Arabic culture in this period is different from what arose in subsequent periods, but in a sense formative of it.

The Modern Period: The 1932 Cairo Congress and the Question of Music Theory

A turning point in twentieth-century Arab music was the first Congress on Arab Music (*Muʾtamar al-mūsīqā al-ʿarabiyya*), held in Cairo in 1932. Convened under the patronage of the Egyptian King Fu'ād I, it brought together leading scholars and musicians from around the world to discuss and debate the principles of Arab music. An interesting issue is Fu'ād's decision to hold a conference on "Arab" music, since prior to this time the more common expression was "Oriental music" (*mūsīqā sharqiyya*). However, Fu'ād wanted to establish the basis for an Arab music in the Arab lands; in many ways this conference was an expression of Arab nationalist sentiment of the period (Danielson 1991: 24–27, 1997: 77). Moreover, referring to the melodic and rhythmic practices of the Arabs as "music" (*mūsīqā*) was not unproblematic because prior to the modern period the term referred primarily to theories of music and not to an autonomous realm of instrumental practices; Arabs tended to call their melodic and rhythmic practices *ghinā'* (song) or *inshād* (chant), revealing the privilege of the voice in Arab aesthetics. Only in the modern period, and as a consequence of the Cairo Congress and the influence of European scholars, has *mūsīqā* come to refer to instrumental music as well as theories about it (Lambert 1997: 26; Shiloah 1995: 59).

Following from the implied focus on "music" (and not song or voice), the participants at the Cairo Congress focused primarily on the precise definition of the Arabic scale, the definition and categorization of the melodic modes (*maqāmāt*), studies on genres and rhythms, the problem of notation, and numerous other technical matters related to the music (S. Marcus 1989; *Kitāb mu'tamar mūsīqā al-'arabiyya* 1933). Leading Arab musicians such as Syria's 'Alī al-Darwīsh and Egypt's Kāmil al-Khula'ī, Orientalist scholars such as Henry George Farmer and Rodolfe d'Érlanger, and such famous European scholar-composers as Bela Bartok and Paul Hindemith attended the conference and gave recommendations for the modernization of "Arab music." Today, many scholars and defenders of modernization celebrate the Cairo Congress as a landmark attempt to modernize the Arab musical heritage; numerous conferences have been held and publications issued on the context, recommendations, and overall importance of this event (for example, Hassan and Vigreux 1992). However, few contemporary commentators point out that the Cairo Congress and its recommendations were not uniformly considered successful when proposed and remain contested today. Indeed, many of the Syrian participants at the congress and later scholars considered it to be limited, if not a failure altogether (Bin Dhurayl 1989: 35, 54; Wīrdī 1948). Why was the Cairo Congress, so celebrated today, considered a failure in its own time?

One reason was the proposed adoption of an equal-tempered 24-note Arabic scale analogous to the equal-tempered scale used in European (tonal) music since Bach. Proponents of the equal-tempered Arabic scale, including the conference organizers and their Orientalist supporters, argued that it would help rationalize Arab music and allow for the use of functional harmony in composition, something seen as lacking in "classical" Arab music, which is largely monophonic (that is, comprising a single melodic line, though heterophony is common in ensemble situations). The adoption of an equal-tempered scale composed of 24 quarter-tones was proposed by the congress organizers, and the equal-tempered scale has been taught as the standard scale in many Arab conservatories ever since (Bin Dhurayl 1989: 34).

Yet a number of musicians and commentators at the Cairo Congress opposed the adoption of the equal-temperament, arguing that it does not capture the nuances of Arab music, which for them does not have uniform pitch intervals (S. Marcus 1989: 178–88). Equal-temperament does not accord with earlier theories of the Arabic scale, such as those of al-Kindī, al-Fārābī, and al-Urmawī, nor the system of fingers (*aṣābiʿ*) and courses (*majārī*) outlined in the ninth century by Isḥāq al-Mawṣilī, for which scale intervals are not uniform (al-ʿAqīlī 1979, vol. 4: 104–64; Bin Dhurayl 1989: 44–53; Shiloah 1995: 110–16; Wirdī 1948). According to a number of contemporary Syrian artists whom I interviewed, imposing an equal-tempered scale on Arab music leads to the loss of its "Oriental spirit" (*rūḥ sharqiyya*), which is one of the defining terms of the aesthetics of authenticity.

Another proposal of the Cairo Congress that aimed to rationalize Arab music was the adoption of a tetrachord model of the modal system. This model proposes that each mode (*maqām*) can be understood as consisting of two tetrachords (*ajnās*, sing. *jins*, from the Greek *génos*), or fixed sequences of four pitches (S. Marcus 1989: 271–322).[16] In this view, the modes can be categorized based on their constituent primary and secondary tetrachords into families (*faṣāʾil*, sing. *faṣīla*) of primary and branch modes.[17]

While some Syrian musicians have adopted this categorical scheme, especially those who have either studied in Cairo or who teach at the national institutes in Syria, many practicing musicians reject this model as too simplistic. At the time of the Cairo Congress, it was also debated (see Wirdī 1948). My Aleppine teachers insisted that although the tetrachord model might be useful in clarifying the relationships among the modes and in understanding some principles of modulation and composition, in practice the treatment of each *maqām* is special and may have little to do with its constituent "tetrachords" (or other subdivisions).[18] A *maqām* is generally more extensive than the scale that represents its constituent pitches, since any given *maqām* can support modulations to a number of related modes whose pitches and intervals are considered extensions of the original. In addition, the modes are flexible in performance and may extend to include tetrachords not found in typical *maqām* scale representations. Some may encompass two or more octaves of the same scale, and others combine different scales according to whether the melody is ascending or descending the scale degrees. According to my Aleppine teachers, reducing the *maqām* as a musical phenomenon to a scale (or a written representation of a scale) ignores important aspects of its dynamism as a performance principle.

The equal-tempered Arabic scale, the tetrachord model, and other proposed alterations to Arab music practice fall short of capturing those aspects of Arab music that many Syrian artists find essential to their tradition. In many ways this is a problem inherent to music theory in general, which constitutes a metadiscourse on music; that is, it represents an attempt to contain and describe in referential terms what are pragmatic and dynamic processes of employing and interpreting various musical rules and guidelines. Even the most creative musical gesture is guided by rules (what Kant (1952) referred to as "enabling conditions"), yet theory can at best approximate these dynamic aesthetic choices; at worst it can lead to performances that are technically correct but aesthetically lacking.

Indeed, many of the Syrian musicians whom I interviewed argued against the notion of a standard theory of Arab music, while being at the same time quite aware of the numerous attempts to create one since the time of the Cairo Congress. For these artists, the importance of local tradition and inherited rules of composition and performance, especially vocal, override any attempt to impose systematicity on the performance tradition. While there are certain rules for music, what some termed "*qawāʿid mūsīqiyya*"—"grammar" for music akin to the grammar of the Arabic language (also a construction)—no music "theory" (*naẓariyya*) per se yet exists for Arab music, according to them. There are systematic rules and agreed-upon principles, yet they are flexible, locally variable, and cannot constitute a theory in the sense of Western music theory. Of course, I do not wish by this to imply that "we" have "theory" while "they" have only "rules." Clearly, European music "theory" is also a cultural construction.

In practice, musicians utilize a number of different variations of the "Arabic scale" and a lot of active debate continues regarding this issue. Musicians may cite different authorities on the idea of an Arabic scale or on the modes. Musicians even disagree greatly on the number of modes and on their character. Some claim that there are only a few basic modes, echoing the simplified *maqām* schedules proposed in 1932 and followed today by many writers (for example, al-Ḥilū 1961; Gholmieh and Kurbāj 1996) Others, usually older and more respected musicians, argue that the modes number in the hundreds; one musician claimed to know and use 540! A "basic" set of about 90 or 100 often are proposed as more essential than others. But the idea that there are primary and secondary modes—reflecting the "family" (*faṣīla*) model—like the theory of tetrachords, is rejected by many practicing Syrian musicians as too simplistic, not in accordance with older treatises, and deaf to the finer nuances of style and spirit that are so important in Arab music.

Moreover, some musicians consider theory—at least as applied to Arab music—to be "foreign," the result of Europeans and their followers who cannot appreciate the richness of monophonic Oriental music and want to add harmony and other elements of Western tonality to rationalize and modernize the music. For these artists, the "authentic tradition" has been inherited over the centuries as a part of the Arab heritage and hence no single theory can encompass it. Moreover, the rejection by Syrian and other Arab artists of the equal-tempered scale, the theory of the tetrachords, and other recommendations of the Cairo Congress indicates the extent to which issues of nuance and spirit, however defined, are important in Arab musical aesthetics, a point that I take up in chapter 5 on emotions and musical performance in Aleppo. Many Egyptian artists also reject the equal-tempered scale and the theory of tetrachords (S. Marcus 1989: 184–87). More important in this context than publications on music are the comments of living musicians and listeners who would critique the performances of others (including my own) for imprecision in the treatment of the modes, among other qualities.

Westernization and the Problem of False Parrots

The debates over the Cairo Congress were in many regards debates over the extent and desirability of modernization and Westernization in Arab culture. A common Syrian reaction to the congress was that the formalization of the music—the attempt to establish a unified scale and system-classification of the modes, among other practices—led to its Westernization, sometimes called *tafarnuj* (from *ifranjī* = Frankish or foreign, an appellation dating from the Crusader period). Critics of over-Westernization abound in contemporary Syria, but the debate in music goes back at least to the time of the Cairo Congress. For example, Tawfiq al-Sabbāgh, the Aleppine composer and self-styled "King of the Violin" (*Mālik al-kamān*[19]) participated in the Cairo Congress and, like many Syrian musicians and scholars, was critical of the results (Sabbāgh 1950; Wīrdī 1948). In a chapter of his comprehensive *General Musical Guide* [*al-Dalīl al-mūsīqī al-ʿāmm*] (1950) entitled "The Music of the East and the West and which of the Two is Best," Sabbāgh decries the excessive "Westernization" (*tafarnuj*) rampant in the modern Arab world. Like many modernists of the age, he argues that while there is much to learn from the West, Arabs should adopt that which is beneficial from European culture and leave that which is not aside. Unfortunately, according to Sabbāgh, Arabs of his day were guilty not only of imitating the West, but of adopting that which was *worst* and ignoring what might be beneficial. The result, he feared, would be total assimilation and loss of a distinct Arab identity. "But I say to them," he writes, pointing to those who would imitate the West, "that the nation that does not preserve its inherited customs tied to its life-style will not hesitate to assimilate and dissolve in other nations and become just a trace to the eye" (Sabbāgh 1950: 13).

To illustrate the dangers of *tafarnuj,* Sabbāgh relates the following anecdote about a bird seller and false parrot:

> I have not seen an example of these Westernized imitators who are not like the bird seller who sells parrots, [and] who one day decided to cheat his customers and took a raven and painted it like a parrot. His imitation was successful and he decided to profit from his efforts, so he displayed the painted bird for sale to his friends, claiming that it was a parrot that he had just bought. However, no sooner had he shown the cage to his friends then the bird flapped its wings, turned over the water dish that was put in the cage for him to drink from, and spilled the water on itself, mixing the colors. His friends practically fell on their backs in their laughter because the raven had become so funny looking. (Sabbāgh 1950: 14)

That is to say, the result of the influence of Western music on Arab music has been an odd mixture of styles and genres that struck Sabbāgh in 1950 and a great many critics since his time as grotesque. Adding a patina of Western melodies or the colors of Western instruments, or imposing Western conceptions of music theory, for example, creates an artificial hybrid music that may at first glance appear to be beautiful but at heart is based on a disingenuous and inappropriate admixture of diverse elements.

This anecdote reveals some of the points of resistance that modernist discourses met in Syria. Yet Sabbāgh and others who were critical of blind imitation of the West were not reactionaries or closed-minded; indeed, he had studied with European teachers, was well-conversant in European music theory, and saw himself not only as a preserver but as an innovator as well, especially in the realm of composition (Mahannā 1998: 151–54). During the period of the mandate when French ideas of modernity were in circulation and resistance to the occupation flared into rebellion on a number of occasions (Khoury 1987), the quest for modernity was more nuanced than simply accepting French and European conceptions of modern culture and discarding the Arabic tradition, or the reverse. Magazines and newspapers from the early stages of the mandate record an avid interest in both the Arabic heritage *and* European discoveries in science and education. For Syria's intellectual elite, there was no harm in learning what was useful from Europe but this did not at the time mean rejecting the Arab cultural heritage.[20] Yet, the dangers of over-Westernization were acknowledged by most cultural leaders of the day, and this has constituted a central theme assuming different values in successive decades, especially after Syria's independence in 1946.

Independence and Assertive Modernity: From *Tafarnuj* to *Kull Shī Faranjī Baranjī*

European visions of modernity began to assume greater importance in Syrian culture and society as a newly independent Syrian government struggled to create a nation from the aftermath of colonialism (Seale 1986). Despite the *nakba* or "catastrophe" of the Arab loss of Palestine in 1948 and continuing political instabilities in Syria, the post-Independence era was one of great optimism about modernity and the possibilities for creating a dynamic and modern nation. With independence came greater involvement in world political affairs, including Cold War relations and engagement in the growing global cultural and political economy dominated by the former colonizing nations. This period witnessed the rise of strongly modernist trends in Syrian culture and a generation of intellectuals came on the scene who had little interest in the Arab heritage, much less in preserving it. Rather, they advocated the modernization of their society and culture, which for many was tantamount to its Westernization even if this came at the expense of tradition. In the arts, European (and in the early years specifically Western European) models of culture were held to be cultural standards and young Syrians increasingly flocked to European academies and universities to study, later bringing home their newly acquired ideologies of art, culture, and social modernity.

With respect to music, the post-Independence generation of intellectuals often saw Arab music as backward in comparison to European classical music, which was held by them to be the standard of civilizational development. A number of prominent Arab artists at the time argued that Arab music represented a "primitive" stage of a musical and civilizational progression of which European art music represented both the greatest achievement and the standard to be emulated (see Berque 1974: 208). Not only did these intellectuals think that Arab music was "primitive," some questioned whether it was even "music" at all. The Egyptian writer Tawfiq al-Ḥakīm disparaged Arab music with remarks that it is merely "party music, born of social gatherings, drinking bouts, and night-time revels, while Western music is born in a more serious, tragic setting" (cited in Berque 1974: 208–209). In this period of high modernist sensibility, Arab music and the Arabic cultural heritage represented a weight on advancement and modernization, not the basis for development.

During an informal gathering in Damascus in 1997, these sorts of comments were aired by a group of Syrian musicians who claimed that when they were growing up in the 1950s they were taught by their parents and teachers to disdain and even to hate the Arab heritage as backward, as a heritage of weakness. These musicians, all accomplished performers of Western classical music and in some cases the children of prominent musicians of the Arab tradition, admitted to having little knowledge of Arab music. When I asked one of them, a cellist in the orchestra of a prominent Arab vocalist, about the mode of a certain song his group performs, he stated that he just plays along with the song and does not even know which mode it is in; in fact, he claimed not to know much about any of the modes. Such indifference (let alone ignorance) would be inconceivable to any of my teachers in Aleppo, but indicates an important disjuncture between discourses of cultural authenticity and musical performance practice in contemporary Syria.

Modernity and "Double Dependency"

The contradictions of a modernizing Syria caught between advocates of heritage and partisans of Westernization resulted in intellectuals becoming caught in what the poet-critic Adonis terms a "double dependency"—dependency on the Arab past as compensation for a lack of creative activity in the present, and dependency on European-American intellectual trends and technology as compensation for the Arab failure to invent and innovate on their own part (Adonis 1992: 80).[21] How to engage European culture successfully while preserving a link to the Arab past characterizes the dilemma of Syrian artists and intellectuals: how to go forward with "modernity" while looking backward to "the past." One contemporary Syrian film critic aptly summarized this dilemma as follows: "In the fifties we used to say '*kull shī faranjī baranjī*' [Everything from the West is Best], but now things are different. There's a lot more interest in heritage and old things."

Heritage and Old Things: Discourses of Authenticity and Modernity in Post-1967 Syria

By "now" this intellectual was referring primarily to the period after the 1967 war with Israel, which represented a humiliating defeat, on the one hand, and an impetus to change and reform, on the other. In many ways, the June War of 1967 dispelled the optimism about modernization that characterized the early post-Independence era. The defeat of the Arab armies by what they considered to be a weaker foe led to a wave of critiques not only of Arab leadership but of Arab culture and society, if not the Arab "mind" itself (al-ʿAẓm 1968, 1969; al-Jābrī 1984, 1986). Like the so-called "shock of modernity," the shock of defeat in 1967 encouraged calls for a renewal of Arab culture from the "slumbering" and decadence into which it had fallen—this time because of an over-reliance on Western conceptions of culture and society and not necessarily because of the so-called "backwardness" of the past; indeed, some critics attributed the Arab losses to *neglect* of their rich past and heritage. As in the *nahḍa,* these more recent calls for reform assumed a number of different forms: Marxist-revolutionary, Islamic reformist, and more moderate calls for a rejuvenation of Arabic culture and society through a return to the cultural roots of Arab society and preservation of its heritage. In the aftermath of 1967, heritage came to play a central ideological position in contemporary Syrian society, for intellectuals of diverse stripes, for politicians, and for individual artists struggling to come to terms with life in the modern age.

As noted above, not all Syrians agree on what constitutes heritage (*turāth*) in the first place. Defenders of "tradition" tend to promote the Islamic elements of heritage, while progressives, on the contrary, often see these same elements as sources of backwardness and instead promote the intellectual and artistic dimensions of heritage. Some intellectuals reject heritage altogether as an impediment to modernity. The term *turāth* is what normally translates into English as "heritage." Derived from the root w-r-th, to inherit, *turāth* denotes patrimony, the inherited customs and traditions of the forefathers (and *turāth* is almost entirely a masculine and patriarchal discourse). In Syria, *turāth* commonly refers to two basic categories of cultural practices:

1. Classical heritage (*turāth klāsiki*): from 750 to 1250 CE, that is, the cultural production of the Arabs from the Umayyad through the ʿAbbasid eras, what is often considered a Golden Age of Arabic culture, including music.[22]

2. Popular heritage (*turāth shaʿbī*): urban and rural practices of the non-elite classes. This might include handcrafts, costumes, storytelling, certain dances and songs, games, and so forth. Folklore (*fūlklūr*) overlaps with "popular heritage" and connotes primarily rural but also urban practices such as storytelling, dance, and costume. In practice, there is often little precise distinction between popular heritage, popular arts, and folklore. For example, in Damascus the "traditional" costumes of the urban dwellers on display at the eighteenth-century ʿAẓm Palace museum are considered "Syrian urban folk-

lore," as are some of the more "traditional" crafts and locales, such as the markets, the public bath houses (*ḥammām*-s) and the people who work and frequent these places (also the subject of display at the ʿAẓm Palace). Other cities have similar displays. In terms of music, the *qudūd ḥalabiyya* (light songs) might be considered to be a variety of urban folk music arising from the cultural heritage of cities such as Aleppo that were major commercial crossroads. Rural songs associated with peasants, such as the pan-Levantine *dalʿūnā,* are also classified as "folklore" and "popular art." The distinctions are fluid.

Given these contradictions, heritage might best be understood as what Alasdair MacIntyre (1984) terms a "tradition." In MacIntyre's understanding, a tradition is a process of cultural selection and memory that implies modes of reasoning about the past, conceptions of selfhood and social identity, and attitudes toward the future. Understood as a tradition in this sense, heritage operates in two ways: as the substantive media through which notions of authentic culture are constructed and transmitted across the generations (for example, genres of music, forms of architecture, styles of painting, modes of narrative, conceptions of honor, gender relations, etc.), and as a process of framing and authorizing interpretations of the self, community, and nation.[23] In this dual sense, heritage has come to figure prominently in attempts by Syrian artists and intellectuals to make sense of their culture and society, to find or impose order on their experiences, and to construct narratives of the past, often by rounding off the rougher edges of what is commonly understood as history.

In many regards, heritage constitutes a discourse of privilege, especially in the context of what Syria's cultural and political elite deem to be "inauthentic" and "vulgar" aspects of contemporary culture, what critics in the West usually refer to as mass or popular culture. As previously mentioned, rarely are such low-brow elements of traditional Arab culture as storytelling, ecstatic religious practices, popular medicine, and traditional dance granted the hallowed status of "heritage." Heritage is the preserve of Arab high culture, "the best that is thought and known," in the Arnoldian sense, and hence also constitutes a privileged discourse in that it lies at the intersection of aesthetic practices and state ideologies of culture and national identity in Syria. Through state patronage of heritage arts in festivals, exhibitions, and heritage ensembles sponsored by the Ministry of Culture, for instance, and through forms of censorship, the state promotes some cultural practices as valued aspects of Syrian national culture that need to be preserved and defended, while excluding others from an already severely limited sphere.

A perceived association with heritage can be profitable for many reasons: local elites have developed a taste for it, as in depictions of the Old City and related lifestyles, and hence may patronize certain artists, while political patronage of selected artists associated in some way with heritage can translate into significant financial remuneration. For instance, a musician performing the "classical" repertoire might be invited to perform for local and international dignitaries and officials. Remuneration might be in the form of permits to travel or more favorable postings for children undergoing mandatory military service, in lieu of or in addition to any actual monetary payment. The key currency here is "*wāsṭa*"—connections and influence, in a way not atypical of patron-client relations elsewhere in the Mediterranean (Cunningham and Sarayrah 1993; Peristiany 1966).[24] In other words, heritage pays.

Heritage pays as well in terms of the great foreign interest in heritage music, festivals, and local "folklore" that provides Syrian musicians and other artists with supplementary income (in some cases primary income) and rare opportunities to travel out of Syria. Foreign remuneration for performances forms a significant informal economy or parallel economy to that of the regular economy—that is, the artists' day jobs, if they have any. To give an example, the director of a music institute might earn perhaps SYP14,000 per month, or $280, from what informants told me.[25] A university professor might earn half this amount. Yet, an instrumentalist might earn anywhere from $200 to $500 or more for a single performance abroad. Well-known artists command at least $1,000 a performance, while Arab superstars such as Ṣabāḥ Fakhrī and others can earn in the tens of thousands of dollars per show. A tour in several European nations might include ten or more concerts and thus several thousand dollars for each performer—far in excess of what they might earn in a year of performances or other employment at home. For this reason, Syrian artists have a strong incentive not only to cultivate their musical heritage but to cultivate relations with foreign audiences and artistic interlocutors (including researchers) that may open potentially very lucrative horizons for them.[26]

Against Heritage

In post-1967 Syria, not everyone is so sanguine about the revival of heritage and its role in saving the Arabs from their cultural and social (not to mention political and military) crises. Adonis (1992) and other critics suggest that Arab fascination with the past has resulted not in its valorization so much as its debasement and reification as heritage. Furthermore, according to many artists and intellectuals, interest in the Arab past contributes to the problems facing the Arab world today, rather than offering any solutions.

Some contemporary artists remain unconvinced that heritage is an important avenue for reconstituting Arab culture. For example, one concert violinist, a member of an elite family and host of a weekly intellectual salon, argued that heritage is merely an "empty discourse." From his perspective, people use the term a lot but without any specific meaning. "I might say I am interested in heritage," he said, "but what does this mean? What do people mean when they talk about heritage? What does it mean to preserve it? Why should we preserve it, and whose heritage should we preserve?" He indicated that the word has come to cover so wide a range of possible connotations and practices that it no longer carries any meaning: it is thus an "empty discourse."

Similarly, a young Aleppine painter of large abstract canvases argued that people talk a lot about heritage but they do not understand it. During a conversation at his studio-home in Aleppo, he criticized a contemporary Aleppine musician who claimed in a television interview to respect heritage but because it is too vast, an "ocean" (*baḥr*), he has to take some little part of it and work on that. His songs, which are modernized versions of folk melodies, are influenced heavily by European and American pop music (I like to think of him as the Lionel Richie of Syrian music). To my artist friend, the problem is that this musician and so many artists and intellectuals like him identify heritage as something tangible, like objects in a museum that you might touch or melodies that can be arranged in different ways. Referring to Moroccan critic Muḥammad ʿAbid al-Jabrī (1991), this artist argued that heritage is an attitude or stance (*mawqif*), a set of ideas and ways of thinking and sets of relationships with other ideas, and not so much the tangible products of these ideas and relationships.

The prominent Syrian philosopher Ṣādiq Jalāl al-ʿAẓm (2000), a leading secular critic, has gone so far as to argue that the focus of Arabs on their once-glorious past and heritage has prevented them from establishing themselves more strongly in the present and preparing for the future. In other words, an exaggerated interest in heritage and a clinging to old or traditional ways of life and thinking has held Arabs back from advancing into the ranks of the modern and secular nations of the world; they are, to use his words, "the Hamlets of the twentieth century" (2000: 11) laying responsibility for their ills at the feet of their dead forefathers and traitorous interlopers. For al-ʿAẓm and others, Arab fascination with reviving and preserving heritage is just another form of escapism and not a magic bullet for reviving and renewing Arab culture and society.

Qafla: Modernity and the Aesthetics of Authenticity

In this chapter, I have outlined some of the keywords that are important in the study of the aesthetics of authenticity in contemporary Syria: modernity (*ḥadātha*), authenticity (*aṣāla*), and heritage (*turāth*). Modernity in Syria must be understood in the historical context of the co-production and co-experience of modernity in Europe and the Arab lands, which began with Napoleon's invasion in 1798 and continues today in Syria's scramble to find a place in the emerging Euro-American–dominated global cultural and political economy. The metaphor of improvisation, or composition in the moment, offers a way to analyze modernity in Syria and elsewhere in the Arab and postcolonial worlds that acknowledges the mutual constitution of the modern condition in the colonial encounter while admitting the dominance of European models of statecraft in recent history. Concern with heritage in its many guises can be seen as one component of the search by Syrian intellectuals for a formula for composing an alternative modernity (though I use the concept advisedly) in which the benefits of modernity and modernization do not mean the disappearance of tradition. In fact, we must understand the concern with heritage and tradition as an integral aspect of the modern condition in Syria. The following chapter explores the ways in which collective memory and narratives of Syrian music history serve to promote modern subjectivities based in creative appropriations of "heritage."

THREE

Constructing Musical Authenticity: History, Cultural Memory, Emotion

Maṭlaʿ: The Time and Place of Authenticity

With my ideas for research in one hand and my oud in the other, I felt that I was prepared for fieldwork in Syria. What I was not prepared for was a common response to my stated research interests in Arab music: Is there even such a thing as "Arab music"? While many Syrians expressed surprise at my choice of Syria as a research site—American researchers are few and far between there—some also expressed doubts about my intentions to study "Arab music." Is the music Arab, or is it Turkish, Persian, or Byzantine, or is it a mixture of all of these? What is "Arab" about Arab music? Because many of the genres commonly performed in the "classical" repertoire have their roots in pan-Ottoman and Persian musical practices, calling them "Arab" is problematic, and many of my interlocutors, musicians and otherwise, pointed this out to me. Moreover, some Aleppines (mostly non-musicians) asked me what I even meant by "music." Emphasizing the latter term, they often asked me if there is such a thing as Arab music—that is, music distinct from song. As mentioned in the previous chapter, referring to the melodic and rhythmic practices of the Arabs as "music" (*mūsīqā*) is problematic since in classical texts the term had referred to theories of music and not to instrumental practices. Because of the privilege of the voice in Arab aesthetics, Arabs have tended to refer to their melodic and rhythmic practices as song.

What many Syrians considered to be Arab or Syrian music, or even "music" itself, depended a lot on their educational, religious, and artistic backgrounds. Some intellectuals argued that Arab music is the inheritor of the music of the ancient civilizations of Mesopotamia and the Fertile Crescent, and therefore authentic. Others argued that it is essentially Turkish music, and therefore inauthentic. Still others claimed different roots, different histories. Aside from causing a certain amount of epistemological self-doubt, these sorts of dialogues opened windows onto discourses about identity that found expression in discussions of music and musical origins. For my Syrian interlocutors, the Arabness of their music had as much if not more to do with conceptions of cultural authenticity, origins, and identity than with more objective musical factors such as tonality, genre, and style.

Chapter 2 explored some of the meanings of the concepts of modernity, authenticity, and heritage, and argued that authenticity is a constructed and contested domain of fluid subjectivities for different groups within Syria. This chapter examines further the construction of concepts of musical authenticity in Syria through an analysis of the spatial and temporal dimensions of discourses on authenticity. I explore a set of important spatial and temporal complexes that serve as orientational centers in contemporary discourses about musical and artistic authenticity in contemporary Syria, then turn to four discourses on the origins of "Arab music" that reveal not only different visions of authenticity but also different understandings of culture, self, and society.

Temporal and Spatial Orientations of Authenticity in Contemporary Syrian Art

Many Aleppine artists and intellectuals support their claims to cultural authenticity by appealing to particular constructions of the origins of the music. Indeed, some make the linguistic link between origin (*aṣl*) and authenticity (*aṣāla*), for the words derive from the same roots. Authenticity itself implies a fixed origin in time and space. In their various discourses about art and authenticity, Syrian artists, critics, and consumers articulate concepts of origin with respect to two orientational centers, one temporal and the other spatial. With respect to temporality, those having an interest in promoting their visions of authentic culture tend to locate authenticity temporally in the past (*māḍī*), or, to be more accurate, in constructions of different pasts—for example, the pre-Islamic era, the early Islamic era, the Ottoman Period, and the early modern period. In general, as Silvia Naef (1996) notes in her study of modernity in Arab fine arts, Arab intellectuals and artists have tended to locate authenticity in the pre-colonial past. But in a country like Syria that has been colonized and recolonized literally for millennia, the pre-colonial past might mean the time prior to the French mandate (1922–1944), the Ottoman Period (1516–1918), and even, for some Christians, prior to the Muslim "occupation" of Syria (beginning in

636).[1] Identifying the pre-colonial with the pre-modern does not suffice, since, as seen in the previous chapter, conceptions of modernity and even the precise dating of the advent of the modern period in the Arab world are debatable. The "authentic past" is hence a shifting and sliding frame that depends as much on one's personal interests as on any specific "objective" historical periodization. Therefore, diverse eras have come to represent authenticity in Syria.

In addition to the association of authenticity with the past and certain sentiments and emotions related to the past (however this past is conceived), Syrian artists tend to identify authentic culture with specific locales and geographical places. For some, the ultimate site of authenticity is the Old City, as in the old neighborhoods of Damascus and Aleppo, whereas for others it is the countryside or the desert. More often, Syrian artists associate authentic culture with a combination of specific places, the people inhabiting those spaces in specific times, and—importantly—the sentiments and emotions associated with these people, places, and times. The temporal, spatial, and social-cultural nexus that defines authenticity thus constitutes an important dimension of the aesthetics of authenticity in late twentieth-century Syrian art worlds.

Syrian Longings: *Ḥanīn*

In contemporary discourse, the modern period is normally not associated with authenticity; indeed, modernity has come to stand for inauthenticity in many discourses of the authentic. As noted earlier, Syrian authors tend to contrast authenticity with contemporaneity or modernity. However, recent Syrian television dramas that depicted modern historical events and nationalist sentiments were praised by many Syrian viewers as evoking an authentic Arab or "Oriental" spirit.[2] What seemed to be important to viewers was the association of particular constructions of the past with particular sentiments. A general association of the old (*qadīm*) and the past (*māḍī*) with authenticity conveyed in these contexts a more basic association of authenticity with particular sentiments such as nationalist commitment, in the example of the television serials, and emotional honesty, in the songs of Umm Kulthūm, for example. Therefore, what makes Arab culture authentic is often the association of particular emotional states with particular times and places and their evocation in the arts.[3]

Syrian artists and intellectuals relate to the past in diverse ways—some positively evaluate the past as a storehouse of tradition, while others negatively view the past as a realm of backwardness. A number of Syrian artworks in diverse media exhibit a romantic if not nostalgic vision of the past. For example, recent memoirs celebrate and memorialize life in the Old City of Damascus, a site par excellence of authentic culture for many Syrians (Qaṣṣāb Ḥassan 1988; Turjumān 1998 [1990]; see Salamandra 2000, 2004). A high percentage of commercial artwork represents street scenes from the Old Cities of Damascus and Aleppo, and Syrians and not just tourists purchase these works to hang on the walls of their homes. Works by more "serious" artists also depict such scenes, though often in a more nuanced and aesthetically interesting fashion (for example, the works of the Damascene artist Naṣīr Shūra from the 1940s and 1950s, and many of Fateh Moudarres' canvases that treat themes from Syrian folklore and mythology).

In general, it seems that Syrian intellectuals and artists consider cultural practices, events, and personalities that they understand to be in time (that is, temporalized as "history") to be less authentic than events that they understand to be out of time (that is, detemporalized as "myth," "legend," and "the past"). One reason for the primacy granted to detemporalized or mythologized aesthetic experience ("the past") might relate to the commonly expressed sentiment in Syria that "history" is written by those who are currently in power, whereas myth and legend, being products of the popular imagination, are more sincere, even if not "real." The gap between "reality" and "truth," at least in the minds of some artists, is an artifact of power. Some intellectuals and artists recognize this and attempt to accentuate the differences between "reality" and "truth" in their works. Some artists play with this tension, for example by using simulacra of ancient symbols and alphabetical characters and not "real" symbols and characters in their works. The state and its apparatuses of truth-production likewise attempt to close the gap by insisting on the truthfulness of "reality" and the reality of "truth." The cult of former President Ḥāfiẓ al-Asad illustrates well how the Syrian state has attempted to impose a patina of truthfulness on the mythologies associated with the "eternal leader."

Artists concerned with authenticity as a personal or artistic vision generally demonstrate a positive relationship to the past and often use the term *ḥanīn* to describe their feelings regarding past locales and times. *Ḥanīn* means a type of longing or yearning, and relates linguistically to *ḥanān* (affection, love, and tenderness) and *ḥanūn* (affectionate, tenderhearted, touching); the sound of the *nāy* often is called *ḥanūn*, for example. *Ḥanīn* often is translated as "nostalgia," and indeed in some cases artists and intellectuals express a relation to past times and places in ways that we might describe as nostalgic. For example, one writer expressed a longing for his childhood home in the Old City of Aleppo—the particular smells, sights, and sounds of his former home and neighborhood—while enjoying the comforts of his modern home in a newer quarter; he was certainly expressing a form of nostalgia when he said he felt *ḥanīn* for his family's former domicile.

Yet, it is important to contextualize and clarify the meaning of *ḥanīn* since nostalgia may not be the best way to describe it. Indeed, nostalgia is often not an appropriate translation of *ḥanīn*. In many instances, what Arabs express as a *ḥanīn* for the past is in fact a gloss of what for them are highly evaluated emotional states and sentiments associated with particular times, locales, social relations, and cultural practices. In English, "nostalgia" may evoke a negative sense of romantic or even naïve attachment to the past, whereas in Arabic *ḥanīn* and other terms such as *ghurba* (homesickness, separation, or exile) carry more positive connotations. Therefore, I use "nostalgia" advisedly to mean a romanticized reminiscence of a past lifestyle or place and time, such as reminiscences of a childhood home. In other circumstances, *ḥanīn* evokes highly positive sentiments about the self and society that reflect an experience of temporal and spatial dislocation.

Spatial and Temporal Metaphors of Authenticity in Syrian Art Worlds

In Syrian art worlds, a number of distinct spatial and temporal metaphors structure discourses about authentic and inauthentic culture; indeed, in many ways debates about authenticity can be seen as debates over different metaphorical understandings of culture, time, and space. As a result of these debates, certain conjunctions of time and space come to represent authenticity, while others become badges of inauthenticity.[4] In contemporary Syrian culture and art, three important and powerful metaphors of authenticity are the pre-modern (Old) city, the countryside, and the desert, with their associated life ways. The metaphor of the Old City (*madīna qadīma*) locates authenticity in the streets and buildings of the pre-modern Old Cities, especially Aleppo and Damascus, and in the lifestyles of the inhabitants of these urban space-times. In the contemporary Syrian literary, cinematic, and popular imagination, authenticity is symbolized first and foremost by the Arab home (*bayt ʿarabī*), consisting of an arrangement of rooms surrounding a courtyard full of citrus trees, a well, and gardens of fragrant plants; indeed, it is the courtyard and the citrus and jasmine trees that grow in it that most prominently excite memories of the older homes. For others, the mosques, public baths, coffee shops, stone walls, and cobblestone streets of the Old City also symbolize authenticity.

Aside from these physical locations, the metaphor of the Old City encompasses the lifestyle of the pre-modern urban elite—the merchants and their culture, including the evening soirées (*sahra*-s) held in expansive Arab homes, as well as the religious scholars and sheikhs performing their duties in the numerous and ancient mosques and Islamic schools (*madrasa*-s). Figures from

Naṣīr Shūra. Untitled, Damascene street scene, c. 1959.

more mundane walks of life are also important indices of authenticity in the Old City metaphor: fruit vendors hawking their produce in the streets, coffee shop denizens smoking *nargīla*-s (water pipes), veiled women with their children, old men on donkeys, and so forth. These scenes of authentic culture and life are found readily in all the major media of Syrian art: painting, literature, television and cinema, and music in its association with the space and time of authentic culture (for example, an evening gathering in an old Arab home). In a way, these locales and characters are thought of as "survivals" of pre-modern lifestyles in Syria, especially by members of the urban elite who reside elsewhere and who look upon them with a mixture of nostalgia, *ḥanīn,* and occasionally even loathing.

Indeed, only a generation ago (pre-1967), the *bayt ʿarabī* symbolized backwardness for those elites who left the Old City for the relative comforts of the newer quarters in the first half of the twentieth century, leaving the older

neighborhoods to the urban poor and poor migrants from rural areas (see Salamandra 2004; Zenlund 1991). In fact, the flight of the urban upper classes and the expansion of the newer quarters gave the older neighborhoods their designation as the "Old City."[5] Only in recent years have the Old Cities of Damascus and Aleppo gained status as sites of authenticity now that they no longer serve as important residential neighborhoods for the Syrian merchant classes and elites. As a result, some elites are now returning to the Old City, not so much to reside there as to convert older buildings into commercial ventures such as restaurants, bars, and hotels (see Salamandra 2004). For some, the identification of the Old City with authentic Syrian culture is a form of nostalgia—especially for the older merchants who, like my writer friend, reminisce about their former homes in the Old City from the comfortable confines of their modern homes—whereas for others it is part of a mission to preserve the Arab cultural and social heritage. The decay of the older neighborhoods and attempts by certain developers to demolish neighborhoods in Damascus and Aleppo and build modern buildings in their place, in conjunction with haphazard attempts to renovate or modernize certain older homes, have led to the establishment of committees for historic preservation with the authority to regulate renovations and new building in these neighborhoods. The positive evaluation of the Old City has arisen in the context of the work of international organizations such as UNESCO to designate these cities as World Heritage sites, restricting building and development within them in order to guarantee their "preservation." No doubt, tourism and the prospect of luring foreigners in search of their own visions (fantasies?) of authenticity has contributed to the commodification of the Old Cities and the conversion of homes and schools into restaurants, coffee shops, and hotels. Yet the number of local and visiting Arabs and foreign tourists frequenting these establishments suggests that the identification of the pre-modern Old City with authentic Arab culture is both widespread and deeply held among Syrians of a range of walks of life.

Another metaphorical time-space of authenticity is the pre-modern (if not pre-historical) countryside, primarily the land and its people, the peasants (*fallāḥīn*), who more than anyone are associated with "folklore" and "authentic" culture. For some modernists, such as the late artist Fateh Moudarres, the rural village constitutes the very location of authentic culture; in his view, one expressed by others as well, Syria's peasants are the inheritors of ancient Levantine and Mesopotamian culture and are therefore the most "authentic" Syrians (indeed, for some, the most authentic humans). The countryside is the source of many of the popular arts, such as the *dabka* or circle dance, songs about harvests, love and marriages, and so forth. These

Fateh Moudarres, *Olive Growers from Qalamun,* 1982.

practices are thought to be timeless and eternal—in a sense without origin, dating back to pre-history. A number of contemporary Syrian fine artists capture many of these figures of authenticity in their works. Important symbols of rural authenticity in recent canvases and sculptures include sun-drenched landscapes, scraggly old olive trees, fields of wheat, peasants bent over in agricultural work, and especially peasant women wearing their colorful "folk" costumes and carrying jugs of water on their heads or ample hips. In these depictions (caricatures, almost), rural life is highly abstracted in terms of temporality, with peasants living in a sort of eternal past, and in terms of space, with "the land" (*arḍ*) coming to represent the nation and Syrian people as a whole, even when it is a highly specific local scene that is depicted, say, in a painting or in a narrative.

A third metaphorical time-space of authenticity is the desert, which plays an important role in defining "Arabness" and hence "authenticity" in contemporary Syrian culture. The desert as a physical space evokes a sense of timelessness,

the nomadism of the bedouin and their camels marching along the dunes suggesting eternal cycles. The haunting sound of the *nāy* frequently is used in such (again caricature-like) depictions of the desert in television and cinematic productions to evoke a sense of timelessness and vastness. Yet, the desert as a physical space is less important than its association with the inhabitants of this space, the bedouin and their particular culture. Bedouin culture conventionally represents "Arabness" (indeed, bedouin often are referred to simply as "Arabs" (*ʿarab*/*ʿurbān*)—through the association of bedouin and Arabs with eloquence, freedom, masculinity, honor, and fierce justice; indeed, there are similarities between urban Syrian and European Orientalist conceptions of the bedouin. Other important components of this metaphorical time-space are the bedouin love for horses and customs of hospitality, drinking coffee, reciting poetry, nomadism, raiding, and so forth. These images are prominent in contemporary "bedouin" television serials as well as Syrian art and literature, where they help to define the cultural space in which questions of authenticity are posed and answered. The bedouin, through their association with Arabness, the vastness of the Syrian desert, and the pre-modern subsistence strategies that they are depicted as utilizing, thus come to represent another important realm of cultural authenticity.

Metaphors of Inauthenticity

Since authentic culture often is defined in contrast to what some may consider inauthentic, we would expect to find certain metaphorical expressions of inauthenticity as well. Indeed, such metaphors exist and sometimes focus on the same geographic places but at different times or with different people. In the Old Cities, the urban poor who moved there after the flight of two generations of middle- and upper-class Syrians following Independence are associated in the minds of these elites with inauthentic culture: crowded and poorly decorated homes, dirty streets, noise, and so forth. Elite Syrians consider the culture of the urban poor in any neighborhood, old or new, to be inauthentic. They also consider the nouveaux riches to be inauthentic because their wealth, as some anciens riches like to point out, comes not from family fortunes and land but from business dealings and especially corruption through association with the new military and political elite (some but not all of ʿAlawite extraction). In this equation, the urban Sunni merchants are authentic, while the newly urbanized ʿAlawites are inauthentic because, while "essentially" rural poor, they have acquired positions by virtue of having political connections. Even their religion is suspect in the eyes of the Sunni majority.

As Raymond Williams notes for England (1973), the "country" may assume numerous valences—as the site of authentic rural culture and the simple, honest people who work the land, or as a source of backwardness and "rural idiocy." These contradictory evaluations find expression in contemporary Syria as well, where condescending portrayals of modern peasants interact with more "pastoral" visions (to borrow Williams' term) of idealized rural life.[6] While some of my Damascene friends claimed that all Syrian families have rural origins, when I mentioned this "fact" to other Damascenes, they reacted with repugnance; for contemporary families to have demonstrable rural roots would disqualify them from being authentic (*aṣīl*), which for the elite means 100 percent urban or even Ottoman roots. Interestingly, Arabness is not necessarily a criterion of authenticity for these elites; it is relationship to centers of power, Ottoman included (but not usually ʿAlawite), that counts. Regarding the bedouin, the old (idealized) bedouin are authentic whereas modern bedouin running around in pick-up trucks and living off the cities, are not. All of these judgments are, of course, laden with class distinctions and reflect the privilege of those who can afford to worry about authenticity in the first place.

The Time and Space of Musical Authenticity: Four Meditations on the Origins of Arab Music

These three primary metaphorical understandings of authenticity structure to a large extent both the production of "authentic" culture and narratives about cultural authenticity in the contemporary Syrian art world and heritage politics that I analyze in this work. Turning to music raises the question of how Syrian intellectuals and artists understand "Arab music" and argue for its authenticity. The question of the authenticity of Arab music often revolves around questions of its origins. Yet there is little consensus about which origin, and therefore whose authenticity, is most authentic with respect to Arab music. For some, the music has clear Arab roots and is hence authentically "Arab" music. For others, the music has diverse, non-Arab roots, which they emphasize to support their claims for other authenticities.

In what follows, I explore four different narratives of the origins of "Arab" music, each of which relies on different (and implicit) understandings and representations of the origins of the music in order to assert claims to a more "authentic" culture than the others. A university professor, a journalist, a bookseller, and a dramatist make claims to authenticity through their diverse understandings of and discourses on the origins of "Arab" music. They employ a variety of rhetorical strategies in their appeals to authority—historical, mythological, and pragmatic, among others—to center a sense of musical identity and personhood with respect to music. Analysis of their claims reveals the implicit understandings and metaphors that structure their narratives and through which they construct and evaluate notions of origin and authenticity. Each draws from different if overlapping narratives of authentic origins that imply particular understandings of the time and space from which the "true" music originated and developed. Whether the music is Arab, Turkish, Kurdish, Christian, or Muslim in origin (or of some other origin) depends in these narratives on particular understandings of the temporality and space of origin. In this manner, the concept of an origin becomes an important—if not *the* important—index of the authenticity of Arab music, however it is conceived (and each has distinct views of what, if anything, is "Arab" about it). Join me as I return to these discussions.

The Return of al-Iṣfahānī

After some weeks in Aleppo, I head back to Damascus and pay a visit to Dr. Saad Allah Agha al-Qalʿah, then Professor of Engineering at the University of Damascus, producer of programs on music and computers for Syrian television, and sometime performer of the *qānūn* from a notable Aleppine family.[7] I want to talk to al-Qalʿah about his recent television program *Nahj al-aghānī* (*The Course of Songs*, 1997b), an encyclopedic and ambitious work that aims to document, analyze, and evaluate the one hundred most important Arab songs since the beginning of the twentieth century.[8] Because al-Iṣfahānī's *Kitāb al-aghānī* documented the one hundred most important Arab songs up to the tenth century, al-Qalʿah sees himself as a modern-day al-Iṣfahānī and his program (an ongoing project with a projected three series) as a modern, multimedia update of the medieval text. For *Nahj al-aghānī*, al-Qalʿah has created a multimedia database of song texts, audiovisual samples, commentaries from published sources, and over sixteen hundred keywords that enable him to search the database for songs based on lyrics, artist, genre, mode, and so forth. Prior to *Nahj al-aghānī*, al-Qalʿah produced programs on Muḥammad ʿAbd al-Wahhāb, the Syrian-born vocalist Asmahan, and on Asmahan's brother, the famed oud player, composer, and singer Farīd al-Aṭrash. *Nahj al-aghānī* has been controversial both because of its content (al-Qalʿah's choice of songs and analysis of them) and because of his heavy reliance on the computer in documenting, analyzing, and presenting his research. But it also has enjoyed a wide pan-Arab audience because of its broadcast on satellite television internationally.

We discuss his programs and his own extensive musical background and career, and I ask him about Arab music and how "Arab" it actually might be. There seem to be a large number of foreign names used in Arab music—for some of the modes, some of the genres and instruments, and some of its great composers—and many people tell me that this proves that there is really no such thing as Arab music. What is "Arab" about the music, or is it merely a congeries of other musical traditions adopted by the Arabs as they moved from the desert and villages to their urban centers in the early Islamic period?

According to al-Qalʿah, evidence of a "pure" Arab tradition can be found in the classical treatises of al-Kindī, al-Urmawī, and others; we must not be misled by the names. Although many of the modes have Persian and Turkish names, this does not meant that they are Persian and Turkish. For example, many of the names of the modes are merely ordinal numeral prefixes, such as the Persian *yakāh, dūkāh, sīkāh,* and *jahārkāh,* which mean "first," "second," "third," and "fourth," respectively. The Arabs once referred to these same modes as *awwal* ("first"), *thānī* ("second"), *thālith* ("the third"), and so forth, according to al-Qalʿah. This is clear in the works of al-Kindī, who wrote in the ninth century, well before there was even a Turkish culture to speak of, let alone Turkish *maqāmāt* to borrow.[9] Moreover, many of the modes have authentic Arabic names. For example, *rāst, bayyātī, ḥijāz, kurd, nawā, ṣabā,* and *ʿajam* are all Arabic names of important and frequently used modes. Similarly, in North Africa *ṭabʿ* and not *maqām* is used to refer to the various modes, which have different names from those used in the Levant. Confusion arises from the fact that the classical theorists used different words from the modern names to identify the same modes; during the Ottoman Period, Arabs adopted the terminology of Ottoman music, applying these new names to the original "Arab" modes.

"What about the Persians?" I ask. Dr. al-Qalʿah replies that Persian civilization is ancient and no doubt there was a lot of sharing amongst Arab and Persian cultures, especially after the rise of Islam. But a strong and independent Arab tradition developed and ample evidence suggests that the modal system—to his ears—is "Arab" in origin, not Persian. Many of the instruments commonly used in Arab and Turkish music, such as the oud, are of Arab origin. For example, according to al-Qalʿah, despite the common claim that the oud has its origins in ancient Egypt or Persia, archaeologists have unearthed evidence of early oud-like instruments dating back several thousand years in the ruins of the ancient Mesopotamian city of Ur. Therefore, there is a strong local (for him, "Arab") tradition that dates back over many centuries, if not millennia.

Not long after visiting Dr. al-Qalʿah, I make my way to an upscale café in central Damascus, the self-styled meeting place of Damascene intellectuals, where a friend introduces me to "George," a young Christian journalist and writer who is seated at a neighboring table. George folds up his newspaper and joins me at my table. We exchange greetings and when our mutual friend mentions my work on Syrian music, he tells me that he has a deep interest in Arab music, or to be more precise, in what he considers to be "authentic Oriental music" (*mūsīqā sharqiyya aṣīla*). George asks me what I am doing, to whom I listen, and what I have "discovered" so far. I proudly name a number of well-known Egyptian and Syrian musicians, having recently acquired some good tapes: Muḥammad ʿAbd al-Wahhāb, Umm Kulthūm, Ṣabāḥ Fakhrī, and Asmahan. George shakes his head and says, "That's not authentic Oriental music!" "But if these prominent Arab stars do not perform 'authentic Oriental music,' who does?" I ask. George sighs and, as if preparing for a lecture, draws out a pen and paper, clears a space on our table, and proceeds to set things straight.

What we know today as "Arab" music had its roots in the early civilizations of Sumer, Babel, and ʿAshura (the Assyrians). Since these civilizations had no musical notation, their music was passed on orally over the generations, "*abban ʿan jadd*" (from father to son), as they say. The early Christian Church played a major role in the notation of this ancient music. To make this clear, George grabs his pen and writes "Babel," "Assyria," and "Sumer," then underneath them draws a line and writes the word "music" (*mūsīqā*). He then writes "the Church" (*kanīsa*) and under it another line, "preserved it" (*jammadat-hā*, lit. froze it, crystallized it). Therefore, what we know as "Arab" music has two major branches that diverged from the early Church: Byzantine and Syriac. Each of these branches influenced later developments of "Arab" music, including Islamic liturgical melodies, especially in Syria and Iraq, the contemporary inheritors of the ancient civilizations. He writes "Byzantine" and "Syriac." Under Byzantine, George writes "Syrian" and "Qurʾānic recitation"; under "Syriac" he writes "Iraqi" and "Qurʾānic recitation." "Aleppo" he locates between these two, since it historically was an important cross-roads between Byzantium and Mesopotamia.

According to George, what most people know as "Arab" music—including the artists I earlier mentioned—is essentially "Turkish" art music that developed in the Ottoman courts and in the homes of the Turkish feudal overlords, the infamous Pashas. As for Egypt, he claims that it has lost touch with its heritage and through the hegemony of its mass media tools has spread its "Turkish" cultural legacy over the Arab world at large. "Everyone thinks it is 'Arab,' but it is really 'Turkish,'" he says. He then writes "'Abd al-Wahhāb" and "Umm Kulthūm" and next to their names, "Turkish." The Egyptian composer Sayyid Darwīsh is for him the only example of a heritage-inspired Egyptian composer; but, claims George, "he got most of his information from Aleppo," where he studied "a number of times." He writes Sayyid Darwīsh and next to it "Aleppo."[10]

True "Oriental" music, according to George, is to be found in the villages, a common sentiment linking the rural areas with authenticity, and especially in the traces of ancient, pre-Islamic musical-vocal practices found in some varieties of contemporary folk and religious song. Everything from the melody of the Islamic call to prayer (*adhān*) to the origins of the music of 'Abbasid Baghdad—the so-called "Golden Age" of Arabic culture in the ninth century—according to George, are to be found in the musical theories and practices of the ancient civilizations. The Church, as he has claimed repeatedly, is responsible for passing them on to us. As an example, George asserts that he has heard Christian funerary rituals in certain Syrian villages whose melodies are identical to the Muslim call to prayer and, ipso facto, must be its origin. Bilal, the first muezzin in Islam, was, after all, originally an Abyssinian Christian, so it comes as no surprise to him that there is evidence of such borrowing, according to George. George suggests Iraqi versions of Qur'ānic recitation and present-day Syriac liturgical melodies are very similar if not identical, and that I could verify this by comparing Iraqi Qur'ānic recitation, the music of the Shi'ite rituals of 'Āshūrā[11] from Karbalā' (in Iraq), and Syriac music.[11]

There is, then, no such thing as "Arab music"; rather, there is "Oriental music," *mūsīqā sharqiyya*, the music of the ancient civilizations preserved and transmitted by Christian Arabs. I should not confuse modern "Turkish" (or turkified) music with "true" Arab music, that is, "Oriental music." I suggest that Persian music also played a major role in the development of Arab music, not just Byzantine music. George grabs his pen and writes at the top of the page, "Nothing is Pure" (*lā yūjad shay' ṣāfī*). "Does this mean that Persian music is just some sort of impurity?" I ask. "No," says George, "just that it is less important than the other influences." In the end, George concludes by writing that "Oriental music" can be divided into two periods: pre- and post-Church music. The Church played an important role in preserving the music of the ancient civilizations in this varied land from over four thousand years ago, a rich heritage that remained oral until the early Church documented it. If I want to get to the heart (*qalb*) of "Arab" music, I should study the music of the Church. George then writes for me a long list of people whom I should consult in this regard, including the Syriac patriarch in Damascus and church leaders in Aleppo and Lebanon.

From the standpoint of a Christian intellectual, the roots of Arab music are ancient and not to be confused with modern accretions from Turkey. The Church played a central role in documenting and preserving this rich musical heritage and remains an important vestige of an ancient but living tradition. From the standpoint of another intellectual from a different background the story is somewhat changed.

Now we are in Aleppo, looking for books in the National Library. It is a few weeks after my discussion with George, and I am heading to the National Library in Aleppo in order to look up some musical references. Friends at the Tourist Café tell me that the library has everything, including al-Iṣfahānī's *Kitāb al-aghānī*. The National Library, situated at Bāb al-Faraj near the Old City, is a prime example of colonial architecture with its red and black striped stones (echoing the *ablaq* style common in Syria) and Oriental arches. Today the building is in a state of disrepair, the entrance used as a ticket booth for local comedy shows. Above the stairs sits a bust of Abū al-ʿAlāʾ al-Maʿārī, the famous blind eighth-century poet and grammarian, who in his present perch seems to turn his nose in disgust from the smell of urine wafting from the public lavatories.[12] I ascend the stairs to the catalogue room and to my dismay find the library closed—it must be yet another national holiday. Sure enough, there is the index of the *Kitāb al-aghānī* dominating the wall over the old-fashioned card catalogue. I leaf through some of the cards and scrutinize the large index to see how it might relate to the cards under my fingertips. Getting nowhere, I notice that there is a small book fair in the main reading room, so I decide to stay and browse awhile. There are only a handful of browsers today and probably because I am the only foreigner in the room, and just as likely out of a mixture of boredom and curiosity, the director, "Aḥmad," comes over and strikes up a conversation with me: "Can I be of any service?" Aḥmad, who has earned a doctorate in Oriental Philosophy from the University of Damascus, works for a publishing house and runs book fairs at the libraries in Syria. In his suit jacket and striped shirt, he looks important if a little uncomfortable in today's heat. "Please take a look around," he suggests, "then join me for tea!" I take a turn around the room and, finding nothing much on music, return to his table, where he offers me a small glass of sweet tea.

We settle into conversation. I tell him of my research and that I had wanted to read some books on Aleppine music, and we exchange views on Arab music and culture. Aḥmad's friend "Luʾay," who studied English Literature at Aleppo University and can recite Shakespeare by heart, joins us for a glass of tea, pondering aloud "whether 'tis nobler in the mind to suffer the slings and arrows of outrageous fortune. . . ." I am half-tempted to finish the line but wonder about its possible implications here.[13]

When no one else is in the room, Aḥmad leans close and whispers, "we are both Kurdish." One cannot advertise that identity too loudly here, they suggest. They ask me who I know in Aleppo among the musicians and how far I have come in my research: What have I "discovered" about the music? When I mention that I have an interest in Syriac music (after my conversations with George) and had just seen a prominent Syriac composer and musician in Aleppo, Aḥmad straightens up and with a concerned look argues, "This musician, like most Syriacs, is zealous (*muta'aṣṣib*) with respect to Syriac music." The "truth," for Aḥmad, is that much of what is claimed to be Syriac culture is originally Kurdish; the Syriacs "stole" Kurdish culture, then recorded it in their churches (that is, they notated Kurdish music), so that today everyone thinks that it is theirs. "Do you listen to Kurdish music?" he asks, and when I reply that I do not, he suggests that I should. Kurdish culture, because it is traditionally oral (*shafahī*), was not written down until the Syriacs came along and by documenting Kurdish culture claimed it as their own. Both Aḥmad and Lu'ay assert (not without justification) that today Kurdish culture is ignored, even threatened by the politics of Arabization in Syria.

Then "Firās," a writer and owner of a publishing house, stops in and we discuss the musics of the world.[14] Aḥmad, Lu'ay, and Firās all agree that music is a "universal language" and hence can be understood by anyone no matter where—"all music speaks to you." There are two aspects, says Aḥmad: realization (*idrāk*), which is mental, and emotions (*'awāṭif*) or spirit (*rūḥ*), which is emotional. "One might not understand the Persian or Hindi languages yet experience *ṭarab* [a state of musical rapture] from the music," says Firās, that is, enjoy its emotional aspect. There is a clear preference and valuation among Aleppines of the emotional over what many described as the "merely rational" aspects of culture that we in the West are thought to value more. However, familiar local music, according to Aḥmad, might not cause *ṭarab*. For example, Aḥmad gets bored with Ṣabāḥ Fakhrī after about ten minutes—it is enough for him. As some say, *mizmār al-ḥayy la yuṭrib*, the neighborhood pipe does not please (cause *ṭarab*); familiarity breeds contempt.

Firās poses the question, "Is there in fact such a thing as 'Arab music' or 'Japanese music' or 'American music,' or is there just 'music,' a universal language?" He proceeds to answer it in the affirmative: music is a universal language. As evidence, he claims that he listens a lot to "world music" and enjoys it, can understand its language.[15] Firās mentions Liszt, Mozart, and other European composers as among his favorite "world composers" in addition to some local artists: I wonder where else one might hear Mozart and the famed Aleppine composer ʿUmar al-Baṭsh mentioned in the same breath. Since he can enjoy both types of music, they must have some commonalities. "Perhaps there's a shared musical spirit," he suggests. Aḥmad then argues that "the Turks claim that Greek music is Turkish, and the Greeks claim that Turkish music is Greek; Each thinks that the other's culture is really theirs! Thus it goes with neighbors!" "Like the Syriac-Kurdish debate we just rehearsed," I think to myself. Yet it is the shared spirit between the neighbors, says Aḥmad, that makes their music similar. Still, if I want to hear real authentic music, I must go to the Kurdish villages to the west of Aleppo. There I would hear the *real* music. . . .

The Arab Tradition: Ancient Roots, Assimilation, and Modern Vitality

Against these and other claims for the "real" roots of Arab music, some of my interlocutors argued that the Arab tradition is not only ancient and vibrant, it is also "Arab." Not long into my stay in Aleppo, I had the good fortune of meeting "Samīr," a locally respected writer and authority on Arab and Aleppine folklore and folk life. I met Samīr at his regular hours (his "*dawwām*," like academic office hours) at the Rendez-vous café. The Rendez-vous—recently redecorated and renamed the Lantern, but everyone still calls it the Rendez-vous—is known as an intellectuals' café and despite its noisy location at a major intersection in downtown Aleppo it usually hosts a number of lively discussions throughout the day and well into the evening. At this table a group argues over the fate of Arabic literature, while over in the corner another debates politics in the global economy. Solitary figures sit at their upper-level tables, hunched over sheaves of loose paper, their cigarettes poised precariously in their fingers while they scratch out drafts of their latest poem-story-play-review. Friends passing by wave through the large glass windows on their way to other appointments; some stop in for a chat, which develops into lengthy discussions and eventually calls for more coffee.

On this sunny afternoon, I find Samīr sitting alone at "his" table upstairs working on a draft of his latest play, one of his several publications. His small glass of coffee sits unsipped to one side of his notebook and a cigarette burns to ashes in his left hand. I introduce myself and he smiles and pulls over a chair from a neighboring table. About fifty-five, he has a calm and friendly demeanor, his eyes full of patience and understanding, and he appears genuinely interested to meet me; none of the usual boisterous welcomes that I have now come to associate with a degree of falseness. "Will you join me for a coffee?" he asks.

I sit and begin to tell him of my research interest in Aleppine music and folklore, and musical aesthetics. I mention a special interest in the development of the Aleppine musical suite (*waṣla*) and its social and cultural importance in Syria from 1946 through the 1960s. The year 1946 marked Syria's independence from France, and the first Syrian radio and broadcasting stations were opened in Damascus and Aleppo in 1947 and 1949, respectively. The period from approximately 1946 to 1970 is considered a high point in Syrian radio and music, a time when many now-famous recordings were made in the radio station's studios by its own orchestras and choirs, which no longer exist. "Well," says Samīr, "that is an interesting, important, and complex topic—in fact, I am working on a similar project for Aleppo Radio," where he works in the mornings putting together various documentary programs for local and national television. "Tell me," he continues, "what have you 'discovered' so far?"

I tell Samīr that I am still in the beginnings of my work but that I have taken on a new interest in Syriac and Kurdish music since they seem to be related to the "authentic" Arab traditions. Samīr chuckles. "You must have been speaking with so-and-so," he adds, referring to a prominent Syriac composer and musician with whom he has done an interview recently. This composer claims that the roots of the many genres of Arab music are Syriac, but Samīr does not agree with him. First of all, in Samīr's view, Syriac culture is "limited." Despite their efforts to revive Syriac language and culture, the Syriacs do not number more than about half a million, so there is "little hope" that they will achieve the cultural revival they hope for. Second, there's too much evidence from medieval Arab writers that most of the genres of the *waṣla* are "local," meaning Arab-Islamic and Levantine, if not Aleppine, but certainly not Syriac.

"But some say," I interject, "that the church played an important role in documenting the music." I have George's remarks in mind. "Certainly," says Samīr, "the Syriac church played an important role in documenting the ancient civilizations, and like the Byzantines developed a system of modes in their religious song (*inshād*) that parallels in many respects the Arab, Turkish, and Persian modal systems." But this is not the whole story, according to Samīr. He adds, "with all due respect to the Kurds, they have never enjoyed civilization (*ḥaḍāra*)." The Kurds, in his view, always have been a mountain people and do not even have an alphabet of their own, let alone a strong musical tradition that could have been the root of Arab music. A well-developed musical tradition is the result of civilization, of *ḥaḍāra,* he asserts. Civilization is the most important factor in creating a strong musical tradition.

"Let me tell you a story" (*baḥkīlak ʾiṣṣa*), he continues.

> There are some old tablets from the ancient [Euphrates] civilization of Mari, located on the Euphrates near the present-day border with Iraq, that date back over four thousand years. One is a letter from a local ruler to the king of Mari asking

> him to oversee the musical education of his three daughters. "Take my daughters, O King, and teach them the art of music in your schools," says the letter. This suggests that there were schools for music at this time. Over four thousand years ago and they had schools for music! Because it was a true civilization, there was a strong musical tradition. Kurdish music, however, is folkloric and popular (*shaʿbī*), not "authentic" music, which comes from the urban civilizational centers such as Aleppo and Damascus.

For Samīr as for others, the authentic musical traditions are primarily urban and not rural, as others sometimes claimed; "civilization" (*ḥaḍāra*) is the key ingredient that makes music authentic, in this view.

"True," says Samīr, "with the exception of the Kingdom of Sheba the Arabs likewise did not traditionally enjoy civilization in this manner." Only after the rise of Islam and through contact with others, especially the Persians, were the Arabs able to create a cosmopolitan Arab-Islamic civilization, he says. Yet, even though this was a civilization built upon the borrowed traditions of others, including the Byzantine and Syriac, "all civilizations are this way"—echoing George's "nothing is pure" remark, that is, authenticity does not necessarily imply purity of origins. The Arab-Islamic civilization moreover assumed a local characteristic wherever it existed: in Baghdad, in Damascus, in Aleppo, in al-Andalus (medieval Muslim Spain), and elsewhere. Pointing out the "foreign" roots of a civilization does not deny its local authenticity (the same way that the presence of European conceptions does not invalidate a "Syrian" modernity).

For example, Samīr says that in Aleppo one can hear a number of different varieties or "colors" (*alwān*) of music. Within the city proper, you have the *muwashshaḥāt,* of which some are Andalusian and some are Aleppine.[16] One also hears the *qudūd ḥalabiyya* in their different forms, many of which are sung in various dialects according to their origin: Aleppine, Damascene, Egyptian, Iraqi, and Turkish.[17] One also hears the *qaṣīda* (classical ode), the *mawwāl* (colloquial lament), and various genres of popular song (*aghānī shaʿbiyya*). These, along with the instrumental pieces that introduce the different genres and the Egyptian *dawr* (a multi-part song in dialectical Arabic), constitute the Aleppine *waṣla.* Even genres that have their origins in the countryside, desert, or outside of Syria have been assimilated into the Aleppine musical culture, taken on an Aleppine character and flavor (*nakha*) appropriate to Aleppine aesthetics, and are hence "Aleppine" genres.[18]

"Are Umm Kulthūm, Muḥammad ʿAbd al-Wahhāb, and others like them essentially Turkish singers," I ask? Samīr looks surprised at my question. "It is true," he says, "that the Ottoman court style of singing prevailed in Cairo and elsewhere in the Ottoman lands in the end of the last century, but the style of

Umm Kulthūm and others has a noticeable *Aleppine* influence. At any rate, they are Arab artists singing in Arabic, so the music is Arab." He did not elaborate on the Aleppine style of Umm Kulthūm and ʿAbd al-Wahhāb other than to reiterate an oft-heard statement that Egyptian singers from the late nineteenth and early twentieth century adopted the Aleppine style of singing, which was less nasal than the then-prevailing Ottoman-Turkish style (Bin Dhurayl 1989: 27–28). Yet, nasality (*ghunna*) was one of the admired characteristics of Umm Kulthūm's voice well into the twentieth century (Danielson 1997: 148).[19]

Constructing Authenticity

The primary metaphorical understandings of authenticity and origin implicit in these dialogues and others like them are the medieval Arab world (such as tenth-century al-Andalus or twelfth-century Aleppo) and the ancient Near East. Both time-spaces support claims to musical authenticity in the present, as if there were an uncontestable link between these two pasts and locales and present-day Aleppo. Indeed, the two metaphors combine to form a sort of spatial and temporal genealogy of musical authenticity and, in other discourses, genealogies of religious and other varieties of cultural authenticity as well. Whereas al-Qalʿah and Samīr trace what is largely a Muslim genealogy that focuses on such Muslim luminaries as al-Kindī and al-Fārābī as well as the role of Muslim artists in modern Aleppine "civilzation" as inheritors of the medieval and ancient civilizations, George and Aḥmad trace different genealogies that emphasize different temporalities, spaces, and peoples.

Dr. al-Qalʿah's main rhetorical strategy is to cite medieval texts to authorize his position on the "Arabness" of Arab music. For example, he cites al-Kindī to support his argument that the tonal system of Near Eastern music is of Arab as opposed to Turkish or Persian origin (while recognizing the influence of the latter cultures on Arab music). His television program borrows explicitly from al-Iṣfahānī; al-Qalʿah envisions himself as producing what is in a sense a second *Kitāb al-aghānī*. He uses the borrowed authority of the medieval authors and texts to support his evaluations of the "best" Arab songs of the twentieth century. Contradictions or contradictory opinions, though explicitly solicited in the television program, play a minor role in his presentation and evaluation of songs. Despite the scientific rhetoric of al-Qalʿah's approach to the music—his heavy reliance on computers in his television program and his "objective" comparisons—in the end it is his "ear" that is the deciding factor: He hears (senses) that the modal system is "Arab" and not Turkish or Persian.

The other primary authorizing source in al-Qalʿah's and Samīr's dialogues is ancient Mesopotamia. Dr. al-Qalʿah claims that the earliest example of the oud has been found there (and others in Syria also made this claim, though I have not seen the published data on these "finds"). Samīr recites the story of the King of Mari and the musical education of his daughters to support his notion of urban civilization (*ḥaḍāra*). In both accounts, temporal and spatial jumps are made from the medieval authorities to the present, and from ancient Mesopotamia to contemporary Aleppo. The result is that physical/geographical Syria is seen as the inheritor of the culture of the ancient Mesopotamian (and Levantine) civilizations, and modern Arab musicians as the inheritors of the theoretical and practical efforts of medieval Arab theorists (one should perhaps write "Arab" theorists since the idea of Arabness in the tenth century was different from contemporary meanings). Especially for Samīr, contemporary Aleppo sits at the end of a complex process of civilizational development based on the assimilation of and borrowing from previous civilizations. Authenticity lies in that quality of "civilization" (*ḥaḍāra*) that transcends the culture of the villages—in urbanism and cultural complexity.

For George and Aḥmad, the genealogy has different roots. For George, the genealogy of authenticity is punctuated by the early Eastern Church's role in codifying the ancient heritage and propagating it generation after generation until today. In this genealogy, Aleppo serves as a meeting point of two early Church-based heritages, Byzantine and Syriac. Yet, he suggests, authenticity can be found in Christian villages, not the city, which in his view is "Turkish" or Turkified. George's remark that he has heard melodies in Christian villages that are similar to the Muslim call to prayer suggests to him that the Christian melody is the root and basis of the Muslim one; he assumes that (a) since Christianity came before Islam, the Christian melody must be older, and (b) rural life does not change, so cultural practices from Byzantine and Syriac culture that found their ways to the villages would remain essentially unchanged over many centuries. He does not entertain the idea that the Muslim call to prayer may have influenced the Christian funerary rite.[20] Yet George is not a purist; he acknowledges that there have been many "outside" factors and influences in the rise of "Oriental music"—after all, "*lā yūjad shayʾ ṣāfī*"—but these are seen in a sense as "outside" if not "impurities," less important than the roots. Again, roots and origins are important in supporting a claim to authenticity; origins thereby serve an authorizing and authenticating discourse.

Aḥmad's version of the history is similar to George's but with a change in the originating culture: Kurdish and not Christian. For Aḥmad, the genealogy of authenticity is interrupted by the early Church's "stealing" of Kurdish culture.

The "true" heritage lives on in present-day Kurdish villages, seemingly untouched by urban-based civilization in the ensuing centuries. In other words, if one were to look behind George's claims and dig a little deeper, one would find that the origin and root of what the early Church codified was in fact Kurdish culture. Aḥmad and his friends posit a timeless Kurdish past, a source that was mined and codified and in their view "stolen" by the early Christians but nonetheless propagated and continued in autonomous Kurdish villages up to the present day. The time frame assumes an eternity that is punctuated by the historical act of codification ("stealing") of the Kurdish heritage by the Syriac Church. The spatial aspect is the same: the villages of Mesopotamia are the sources of authentic culture. However, their construction of an originary and authentic Kurdish culture is compromised by their discourse on music as a universal language. If music is in fact a universal language, would not its universality contradict claims to a specific origin or authenticity? If it is universal, can we even speak of Kurdish or Syriac or Arab or Persian music? These genealogies of musical authenticity were reiterated at a conference on Arab music sponsored by the International Council on Traditional Music and held in Aleppo in the spring of 2000. A number of the Syrian participants argued for similar histories of Arab music to support implicit claims for Syria (if not Aleppo per se) as the inheritor of an authentic, ancient, and now Arab tradition—"Arab" in the sense that the Arabs have inherited it and made it their own, as in Samīr's remarks.

Qafla

Aleppo lies at a crossroads where constructions of authentic selves meet constructions of the modern Syrian nation. Examining the temporal and spatial dimensions of musical and cultural authenticity in contemporary Aleppo reveals the ways in which collective memories and understandings of the past can be harnessed by cultural agents to project divergent visions of the contemporary nation. Yet the nation is rarely the subject of such discourses. Rather, the city (Aleppo), region (Mesopotamia), and religious and ethnic groups (Syriac, Muslim, Kurdish) are the primary referents for genealogies of musical authenticity.

I turn now to a specific cultural space that assumes significance as an originary space for Aleppo's musical heritage: the Sufi *dhikr* or ritual invocation of God. Many of my musician friends in Aleppo told me that if I wanted to understand their music properly I needed to attend the Sufi *dhikr,* which, for them, represented the origin of contemporary musical practices. If the roots of the *waṣla* were to be found in the *dhikr,* as some claimed, then I needed to learn more about this special performance realm in Aleppo. Chapter 4 explores the Sufi *dhikr* both as a site for religious ritual observance and as a site for musical performance intimately related to the performance of music in other domains of life in contemporary Aleppo. It also serves as a space for the formation of moral and musical selfhood.

FOUR

Body Memory, Temporality, and Transformation in the Dhikr

The heart of man has been so constructed by the Almighty that, like a flint, it contains a hidden fire which is evoked by music and harmony, and renders man beside himself with ecstasy.

—al-Ghazzali, *The Alchemy of Happiness*

Maṭlaʿ: A Journey Toward Remembering and Forgetting

Many of my friends and teachers told me that if I wanted to understand the roots of "authentic" Arab music then I should listen to and study the music and song of the Sufi *dhikr*, the ritual invocation and remembrance of God.[1] They claimed a close relationship between the secular repertoire of Arab music and the songs and rhythms of the *dhikr* and the melodious style of Qurʾānic recitation known as *tajwīd*. In addition, Aleppo's numerous *zāwiya*-s or "Sufi lodges" have played an important role in preserving "traditional" Arab music, especially in times of change when traditions have been cast off in favor of the new.[2] Even at the beginning of the twenty-first century, argue many Aleppines, the *zāwiya* continues to preserve the traditional song forms and spiritual life of the city.

Sufism (*taṣawwuf*) expresses the "mystical dimensions of Islam" (Schimmel 1975), which is to say that it focuses on the esoteric meanings of sacred texts and spiritual practices in addition to their exoteric or literal meanings. Muslim mystics or Sufis—the word is generally thought to derive from the wool garments early mendicants wore, *ṣūf* meaning wool[3]—can be found in both the Sunni and Shiʿite traditions of Islam in many areas of the Muslim world. Despite important Shiʿite groups in Syria, it is the Sunni branch of Islam that constitutes the majority of Syria's Muslim population. Not all Sunni Muslims have

Sufi or mystical leanings and therefore do not attend *dhikr,* but at the same time, many of those who do attend *dhikr* do not consider themselves to be especially mystical or "Sufis" either. Rather, they participate in *dhikr* as a form of spiritual practice inherent to the *sunna* or orthodox obligations of Islam.

Syria has been home to numerous famous Muslim mystics, from the great master Muḥī al-Dīn Ibn al-ʿArabī, Shams al-Dīn al-Tabrīzī, and Jalāl al-Dīn Rūmī in Damascus, to al-Fārābī, Suhrawardī (al-Maqtūl), and others in Aleppo.[4] Aleppo is considered to be the second city after the Turkish city of Konya for the Mawlawiyya or "whirling dervish" sect of Sufism founded by Rumi in the thirteenth century. Today, Aleppo is home to numerous *zāwiya*-s of different orders (*ṭuruq,* sing. *ṭarīqa*), such as the Qādiriyya, the Rifāʿiyya, the Badawiyya, the Mawlawiyya, and others.[5] Popular worship of Sufi "saints" (*wālī*-s) or mystical leaders is common as well. One man, a local heritage buff, claimed that in Aleppo one can find the tombs of over 150 *wālī*-s, each specialized in providing certain services to devotees, including healing and curing disease, granting success, and even one—he claimed sardonically—thought to have the power of warding off the American army.[6] *Dhikr* is held almost daily in Aleppo at the different *zāwiya-s,* though usually only once a week at each, as well as in private homes and at the tombs of certain "saints." The *dhikr*-s that I attended were primarily held on Friday, the Muslim Sabbath, although I also attended *dhikr* on certain holidays and feast days.

I had attended some of the more public *dhikr*-s held near the Mosque of Hussein in Cairo but personally found them to be noisy affairs. I was assured by friends that the *dhikr*-s in Aleppo, unlike those in Cairo, were austere, serious, and yet energetic. However, they told me that the *dhikr* is a relatively closed world; it would be best for me to find a local participant to accompany me to the *zāwiya* rather than to go alone. Requests to friends and teachers were met with warm encouragement but not fixed appointments: "Tomorrow, God willing," was the usual response, meaning, "some day . . . maybe." Indeed, the *dhikr* remains a closed world to many locals because of their distance from this dimension of Muslim spirituality.

While I was asking around about the *dhikr* in Aleppo, I became somewhat fixated on the so-called Most Beautiful Names of God (*asmāʾ allāh al-ḥusnā*), and what we prosaically translate as "The Ninety-nine Names of God."[7] Earlier in my wanderings, I had seen numerous little booklets on the Names scattered among the sidewalk book stalls in Damascus and Aleppo, as well as in the small book shops located near the Umayyad Mosque at the farther end of the Sūq al-Ḥamidiyya,the main covered market in Damascus. Perhaps conversations with a Sufi friend in Damascus about Ibn al-ʿArabī and his interpretation of the Names led me to wonder what they were and to try to learn and memorize them. It would also help my Arabic, I thought, trying to find some justification for my arcane interest—arcane because few Syrians whom I know can recite all the Names. But now that I wanted to learn them, I couldn't find any of the booklets, and when I asked around for them I was told that there were none, or that I should come back later. Where did they all go?

Stymied in my attempt to procure a book (my favorite modus operandi), I tried to remember the few Names that I had heard before as well as imagine what might be probable Names. I already knew a few: The Merciful (*al-rahmān*), The Compassionate (*al-raḥīm*), The Great (*al-ʿaẓīm*), The Beloved (*al-ʿazīz*), The Omniscient (*al-ʿalīm*). I soon realized that a number of famous Arab musicians had names that revealed some of the Names of God. Muḥammad ʿAbd al-Wahhāb, for example, pointed me toward The Endower (*al-wahhāb*); ʿAbd al-Ḥalīm Ḥāfiẓ suggested The Gentle (*al-ḥalīm*) and The Guardian (*al-ḥafīẓ*); Muḥammad ʿAbd al-Muṭṭalib, The Beseeched (*al-muṭṭalib*); ʿAbd al-Fattāḥ Sukkar, The Opener (*al-fattāḥ*), and so on. After a while, I ran out of vocalists and began searching street signs and trying to recollect the names of characters in novels that began with *ʿAbd* ("servant of"), which would be followed by one of the Names of God: ʿAbd al-Munʿim, The Benefactor (*al-munʿim*); ʿAbd al-Razzāq, The Provider (*al-razzāq*); ʿAbd al-Ṣamad, The Everlasting (*al-ṣamad*). This got me to about thirty-three Names. Ninety-nine seemed a lot.

I soon found myself on yet another bus ride from Damascus to Aleppo, this time accompanied for the fifth time by Ahmad Zakī playing Jamal ʿAbd al-Nasir in the movie "Nasir '56." Trying to ignore the film, though it gave me another Name (The Victorious, *al-nāṣir*), I pulled out the rosary that a Muslim friend had given me and began counting off the Names that I knew on its ninety-nine beads. By the time I reached Aleppo almost five hours later, I had come up with only sixty-one Names. Where on earth were those little books when I needed them? Disappointed, I headed over to the Tourist Café to say hello to whoever might be there. To my surprise I ran into my main music teacher, Muḥammad Qadrī Dalāl, who normally sat at another nearby café. He invited me for coffee and we fell into talking about what I had been doing in Damascus, what was new in Aleppo, news of mutual friends, and the like. I reminded him of his promise to take me to see the *dhikr* and he suggested that we go to one the following morning. His father had been an important sheikh, and Dalāl, though he seldom attends the *dhikr* today, remains a well-known figure in Aleppo's religious communities and would therefore be an appropriate guide.

We met the next morning at the café and headed off to the Old City in his car. We parked near one of Aleppo's ancient gates, then made our way into the old stone neighborhoods on foot. Winding our way through the myriad alleyways and thoroughfares of the Old City, which were mostly silent that Friday morning, we talked about music, about the importance of the *dhikr* as an institution that helps preserve the old ways: "As long as there are children attending the *dhikr*," he suggested, "no one need worry about the future of Arab music."[8] After about twenty minutes and once I was totally lost in the veritable labyrinth of lanes, we ducked into a narrow opening in a plain stone wall and found ourselves in the small courtyard of the *zāwiya*.[9] A group of men young and old mingled amongst a number of old tombstones in the courtyard, their white *jalabiyya*-s suggesting purity and simplicity.[10] Dalāl introduced me to some of the men, and I asked about the tombs. I was told that they were the tombs of the founder of the *zāwiya* and his successors, the earliest dating back over five hundred years. The current leader (*shaykh al-zāwiya*) is a direct descendant of the founding sheikh, near whose tomb we were standing. Sayings from the Qurʾān and Prophetic traditions (*ḥadīth*) as well as poems were inscribed on the tombs in the simple *naskhī* script. I was told that, following the principles of Islamic numerology (*ḥisāb al-ḥurūf*), which assigns numerical values to each of the twenty-eight letters of the Arabic alphabet, the last letter of each verse would add up to the year in which the deceased person had passed away.[11] For those who know how to read them, these sayings are signs of divine will and further proof of the sacred character of the Arabic language.

In the background, we could hear the slow chanting of "The Cave" (*Sūrat al-kahf*) from the Qurʾān. In many ways, the *zāwiya* seemed like a cave to me, its dark interior contrasting with the brightness of the sun-drenched courtyard. Men and boys drifted in and out of the main room, while others prostrated themselves in prayer in the smaller adjoining rooms. A group of doves circled above the high wall, swooping over the housetops of the Old City in their seemingly never-ending journey. After a short while we removed our shoes and walked in.

The *zāwiya* measures about 30 feet square with a high, domed ceiling. Dark wooden bookcases filled with old manuscripts and copies of the Qurʾān line the walls, rich carpets cover the floors, and a number of ceiling fans circulate the air on this hot day. A group of older men file in and stand along the back wall; these are descendants of the founding sheikh and each wears a beige turban, as does the main sheikh, who sits on the floor just in front of the back wall, which contains the prayer-niche (*miḥrāb*). Others line the side walls, and the rest of us sit on the floor facing the main sheikh. As people enter, they approach the sheikh, kiss his right hand and then press their foreheads to his hand, repeating this two or three times in a rapid motion. Others, usually older men, attempt to do the same but the sheikh quickly removes his hand before it can be kissed, refusing this sign of deference, and instead kisses his own hand and then places it on his own forehead. He indicated to older members that they should sit closer to him, while others take spaces nearer the walls and door of the *zāwiya*. While my teacher goes to kiss the sheikh's hand, I take a seat, uncertain whether it would be appropriate for me to do so as well.

Once seated, I am taken aback to find the Most Beautiful Names of God written along the side and back walls in beautiful, large *thuluth* script, the elegant black lettering standing out against the light marble in which they are engraved.[12] What I have been trying to recollect and memorize for the past week is now written in front of my very eyes. Is this some kind of sign? The Qur'ān says: "And we shall show them Our signs in the horizons and in themselves, that the Truth may be manifest to them" (XLI: 53). Looking above me, I find "There is No God but Allah" (*lā ilāha illā allāh*) written high across the back wall in green neon letters. Below, it small white bulbs announce Allah and Muḥammad. The four corners are graced by plaques bearing the names of the Rightly Guided Caliphs: Abū Bakr, ʿUmar, ʿUthmān, ʿAlī. The writing reminds me of Michael Gilsenan's discussion of the green neon writing he found in an Egyptian mosque, and "Gilsenan (1982)" comes to mind, which annoys me. When I should be focusing on the words and sounds and like those around me trying to open my heart to the spirit of the *dhikr*, Anthropology comes crashing in to break the spell and distract me. . . .

The recitation of the Qur'ān concludes and the ensemble begins chanting the Most Beautiful Names, slowly and in a low voice: *Yā raḥmān! Yā raḥīm! Yā ʿalīm! Yā ʿaẓīm*![13] The hair on my arms stands on end and a shiver runs over my shoulders and up the back of my neck. How strange a sound—how otherworldly it seems! I try to follow along by reading the Names on the wall. A child at my right, perhaps ten years old, chants in a loud treble voice: *Yā ḥayy! Yā qayyūm*![14] Eyeing me suspiciously as I sit transfixed and mute, he leans over and offers me a small booklet that contains the prayers and the Most Beautiful Names, like the one for which I had been searching. He tries to give a copy to my teacher, apparently not knowing him, but is brushed off with a reproachful glance and that ubiquitous Syrian hand gesture that means something like "Hold your horses!" I take a copy and soon find myself chanting along with them, mechanically fingering the beads of my rosary: *Yā waḥid! Yā wājid*! (The only one! The finder!).

The Names having been recited, the participants begin chanting the first part of the proclamation of faith (*shahāda*): There is No Deity but God (*lā ilāha illā allāh*). The chanting follows a syncopated rhythm, the "*ha*" of "*ilāha*" aspirated to provide a rhythmic stress: ha! Over this chanting, the vocalists begin to sing a *muwashshaḥ* and the rhythmic chanting of the *shahāda* provides a background tempo for the singing.[15] Finishing this *muwashshaḥ,* the vocalists (*munshid*-s) begin another one, then another, the pitch subtly rising, gradually, stepwise. The lead vocalist (*rayyis*) stands before the main sheikh and slaps out the tempo with his right hand on the back of his left until it turns red; I imagine it must get sore from all the vigorous slapping. As the pitch rises, the tempo accelerates and the chanting gets louder. The men along the walls, now numbering over seventy, begin to sway their upper bodies in coordination with the tempo, first to the right, then to the left, to the right, to the left, right left, right left. The effect is astounding: a circle of motion and sound swirling around a stationary center from which rise the voices of the young vocalists. They finish singing and the entire ensemble chants the proclamation of faith—shouts it!—proclaiming the Unity of God. I look over to the back wall and find that one older man's eyes have turned up into his head, his body moves spasmodically—right . . . left, right; left—and his mouth dangles open in a sort of grin. Another repeatedly knocks his head against the wall, seemingly oblivious to the tempo of the chanting. The main sheikh, earlier composed, now rocks back and forth on the carpet and shouts out *allāh! aywa! allāh! aywa!* (Allah! Yes!). The tempo increases to a frenetic pace, the volume increases to a veritable roar, and the men are nearly screaming: *lā ilāha illā allāh! Lā ilāha illā allāh*! The center begins to sway and I find myself moving along with my companions on the carpet, right, left, right, left, *lā ilāha illā allāh! lā ilāha illā allāh*!

Suddenly the main sheikh shouts *Allaaah*! and everything stops. The group falls silent and still. Only the sound of the ceiling fans can be heard swishing the hot air around. The sheikh then proclaims: "Pray to the Prophet!" All relax and murmur the standard prayer: "Pray to the Prophet Muḥammad and to his Family and Companions, and Grant Him Peace!" After a momentary pause, the *rayyis* takes up another *muwashshaḥ,* slapping out the slow, heavy rhythm on his bare hands. The participants begin to chant *allāh hū! allāh hū*! (He is God!) and the men along the walls slowly begin to move again, first to one side, then to the other, one side, then the other. . . .

And so began an Aleppine *dhikr,* a series of invocations, prayers, songs, and movements that reached several climaxes within the space of almost four hours. I left in a strange state, a mixture of awe, confusion, joy, and exhaustion from sitting and chanting in a hot, sweaty room with about two hundred others. Afterward, as we headed back to the café, Dalāl and I discussed the *dhikr,*

Dhikr, Damascus, 1998.

not so much as a religious ritual but as an artistic work. We compared notes on the different songs that were performed, the modes and meters used, the elevation of the pitches and acceleration of the tempos, the dance steps, and other aspects of the *dhikr,* and agreed to attend *dhikr* at other *zāwiya*-s in the coming weeks. The experience of having thought about the Names of God for a week and then finding them inscribed and invoked before me (within me?) in the *dhikr* left me questioning: Was this somehow meaningful or merely a coincidence? A meaningful coincidence? I shyly asked Dalāl and he replied that it must have been a "correspondence of ideas" (*takhāṭub al-afkār*). I'm still not sure what that means.

The *Dhikr* Defined

Dhikr is the ritual invocation of god and divine authority and power by Muslims through the repetition of the Most Beautiful Names of God, and usually accompanied by the performance of chanting and bodily movements known collectively as *samāʿ* (audition). Although *dhikr* may take place anywhere and indeed Muslims are commanded to "be ever mindful of God"—that is, to make every act itself a form of *dhikr* and invocation—*dhikr* usually takes place in a mosque or *zāwiya*, the Sufi lodge (literally a "corner" of a mosque) where it constitutes one aspect of a larger sequence of prayers, recitations, and songs accompanied by specified bodily motions. In Aleppo, the entire ritual sequence is generally known as the *dhikr*, though technically *dhikr* is one component of a larger ritual sequence known as *ḥaḍra* that includes the recitation of devotional formulas (*wird*) as well as the *dhikr* and *samāʿ* (see Pinto 2002: 198). *Dhikr* is held around the city at different times and on different days (indeed, every day), but most participants attend *dhikr* once a week. The *dhikr*-s on which I base the following remarks are held on Fridays after the main *jumaʿ* or congregational prayer and before the advent of the *ʿaṣr* or afternoon prayer: that is, they last approximately three to four hours. Others are held in the evenings on different days, often in private homes, and may be of longer or shorter duration. Some are accompanied by extreme forms of ecstatic worship such as piercing the skin with skewers (known as *ḍarb al-shīsh*), chewing glass or hot coals, self-flagellation and immolation, and other acts (Pinto 2002).

In Arabic, the word *dhikr* derives from the trilateral root dh-k-r, which also produces such cognates terms as *dhikra,* remembrance; *dhākira,* memory; *dhikrà,* memorial, commemoration; and the verb *dhakara yadhkuru,* to mention, to name, to invoke, among others. While wishing to avoid any simple correlation between linguistic meanings and the meanings of cultural practices, the relationship of the practice of *dhikr* to processes of remembering, remembrance, and commemoration has been taken up by scholars and "Sufi" commentators.[16]

Performing *dhikr* fulfills the divine injunction to "Be Ever Mindful of God" (Sūrat al-aḥzāb XXXIII: 41). Aside from cultivating this state of "mindfulness" in everyday life, Muslims around the Islamic world participate in regular and codified *dhikr* rituals that incorporate sequences of recitation, invocation, supplication, chant, metrical and non-metrical song forms, and codified bodily motions, though few would equate the practice of *samaʿ* with dance (*raqs*). According to some Sufi manuals and commentaries, the ultimate goal of the *dhikr* is oblivion (*fanāʾ*) of the individual "self" with the simultaneous remainder (*baqāʾ*) of the higher Self and its union (or *tawḥīd*) with the Divine Reality (*al-ḥaqq*) (Baldick 1989: 3; Nasr 1972; Schimmel 1975: 178; SEI 1995: 189). Paradoxically, some texts refer to this final state as the simultaneous remainder of the "higher self" and the oblivion or obliteration of the "lower self," both, presumably, called *nafs* (Baldick 1989: 3; Schimmel 1975: 178; SEI 1995: 189). Most orthodox Muslims would reject the claim that the human soul can literally unite with the divine essence because that would imply a sharing of the divine essence (*shirk*), which is incompatible with the doctrine of the Unity of God.[17] Metaphorically, however, union refers to states of proximity to the divine, or even to a form of mystical knowledge or gnosis (*maʿrifa, mushāhada*) of the divine reality gained as a result of the spiritual practices and devotions of the Sufi path.[18]

As one component of this path, performing *dhikr* is thought by some commentators to bring the believer to a realization of divine truths such as the unity of God and the unity of existence (*waḥdat al-wujūd*)—this is especially the case in the theology of Muḥī al-Dīn Ibn al-ʿArabī, the great twelfth- to thirteenth-century Muslim sage of Andalusian origin who settled in the Levant and died in Damascus in 1240 (see Chittick 1989, 1998). Since these truths are eternal and unchanging, the participants in the *dhikr* must have paradoxically "forgotten" what they must accept as articles of faith, and hence need to be reminded (made "mindful" of God, as the Qurʾān states). Practicing the *dhikr* reminds them (the verb *dhakkara* can mean "to remind someone of something") so they will not "forget" again these truths about themselves and about reality.[19] The *dhikr* in effect accomplishes this by bringing the faithful from a state of ignorance (*jahl*) to a state of knowing (*maʿrifa*), just as the advent of Islam brought the faithful from the *jāhiliyya* of the pre-Islamic "Days of Ignorance" to the knowledge of divine will. The Qurʾān, also known as "The Wise Remembrance" (*al-dhikr al-ḥakīm*), serves as a reminder to the children of Abraham of their earlier covenant, and as a warning to humanity to follow the Straight Path (*al-ṣirāṭ al-mustaqīm*).

Therefore we can understand *dhikr* as a form of ritual remembrance, indeed an unveiling (*kashf*[20]), of eternal truths that remain buried within us, but which are revealed and re-membered though the embodied practices of the *dhikr*. The Sufi path, the practice of *dhikr,* the acts of invocation, effects this transformation from ignorance/forgetting to knowledge/remembrance. As Nasr writes (1972: 17), Sufi practices allow one "to become aware of what one has already been from eternity (*azal*) without one's having realized it until the necessary transformation has come about." While prayer and constant meditation on the Most Beautiful Names of God may lead to a state (*ḥāl*) of annihilation and perseverance, it is the particular musical and kinesthetic elements of the *dhikr*—the practice of *samāʿ*—that Muslim commentators such as al-Ghazzali most often cite as having the power to effect this transformation (al-Faruqi 1985/1986; al-Ghazzali 1901–1902; Qureshi 1995: 82–84, ff.; Schimmel 1975: 168–76). *Samāʿ* is thought capable of triggering an ecstatic state known as *wajd,* literally "finding."[21] That is, Sufis "find" (*wajada*) God and attain a state of peacefulness (*iṭmiʾnān*)—a state reflected in the stillness of the *qafla,* which comes after the expense of considerable energy in the performance of the *dhikr*. This peaceful state can instill such a sense of happiness that adepts fall into ecstasy; hence the paradox of an ecstatic peacefulness.[22] Behavior associated with this state varies from quiet, still, and trance-like paralysis to violent spasmodic movements of the limbs, shouting, and occasionally such extreme acts as slashing the head, chewing glass, and inserting swords or skewers in various parts of the body (*ḍarb al-shīsh*) (Crapanzano 1973; Gilsenan 1982; Pinto 2002). As mentioned, in the Qādiriyya *dhikr*-s that I attended in Aleppo, I did not note more than a few rolled eyes and spasmodic movements, with an occasional knocking of a head against a wall, though more extreme acts such as *darb al-shīsh* and chewing glass are not unknown in Aleppo (Pinto 2002).

The Participants

The main sheikh (*shaykh al-zāwiya*) leads the *dhikr*, receiving participants as they arrive, seating the prominent members near his side, and initiating the opening and closing of the *dhikr*. As a direct descendant of the founding sheikh, he along with the other descendants form the spiritual core of the *zāwiya*. His distinction is marked by his position in the center of the *zāwiya*—either seated on a rug or standing just before the back wall—as well as by his wearing of the special beige turban. The other living descendants of the founding sheikh stand along the back wall behind the main sheikh and wear similar turbans; the other participants, if they wear any head covering, place simple white scarves over their heads.

The chanters gather in a circle around the main sheikh with the *rayyis* or lead vocalist at the center, usually standing in order to lead the participants in the chanting and singing. The others are known as the "wings" (*ajniḥa*, sing. *jināḥ*) and alternately lead the singing or serve as a chorus for when another vocalist solos. The "wings" are chosen from among the participants for their strong voices, and older, established vocalists may join as members of the "wings." Many of Syria's prominent singers began as members of the "wings" in Aleppo's *dhikr*-s.

The remaining participants stand along the walls or sit in a roughly semicircular pattern on the floor in front of the singers and main sheikh. The *dhikr* is a well-regulated social space, and the main sheikh and his assistants ensure the proper placement of individuals in the *zāwiya* according to their spiritual and sometimes social stature. Because I was allowed to tape one session, I was seated to the left and center of the main sheikh, one row behind the vocalists. One singer, seeing me assemble my recorder, moved the microphone into position just in front of the main sheikh, who acknowledged me with a brief nod. Behind me and to my sides sat a mixture of men and boys, most wearing long white or blue robes, only a few being in street clothes. Toward the back sat a man with his young daughter of perhaps six years standing by his side, her head covered in a light scarf. She was the only female in the *zāwiya* that day; women may participate but must do so in a separate room on the other side of the courtyard (though some *zāwiya*-s do not have a separate room for women, precluding their participation; Pinto 2002: 204).

The *Dhikr* as Performance

The Aleppine *dhikr* follows a set structure.[23] *Dhikr* always begins with recitation of passages from the Qur'ān, often an entire chapter in the melodious *tajwīd* style. This style closely follows many of the modal principles of Arab music, though devout Muslims deny that the Qur'ān is chanted, sung, or musical at all; as mentioned above, performers of Aleppo's "secular" repertoire closely follow the rules of Qur'ānic recitation in their singing, so there is considerable overlap in terms of the aesthetics of performance in both contexts. Recitation of the Qur'ān itself generally is preceded by the recitation of a prayer to ward off Satan, and then the first and shortest chapter of the Qur'ān (the *fātiḥa*), which "opens" the recitation.[24] Indeed, recitation of prayers and the Qur'ān also opens the sanctified space of the *dhikr,* purifying the *zāwiya* and the hearts of the participants. In one *zāwiya,* the walls were covered with ornate inscriptions of the Most Beautiful Names and names of the Prophet and Rightly Guided Caliphs. This writing delimited the space of the *zāwiya* (itself not more than about 30 or 40 feet on a side) as sacred, forming a scripted enclosure for the oral and kinesthetic acts of recitation and remembrance that constitute *dhikr*.[25] Prayers of supplication (*ibtihālāt*) or forgiveness (*istighfār*) follow recitation of the Qur'ān, then the participants recite the devotional formula of the Order.

Once these preparatory prayers and invocations are completed, the participants enter the main sequences of the *dhikr* and embark on their spiritual (and musical-kinesthetic) journey. When this journey occurs in the hot summer months, ceiling fans whir above the heads of the participants, and young boys walk around dispensing cups of cool jasmine-scented water. The *zāwiya,* already hot from the summer air, becomes almost intolerably so once the room fills with up to two hundred participants seated side by side on the floor and standing shoulder to shoulder against the wall, all chanting and swaying to the rhythms of the *dhikr*. Bodies touch, sweat pours from brows and necks, the air is choked with a melody of smells: sweat mixed with the perfume of the jasmine water, mixed with wafts of a particularly strong aftershave, mixed with the strong scent of musk perfume that some of the boys rub on the forearms of participants and which has a strong correlation with Muslim piety.

The *dhikr* consists of a number of sections or movements (*fuṣūl*, sing. *faṣl*). Each section consists of specific sequences of prayers and songs accompanied by particular movements of the body. There are six primary sections in the Aleppine *dhikr*, and potentially many secondary sections. The first, "Majesty" (*al-jalāla*), comprises the rhythmic and repetitive invocation of the first segment of the proclamation of faith: *lā ilāha illa allāh* (There is no God but Allah). These words are chanted in 8/4 tempo to a particular rhythm.[26] Melodically, the syllables are chanted to three pitches that correspond roughly to the first (tonic), sixth (superdominant), and seventh (subtonic) tones of a major scale, beginning with the first, descending to the sixth, then ascending through the seventh back to the first.[27]

This section is accompanied by particular body movements, beginning with a bend to the right on the first two beats followed by a return to center on the third and fourth beats, then a bend to the left on beats five and six and a return to center on the seventh and eighth beats. The overall motion appears as a swinging from right to left, right to left. Like so many ritual motions in Islam, the motion of the *dhikr* begins to the right side, associated in Islamic tradition with goodness and purity, whereas the left side has connotations of evil and pollution. In a similar fashion, one enters a home or crosses a threshold with the right foot, eats and writes with the right hand, and circumambulates the Kaʿaba (*ṭawāf*) during the *ḥajj* or pilgrimage to Mecca by proceeding counterclockwise, that is, to the right.[28] The chanting, regulated by the *rayyis*, provides the tempo for these movements, and as the chanting picks up tempo, the participants move more quickly.

The vocalists sing suites of religious songs while the participants recite the proclamation of faith; a suite may consist of a single *muwashshaḥ* or several sung sequentially without pause.[29] At the end of each suite, the lead vocalist elevates the pitch of the chanting in a step-wise fashion, modulating from one mode to another during the chanting of the sections of the *dhikr*. This process, known as *tarqiyya*, occurs at the conclusion of each suite of songs in a given mode, when the leader will modulate to a new mode and the vocalists will perform another suite.[30] This melodic modulation or elevation proceeds according to one of three fixed patterns of modal progressions based on the initial mode and tonic pitch (Dalāl n.d.: 8–10).[31] In addition to elevating the pitch of the chanting and singing, the *rayyis* also accelerates the tempo of the chanting and singing, a process known as *karta*.[32] The *rayyis* usually accomplishes this by proclaiming *mawlāyā*![33] (My Master!) and slapping the back of his hand with increased vigor.[34] The participants continue to chant on the new melodic mode and faster tempo, although with slightly altered rhythms and accentuations.[35]

The twin processes of melodic and rhythmic modulation continue until the participants reach the highest pitch of the mode series and a very quick tempo. At this point they are practically shouting, the high pitch and quick tempo of the chanting blending their voices into a single Voice, beyond pitch and rhythm. Those standing along the walls swing right and left, while those seated on the floor sway back and forth, creating swirling and contrasting currents of motion. Sound and motion intensify until there is but noise and a blurring, the climax of the section having been reached. Then the main sheikh pronounces allāh! (lengthening the "ah") and the section comes to a close.

In a similar manner, the other principal sections begin either with a *muwashshaḥ* or with prayers followed by a *muwashshaḥ* or sung poem (*qaṣīda*).[36] Prayers and songs are accompanied by different chants and proceed through the stages of the section until the sheikh calls "Allah" and it ends with a closure (*qafla*). Secondary sections, as many as twenty, can be interspersed between the second and third principle sections, thereby granting the *dhikr* a flexible, open-ended structure.[37] Each secondary section follows a similar structure to the other sections and includes suites of songs, prayers, and invocations.[38] Toward the end of the *dhikr,* someone may perform the "whirling dervish" dance, donning a black robe and twirling in front of the main sheikh until closure.[39]

Finally, each section ends with a closing sequence or *qafla* (lit. "lock" or "closure") at which point the participants rest before opening the next section or concluding the *dhikr*. However, closure in the *dhikr* is never final. The *qafla,* like musical closure, marks a temporary pause before the opening of another section or of another *dhikr,* if it is the *qafla* of the last section. The end of the *dhikr* itself is not marked with any sort of finality. When the last section concludes, the participants recite the *fātiḥa* prayer, which in this case "closes" the *dhikr* (whereas it opens and closes other Islamic rituals) then arise and exit the *zāwiya*. Some linger in the courtyard and chat before the next call to prayer brings them back inside for prayer—the *dhikr* usually being held between the noon and afternoon prayers, though some *zāwiya*-s hold their *dhikr*-s between the afternoon and sunset prayers. Others remain and perform supererogatory prayers (*nawāfil,* sing. *nāfila*), while still others head off home or to tend to affairs. Far from being an isolated ritual event, a given round of *dhikr* constitutes one moment in a general process of *dhikr* that recurs week after week, indeed day after day in Aleppo and throughout the Islamic world.

The Meanings and Symbolism of the Aleppine *Dhikr*

The Aleppine *dhikr* presents a rich domain for analysis, with its intricate musical, kinesthetic, and "ritually charged" atmosphere. However, studies of Islamic rituals such as the *dhikr* have tended to reduce its dynamic to such functions as the mystification of power relations or their legitimization (for example, Gilsenan 1973, 1982). Others have tended to reproduce Sufi ideologies, in particular those that claim that the aim and function of *dhikr* is to achieve union with God (for example, Nasr 1972). Moreover, until recently, analyses of ritual behavior have tended to assume a strict division between ritual thought, on the one hand, and ritual action on the other. As Catherine Bell (1992, 1997) and Talal Asad (1993) have shown convincingly, most anthropological analyses of ritual have granted primacy to ritual thought and considered ritual action to be a peculiarly thoughtless variety of action. Witness, for example, the long tradition of studying myths as "charters" for ritual, blueprints for and of action, to borrow Geertz's metaphor (1973) for the function of religious symbolism. The meanings and connotations of *dhikr* arise in its enactment and through the performance of its various sequences. The *dhikr* does not merely reflect the context in which it is enacted, it simultaneously creates and transforms this context so that meaning—if we can even speak properly of the meaning of such a rich and complex domain of spiritual practice—is continually suggested and deferred, in the Derridian sense (Derrida 1981; 1978). The multiple significations of the *dhikr* arise in their practice and are lent semantic continuity by the texts, authorities, and traditions of Sufism and the particular Sufi order (in this case, the Qādiriyya) that structure and legitimate the context in which participants undergo ritual embodiment and transformations.

Yet, the *dhikr* does not so much reflect these relationships and contexts of power and authority (let alone mystify them) as participate in their construction (Bell 1997: 82). The process of deferred signification is not open-ended; "tradition" defines (or attempts to define) the boundaries of practice and interpretation, but the complex and changing world in which the *dhikr* takes place raises the possibility for numerous novel interpretations and meanings to arise in the course of the performance of the *dhikr* and other spiritual and cultural practices.

Study of the musical and kinesthetic elements of the *dhikr* reveals that the spiritual truths of Islam and the moral values to which they give rise cannot be understood as concepts abstracted from lived experience. Rather, Islamic spiritual practices and values are mutually constituted through the specific acts that we call "rituals," of which the practice of *dhikr* is only one. The *dhikr* participates in a wider field of spiritual practices—prayer, recitation, fasting, study, almsgiving—that engender in participants specific Islamic virtues. In this regard, what we might treat as a question of belief (and especially as inner belief as opposed to outer behavior) is less relevant than the question of participation. Participation in the *dhikr* and other "rituals" inculcates or engenders those states of spiritual experience that we might translate as faith (*ʿaqīda,*[40] *īmān*) but which are not merely inner beliefs understood as separate from external actions and prior to them in the hierarchy of religious obligations (see Asad 1993; Bell 1992, 1997). Faith and ritual action are mutually constituted in the *dhikr* through its specific structure and through the various techniques that provide its dynamic, among them song and dance (*samāʿ*).

Embodying the Moral and Musical Self

The performance of *dhikr* aims to condition the moral self of participants. In the course of this habitual conditioning, it also enacts a "remembrance" or "remembering" of spiritual truths—divine power, the unity of existence. Participating in the *dhikr* also cultivates a musical self and provides a space for cultivating habitual body memories that are linked strongly in discourse and practice to musical performance both within the *zāwiya* and in the context of Aleppo's famed "secular" musical traditions. Indeed, the *dhikr,* as some musicians argued, serves as a rehearsal space and de facto conservatory (in the sense of conserving through training) for the modal and rhythmic cycles of Arab music. This latter aspect is paradoxical given the ambiguous relationship of music in Islamic theologies. Yet, the spiritual states articulated, cultivated, and performed in the course of the *dhikr* not only are related to the formation of musical and kinesthetic competencies, they require them. It is via the aesthetic practices of performing *dhikr*—the acts of the sensate, sensual body in time and space, conditioned by specific aural, kinesthetic, olfactory, and tactile experiences—that effect this moral-musical conditioning, and move participants toward a state (ephemeral, always in need of re-enactment) of remembering their higher Self and the divine truths of existence.[41]

The chanting and ritualized body movements constitute a form of ritual discipline, "techniques of the body" (Mauss 1979) through which adepts simultaneously embody and express a relationship to the divine. By the conclusion of the *dhikr,* participants have been cleansed spiritually and disciplined, according to al-Ghazzali and other commentators (Schimmel 1975), and thereby are prepared for their return to profane life (*al-ḥayāt al-dunyā*); performance of the

Wedding *munshid*-s, Aleppo, 1997.

dhikr thus disciplines a moral self. Repetition of the *dhikr* every week, if not every day, further inscribes these practices into the participant's spiritual and physical memory—it re-members spiritual truths paradoxically forgotten—and aids the progression of the soul to its final stage of "serenity." The language of higher truth and transcendence evoked in the *dhikr* expresses not only participants' relationship to the divine, but to themselves as well. Therefore, we should understand the *dhikr* as intimately related to the complex processes of self formation, via moral discipline, and also self characterization and presentation since, as Crapanzano (1992) and others have shown, conceptions of the self and personhood arise in the dialogical engagement of self and other that has an important presentational element.[42]

Following Asad (1993), Bell (1992, 1997), Mauss (1979), and others (Csordas 1994; Mahmood 2001, 2004; Stoller 1997), the *dhikr* needs to be understood as a form of "embodied practice" that conditions or disciplines a moral and musical self. The disciplining of the self is accomplished through the repertoire of aesthetic practices that constitute the experiential heart of the *dhikr:* music and rhythm, dance and motion, olfaction and tactility. The spiritual elements of the *dhikr* cannot be understood as separated from the aesthetics of *dhikr* performance and performativity. The spiritual truths and states of being require the aesthetic practices, which in turn draw their legitimacy from their role in promoting spiritual states. These states, which can be thought of as constituting a form of memory or remembrance of spiritual truths "forgotten" as a result of a fundamental human state of *méconnaissance,* arise in the production and reproduction (indeed, to borrow a musical term, "rehearsing") of what Edward Casey (2000), following Merleau-Ponty (1962), calls "habitual body memory." Habitual body memory, according to Casey, is "an active immanence of the past in the body the informs present body actions in an efficacious, orienting, and regular manner" (Casey 2000: 149). In the context of the *dhikr,* it is not a defined past memory or experience that is immanent in the bodies of participants. Rather, participants remember and commemorate spiritual truths and articles of faith. By performing *dhikr* in its full aesthetic experience, participants are remembering habits and dispositions inculcated from an early age (most participants have attended *dhikr* from the age of five or six). In a very basic sense they are remembering not abstract spiritual truths but the embodiment and naturalization of these spiritual truths in their physical, sensate bodies.

Temporal and Spiritual Transformations in the *Dhikr*

In the Aleppine *dhikr,* the combination of melodic and rhythmic intensification contributes to this sense of spiritual transformation by altering participants' perception and experience of time and temporality. The gradual increase in both the pitch and tempo of chanting, and thereby of the accompanying bodily movements, contributes to the experience or expectation of states (*aḥwāl*) of heightened emotional energy. In such states, the finite and linear temporality of the *dhikr* and its constituent sections—from opening prayers to closure—coexists with numerous non-finite and non-linear temporalities: of Creation, the eternity of the Qurʾān, for example, as well as the open-endedness and flexibility of the *dhikr,* suggesting cycles of *dhikr*-s and a continuing process of invocation and remembrance. As participants approach closure, they reach what Ibn al-ʿArabī termed the *barzakh* or margin between the human and the Divine, between the finite (*nihāʾī*) and the Infinite (*lā nihāʾī*).[43] At this *barzakh,* participants move from linear, measurable time toward eternal time, and back again. In a mathematical sense, this progression describes an asymptote, a state of perception (*mushāhada*) in which participants may experience the unity of existence, and the unity of diverse temporalities and causalities, and thereby fall into ecstatic states. In this way, musical processes aide participants' spiritual elevation.

The experience of temporal transformations in the course of the *dhikr* contributes to the production of the experience of transformations in the body. Although not all participants experience trance states or engage in ecstatic behavior, as noted, the experience of heightened emotionality in the *dhikr* is narrated both in textual commentaries such as al-Ghazzali and by participants as "ecstasy." Yet, the experience of transformation or transition in the course of performing *dhikr*—what in Arabic is termed variously *wajd* (rapture), *tawājud* (finding), and *tajallī* (manifestation)—corresponds not to an experience of transcendence related to objects outside the body, what Merleau-Ponty calls *ek-stase* (1962: 70, 419), but rather of more closely realizing the interiority of divine truths within the body. Paul Nwiya (1972) has called this a state of "instasy."

Artistic, Dramatic, and Social Aspects of the *Dhikr*

Yet, this abstract reading of Sufism and the functions of the *dhikr* notwithstanding, it is important to note that performing *dhikr* does not necessarily have mystical or even spiritual meaning for all participants. Few participants whom I interviewed described its meaning for them in Sufi terminology, though some did argue that the *dhikr* brings them to a state of spiritual elevation (*sumūw rūḥānī*). They described this state as a sort of floating or hovering (*taḥlīq*). Interestingly, as I examine in chapter 6, many musicians use the same terms to describe the process and experience of improvisation. Yet, none of the participants with whom I spoke suggested that unity with God was the true goal of the *dhikr*. Some suggested that nearness (*taqarrub*) to God was possible but that union with the divine was not (perhaps in line with Sunni teachings that deny the possibility of unity with God). In fact, many did not claim to have a particularly strong identification with Sufism at all. For them, performing *dhikr* is a Sunni obligation, part of what they consider to be a normative and not particularly mystical variety of Islamic worship. Just as Crapanzano (1973) found that the dramatic rituals of the Ḥamadsha Sufi lodges in Morocco had more to do with notions of spirit possession and exorcism than with divine union, in Aleppo the *dhikr* has a practical and non-mystical meaning or effect for many of its participants. Labeling the *dhikr* a "Sufi ritual" in some ways obscures for us its potential meanings.[44]

For example, some Aleppines attend the *dhikr* more for its artistic than for its spiritual content. This includes Muslims and some non-Muslims interested in the musical or performance aspects of the *dhikr*. The director of the Arab Music Institute in Aleppo, a Syriac Christian, claimed to have attended *dhikr*-s for many years as part of his field research on Oriental (*sharqī*) melodies and rhythms. Contemporary musicians study the genres and melodic and rhythmic processes of the *dhikr* as a basis for their compositions and performances. Some musicians suggested that the step-wise melodic progressions of the *dhikr* might provide the basis for novel modulations in Arab music composition and improvisation, which seldom follow step-wise progressions (S. Marcus 1992).[45] For devout and non-devout participants, attending the *dhikr* provides a solid training ground for acquiring a strong voice and learning the *maqāmāt.* As previously mentioned, most of the prominent Aleppine vocalists and musicians of the past century received their primary musical training in the *zāwiya.* The younger generation continues this tradition.

Catharsis: *Fishsh al-Qalb*

Aside from its artistic aspects, an important function of the *dhikr* for some participants is what is known as *fishsh al-qalb,* the cathartic release of tension from the heart (*qalb*) "like air from a balloon," as one friend put it—"*fishsh*" being this sound.[46] Another explained that performing the *dhikr* releases emotional tension and energy that otherwise might be released in violent ways; evoking Aristotle's discussion of catharsis in the *Poetics,* he argued that the *dhikr* is a form of drama.[47] The progression from slower to faster tempos and from lower to higher pitches in conjunction with repeated bodily movements has the effect of generating and releasing psychic and physical tension, according to many participants. Some further argued that *dhikr* is a good form of exercise, beneficial practically as well as spiritually.[48] These evaluations make sense given the high energy of the *dhikr* and the fact that it can be demanding physically, let alone spiritually. Chanting and moving for three or more hours with two hundred others in often intense heat can be exhausting, to say the least.

Healing

Occasionally, participants attend the *dhikr* to seek the cure of a physical or spiritual ailment. In some *zāwiya*-s in Aleppo, the main sheikh is thought to be able to cure illness because of his unique endowment of *baraka,* a special spiritual power and presence.[49] Before the first section commences and while the Qur'ān is being recited, people afflicted with back aches, paralysis of limbs, spirit possession, or other (usually somaticized) illnesses, gather round the sheikh. The afflicted sits before the sheikh and either he or a caretaker whispers the particular ailment in the sheikh's ear. The sheikh then lays his hands upon the afflicted part of the body and recites certain prayers or puffs a breath of air into the face of the afflicted person. It is believed that the sheikh's touch, prayers, and even his breath—energized by his *baraka*—will thereby effect a cure. The link between the sheikh's breath, his *baraka,* and his power to cure reflects the correlation in Arabic between the words for soul (*nafs, rūḥ*), on the one hand, and breath and wind (*nafas, riḥ*), on the other.[50]

Social Aspects

For many participants, the *dhikr* is an important social ritual that brings people together to share in a sense of community. In recent times, when having a strong Islamic identity has been officially suspect, the *zāwiya* has served as an important domain for collective forms of worship. This is especially the case after the "events" of 1982, when the city was blockaded by the Syrian army for a month and large sections of traditionally Islamic neighborhoods were razed, including the neighborhood near one of the *zāwiya*-s at which I attended *dhikr*. The government hoped thereby to prevent a feared uprising by the Muslim Brotherhood against the regime, as happened elsewhere in Syria, most notably in the city of Hama. In the context of these events, the *dhikr* brings people together for prayer and invocation, for song, for psychic and physical release, and to strengthen their commitment to Islam and to one another, and to help raise a new generation in the spiritual (and, as my teacher remarked, musical) traditions of the city.

Performing *dhikr* brings participants together, but it also effects certain temporary transformations in the social order as well. Within the *dhikr,* social hierarchies are ritually erased, as rich and poor, who outside the *dhikr* might not have any social contact, sit side by side on the carpets invoking the names of God. At the same time, spiritual hierarchies are raised within the *zāwiya,* and the materially poor may occupy a higher spiritual status than the materially wealthy. This is especially true for descendants of the founding sheikh, who stand in the privileged position along the back wall of the *zāwiya* during the *dhikr* and who, along with the main sheikh, wear a uniquely colored turban. Even the wealthiest of the local merchants, such as the merchant who showed me his five hundred-year-old genealogical scroll, pay ritual deference to the poorest of these descendants, the so-called *darāwīsh,* which in the local dialect means at once "spiritual mendicants" and "impoverished people." In this way, the *dhikr* bends and often breaks the normal rules of social intercourse, emphasizing brotherhood through piety, community through adherence to a common tradition, but also a spiritual hierarchy in which descent (*naṣab*) plays a role alongside piety in determining one's rank (*ḥasab*).

Certainly, the above remarks pertain to those believers who attend the *dhikr* for spiritual reasons as well as out of any interest in its artistic aspects. We should not, however, romanticize the sense of community that the *dhikr* might create despite whatever states of communitas the participants in the *dhikr* might achieve or evoke. Individuals attend the *dhikr* for numerous reasons, not all of them mutually compatible, and it would be naïve to suggest that a weekly ritual could eliminate the potentiality for discord and difference within any community of believers. Social tensions are not ameliorated in the *dhikr* and may even be exacerbated. For instance, the formation of spiritual hierarchies that grant descendants of the founding sheikh higher status within the *zāwiya* than they might enjoy outside of it might cause tension. Differences often arise within the *dhikr* among the vocalists. A now-famous dispute arose some years ago between two well-known religious singers in Aleppo, leading to tensions within the various *zāwiya*-s when either one attended the *dhikr*. Attempts to reconcile the two have failed. The *zāwiya* therefore can be the domain of discord as well of communal feeling.

As Qureshi (1995: 128–29, ff) notes for Qawwali practice in India, the erasure of social hierarchies from outside the *dhikr* during performance is temporary, and musical-spiritual practices such as *dhikr* usually serve to reinforce social hierarchies even while temporarily suspending them in the course of performance. Following scholars of carnivalesque inversions from Bakhtin (1984) to Turner (1987), and Stallybrass and White (1986), among others, the ritual inversions that occur in ritually charged environments such as the *dhikr* must be analyzed in terms of how they relate to social pressures and configurations outside the realm of ritual behavior and practice. Indeed, spiritual hierarchies enacted in the *dhikr* may exacerbate those found in the market.

In the context of late twentieth- and early twenty-first-century Syria, participation in *dhikr* can be interpreted as a form of resistance to the inauthenticities of a secular, Baʿthist Syria through the performance of "authentic" spiritual practices associated with long-standing Muslim identities. At same time, the *dhikr* serves as a vehicle for the discipline of moral and musical selves in which social hierarchies from outside the mosque (especially the market) are at once subverted and reaffirmed. The recontextualization of social and spiritual hierarchies though this performance practice must be analyzed in terms of how it relates to "secular" music and to the broader issues of modern subjectivities in the contemporary Arab and Islamic worlds. The *zāwiya* is not isolated from other arenas of social life and needs to be understood as an extension of them; this sort of analysis upsets the simple dichotomies between "religious" and "secular" so prominent in Western social and cultural analysis.[51]

One example of the contradictions surrounding the practice of *dhikr* is that many Sunni Muslims avoid the *zāwiya*-s and denounce *dhikr* as being outside the normative tradition. When I mentioned my interest in attending *dhikr,* not a few Syrian Muslims (echoing the remarks of some of my Syrian Christian interlocutors) argued that it was a domain of backwardness and mystical escape, if not unorthodox.[52] Although as Muslims they accept the Qurʾānic command to perform *dhikr,* these Syrians interpret it to mean the quiet "*dhikr* of the heart" (*dhikr al-qalb*)—as opposed to the louder "*dhikr* of the tongue" (*dhikr al-lisān*) associated with *fishsh al-qalb.* Those identifying themselves as "secularists" (*ʿilmānī*), for their part, often ridiculed those who attended the *dhikr* as backward, overly emotional, and—ironically, given their professed lack of faith—unorthodox. Many contemporary Syrians are content to watch *mawlawiyya* dancers twirl in a restaurant to the sounds of the oud, *qānūn,* and *nāy,* instruments never found in Syrian *zāwiya-s,* but very few would attend the *dhikr* themselves or even encourage their children or siblings to do so, or even to learn one of these instruments.

Qafla

"Moral virtue . . . is formed by habit," argued Aristotle (§1003a; 1962: 33), considered by Muslims to be the First Master. Music and dance, according to al-Ghazzali, and the habits they inspire, prepare adepts for the encounter with spiritual gnosis (*maʿrifa*) that cannot be accessed through reading of texts alone. The mutisensorial experience of the *dhikr*—its sights, sounds, smells, feelings, and tastes—constitutes the experiential ground for the realization of these higher states of knowledge and awareness, producing a condition of "mindfulness" (Be ever mindful of God) in the body.

In this chapter, I have analyzed the *dhikr* in Aleppo as a type of embodied practice in which the spiritual transformations and transitions of Sufi discourses are understood as mediated by specific repertoires of musical, kinesthetic, and other bodily and sensual practices. In the course of the Aleppine *dhikr,* the dual processes of melodic modulation (*tarqiyya*) and rhythmic acceleration (*kartah*) in conjunction with particular kinesthetic, visual, olfactory, and tactile cues produce an experience of temporal transformation that evokes states in participants that they narrate as "ecstasy." These specific practices as well as the general sensory context of the *dhikr* inculcate embodied memories of transformation and simultaneously condition a spiritual-musical self.

The specific aesthetic repertoires that structure the Aleppine *dhikr* construct an experiential world in which Islamic values are evoked, performed, and inscribed in the bodies and memories of participants. As a variety of spiritual practice, the *dhikr* allows participants to transcend their mundane existence and approach a realization of their "self-ness" and—to borrow a phrase from al-Ghazzali—acknowledge the signs of truth in the world and in themselves and thereby re-enact and memorialize themselves through experiences framed as fundamentally spiritual. This can be understood as a form of ritual memory making and re-membering that results in the disciplining of a locally specific understanding of moral selfhood. Performing *dhikr* also conditions a musical self, and paradoxically it is this musical-aesthetic self that allows for the conditioning and habituation of the spiritual self. This suggests the importance of investigating the interface of embodied practices, temporality, agency, and the experience of heightened emotional states in a variety of contexts, "sacred" and "secular."

I have modulated, to borrow a musical metaphor, to the topic of the *dhikr* in order to suggest the centrality of the idea of the *dhikr* as a source of authenticity in Aleppo's musical culture. As I indicated above, many Aleppine musicians consider the *dhikr* to be an origin of their "secular" musical practices and a veritable "conservatory"—both in the sense of a music institute and as a domain of preservation—for learning the particular musical arts that comprise the "sacred" and "secular" repertoires (keeping in mind the slipperiness of this distinction). Moreover, Sufism in general serves as a strong metaphor of authenticity for a number of contemporary Syrian artists and intellectuals for whom spiritual practices such as *dhikr* refer to a broader realm of experience that believers, musicians, and promoters of heritage cultural politics alike consider uniquely authentic.

The temporal transformations that occur in the course of the *dhikr*, the simultaneous evocation of finite and infinite temporalities, and the transformative power of the *barzakh* or bridge between the physical and the spiritual domains engage in the broader discourses of authenticity in which detemporalized experience ("myth," "the past") is thought of as more authentic than temporalized experience ("history"), as discussed in the previous chapter. The *dhikr* evokes these same correspondences between suspended or transformed temporal orientations and authenticity in a space uniquely spiritual, thereby providing yet another metaphorical time-space of authentic culture: the *zāwiya* as a locus of the authentic and, as in my teacher's remarks, a defense against the inauthentic and a preserver of authenticity for future generations. Finally, the *dhikr* also becomes a site of authenticity through its association with the spirit (*rūḥ*) and the extensive domain of emotional life that many Syrians value. The following chapters on the performance of the secular repertoire and the concept of *ṭarab* explore how conceptions of the emotions and the discourse of emotionality and transcendence conveyed in such domains as the *zāwiya* and the musical gathering known as a *sahra* metaphorize intricate processes of social interaction and self-presentation that contribute to Aleppine understandings of musical and social authenticity.

FIVE

Authentic Performance and the Performance of Authenticity

Maṭlaʿ: The Master in Concert

It's another hot July day, and as I zip along the streets of Aleppo in a packed minibus I notice a colorful sign draped across the light posts at an intersection. Usually these signs announce upcoming concerts by local singers, generally those who sing in the modern pop style: "An Evening with Vocalist Nawāl al-Zughbī, with a Luxurious Meal, at the Miami Club!" is just one example. Such placards are common in Damascus and Aleppo, especially at major intersections and plazas. One older musician expressed his dismay that today singers are presented as "just another dish" in the evening's offerings. For this reason, I am a little surprised to find that the proffered artist is none other than "The Great Arab Artist Ṣabāḥ Fakhrī, for One Show Only at The Freedom Club, 31 July 1997." No mention was made of food. . . .

The next day, I make my way to the Freedom Club, which, along with the Resort, Miami, and the Springtime, is one of Aleppo's premier clubs (*nādī*-s). These establishments are combination social and health clubs, often featuring large swimming pools, gymnasiums, meeting halls, lounges, and often fancy restaurants. Usually only members can use the facilities during the day, but clubs often open their restaurants to the public in the evenings. However, the expense of dining there means that only certain classes ever go. Another common function of the Aleppine clubs is to host evening concerts. In many ways, this distinguishes Aleppo from Damascus, where most shows are held in hotel nightclubs and certain cabarets in the foothills surrounding the Rabwa Valley on the city's western outskirts, and along the highway to the airport to the southeast.

Arriving at the front entrance, I find a small number of people gathered about who, like me, have come for tickets. When my turn comes, I am presented with the option of sitting in the "youth" (*shabāb*) or "families" (*ʿāilāt*) sections. Since I will be going alone, I must sit with the youth; were I going with a group of adults, including married women, we would sit in the "families" section, since women, married or otherwise, cannot sit with the *shabāb*—what would people say? Plus, at 500 līra (approximately $10—a considerable sum in local currency), sitting with the youth is a cheaper than the 750 līra "families" seats.

The ticket says that the show begins at 9:00 P.M. Although I have become accustomed to Aleppine conceptions of time (most appointments are afforded at least a half-hour leeway), I show up at 8:30 in order to make sure to get a good seat. Not only am I early, I am the first person in line, and they haven't even begun to set up for the show. I stand at the gate for about half an hour before a few others begin to trickle over, including a young singer whom I frequently run into at other concerts. He sometimes sings in Ṣabāḥ Fakhrī's chorus and studies with him in his monthly workshops in Aleppo. He doesn't have a ticket and hopes that "Ustāz Ṣabāḥ" will let him in for free, but the master has yet to show up and the young guy is stuck standing at the gate with the rest of us; he would later get in. About 9:30, they finally open the gates and a number of us wander in.

The club consists of a large outdoor swimming pool enclosed on four sides by low buildings, a cafeteria, and a gym. At one end of the pool is the stage, and before it and to either side of the pool are set a number of tables with white table cloths—the "families" section. At the opposite end of the pool are about a hundred plastic chairs arranged in neat rows—the "youth" section. It's a good 40 meters from the first row of the youth section to the stage, but it affords a nice view of the performers and the audience. I grab a seat right on the edge of the pool, but later I will regret my decision when evening finally falls and cool winds begin to blow across the waters and chill me to the bone. But for now I am quite pleased with my location, get my notebook and camera ready, and take in the scene.

Not long after I sit down, I group of *shabāb* (youth)[1] file in next to me. Each has brought along the hose pipe and mouthpiece for a *nargīla* (water pipe) and are anxious to get one of the club staff to bring lighted *nargīla-s* over to poolside so they can begin their evening's entertainment in earnest. Once they are settled in and happily puffing away—their pipes making that familiar gurgling sound—one of them, a young man of about thirty years dressed smartly but casually (and warmly—evidently an experienced concert-goer), notices my note pad and camera and asks me what I am up to. I describe my research on

Syrian music, and he begins a long tale of how he is obsessed with the music. He is the closest I have met in Syria to what might be called a Ṣabāḥ Fakhrī groupie, for he claims to attend over thirty of his shows a year and has traveled as far as Lebanon, Jordan, and Egypt to hear him sing. I ask him why he goes to so many concerts, and he replies, "I am one of the true 'cultivated listeners' [*sammīʿa*]. I cannot live without the music."

At around 10:15, a group of musicians comes onto the stage and begins to get set up. The audience applauds weakly, while a couple of *shabāb* get up and begin a mock dance even though there is as yet no music, earning jeers and laughter from their compatriots, then sit back in their plastic chairs. The *qānūn*-player, whom I had befriended at his cassette shop a few weeks earlier, takes a seat center stage. To his right sit five violinists, and to his left two cellists, an oud-player, and two percussionists, who set a variety of drums before them, including the *riqq*, *ṭabla*, and *daff*.[2] Five vocalists appear behind microphones stage-right while the instrumentalists tune their instruments. One of the vocalists begins to sing "O night! O eye!" (*a layālī*), while the *qānūn*, oud, and violin play a drone note and improvise behind him. No sooner has he started then he stops, and the orchestra begins playing a well-known instrumental prelude (*samāʿī*). It is just a sound-check, and after a few minutes they leave the stage. I try to occupy myself by drawing a map of the club and the locations of the performers on stage, but my *nargīla*-smoking neighbor, looking at my obscure drawing, shakes his head and laughs lightly, as if to say, "What on earth are you doing? Have some fun!" and offers me a drag on the *nargīla*. Its pungent yet sweet apple flavor gets me more into the evening's mood.

By 10:30, the wind has begun to pick up and I am getting rather cold. A few drags on the *nargīla* help a bit, but I am wondering when the show will really start. The club is now full: families sit at their tables waiting patiently or engaged in discussions, while the *shabāb* sit nervously chatting, getting up to get colas or shawarma sandwiches from the cafeteria, ordering more *nargīla-s*.

The show finally begins at 11:20 when a man—apparently the emcee—comes on stage and after welcoming everyone to the club recites a poem on Aleppo. I can't understand what he is saying, and neither can my neighbor—when I ask him what the poem is, he says, "some old poem on Aleppo." Nearly every public event I have attended in Aleppo has begun with the recitation of a poem about the city, usually a classical ode (*qaṣīda*) by such poets as al-Mutanabbī and Abū Firās al-Ḥamdānī, and sometimes contemporary poets. The emcee then speaks about the Andalusian *muwashshaḥ* and the role of Aleppo as a preserver—*the* preserver—of the great Arab-Andalusian musical-poetic tradition. Some of the *shabāb* shout *Yā ʿaynī*! (O my eye!), *Yā rūḥī*! (O my soul!) in what seems to me to be a satire of the traditional responses to vocalists

Ṣabāḥ Fakhrī campaign poster, Aleppo, 1994.

and musicians when they perform well and cause musical rapture (*ṭarab*).[3] The man then introduces Ṣabāḥ Fakhrī as "The Righteous Son of Aleppo" (echoing the slogan on Fakhrī's campaign posters when he ran—unsuccessfully—for a seat in the Syrian parliament a few years earlier). The audience, *shabāb* and families alike—break into spirited applause.

Yāsīn al-ʿĀshiq, a composer and Ṣabāḥ Fakhrī's lead violinist, comes before the microphone and with a wave of his bow the orchestra begins to play his composition "The Dreams of Youth" (*Aḥlām al-shabāb*), an instrumental piece that traditionally opens Ṣabāḥ Fakhrī's concerts. It features changes in mode, meter, and has several sections of improvisation by the various instrumentalists, including the percussionists; in fact, it is the measures of percussion "breaks" or solos that really get the *shabāb* off their feet, clapping and dancing, establishing a mirthful atmosphere while the aging al-ʿĀshiq leads the orchestra with his affable stage presence and sardonic humor on the violin.

As "The Dreams of Youth" comes to a close, the family section suddenly bursts into applause and cheers: Ṣabāḥ Fakhrī has appeared in the wings. A group of white doves are released and flutter about confusedly for a moment before scattering to the tops of the club buildings. The great artist acknowledges the applause, raising his arms over his head in the fashion of a political leader and bowing, then mounts the stage as the music ends, turning his back to face the musicians. Seeing him on stage, the *shabāb* yell and scream too.

The orchestra begins to play a short introductory piece (*dūlāb*) in the mode *ḥijāz kār* and Fakhrī cocks his head to one side as if listening intently. He pays special attention to the percussionists, standing before them and having them adjust the volume of their playing. He then walks over and listens to the violins, says a word or two, and several of them retune their instruments. The *qānūn* player embellishes a descending phrase with quick finger work, and Fakhrī nods to him in appreciation. As I begin to scribble some notes on my notepad, my neighbor leans over and, smiling, says, "*ḥijāz kār*!" then leans back in his chair and puffs on the *nargīla*. Its gurgling makes for an interesting counterpart to the orchestra.

Once the piece ends, Fakhrī—Ustāz Ṣabāḥ—begins to sing the first *muwashshaḥ* of the evening: "*Murr al-tajannī*" (Bitter is the accusation).[4] It is a song of passionate love—a typical theme for a *muwashshaḥ*—and sung in the formal dialect of Arabic. I ask my neighbor what the lyrics mean, and he replies, "By God (*wallāhi*), I don't understand all the words, because they're difficult. But it's about love. We don't always understand these old songs, but we like to listen to them anyway." I ask why, and he says, "They're 'sweet' (*ḥilwa*)," using that all-purpose aesthetic term to describe the music. We return to listening.

Aside from a few *shabāb* who are settling in their seats with sandwiches or soft drinks, the audience is quiet and somewhat subdued, sitting and listening to the great master vocalist and the smooth sounds of the orchestra. This *muwashshaḥ*, while not among the slower in the Aleppine repertoire, has a stately meter (approximately 70 beats per minute). Its mode—*ḥijāz kār*—hovers in the upper register before finishing in the lower, suggesting a reflective mood, complaint, the bitterness of the accusation resolving in a flood of passion as the orchestra descends to the lower register. As is common in this genre of song, the poetic and musical meters do not coincide precisely, so "filler" words (*tarl*) such as *amān* (peace) and *Yā layl* (O night) are added either at the end or between hemistiches of the poetic verse. These afford the vocalist the opportunity to display his skill and vocal range. The first lines of this *muwashshaḥ* end in *amān*, and when Ustāz Ṣabāḥ finishes them with a melismatic flourish, the audience shouts its approval. A couple of men in the family section jump out of their seats and raise their arms, then sit back down with sheepish grins on their faces. It is only midnight, still early in the evening.

The *waṣla* proceeds through two more *muwashshaḥ*-s in the same mode. In fact, the entire *waṣla* remains in the same mode with the exception of modulations to related modes during instrumental improvisations (*taqāsīm*), for example, or solo singing. The latter songs are much faster, and the audience claps along. Some of the *shabāb* arise and dance, and another group shouts out a traditional wedding chant as an expression of joy and not a little bravado. A couple of men in the family section sing along with the artist, and another plays "air *ṭabla*," mimicking the rhythm of the percussionists with his hands. Ustāz Ṣabāḥ waves his arms as he sings, and people shout *Aywa*! (Yes!) and *Yā ʿaynī*! (O my eye!) in encouragement. A young man to one side of the pool gets up and begins what I have come to term the "semaphore dance," waving paper tissues with his hands up and down, side to side, as if directing a wayward airplane with vague and confusing signs. He seems a little odd since no one else around him is dancing, though others look on smiling and he clearly is having a good time.

At the conclusion of the last *muwashshaḥ*, the orchestra pauses and the audience bursts into applause. Fakhrī bows and raises his arms, then turns to the orchestra. He has the cellists retune, and says a few words to the *qānūn* and oud players. Then the orchestra begins the next section of the *waṣla*, consisting of the song *Yā nās ana mutt fī ḥubbī* (O people, I have died in my love) by the Egyptian composer Sayyid Darwīsh (1892–1923); the folksy Egyptian song *Yā mariya* (O Maria); and the formidable *dawr* (multi-part colloquial song) *Yā mā inta waḥishnī* (O you whom I miss), by the nineteenth-century Egyptian composer Muḥammad ʿUthmān. These songs are composed in the Egyptian style and sung in the Egyptian colloquial dialect. Musically, this means a sense of lightness and modernity as opposed to the heaviness and antiquity of the *muwashshaḥ* genre, though these popular songs nonetheless require great skill and mastery. The meters of these songs tend to be simpler and the melodies lighter if still complex, especially the multi-part *dawr*, which also includes extended vocal improvisations and exchanges between the artist and the chorus. In the section of the *dawr* when the vocalist and chorus exchange operatic "Ahs" throughout the range of the mode, the audience responds energetically by singing along, clapping, dancing, and shouting encouragement. The mood is much more enlivened, though still somewhat restrained; everyone is having a good time, but I have a feeling that we still have not reached the heart of the matter.

After the conclusion of the *dawr*, the orchestra takes a five-minute break. It is nearly 1:00 A.M. and now that I am not writing in my notepad, I realize how cold it is; I curse myself for not having the foresight to bring at least a sweater. My neighbors get up to stretch their legs, we exchange a few words about the *dawr* and how great Fakhrī sings it—"Better even than the Egyptians," says the groupie, with obvious pride. "No one sings it like him, except maybe the late Muḥammad Khairi," the well-known Aleppine singer and contemporary of Fakhrī's who died in 1981.

While Fakhrī is still off stage, the orchestra returns and commences the second suite with a prelude in the *maqām rāst*. The mood is immediately lively and the instrumentalists perform with gusto, adding numerous embellishments. The great master returns to great applause and launches into the *muwashshaḥ* "*Aḥinnu shawqan*" (I Long with Yearning). It is a slow number (about 60 beats per minute) and the audience seems a bit distracted: conversations ensue, *nargīla*-s are refilled, we are settling in for the rest of the evening. This is the only *muwashshaḥ* of this suite, since at its close the oud player begins a solo improvisation (*taqsīm*). Beginning low in the register of the mode, he strums out a long drone on the tonic note (middle C). He then proceeds slowly to explore the mode's lower range, then its mid-range, modulating briefly to a related mode before closing back on the tonic. He then progresses back up the mode until he is in the upper range, now employing a great deal of fast trilling (*rashsh*) with the plectrum as he modulates through a number of *maqāmāt.* Unlike many players, he does not make dramatic pauses between sections but plays right on, buzzing like a bee with all the *rishsh* and showing his fancy technique by playing in the highest register at the inner positions near the body of the instrument. The audience comes alive to his technical fireworks and shouts encouragement, "*Aywa*!" "*Yā rūḥī*!" Finally, he makes a dramatic ending by coursing through some difficult arpeggios all the while maintaining a constant bass drone and lightning-fast *rishsh,* then closes on the tonic. The audience erupts into wild applause as the oud player settles into a quiet droning, and the *qānūn* joins in.

Ṣabāḥ Fakhrī then begins to sing the classical ode (*qaṣīda*) *Salū fuʾādī* (Ask my heart), a lover's complaint. In the *qaṣīda,* the artist improvises the melody, usually accompanied by an instrumentalist with whom he engages in a sort of improvisational dialogue.[5] He seems entranced by the mood and stands almost frozen on the stage listening to the oud player, who states simple phrases in the mode. Musicians refer to this state as *salṭana,* when the mood of the mode dominates the artist's emotions.[6] Especially when there is good rapport between the artist and the audience, in particular the skilled listeners known as *sammīʿa,* the artist can enter the state of *salṭana* and evoke a corresponding state of *ṭarab* or musical rapture in listeners.

As he sings the verses of the poem, the master evinces great emotion in his visage and through the movement of his arms and hands. The audience seems enthralled: all eyes are on him. At one point, Ustāz Ṣabāḥ sings one phrase with considerable feeling and a man from the family section jumps out of his seat with a shout of "allah!" hops up on the stage and hugs the great vocalist, then returns to his seat. The audience applauds in appreciation, some of the *shabāb* shout *Yā ʿaynī*!, while a couple of others laugh. Ustāz Ṣabāḥ proceeds into a *layālī,* singing *Yā layl Yā ʿayn,* while the oud player responds with choice phrases. When they reach a particularly high pitch, well above the range of

Ṣabāḥ Fakhrī in concert, 1997.

most singers, the audience is transformed into a cacophony of "*Allāh!*," "*Yā salām!*," and "*Aywa!*"

Ustāz Ṣabāḥ then closes with a flourish and descent from the high to the low register of the mode, the audience roars, and the orchestra immediately begins playing the *dawr* "*Aṣl al-gharām naẓra*" (The Root of passion is a glance). No sooner does Fakhrī start than people hop up and start dancing. Up near the stage, a handful of men dance together, while over on the side, that same younger man does the "semaphore dance" again; several of the *shabāb* rise and clap, some dance. At one point, Ustāz Ṣabāḥ sings a phrase with a noticeable cry (*bukā'*) in his voice, and the *shabāb* near me cry out, "*Ya ḥabībī!*" (O My Beloved!) This goes on for almost ten full minutes—Ustāz Ṣabāḥ singing the same line and the audience reacting with various cries and shouts.

Then it happens: Ustāz Ṣabāḥ begins his trademark *salṭana* dance, turning his back to the audience, making a few quick steps with arms spread wide, spinning around, first in one direction, then the other, and then more quick steps. It is far from elegant, but the audience roars with approval: the great singer is "*mitsalṭan,*" experiencing *salṭana* under the influence of the mood and atmosphere of the evening. This reflects well on the audience, for they have contributed to the atmosphere with their shouts and cries. A number of listeners sit and rock their heads back and forth to the meter of the stately *dawr;* many gyrate and wave their arms around; semaphore signals are sent; *ṭarab* is in the air. There is a definite groove in the air and I find myself getting into it.

A few minutes later, they are performing the light song (*ṭaqṭūqa*) *Ib'at lī jawwāb* (Send me a reply) by the Aleppine composer Bakrī al-Kurdī (1909–

Shabāb at Ṣabāḥ Fakhrī concert, Aleppo, 1997.

1978). Light, energetic, and in the modern Egyptian style that was popular among Aleppine composers in the 1950s and 1960s, it is easily the most popular of the traditional songs in Aleppo, and is well known outside Syria (I found that it is extremely popular in Morocco, for example). While the orchestra establishes the mood, Ustāz Ṣabāḥ comes out of his *salṭana* and adjusts one of the speakers that seems somehow off. One man dancing near the stage offers him a rosary, which he politely refuses by placing his hand over his heart and bowing his head. Things begin to heat up again as the audience sings along with the artist. Now almost everyone is dancing. In the family section, a few women dance with their daughters, husbands, and other family members. Two young men on the opposite side of the pool from the semaphore dancer get up and dance in a style reminiscent of women's dance (what we inappropriately term "belly dancing"); in a parody of feminine grace and motion, they gyrate their hips, shake their flat chests, and move their hands and wrists in quick circles. This sort of burlesque (if that is an appropriate term for it) inevitably occurs at public concerts, especially during the lighter portions of a *waṣla*. The *shabāb* laugh at them while their neighbors look on with mirthful grins on their faces. The dancers apparently are enjoying themselves immensely and this goes on for several minutes. It is now about 2:00 A.M.!

Ustāz Ṣabāḥ then launches into a *mawwāl*, a colloquial poem sung, like the *qaṣīda*, to an improvised melody with the accompaniment of an instrumentalist and modulation into a *layālī*. The audience stops dancing, but their engagement with the vocalist is still high, for many attempt to sing along with him, sighing "*Āh*!" and "*Allāh*!" after each phrase. Some in the front wave their arms in a peculiar manner, as if unfolding reams of cloth or drawing out something from their chest, each hand alternating with the other in a outward flowing circle. I noticed this as well in Cairo and it seems to be a trademark motion of the *sammīʿa*. Finishing his *mawwāl*, Fakhrī seamlessly leads the orchestra into a *waṣla* of the light Aleppine tunes known as *qudūd ḥalabiyya*. Beginning in the mode *rāst*, he sings some of the most popular songs in Aleppo: *Yā ṭīra ṭīrī* (O Bird, fly) and *Yā māl al-shām* (O treasures of Damascus!), both Arab standards by the famous Damascene composer Abū Khalīl al-Qabbānī (1832/5–1904). These light and fast tunes get everyone up out of their chairs. I have forgotten the evening's chill and am standing pool-side clapping and watching the semaphore dancer. Ustāz Ṣabāḥ takes another turn at dancing, people shout, and the atmosphere is mirthful and carefree.

At last, after modulating through a number of folkloric songs in the mode *bayyātī*, Ustāz Ṣabāḥ brings the concert to a close with an impressive ascent to the note D two octaves above middle C (*jawāb al-muḥayyar*, in Arab musical parlance)—well above the range of singers half his age. It is now 4:00 A.M. and he has been singing almost non-stop for over five hours. Fans are quick to point out that this is not unusual for Fakhrī; in fact, many claimed that he holds a Guinness World Record for endurance singing, seventeen hours non-stop at a concert in Venezuela in the 1980s.[7] Putting away his *nargīla*, my neighbor exclaims "It's still early!" and slaps me on the back as he makes his way toward the exit.

Friends and families pile into cars and taxis, parents hold sleepy children in their arms, some head off to the mosque to pray the dawn prayer, an anthropologist walks home. Yet there is an air of expectation for the next *waṣla* concert; indeed the term *waṣla*, which means a connection, a tie, implies a continuity between the past performances and those yet to come. This is an important aspect of the *ṭarab*-culture: ever-evolving contexts for experiencing the joy of great music that comes "from the heart" (*min al-qalb*), and is authentic and honest.

This chapter discusses how Aleppines evaluate what makes a good song "good," and what makes it "authentic." Basing my remarks on attendance at numerous concerts such as the above-described evening with Ṣabāḥ Fakhrī, I examine the musical and performative dimensions of the *waṣla* as the epitome of musical authenticity in contemporary Aleppo. Although Aleppines utilize a specific musical terminology when discussing songs, what makes a song both "good" and "authentic" depends on the context of its performance as much as on its specific musical properties, though these also serve an important function as what Kant (1952) termed "conditioning concepts" that frame aesthetic discourse. More specifically, despite the well-established tradition of aesthetic discourse on the modes, rhythms, and performance practices in Arab music (for example, Sawa 1989; Shiloah 1995), for contemporary Aleppine musicians and listeners, the most important factor in determining the aesthetic value of a song is the actualization of culturally valued emotional states in performers and listeners. This constitutes an important dimension of the "*ṭarab* culture" of the Arab East (Racy 2003: 191–93), referring to special intersubjective musical-cultural practices and values through which performers and listeners engage in a dialogue of the emotions and the self. Through music, performers enact and present culturally specific cues that are understood by listeners as evidence of internal emotional states, especially "Oriental spirit" (*rūḥ sharqiyya*) and *salṭana*. For their part, listeners present certain culturally understood cues of internal emotional states, in particular that of *ṭarab*, which participants, artists and audiences alike, read as the prime index of a successful—and authentic—performance.

The *Sahra* and the *Ḥafla:* Genres, Venues, and Patronage

Fakhrī's concert exemplifies the predominant genre of musical performance in contemporary Aleppo, the *sahra*. Literally meaning an evening gathering or soirée, *sahra* refers colloquially to a gathering of friends and family for a mirthful event such as a birthday, engagement, wedding, or graduation. As a social institution in contemporary Aleppo, as elsewhere in Syria, the *sahra* is governed by elaborate rules and etiquette, as the anthropologist soon discovers when he transgresses most of them at first: particular dress codes, forms of conversation, culinary and other gustatory practices, and a distinct temporality. A *sahra* is a semi-formal, semi-public affair usually held in someone's home whose key ingredient, if anything, is the concept of closeness or intimacy.[8] Not simply a party, the *sahra* is an opportunity for members of a certain class—usually middle-class and elite men—to engage in forms of polite behavior that fall under the category of *adab* (Bonebakker 1988). Of course, the poor and working classes also hold *sahra*-s, but they tend to be less formalized. In addition to *sahra*-s held for special occasions, some Aleppines host varieties of weekly *sahra*-s. One type is the *sahra bishmariyya,* in which a group of friends take turns hosting a *sahra* every week in one of their homes, or, alternatively, one will bring food and everyone will split the cost. Another type is the *sahra ṣaḥaniyya,* for which everyone brings a dish (*ṣaḥn*) of food, like the American "potluck" dinner. Both varieties feature food, conversation, and music.

In the "Golden Age" of Aleppine music[9]—from approximately the middle of the nineteenth century through the first half of the twentieth century—wealthy merchants entertained guests with fine food, conversation, and music. In this period, the *sahra* was a domain reserved almost entirely for the men of Aleppo's commercial and religious families. Women hosted analogous women-only *sahra*-s, such as morning women's gatherings (*ṣubḥiyyāt nisāʾ*), the adornment of the bride on her wedding night (*talbīsa*), women's reception (*istiqbāl*), and others.[10] The musicians generally would not be paid for their services, though they would be provided food. Many were not professional in the sense of deriving their primary income from performing but were rather what we call "amateurs" who had other jobs. For example, many vocalists have served as imams or muezzins at local mosques, and many were also merchants or tradesmen. The famous composer and singer ʿUmar al-Baṭsh was a stone engraver who later earned a modest income from training students in the art of singing and composition. Artists and patrons thereby participated in a system of reciprocity, however unbalanced, which was the context for the production of what some Aleppines consider to be the most beautiful music and song.

As a context for the performance of the *waṣla,* the public or commercial *sahra* has come to all but replace those held in private homes. Today, the *sahra* tends to be held not in private homes but in public or commercial venues at which admission fees usually are charged. Both men and women attend these medium- to large-scale events (though women usually are found only in the "families" sections). *Sahra*-s less frequently are held in private homes today than in the period of Aleppo's "Golden Age." Many musicians and music lovers in Aleppo attribute its decline as a context for music-making to Aleppo's commercial-economic and cultural decline, which, as mentioned in chapter 1, began with the opening of the Suez Canal in 1869 and continues today as political and economic power has consolidated in Damascus. To get a clearer idea of role of the *sahra* in contemporary Aleppo, I asked my teacher Muḥammad Qadrī Dalāl about the reasons for the decline of the musical *sahra* in contemporary Aleppo. He replied:

> There are a lot of reasons, such as that many of the people that used to have good relations together have gotten busy with work, left, traveled, and the world is no longer the way it was . . . There is also a big economic depression overall. People are busy thinking about how to make a living. The other problem is that in the

beginning the food could be anything. Today, no—other things have to be present. For example, we used to eat *mujaddara* [a simple dish of lentils and cracked wheat], whereas today *mujaddara* is not enough; there has to be salad and other things [meat *kabābs* are common fare]. We used to eat falafel, but now it's become a sandwich, and so on. So even with respect to the food it has become different.

Today, as Aleppo struggles to revive its economic position, mostly through developing agriculture, construction, and tourism, the remaining merchant and commercial classes either do not have the time or money to host regular gatherings or no longer reside in the old Arab homes in which they were traditionally hosted, according to numerous informants. Economic decline and the social changes of the last century have meant that fewer Aleppines are capable of hosting them. Moreover, Dalāl implied that those who can are no longer satisfied with the simpler pleasures of the old days; he was not alone in indicating that today well-off Aleppines, the ones most likely to host a *sahra,* like to show off their wealth and are becoming not a little "conceited" or "showy" (*mufazlakīn*).

As a result, musical performance has shifted almost entirely from the private home to the stage, with recitals and concerts now held in performance halls or public venues, not private homes. This marks a radical change in the contexts for music making, especially those associated with the experience of *ṭarab.* Public venues for the performance of music did not exist in Aleppo or in Syria as a whole until after the first third of the twentieth century and the establishment of cafés and theaters in the major cities; before then, most music was performed in the context of private homes or in the confines of the *zāwiya*-s. Even today, relatively few concert or recital halls in Syria are devoted exclusively to the performance of music or related arts. For example, Damascus boasts a recital hall in the Asad National Library, the auditorium of the High Institute for Music, and a newly completed opera house, in addition to multipurpose halls and conference rooms at hotels and cultural centers, and a handful of theaters. Aleppo, for its part, has no single performance space devoted exclusively to music. Performances are held in a variety of multipurpose venues, including the renovated auditorium of the National Library, the aging Muʿawiya Hall, and also the amphitheater and reception hall of the Citadel and various "heritage" buildings that are being restored currently to serve as performance spaces.[11] The numerous clubs, hotel lounges, nightclubs, and cabarets provide another set of venues, though they hardly can be considered designed especially for the performance of music (as my description will have implied).

Nonetheless, a concert held at a hotel lounge, nightclub, or cabaret might also be called a *sahra,* in order to suggest the more intimate setting of a private gathering. In fact, restaurants that feature music often present it as a *sahra* as well. A large concert generally is called a *ḥafla,* since the degree of intimacy implied by a *sahra* is not expected at a *ḥafla,* nor are there as many social rules as in a *sahra*. Women may attend these events freely, though often they do so in the accompaniment of male relatives in "family" sections. In the end, the difference between a *sahra* and a *ḥafla* may only be a matter of scale and expectations. If the musical setting is intimate or if intimacy is an important aspect of the performance atmosphere, then it is likely to be labeled a *sahra* and occur in a place where you can easily see and possibly interact personally with the singer. If the concert is held in a large venue such as a sports arena in which the singer is separated from the audience by a great distance with little or no probability of interaction, it will be called a *ḥafla*. For example, a multi-vocalist show at the Fayḥāʾ Sports Complex in Damascus was billed as a *ḥafla,* while the previously described Ṣabāḥ Fakhrī concert, at which there was continuous interaction between artist and audience, was a *sahra*. The difference between the two genres may also be a matter of repertoire and orchestra; the *waṣla* tends to be performed primarily at *sahra*-s, whereas modern songs and larger orchestras appear in *ḥafla*-s.

In contemporary Aleppo, *sahra* and *ḥafla* performances take place in the context of the ideologies, rhetoric, and practices of the Syrian state. These include active sponsorship of concerts, exhibitions, festivals, and literary publication through systems of official patronage under the auspices of the Ministries of Culture and Media, and exclusionary practices such as the numerous and inauspicious forms of censorship organized under the same authorities. Through these and other practices, the state attempts to control the allowable or imaginable discourse in the public realm in order to frame people's views of social life and establish guidelines for compliance with official views, or resistance to them (Wedeen 1999: 45). Even when we acknowledge the ambiguity—indeed, the absurdity—of many of these practices and discourses, nevertheless the cultural arena is, to use Wedeen's apt phrase (1999: 33), "cluttered" with official rhetoric, making efforts to navigate the contemporary Syrian cultural scene somewhat clumsy. Hence the move of the context for music making from the home to the stage, from "private" domains to cluttered "public" domains, has had important political implications for musical aesthetics.

The political implications of these changing contexts become readily apparent when we consider the nature of patronage and the social relations of the performers and audiences in these different performance domains. On the one hand, as indicated above, intimate *sahra*-s engage forms of reciprocity, as in the rotational or "potluck" varieties of *sahra* in Aleppo. The important point is that in these contexts patronage is local and directly involved in relationships of reciprocity, usually revolving around food-for-music, music-for-food. On the other hand, many public performances both large and small are sponsored by political figures such as the mayor or leader of the local branch of the Baʿth Party. As previously mentioned, nearly all recitals and artistic exhibitions in Syria occur under the patronage of the Minister of Culture, the local Baʿth Party leader (especially outside of Damascus), or the mayor. Often they celebrate national holidays. The above-mentioned multi-vocalist concert at the sports complex in Damascus celebrated the fiftieth anniversary of the establishment of the Baʿth Party and included numerous encomiums to then-President Ḥāfiẓ al-Asad.

The *Waṣla:* Aesthetics and the Performance of Authenticity

The *waṣla* is the primary context for the performance of what Aleppines and many non-Aleppines consider to be the best and most authentic form of Arab music.[12] A great amount of variety exists with respect to the order and number of each genre, though the overall structure remains one of a movement from heavy and slow meters and complex melodies to light and fast meters and simpler melodies, as in the *dhikr,* with which it shares numerous structural features. The typical *waṣla* involves an overall alternation of fixed and unfixed meters and forms; that is, pre-composed songs and vocal improvisations, pre-composed instrumental pieces and improvisations (Touma 1996: xx). A given *sahra* may comprise more than one *waṣla,* and some twenty-two are known in Aleppo—one each for twenty-two different *maqāmāt* (Rajāʾī and Darwīsh 1956; Touma 1996: 84). Ṣabāḥ Fakhrī presented two (*ḥijāz kār* and *rāst*) in the course of five hours, each comprising songs selected from much larger repertoires in the same modes that are also called *waṣla*-s.

The *waṣla* generally begins with an air of gravity and grandeur evoked by the slow, heavy rhythms of the instrumental preludes and the *muwashshaḥ.*[13] Of putative Andalusian origin, they often are referred to as "Andalusian *Muwashshaḥāt*" (*muwashshaḥāt andalusiyya*). However, in Aleppo the *muwashshaḥ* has assumed a distinctive local style, what many Aleppines refer to as an Aleppine *nakha* or flavor, especially in the hands of famous composers such as ʿUmar al-Baṭsh, who composed over a hundred. Since the lyrics of the *muwashshah* allow for numerous interpretations, many of them are performed in both "sacred" and "secular" contexts in Aleppo; for example, some are performed in both the *dhikr* and the *waṣla.*[14]

Indeed, a firm distinction between "sacred" and "secular" is hard to maintain with respect to Aleppine music, both because of the interrelationships between spiritual and non-spiritual realms in Islamic culture and because most prominent Aleppine vocalists have come from strong religious backgrounds (see Shannon 2003b, and below). Despite the avowedly "secular" venues of *waṣla* performances—concert halls, theaters, Aleppo's famous clubs—the atmosphere in the beginning of the *waṣla* is subdued if expectant, as in the *dhikr*. Audience members still may be arriving, the orchestra and vocalist still "warming up," the special emotional state of *ṭarab* yet to be established. Therefore, we need to treat the secular-sacred distinction, as the public-private, with caution; each pair of binaries expresses social and cultural potentialities that artists and audiences actualize and manipulate in specific performance situations. For this reason, one may find "whirling dervishes" on a concert stage and people performing adaptations of popular songs in the *zāwiya*.

As the *waṣla* moves into its middle sections—the *qaṣīda, ughniya,* and *dawr*—performers and members of the audience gradually become more energized and establish a mood, set a groove.[15] This is not unlike the mood of the middle sections of the *dhikr* once the participants have "warmed up" with the chanting of the opening portions of a particular section. Indeed, some musicians refer to this early period as *taskhīn,* warming up, preparing for more energetic phases to follow. At this point, some people begin to dance, spontaneously rising in their seats or dancing together in groups, while others shout encouragement, *Aywa*! *Allāh*! *Yā salām*!—phrases also uttered in the *dhikr* to express delight, awe, and ecstatic rapture. The musicians, now loosened up, may fall into a groove and the artist may dance about on stage (as with Ṣabāḥ Fakhrī's trademark twirls) and talk with performers and audience members, the general atmosphere becoming highly charged, joyful, mirthful.

In the latter genres, especially the section of popular songs, the pitch may rise and modulate to different modes, as in the melodic modulation (*tarqiyya*) of the *dhikr*. In the Ṣabāḥ Fakhrī concert, for example, the first *waṣla* was in *hijāz kār* and the second ended in *rāst* and *bayyātī*. In a process similar to rhythmic accelerando (*kartah*) in the *dhikr,* the tempo of the latter segments of the *waṣla* invariably increases, usually involving the use of quick and simple duple meters that also are used in popular music today (especially the *baladī* beat, which has folkloric connotations). As in the *dhikr,* these lighter meters are accompanied by body motions and forms of dance; the faster tempos tend to bring large numbers of audience members to their feet. Moreover, because the lyrics of these songs are in colloquial Arabic, just about everyone understands them and many sing along; they are far more participatory than the heavy and archaic *muwashshaḥ* of the beginning of a *waṣla,* the lyrics of which are sometimes incomprehensible even to many native speakers and enthusiasts. Finally, the *waṣla* concludes with a closing sequence (*qafla*), but as in the *dhikr,* it is temporary, since each *waṣla* performance connects with those that have come before and suggests those yet to come.

The structural similarities between the *waṣla* and the *dhikr* point to shared aesthetics if not shared origins for these forms of cultural practice. Yet, as Racy notes (2003: 195–98, ff.), the experience of *ṭarab* in many ways differs from the experience of ecstatic states in the *dhikr:* usually less extreme in form and intensity, not generally associated with a spiritual trajectory or practice aiming at perfectability, and not as codified ritually (though of course the *ṭarab* culture has its rules and ritualized behaviors). Yet, the *dhikr* and *sahra* are both arenas for the disciplining of moral and musical selves, primarily through the act of creative and imaginative listening, reinforced through other sensory and sensual practices such as bodily motions. Not coincidentally, participants in both domains in Aleppo use similar metaphors to describe the experience of a *sahra* and those of the *dhikr,* suggesting a close narrative and experiential linkage between the domains. A primary metaphor used in both the spiritual and "profane" contexts is *dhawq,* "taste." Aleppines, like their counterparts in other Arab and Muslim lands, use the metaphor of taste to describe musical delictation as well as the experience of closeness to the divine. In this way, an auditory sense of taste akin to "auditory vision" is intimately linked to the dynamic construction of subjectivities in contemporary Syria.[16]

The Three Keys to a Good Song

Returning to the music, why do so many Aleppines flock to concerts to hear the songs of the *waṣla*? Why, especially, was the *shabāb* section full when so many critics have pronounced the death of traditional music and the dominance of the modern pop song in the hearts and minds of Syria's youth? Why are these genres considered by many to be exemplars of musical authenticity and standards of musical taste?

Aleppine musicians and music lovers, like their counterparts in Cairo and elsewhere in the Arab world, evaluate music through the use of a specific aesthetic vocabulary or *qāmūs*. In Aleppo, this aesthetic lexicon comprises a set of terms that I call the "Three Keys" to a good song: melody (*laḥn*), words or song lyrics (*kalimāt*), and voice (*ṣawt*).[17] Racy (2003) explores the complex and nuanced relationships between tonality, lyrics, and emotional economies among performers and listeners in the *ṭarab* culture. His analysis focuses primarily on master artists and skilled listeners, and how musical mastery, culturally rich song texts, and the vagaries of social life can come together to produce ecstatic emotional reactions in the course of performance. In a similar manner, I found that a broad base of listeners and performers, and not only the most skilled, understand a good song to be the result of a felicitous conjunction of melody, lyrics, and voice. These components seem to constitute a minimal requirement for good Arab song around the Levant, though what constitutes a good melody, strong lyrics, and good voice may vary from one locale to another, or according to social class and personal tastes.

My interest is not in reiterating well-known musical features but in exploring how this basic (and admittedly over-simplified) musical-critical lexicon articulates a more fundamental discourse on the emotions that determines the aesthetic value and authenticity of a given performance. The "Three Keys" act as a metalanguage that articulates in musical terms what are performative qualities of the musical engagement, especially emotional honesty (*ṣidq*), rapture (*ṭarab*), and what many Syrians refer to as Oriental spirit (*rūḥ sharqiyya*).[18] Closer examination of critical discourse in the context of specific musical performances in Aleppo reveals that the musical elements of performance are often not the decisive factors in determining aesthetic judgments of a performance's value or authenticity, nor are they always important in producing the experience of *ṭarab*. Rather, the overall social context of performance is more often the strongest factor in the Aleppine aesthetics of musical authenticity. The actual music may be incidental to the experience of highly charged emotional states in the course of performance—music lovers, as indicated above, may not even understand the lyrics or know much about Arab music tonality yet nonetheless enjoy the music. This qualifies an ideal-type analysis of *ṭarab* culture from the perspective of only the most skilled practitioners, including the fabled *sammīʿa* and master performers such as Ṣabāḥ Fakhrī. This is not to deny the historical importance of creative listening and masterful performance in the constitution of the *ṭarab* culture. Rather, my aim is to shed light on the processual elements and discursive strategies through which participants construct musical experience and narrate it as authentic.

Melody (*Laḥn*)

The Arab tradition is rich with treatises that discuss the theoretical basis of the music, and especially the melodic and rhythmic modes that are the basis of the classical music (Abū al-Shāmāt 1997; al-ʿAjjān 1990; al-ʿAqīlī 1979; al-Ḥimṣī 1994; al-Khulaʿī 1993 [1904]; al-Mahdī 1993; Racy 2003; al-Sabbāgh 1950; Sawa 1989; Shiloah 1979, 1995; Touma 1996; Wirdī 1948). Despite numerous efforts in the twentieth century to systematize and classify the modes and meters, especially after the landmark Cairo Congress of 1932, Aleppine musicians and music lovers still debate the precise number of modes and their interrelationships, as well as their postulated emotional connotations. The rhythmic modes engender less debate, and numerous treatises on them specify both their arrangement of accents, duple and triple meter components, and occasionally their origin in certain natural phenomena and cultural practices, such as the rhythm of the camel's gait, the weaver's loom, or the rocking of a crib (Abū al-Shāmāt 1997; al-ʿAjjan 1990; al-ʿAqīlī 1979; al-Ḥimṣī 1994).[19]

However, mode and rhythm alone do not a good *laḥn* make. A good melody results from the ways these and other features are employed to express musical ideas. The art of composition (*talḥīn*) requires mastery of the modes and rhythms, to be sure, but it also requires imagination (*khayāl*) and the ability to create new musical ideas. When I questioned Aleppine and Damascene composers about the most important factors in composition and how they go about composing songs, many remarked that mastery of the technical language of the music is a first step, but that the art of composition depends more importantly on a strong sense of Oriental spirit and having a good musical ear, which develops only through intensive listening and as a result of God-given talent. This talent may be developed through study and formal lessons, and many contemporary composers have pursued lessons in music theory and composition in Syria, Egypt, and various European and American academies.

It should be pointed out that this does not necessarily imply knowledge of musical notation and orchestration, as is the case in European "classical" music. In fact, many well-known twentieth-century Aleppine composers have had little or no training in music theory and notation. The oral transmission of melodies and their memorization by choruses and instrumentalists was the primary mode of composition and study and remains practiced today among older and even some younger singers and composers; in fact, some musicians expressed a distrust of notation, preferring what they perceived to be the "certainty" of learning via listening (*samāʿ*) and dictation (*talqīn*) from a master teacher. As mentioned previously, the mosque and *zāwiya* have been important musical training grounds for generations of Aleppine vocalists and composers, a role only recently being assumed by formal schools of music in the major cities of Syria.

Lyrics (*Kalimāt*)

The most important function of the melody, however, is to convey the meaning of the words (*kalimāt,* sometimes *kalām*). In fact, most people with whom I spoke argued that the words are the most important component of a good song. Without meaningful words, even the best melody sung by the best vocalist will not be good. But what are meaningful words? How does a melody express their meaning?

The lyrics of the *waṣla* repertoire often derive from classical poetry or contemporary poetry that follows the classical conventions of meter and rhyme. The link between the classical poetic tradition and such genres as the *muwashshaḥ* and *qaṣīda* grants these songs special authority as "authentic" and provides a model of authenticity for contemporary musicians and composers who aspire to emulate this standard. The esteem granted classical poetry and poets in Arab culture helps us understand why the words to a song might be so important to these artists and listeners, for they relate to deeply held notions of what it means to be an Arab—eloquence (*faṣāḥa*), imagination (*khayāl*), and sincerity (*ṣidq*) being highly valued characteristics. However, other genres of the *waṣla* are sung in colloquial Arabic, such as the different varieties of *mawwāl, ughniya, dawr,* and the *qudūd* and other light songs that close the performance of the *waṣla*. In these genres, authenticity lies not in the eloquence of the classical language but in the meaning and meaningful rendition of the colloquial words themselves. Indeed, as mentioned above, many Syrians claim that they cannot understand the words of the *muwashshaḥ* and *qaṣīda* because the language is too archaic.

One evening as I was taking a stroll in downtown Aleppo, I heard someone shout out, "*Yā ustāz*!" ("Hey teacher" or "Mister"—a common honorific). I stopped and a young man came up to me and asked, "Excuse me, but aren't you the one who appeared on TV a few days ago?" I had been interviewed on Syrian television that week and the show had aired the previous morning. All day long I had engaged in similar conversations with taxi drivers and newspaper vendors and was feeling a little self-conscious; "Here we go again!" thought I. Soon there gathered about me a group of five earnest young men. We shook hands and they asked me about the TV program and my work in Aleppo. When I told them that I was interested in Aleppine song, one, wearing a t-shirt with the word "Jazz" written on it in big bold letters, claimed to love the older songs. I asked him if he also likes jazz, pointing to his t-shirt, but he replied with an emphatic "No!" Another replied, "You sang some old song on TV, right?" I said that I had tried to sing part of an old *muwashshaḥ*, but that it is very difficult. Another told me that whenever he hears that song he just shakes his head, demonstrating for me by shaking his head violently from side to side as if confused. "It is just too heavy for me," he said. "I prefer the popular songs because they are lighter." Even the Ṣabāḥ Fakhrī groupie at the concert did not understand all of the words of the *muwashshaḥ*-s and showed greater interest in the *qudūd*, for example by dancing and singing along with them. This is not uncommon, since indeed the language is difficult.

Why, then, should the words be singled out as the most important factor in a good song if often they are incomprehensible to many native listeners? First, not all the words are so difficult that most native listeners cannot pick out certain phrases and verses that the vocalist repeats. Some are based on well-known poems that students may study in school and have memorized. Second, the cultural valuation of poetry in the classical language grants these songs the seal of authenticity as part of Arabic high culture. Despite (or because of) its highbrow implications, I found that this valuation is shared by members of different classes. College graduates, newspaper vendors, hotel workers, taxi drivers, and manual laborers all impressed me with their ability to speak the standard variety of Arabic.[20] In Syria, unlike in Egypt, where literature and song in the Egyptian colloquial have played an important role in popular expressions of nationalism (Armbrust 1996), the ability to speak standard Arabic is an important component of Syrian national and pan-Arab sentiments. The Syrian government places heavy emphasis in the schools on learning standard Arabic. For example, a student must pass the Arabic portion of the end-of-year examinations to continue to the next grade while being required to pass only two of three subjects in other fields. On the notoriously difficult Syrian Baccalaureate exam, students must pass the Arabic portion in order to graduate.[21]

Nevertheless, I found that the colloquial genres remain the most popular. Numerous Aleppines and other Syrians claimed that the lighter songs in the colloquial language express the conditions of daily life more than the *muwashshaḥ* and are therefore more authentic for them. Hence the great popularity of the *qudūd ḥalabiyya* among young and old listeners. Through their association with local and pan-regional urban "popular arts" (*funūn shaʿbiyya*), they are considered by many Aleppines to be more authentic and sincere than the urban high-culture genres because they are "closer to the people."[22]

Musical Expression (*taʿbīr mūsīqī*)

Aleppine musicians and music lovers commonly stated that a melody should express the meaning of the words it accompanies. Some critics have argued that Arab music, unlike European music, is not capable of expressing emotional states (Shiloah 1995). Others have argued that, on the contrary, Arab music is highly expressive, employing numerous compositional techniques to suggest emotional states such as sadness and passion, natural conditions such as the wind and rain, and so forth.[23] For my purposes, it is less important what these techniques are than that musicians and listeners engage in discourse about musical expression and expect that there should be a relationship between a song's melody and its words. Classical treatises argued for a correspondence between the melodic modes and moods; today some artists assert that certain *maqāmāt* are associated directly with the experience of specific moods (see Racy 2003: 96–100). For example, I was told that the mode *ṣabā* evokes sadness, while *rāst* instills bravery and courage. Touma (1996: 43–44) reports that Arab listeners conventionally associate *bayyātī* with "vitality, joy, and femininity," while *sīkāh* conjures "feelings of love" and *ḥijāz,* "the distant desert." While some contemporary Aleppine musicians argue that the medieval theories are valid and others that they are not much more than myths, cultural conventions do associate certain modes with certain moods, some of which may even be cross-culturally valid (Touma 1996: 44).[24]

However, in terms of musical expression and the association of lyrics and melody, there is actually quite a degree of variation that suggests that the sorts of associations that Touma reports in his survey of Arab musicians may not always be practiced. For instance, I asked a well-known composer about the association of the melodic modes with certain moods and how this may influence his choice of mode when fitting music to words. He picked up an oud and played a melody in the mode *zinkūlāh* (sometimes called *zinjirān*), which has a resemblance to *ḥijāz* and *ḥijāz kār* and thus, according to Touma's survey, should conjure "the distant desert." Indeed, the melody sounded sad, mournful even. However, it turned out to be the melody of a song by the Egyptian composer Zakariyyā Aḥmad called "*Yā ḥalawat al-dunyā*" (How sweet the world is!) whose words are decidedly upbeat and cheerful. In this instance, barring the deliberate and ironic utilization of a "sad" mode to sing about the sweetness of life, there is no relationship between the mode and the mood of the lyrics. A good composer, according to this artist, can compose any type of song in any mode. The cosmological models, he suggested, are myths; there is no necessary relationship between modes and moods. Echoing a common modernist sensibility, he asserted that musical expression relies on the genius of the composer and the poet-lyricist, and then ultimately on the skill and sensitivity of the artist to convey it in performance. Certainly audience expectations play a large role in the production of affective associations between lyrics and melody, but the modal system offers much room for negotiation and interpretation among performers and listeners.

Voice (*Ṣawt*)

The interpretation of lyrics and the apt expression of their meaning in the melody is the responsibility of the composer, but the meaning of the lyrics and the beauty of the melody become apparent only through the voice of the artist. Hence, the human voice and vocal qualities are important components of musical aesthetics in Aleppo. Not surprisingly, Aleppines have an extensive and precise vocabulary for describing the human voice. One text lists over thirty different vocal characteristics, both positive and negative (Abū al-Shāmāt 1997: 221–22). These include:

shajī: "the best of the voices and the sweetest, clearest, and most melodious of them."
mukhalkhal: "a high and sharp voice with strength and sweetness."
ajashsh: "a low voice with pleasing huskiness and grand melodiousness."
karawān: "that which resembles the voice of the plover bird (*karawān*) in precision, clarity, and fluency."
raṭb: "that which is like freely flowing water, and sweet."

Other, less desirable, characteristics include:

musahrij: "like a heavy scream without embellishment or melody."
muqaʿqaʿ: "that which resembles the speech of bedouin, without any sweetness."
ṣarṣūrī: "a fine, high-pitched, and ugly voice." (from *ṣarṣara,* to squeak, and *ṣarṣūr,* cricket).
murtaʿid: "a voice as if the singer is chilled with a fever" (*maqrūr biʾl-ḥummā*).
luqmī: "a voice as if the singer has a bite of food (*luqma*) in his mouth."
akhann: "a voice as if the singer's nose is clogged."
muzlim: "that in which there is no melody and which is barely audible."

There are numerous popular terms for describing the voice as well, some that overlap with the above terms (such as *shajī*). Most common, however, are general terms that are applied to many different domains of cultural life, such as the ubiquitous *ḥilū* (sweet), which commonly describes anything considered good or beautiful: a voice, person, house, car, song, dog, painting, dress, food, the Moon. Other terms are *ḍaʿīf* (weak), *nāʿim* (delicate, tender, or smooth), *ḥassās* (sensitive), *rakhīm* (mellow, melodious), *ṣāfī* (clear), *qawī* (strong, loud), *ʿālī* (high or loud), *ḥadd* (high and sharp), *ghalīẓ* (low, bass, or coarse), *nashāz* or *nāshiz* (discordant, out of tune), and others.[25]

As mentioned in chapter 2, Aleppines consider the best singers to be those who have a strong religious background, especially those trained in Qurʾānic recitation and Islamic spiritual song. Virginia Danielson (1990/1991; 1997: 21–27) discusses the common Egyptian belief that their best artists, from Sayyid Darwīsh and Zakariyyā Aḥmad to Umm Kulthūm and Muḥammad ʿAbd al-Wahhāb are "*min al-mashāyikh,*" that is, "from the sheikh's." In a similar manner, many Aleppines argued that their best vocalists are those who have had religious training in such Islamic aural practices as *dhikr, adhān* (call to prayer), *tajwīd* (Qurʾānic recitation), and *inshād* (religious song). Examples include the artist Sabri Moudallal, who is the main muezzin at the Great Mosque in Aleppo and a well-known *munshid;* Ḥassan al-Ḥaffār, also a muezzin and *munshid* in Aleppo's Great Mosque; Adīb al-Dāyikh (d. 2001), who became famous for his pre-dawn supplications (known variously as *ibtihālāt, tadhkīr,* and *tasbīḥ*) and for his renditions of the *qaṣīda*. Other great vocalists also have served at one point or another as muezzins, including Bakrī al-Kurdī, Ṣabāḥ Fakhrī, Muḥammad Khairī, and others. Many younger vocalists in Aleppo also have been or continue to serve as *munshid*-s or have training in Islamic song. Some well-known vocalists actually made the reverse progression, becoming muezzins later in life when they could not find work as singers in clubs (Mahannā 1998). This indicates the fluidity of the boundaries between sacred and spiritual domains in Aleppo, as well as the value placed on the human voice for rendering the word of God and in praising Him.

Reference to the religious background of a singer is exceedingly important in Aleppine discourses of musical authenticity. Often when a young singer begins to make a name for himself as an artist, his religious background will be cited as the decisive early conditioning factor. For example, in a biographical entry on the young singer Nihād Najjār (Mahannā 1998: 294–95), the first few paragraphs are actually descriptions of the religious school he attended, which has produced numerous well-known singers in its time. Even though this singer does not now perform what Aleppines would identified as primarily spiritual genres of song (*inshād, dhikr*), his roots in the religious school are emphasized as the most important factor in his success (and authenticity) as an artist.

This is the case for non-Muslim artists as well, who are plentiful in Aleppo with its numerous and venerable Christian communities. For example, Shādī Jamīl (né George Jubrān) is described in a musical biographical entry on him as having developed his "heavenly throat" *(ḥanjar ʿanān)* in the choir of the Orthodox Church in Aleppo (Mahannā 1998: 290–92). Yet, the biography does not hesitate to state that Jamīl, who like so many other young singers today performs in the style of Ṣabāḥ Fakhrī, studied the art of Qurʾānic recitation and other genres of spiritual song in addition to the great Aleppine musical heritage at the hands of some of Aleppo's great Muslim teachers. By emphasizing his professed links to the Islamic tradition, the biographical entry grants him an added degree of authenticity.[26]

Religious training is thought to inculcate proper pronunciation (*lafẓ, nuṭq,* or *ilqāʾ*), skill in the interpretation of the lyrics (*taṣwīr al-maʿnā*), and a proper moral stance (*khulq, ikhlāqiyya*) in order to interpret the words and convey their meaning sincerely to an audience. As for the latter quality, Nūr Mahannā's own biographical entry (Mahannā 1998: 296–98) clearly states that his father would allow him to pursue a career as a singer only if he abided by the strict moral standards to which a "great artist" should adhere: honesty, dedication, and morally upright behavior. Regarding proper pronunciation, Danielson notes that Umm Kulthūm, who had a strong background in Islamic song, was known for the clarity of her pronunciation (1997: 96).[27] Similarly, a musician friend with whom I attended a Nihad Najjar concert commented extensively on the young singer's proper and clear pronunciation. Other vocalists cannot pronounce them properly, he complained, though it is very important in his estimation to be able to do so. "The true artist," he said, "must be cultured (*muthaqqaf*) and know how to appreciate (*dhawq,* lit. taste) the meaning of the words and pronounce them properly." Along with so many other critics of the modern pop song, he argued that few contemporary pop stars are able to sing these kinds of songs properly; either they do not have the culture or the background that would prepare them for this, meaning a religious background. "ʿAmru Diab," he claimed, commenting on one of the biggest stars in the contemporary Arab pop music scene, "doesn't have a good voice. It's weak and discordant (*nashāz*), but they are able to fix it in the studio." Nor does Diab have a recognized connection to the *mashāyikh*. "Voice," then, comes to represent a set of cultural and spiritual practices that condition a musical and moral-ethical state in the would-be artist; hence the importance of training in such "conservatories" as the *zāwiya*. Voice is also a prime index of a performer's authenticity (or, as in the case of Diab, whose voice must be "fixed" in the studio, his inauthenticity). This becomes apparent not only through study of biography but in the act of performance as well.

Emotions and Music

There is one essential ingredient that "makes or breaks" an Arabic song, even if the above components are present: emotional sincerity (*ṣidq*). The best of lyrics sung to complex and expressive melodies by a strong yet feeling-less and insincere vocalist will fail to inspire listeners. Time and again, when I asked people at concerts or music conferences what they found most appealing about a certain artist or song, they mentioned this quality of *ṣidq*. Sharing linguistic roots with the word *ṣadīq* (friend), and *ṣādiq* (honest or sincere), *ṣidq* implies genuine feeling, a lack of artifice, and a surrender by the vocalist to the true meaning of the words of the song. *Ṣidq* implies that the artist understands the words and is able to express their meaning to listeners by translating them through his own feelings. To be authentic, an artist must be *ṣādiq*, endowed with *ṣidq*. In fact, this is what some Aleppines argued distinguishes a mere singer-performer (*mughannī, mu'addī*) from a true artist (*muṭrib*), who can evoke *ṭarab*.[28]

In Aleppo, all the great vocalists are considered to have a high degree of *ṣidq*, whereas most contemporary singers are thought to lack this quality. This sentiment was echoed in discussions I had with critics and journalists at the Syrian Song Festival, held annually in Aleppo and which I attended in 1996 and 1997. One woman journalist despaired at the majority of the performers and their songs. "So many of them are nonsense" (*ḥakī fāḍī*, lit. "empty speech"), she said. "A lot even lip-synched on stage instead of performing live." I agreed that the lip-synching was unfortunate but asked about those who did perform live. "Most of them lack sincerity (*ṣidq*)," she claimed. "A true artist (*muṭrib*) should be sincere (*ṣādiq*)." Samīr, whom we met in chapter 3, claimed that modern singers may sing of love, but "they don't know real love." In his estimation, these new singers are at best mimicking true love, and at worst fabricating the experience; theirs is false love. Others also indicated the insincerity of modern vocalists who sing of love but "are really only interested in sex." Hence, the more these artists portray sexualized love in their songs, the less sincere they are thought to be. "True" emotion therefore would seem to be another condition of authenticity, and more importantly, the public expression of sincere emotional states.

The composer and performer 'Abd al-Fattāḥ Sukkar, one of the artistic directors of the Festival, also mentioned the importance of *ṣidq* in our long conversations about music in Syria. According to him, what distinguishes the good from the bad in any art form, whether a composition, a poem, or a painting, is this quality of sincerity. Why aren't a lot of the newer songs and singers sincere? "Before a singer can be sincere with the audience," he argued, "he must be sincere with himself. These days it is getting harder for people to be honest with themselves, so how can they produce good art?"

A number of Aleppines cited Bakrī al-Kurdī as the foremost example of a sincere artist. Known for having a weak and delicate voice, Sheikh Bakrī, as he is called, could produce *ṭarab* in listeners nonetheless because they felt that he was singing "from the heart." Some musicians criticized Ṣabāḥ Fakhrī as insincere because in their view his voice is strong (*qawī*), but devoid of feeling. Others (the majority) react more positively to his singing, such as the man who jumped on stage to hug him after Fakhrī sang a particularly moving phrase. Some Syrian artists and music fans even described the great Umm Kulthūm as "insincere" (*muftaʿala,* fabricated, artificial), despite her being almost universally recognized as among the outstanding voices of the twentieth century. One prominent artist claimed that he cannot listen to her for more than five minutes because she is overly emotional; her feelings are exaggerated, insincere, artificial. Interestingly, for the same reason he claimed that he cannot read Naguib Mahfouz for more than a few pages—the Egyptian novelist is just too maudlin for his tastes.[29]

Sincerity (*Ṣidq*) and Oriental Spirit (*Rūḥ Sharqiyya*)

According to numerous Aleppine musicians and music lovers, sincerity (*ṣidq*) is intimately related to a performer's Oriental spirit (*rūḥ sharqiyya*). Aleppines describe the person endowed with Oriental spirit as emotional and sensitive, someone who uses intuition and understands instinctively the nuances of the melodic modes. The Westerner, on the contrary, they describe as rational, direct, and logical, someone barely capable of understanding the modes, if at all. If these descriptions strike the Western reader as auto-Orientalist characterizations, for many Aleppines and other Arab musicians I have known elsewhere they are matters of both fact and pride. Who wouldn't want to be emotional, sensitive, and intuitive? Although many Syrians criticize this characterization, for many Aleppine musicians, emotionality is as matter-of-fact as the richness and beauty of their music.

The longer I stayed in Syria and the more I studied the music, the more I was asked by friends and acquaintances to play something on the oud or sing in order for them to assess my knowledge and see to what extent I possessed any "Oriental spirit." It initially seemed that one possesses this spirit rather than develops or acquires it, or is possessed by it, as in the concept of *duende* in Flamenco deep song (see García Lorca 1998).[30] At best my interlocutors would encourage me politely in my efforts; usually I failed the "test" and they would pronounce my lack of Oriental spirit. Saddened by this, I asked my teacher what it meant not to have this spirit. "If you're playing and someone says to you, "There isn't any spirit" (*mā fī rūḥ*), he said, "this means that you still haven't entered the music or represented it fully so that your personality and presence can come through in it." Toward the end of my field research, one of my personal high points came when I was asked to play after giving a public lecture in Damascus. Afterward, a member of the audience, a respected Syrian dramatist, told me that had his eyes been closed while I played he would not have known that I was not Syrian because I demonstrated Oriental spirit. So maybe it can be acquired after all. . . . At any rate, having Oriental spirit is tantamount to having sincerity as a performer; the latter presumes the former. Sincerity arises in performance and is measured by the artist's ability to induce *ṭarab* in listeners; in fact, *ṭarab* is a sort of Aleppine "litmus test" of a vocalist's sincerity, and hence of his or her Oriental spirit and authenticity.

What, then, is this thing called *ṭarab*? That is the subject of the following chapter.

Qafla: The Importance of Performance in Aesthetic Judgments of Authenticity

This chapter has outlined the "Three Keys" to a good Arabic song and shown how they are in effect a metalanguage for discussing emotional conceptions of musical culture. The aesthetic lexicon of melody (*laḥn*), lyrics (*kalimāt*), and voice (*ṣawt*) attempts to account for what are fluid processes of musical creation and reception that emerge in specific performance situations. It is in performance that these aesthetic values are enacted and a song or performer becomes "good," "authentic," or otherwise. In fact, despite informants' emphasis on the musical qualities of song, it is a song's performative dimensions that actually determine its aesthetic merit. The three essential elements alone cannot ensure a good and authentic song; the added "special ingredients" are emotional sincerity (*ṣidq*) and the elusive Oriental spirit (*rūḥ sharqiyya*), qualities that emerge in performance. Performance and the performance context are, in the end, what make a good song "good" and an authentic song "authentic;" that is, meaningful, sensitive, and sincere performance determines a song's aesthetic value and authenticity.

The physical place of performance also determines to a large degree the expectation of intimacy and emotional sincerity. In the transformation of the space of the *sahra* from the private home to the club or concert stage, many of the ingredients of intimacy potentially are lost: the eye-to-eye contact and direct personal interaction between artists and audience members, the overall atmosphere (*jaww*) of intimacy and closeness that characterize the private *sahra*. Nevertheless, audiences in Aleppo may still experience *ṭarab* in the context of these novel performance settings, suggesting that the physical space of performance may not be as critical in judgments of authenticity and emotional sincerity as expectations of authenticity. The following chapter explores the performative qualities of authenticity and the link between emotion, especially the experience of *ṭarab*, and the context of performance to further question what it is that makes a given performance authentic.

SIX

Ṭarab, Sentiment, and Authenticity

Maṭlaʿ: Ṭarab and *Samna*

It is a late autumn day in Damascus, and I am back paying a visit to my friend ʿĀdil al-Zakī, owner of the Shām Dān cassette shop. Mr. Zakī has "everything" in his shop, including nearly a million recordings in a variety of formats, mostly cassettes, of older Arab music and music from around the world. Zakī is a jocular man, somewhat round of belly and quick of smile, and a great enthusiast of Arab music—the "good music," as he would put it, and not the modern popular songs for which he has little regard. Whenever I visited him, I generally would sit for an hour or so while we listened to various artists—whomever he happened to be making a tape of at the time, or others according to his mood: the great Egyptian artists Umm Kulthūm and Muḥammad ʿAbd al-Wahhāb, of course, but also Indonesian Qurʾān readers, Persian oud players, all-women orchestras from Tunisia, and others both famous and obscure. We'd sip little glasses of coffee, sit back in our chairs, and enjoy the music—as we did that autumn afternoon.

I have come to get some cassettes of songs by Aleppine composers recorded by Aleppo Radio in the 1950s and 1960s. When I ask Zakī if he has anything by Aleppine composers, he says, "Uncle, I have everything! Who are you looking for?"[1] He then rattles off a long list of names and has his son bring down several boxes of tapes from the shelves, each precisely numbered, catalogued, and arranged according to the artist or genre.[2] Peering through the boxes, he selects some tapes for me and begins putting them in a tape player so we can listen to them. As Muḥammad Khairī sings about lost love, Zakī exclaims, "What a voice!" and waves his arms around in a gesture familiar to aficionados of Arab

ʿĀdil al-Zakī in his store, Damascus, 2004.

music. "*Ḥilū*," I add, "Sweet."[3] "Do you want to hear some real *ṭarab*?" he asks me. Of course I do, and he says, "Here's an old-time singer from Homs, not well known, but he could really sing!" and he puts in a cassette. The tape is a recording from the 1950s of ʿAbd al-Wāḥid Shāwīsh, a vocalist from the central Syrian city of Homs. He is singing a *qaṣīda* and when he finishes each phrase the audience on the tape bursts into oohs, aahs, and shouts of encouragement—like Zakī's arm-waving, typical *ṭarab* responses. Zakī is all smiles as he leans back in his chair, his hands moving ever so slightly along with the singer—a shadow conductor of the emotions.

When the song is over, he turns to me and asks, "Well? Isn't is good?" and I respond by shaking my head in amazement and saying "Very nice!" I ask if there were others like Shāwīsh in Homs and elsewhere in the 1950s, aside from the big names from Aleppo and Damascus, and he says "There were a lot, but now there aren't that many voices like that—that can cause *ṭarab*." He adds, "there are only a handful today, nothing like the old days." "Why?" I ask. Leaning back in his chair and patting his paunch, he says, "The reason is that today no one eats enough fat." I look surprised, so he continues.

> Look, Uncle. In the old days, we used to eat *samna baladī* (clarified butter), but today everyone eats Mazola. It's just not the same! You need fat to have a good voice. God made sheep so that for every 15 kilos of meat you have 5 of fat. That's one-third fat—33 percent. We need to eat fat! Today all these singers are skinny and their voices weak. So how can they cause *ṭarab*? They need to eat more *samna*!

He laughs with a sparkle in his eye that says he is only half joking. I collect my tapes and leave. Over the coming weeks, I can't help noticing that many of the good artists, old and young, appear to be a little fat. Do they eat *samna*? Is this the secret to *ṭarab*?!

As I have shown in the previous chapters, Aleppines associate musical authenticity with their perceptions of the emotional sincerity of artists more than with specific musical features. *Ṣidq* and *ṭarab* constitute the two most important ingredients for a successful and hence "authentic" performer. But the test of the authenticity and quality of a performer is his or her ability to induce *ṭarab* in listeners—a test that arises in performance. *Ṭarab,* then, is a key term in musical aesthetics in Syria—and especially in Aleppo, which locals refer to as "The Mother of *ṭarab*" (*Umm al-ṭarab*).

This chapter examines the concept of *ṭarab* in Arab music and explores its dynamics in the context of performance in contemporary Aleppo. Discourse on *ṭarab* (both in Syria and in ethnomusicological literature) tends to focus on the influence of melodic modes, song lyrics, and the specific qualities of performers (including, in the above example, their gustatory habits) in the production and experience of emotion in Arab music. Following ethnomusicological research on emotion and music making in the Arab world (Danielson 1997; Lambert 1997; Racy 1991, 2003), I analyze *ṭarab* in Syria as an index of the social relations of musical performance, and not merely the product of configurations of melody and rhythm. From the perspective of audience members, *ṭarab* and its associated emotional and gestural responses are means of self-presentation through which valued emotional states are given linguistic, paralinguistic, and kinesthetic expression. Moreover, *ṭarab* rhetorically confirms individual claims to cultural authenticity and emotional transparency and operates as a frame for the enactment of conceptions of the self. Although musical elements of performance may at times be secondary in the production, experience, and presentation of *ṭarab,* musicians commonly employ repertoires of stock phrases and other melodic and rhythmic techniques to elicit *ṭarab* responses in audiences. I suggest that these strategies and techniques produce *ṭarab* responses by altering the perception of temporality in the course of performance. In many ways, *ṭarab* responses index these transformations in the experience of time as well as the social context of music making itself. Finally, *ṭarab* plays an important role in the Syrian aesthetics of authenticity, serving as an important and highly contested metaphor for what many Syrian artists, intellectuals, and patrons understand to be a realm of cultural difference from the West—one infused with Oriental spirit. I suggest that the concepts of *ṭarab* and Oriental spirit and the debates they engender must be understood in terms of competing conceptualizations and practices of modernity in the context of the Syrian nation-state. In this manner, close ethnographic investigation into forms and processes of self-presentation and the specific musical features that enact these presentations can reveal how music and other aesthetic practices engage broader theoretical questions of self, community, and national-identity formation in Syria and elsewhere in the postcolonial world.

Ṭarab Defined

Ṭarab is a difficult term to translate, for it connotes a number of concepts (see Racy 2003). In Arabic, *ṭarab* refers linguistically to a state of heightened emotionality, often translated as "rapture," "ecstasy," or "enchantment" but which can indicate sadness as well as joy. *Ṭarab* also describes a style of music and musical performance in which such emotional states are evoked and aroused in performers and audiences.[4] Finally, *ṭarab* constitutes a general term in Arab aesthetics that describes a type of aesthetic bliss or rapture with respect to an art object: One may, for example, experience *ṭarab* when hearing a poem or even when regarding a painting, as well as through listening to music, though usually *ṭarab* is restricted to acts of listening. Historically, *ṭarab* was a term associated primarily with the recitation of poetry and the Qurʾān.[5] Given these different connotations of the term, some scholars refer to a "*ṭarab* culture" of shared social, cultural and aesthetic practices and sentiments related to performing and listening to music and other aural arts (Danielson 1997; Racy 2003).

As one Aleppine vocalist put it, "*Ṭarab* is the feeling you get when you listen to music, and it just makes you want to say Ahh!!" There is a sense that listeners cannot help themselves—they are moved to shout, sigh, and wave their arms about. Indeed, *ṭarab*-style musical performances often are accompanied by a running commentary of shouts, exclamations, sighs, and gestures that are thought to express emotional states aroused in listeners by performers, who read these expressions as encouragement to continue a masterful performance. Like jazz and so many other musical cultures (Berliner 1994; Monson 1996),

Arab music is a highly sociable form of music making and audience participation is a key ingredient in the *ṭarab* culture.

Ethnomusicologists have described *ṭarab* as an emotional state aroused in listeners as a result of the dynamic interplay between the performer, the music, song lyrics, the audience, and certain other factors—what Jihad Racy (1991) describes as an "ecstatic-feedback model" of the *ṭarab* culture. Since Arab music is primarily vocal, analyses of *ṭarab* tend to focus on the role of the vocalist (the *muṭrib,* literally "one who causes *ṭarab*"), in reaching a state of *salṭana* (melodic flow, or "groove") that can in turn allow him or her to induce *ṭarab* in listeners. In this model, audiences must be both cultivated in the specific repertoire and emotionally responsive to the vocalist's performance—these are the astute and cultivated listeners (*sammīʿa*) for which such cities as Aleppo and Cairo are famous (see Racy 2003). In the *ṭarab* culture, listening itself is a performative and creative act that is equally important to the construction of the musical experience as the performance of the musicians. Certain other factors, such as the particular musical modes being performed, the occasion for music making, the time of day, and the vagaries of human social interaction, are also thought to be important in establishing an appropriate atmosphere for the experience of *ṭarab* (Racy 1998: 100).

As Racy argues (2003), musical and non-musical circumstances converge in Arab music making to evoke *ṭarab*—a state that one commentator termed an essential element of "Arabitude" (Racy 2003: 13). The pan-Arab dimensions of *ṭarab* as emotional experience are readily apparent in the shared discourses of *ṭarab* from Egypt and Syria to Morocco, where one can hear "Andalusian *Ṭarab*" (*ṭarab andalusī*) and "Granadan *Ṭarab*" (*ṭarab gharnāṭī*), though comparative study of the nuances of *ṭarab* in these different contexts has not been made. Racy's analysis reveals the shared discourses and ideologies of *ṭarab* among Levantine and Egyptian Arab artists and audiences, especially because of the great influence of Egyptian media and artists associated with the "Golden Age" of *ṭarab* music (c. 1925–1975), most importantly Umm Kulthūm. Yet, the experience of *ṭarab* is not necessarily shared by all audiences or experienced in the same ways everywhere. As Steven Feld (1994a) has argued, every occasion of listening has a biography, a specific history, and these biographies and histories are situated in specific locales that produce particular social and emotional experiences of music. For this reason we can expect that *ṭarab* culture will assume different characteristics in different locales, and the experience of *ṭarab* in Cairo or Beirut to be somewhat different from its experience in Aleppo because of the different musical and social histories of these cities.

Within Aleppo, *ṭarab* is experienced in a wide range of contexts and in a variety of ways that influence evaluations of musical authenticity. Until the

Ṭarab in Aleppo: Ensemble Urnīnā, 2004.

middle of the twentieth century, the primary context for experiencing *ṭarab* in Aleppo was the *sahra*. Today, as I explored in the previous chapter, the *sahra* has diminished in importance and many Aleppine music lovers (perhaps the majority) experience *ṭarab* in the context of listening to mass-mediated music, chiefly through cassettes and radio broadcasts. Thus, rather than speaking of a single *ṭarab* culture, we must attempt to understand how diverse *ṭarab* cultures are formed through musical performance and mass mediation. Below, I examine some of the elements of *ṭarab* culture in Aleppo and the factors that Aleppine artists indicate are the most important in the experience of *ṭarab* in their city. I also explore divergent understandings and experiences of *ṭarab* by skilled *and* unskilled listeners, to offer a broader picture of the social importance of *ṭarab* in constructions of modern subjectivities in Syria today. Scholars of Arab music in other contexts will recognize many of the features of the Aleppine *ṭarab* culture. My aim is not so much to rehearse familiar arguments as to reveal how discourses of *ṭarab* and musical experience in Aleppo relate to deeper conceptions of selfhood. Moreover, these conceptions are fundamental to the elaboration of social and political projects of modernity in Syria.

An Aleppine Perspective on *Ṭarab*

During my fieldwork in Aleppo, I studied the oud with the master performer and music researcher Muḥammad Qadri Dalal. During an early lesson, I asked him about *ṭarab:* What it is, and how it is experienced by performers and audiences in Aleppo? According to Dalal, the first question we must ask when investigating *ṭarab* is, "Does a connection (*tawāṣul*) exist between the artist and the audience?" All of the great artists he has known and listened to have had the ability to connect with their audiences and evoke *ṭarab*. This then leads to the question, "Is *ṭarab* to be found in the connection between the performer and the audience, or is it a characteristic of the performer alone, the music, or what?"

To illustrate and investigate the concept of *ṭarab* in Aleppo—an area of interest to Dalal in his capacity as a music researcher and performer—he gave me some examples of Aleppo's *ṭarab* culture from his own experience as a performer with many of Aleppo's great singers. Regarding the state of the performer, sometimes an artist may not be in touch (*mittaṣil*) with himself during a performance and *ṭarab* won't arise. For example, Ṣabāḥ Fakhrī once complained during a concert that it wasn't working out, meaning that something was wrong either with his voice, the orchestra, or the audience. There just wasn't any *ṭarab*. However, the singer Muḥammad Khairī would be "*mitsalṭan*" (experiencing *salṭana*) whether his voice was on or off, whether the orchestra was in tune or not, and the audience would fall into *ṭarab,* shouting their Oohs and Ahhs almost regardless of the musical aspects of the performance. It didn't matter what was happening: he could always produce *ṭarab*. In addition, the great composer and vocalist Bakrī al-Kurdī, though his voice was delicate (*nāʿim*) and weak (*ḍaʿīf*), could get the audience to cry Ahh! "with one phrase." Hence, Dalal argued, it seems that the artist's relationship with himself, his internal harmony (*insijām*), is what determines the ability to be creative. This reflects on the audience and they react to it with *ṭarab* responses.

Dalal seemed to place great emphasis on the artist's ability to cause *ṭarab* in audiences. A true *muṭrib* must achieve a state of being connected with the audience and in harmony with himself in order to effect *ṭarab* in listeners. As in Racy's ecstatic-feedback model of *ṭarab,* the state of *salṭana* or melodic groove derives from an internal state of harmony that is then reflected onto the audience, who experience *ṭarab*.[6] Emphasizing the processual nature of *ṭarab,* Dalal argued that a vocalist needs time to warm up before getting into a state of internal harmony and thus having the ability to effect *ṭarab* in others. For example, Bakrī al-Kurdī would warm up in private musical evenings first by playing instrumental pieces and then by improvising on the oud. After the improvisations, he would then sing a *muwashshaḥ* or two, and this would have the effect of making him "*mitsalṭan*"; "the mode and *ṭarab* would dominate the *sahra*," said Dalal. "All it took was for al-Kurdi to sing *Yā laylī! Yā layl*! (O my night! O night!) and the listeners would explode, *Ahh*!"[7] "It's strange," he claimed. "When a vocalist sings a beautiful phrase or a line from a *qaṣīda*," he continued, "the audience doesn't just react with him—they are prepared to do *anything* as a result of the *ṭarab*."

In this scenario, the *ṭarab* felt by the audience is a product of the internal state of the vocalist, itself a result of warming up to a modal groove; the vocalist—or rather the voice—is the medium for the expression of deeply moving emotional states. Nevertheless, it is a "strange" process, and even for this experienced artist *ṭarab* presents some mysteries. *Ṭarab* appears to have a magical power to move, such that audiences, when they feel it, are prepared to do "anything." What extreme acts might be associated with *ṭarab* was never clarified to me, though stories circulate in Aleppo of people dying from being overpowered by strong emotions while listening to a song. As I have indicated, it is not uncommon for people to shout, scream, cry, moan, dance, and otherwise exhibit behavior that we might define as "ecstatic." Certain parallels also exist between the conventional *ṭarab* responses and behavior in the Sufi *dhikr*, such as shouting Allah! or making certain gestures. In Dalal's account, a lot depends on the individual artist's internal emotional-musical state, especially his sincerity and "Oriental spirit." Certain artists feel *salṭana* and cause *ṭarab* quickly and easily, while others do not. For example, Muḥammad Khairī could get into it right away even if the conditions weren't favorable, while Ṣabāḥ Fakhrī might not be able to because of some problem. The audience, at first seeming to play a central role in determining the connection between them and the artist, now seems to be a reactive, secondary agent in the *ṭarab* process. The artist's internal state is most important.

Switching emphasis to the music itself, I asked Dalal how he experiences *ṭarab* and *salṭana* as a performer, and when and where he first experienced these feelings. He related to me the following story:

> I remember when I was young, like ten, and there used to be *sahra*-s in our house and some of the big names would come—Bakrī al-Kurdī, Muḥammad Khairī, others—and, for example, they would do a *waṣla* in [the mode] *bayyātī*. *Bayyātī* would ring in my mind, in my head for a week afterwards! A full week and my head would be full of *bayyātī*! That's *salṭana*!

Dalal described an experience familiar to anyone who has been possessed by a particular tune for days on end. This is one aspect of *salṭana*—the idea that the tune or melody or even mode will remain in one's head almost despite oneself.

It would seem, then, that one would need some familiarity with the modes before being able to experience *salṭana* for a week by a single mode, and that therefore the experience of *ṭarab* indeed may require a certain fluency in the melodic system of Arab music. This fluency would be acquired through a history of interaction in the *ṭarab* culture as a performer and listener. This confirms Racy's suggestion that the *sammīʿa* (skilled listeners) are the arbiters of musical taste and *ṭarab* in Arab musical cultures.

I asked Dalal where he first learned the modes. He said that he first learned the them in the *dhikr* as a child.

> I would go to the *dhikr* with my father when I was five years old. The *zāwiya* would be packed, maybe five hundred people, sometimes six hundred!, all participating in the *dhikr*. [There were always] good singers. My father would recite a *qaṣīda*—my father was a strong personality and had a good, strong voice—and the *dhikr* would turn into a mass of emotion (*kutlat mashāʿir*). Something very strange! I would feel scared and frightened. The *shaykh al-zāwiya* would open up his wallet and give me a quarter lira (which seemed like a lot to me then) so that I would come back! I would be really happy going with my father, like when I worked with Sabah Fakhri. I'd be happy when he sang [because of the feelings], not because of the money.[8]

As mentioned in chapter 4, the *dhikr* has served as an important training ground for Aleppine musicians for many decades. In contemporary discourse, the *dhikr* often serves rhetorically as a site of musical and cultural authenticity; the claim to having learned the *maqāmāt* and the Aleppine repertoire in the *zāwiya* testifies to one's authenticity as a Aleppine and as an artist. Moreover, it is in the *zāwiya* where the intimate connection between strong (even fearful) emotions, the human voice, and the musical modes are first forged for many artists—a connection that extends outside the *zāwiya* to include *sahra-s* and other performance venues. Indeed, as Racy notes (2003: 203–206), *ṭarab* has been understood by Arab commentators over the ages as combining strong emotions such as joy (*faraḥ*) and sadness (*ḥuzn*)—a process he terms "transformative blending" and which we also might understand through Needham's (1975) notion of polythetic classification. For Dalal the child participant of *dhikr,* the experience of strong emotional states in the *zāwiya* and instruction in the modes and song forms of Arab Muslim devotional music translates for Dalal the adult performer into a foundation for understanding how artists can evoke *ṭarab* in performances. The emotions that made Dalal happy or fearful arise from a combination of the specific musical modes being performed (such as *bayyātī* in Dalal's remembrance) and the social environment of the *zāwiya; ṭarab* is hence a musical-social phenomenon.

What about the audience and its role in creating the appropriate atmosphere for *ṭarab*? To what extent do the audience and the physical location of the *sahra* affect the probability of attaining *salṭana* and *ṭarab*? Dalal compared two different performances at which he participated to illustrate how the people and atmosphere can influence the outcome considerably. Every Thursday evening for over twenty years, he and a group of friends have met for an evening of food, conversation, and, of course, song. "We sing the songs we like," he said, "and everyone has a good time." "It's something well known about the Aleppines," he continued. "We love evenings of good conversation, food, and *ṭarab*." This same group once attended a *sahra* at the house of a foreign music lover and performer who was hosting a foreign diplomat from Damascus. Local television was even going to come and film some of it, so Dalal brought along the venerable vocalist Sabri Moudallal and Moudallal's prodigy, ʿUmar Sarmīnī, in addition to his oud. One would expect that with such talent the evening would have been a great success. Dalal commented on the second performance:

> We had a good time, but it wasn't the same [as the Thursday night event]. Everything was fine with respect to the form (*shakl*) and movement (*ḥaraka*) of the *sahra*. People felt good (*kān fī basṭ*, lit. "there was happiness"), but there wasn't anything inside us (*mā kān fī shī juwatnā*), not the atmosphere . . . you know. The TV cameras were there filming and so on. It became artificial (*muftaʿala*).

The atmosphere (*jaww*) of the first performance was more conducive for *ṭarab* than that the second, even though pretty much the same individuals were present and some of Aleppo's finer artists performed familiar and beloved songs. But because the atmosphere was artificial—with the television cameras and perhaps the presence of foreigners and a foreign diplomat—the participants did not achieve the same state of *ṭarab* that they normally experienced in their weekly gathering. Or rather, the existence of a good feeling externally (*kān fī basṭ*) was not sufficient to produce an experience of *ṭarab* internally (*mā kān fī shī juwatnā*) because the atmosphere was constructed, artificial. In a similar vein, Racy remarks that Arab musicians commonly explain a lack of creativity in a given performance by the absence of "*jaww*," often as a result of stifled or stilted interactions between the artists and the audience (Racy 1998: 102). But the atmosphere has to be authentic—spontaneous, from the heart—in order to elicit the internal states associated with the experience of *ṭarab*.

Admitting the importance of the performer, and especially the vocalist, in eliciting *ṭarab,* Dalal argued that in the end it is the connection between performers and audiences that best explains *ṭarab*. To illustrate how the relationship between artists and audience members and not the quality of the music or even the artists determines whether or not participants will experience *ṭarab,* and whether or not a given performance will be considered successful, Dalal told me the following story of a particular evening:

> Once Sabah Fakhri was invited to our house . . . and he came with his ensemble, maybe four people. Everyone present went crazy. It was really outstanding. So once [years later] when I saw Sabah I asked him, "You remember that great *sahra* back in 1970, '71?" He told me, "Yeah. It was bad." I said, "You mean that *sahra* in which we had such a good time?!" "Yes," he said, "it was *very* bad." I was surprised. We had such a great time, we were happy, we felt *ṭarab*. So I went and listened to a tape of the *sahra,* and it turned out to be bad!

Turning back to the cassette tape of the performance, Dalal discovered that, from a strictly musical standpoint, Fakhri was correct: it was bad (perhaps even *very* bad). He nevertheless remembered having a great time and that other participants also experienced *ṭarab*. Hence a low level of artistry combined with a high level of intimacy and whatever else contributed to creating the right atmosphere led many of the participants (if not the vocalist) to experience *ṭarab*. In a similar vein, Dalal argued that a musically exemplary performance might not necessarily guarantee that participants will experience *ṭarab*. It is the relationship between the artist and the listeners, the connection (*tawāṣul*), that is important, more so even than the music itself—and more important than the mere semblance of an appropriate atmosphere, as in the previous example. "The cassette doesn't record the presence of the people and their emotions, the atmosphere," said Dalal. Some performers can elicit *ṭarab* with ease because of their relationship with their audiences, even when their performances are less than stellar. Aleppines remember them as great artists endowed with a high degree of emotional sincerity (*ṣidq*), and their performances as great, independent of evaluations of their precise musical qualities.

However, Fakhri, the consummate master, seems to place greater emphasis on the music itself and to have more discriminating standards. But regardless of the merits or lack thereof of a given performance, an audience may indeed experience *ṭarab,* as Dalal's story illustrates, if the relationship between the vocalist and the audience is right. The internal state of the vocalist—what ethnomusicological discourse has argued is the primary factor in evoking *ṭarab*—seems to be an *effect* of his or her relationship with the audience, and not the cause of it; in other words, *ṭarab* is produced in and by the relationship between audiences and performers, and not aroused in listeners by the performer alone. This relationship at once reflects and produces the musical, social, and emotional states that allow artists and audiences to experience the feelings they gloss as "*ṭarab*."

Ṭarab, Sentiment, and the Presentation of Self

Dalal's narrative presents one Aleppine perspective on *ṭarab;* a highly reflective one by a well-known performer and music researcher. In many ways, it coincides with ethnomusicological descriptions of *ṭarab* such as that of Racy, himself an exemplary performer of Arab music. Both views, which to some extent we can consider informed "insider" views, emphasize the importance of the connection between artists and audiences, the familiarity of audiences with the complex modal systems of Arab music, and the special quality of atmosphere (*jaww*) in conditioning the evocation and experience of *ṭarab,* understood as an internal state. However, in Dalal's narrative, we discover that often times the music is not a primary factor in the experience of *ṭarab*; in fact, it may be irrelevant except to the extent to which music making is the context for the experience of emotional states such as *ṭarab.*[9] His narratives suggest that extra-musical factors are critical in determining the experience of music. Nonetheless, most musicological models of emotion in music assume an ideal listener with complete knowledge of the musical culture and a degree of emotional transparency that facilitates the expressions and articulation of emotional experience (for example, Davies 1994; Kivy 1989). Racy's ecstatic-feedback model of Arab music making (Racy 1991) is based on the responses of cultivated listeners (*sammīʿa*) and his interviews with the master performer Ṣabāḥ Fakhrī. I found that many of the people with whom I listened to music, both live and mediated, were not such "ideal" listeners and did not understand the modes and even the lyrics of many of the songs we heard, but they nonetheless experienced *ṭarab*—or, importantly, presented in the course of performance the signs of *ṭarab.* Some musicians whom I interviewed also claimed not to know the modes or understand the lyrics of certain songs they performed. For these "uncultivated" listeners (who constitute the majority in Syria and the Arab world), and even for many performers, the sound of the song lyrics and the quality of the voice, divorced partly or entirely from meaning, can produce emotional states of bliss and rapture that are expressed as *ṭarab.* Listeners also may appreciate a melody without knowing its modal characteristics; in fact, I found that in general the rhythmic qualities of song were the most aesthetically compelling aspect of performance—getting people on their feet to dance or to sway in their chairs.

Of course, certain musical elements have come to be associated conventionally with the *ṭarab* culture and on which performers will draw strategically in order to produce *ṭarab* responses in audiences, "musical tools of ecstasy," as Racy terms them (2003). I discuss some of these below, especially their role in producing the experience of transformations in temporality that are a precondition for experiencing *ṭarab*. But what comes out most strongly in Dalal's narrative is that, in Aleppo, whether listeners experience *ṭarab* is determined by the extent to which they experience a good connection between themselves and the performers. When such a connection exists, listeners are more likely to consider a given performance to be successful and an artist to be "authentic," which usually means that he or she is endowed with emotional sincerity and Oriental spirit. In other words, the connection between artists and audiences becomes the major focus of aesthetic judgment, and "*ṭarab*" comes to gloss the highly complex and intersubjective process of forming this connection—of achieving what Alfred Schutz (1977) called the "mutual tuning-in relationship," the experiential "we" established during music making.

Emotional states such as *ṭarab* that Aleppine artists and audiences reported experiencing in the context of musical performance (and, as noted, other emotional states may be experienced in addition to or in lieu of *ṭarab*) can be understood as metaphorical expressions in conventional language of the pragmatic elements of the musical engagement; that is, they are meta-pragmatic glosses of pragmatic, context-driven and context-creating processes of musical and social engagement. Such terms as "*ṭarab*" are abstractions not so much of the internal emotional states of listeners and performers (which we cannot verify anyway), but of the intersubjective processes of the "mutual tuning-in relationship" itself. The language, para-language, and gestures associated with *ṭarab* are in effect social-emotional metaphors of authentic music; they gloss the complex and positively valued sentiments and the social and musical interactions that give rise to them in performance. For example, when listeners shout Allāh!, sigh, make elaborate hand motions, or dance, they may be expressing to themselves and to those around them their internal emotional states, but in the overall context of performance these actions also serve to index the atmosphere of the performance, the connection between artists and listeners, and, by extension, the participants' and performance's authenticity: The more the conventional responses of the *ṭarab* culture are manifested in performance, the more that performance and the artists and audience are judged to be successful and "authentic."

In one sense, conventional *ṭarab* reactions metaphorically link the domains of musical performance and emotional experience; one might describe them as "internal metaphors" that gloss the experiential states of individual listeners who present *ṭarab* responses. In another sense, they can be thought of as marking a metonymic or part-whole relationship between the listeners and the overall performance; the shouts and gestures that occur within the context of a performance may come to stand for the performance itself. In a similar manner, a given performance may come to stand for an entire genre, and indeed for "heritage" and "cultural authenticity" as a whole. It is this music-culture synecdoche that allows a given performer or performance to insinuate itself into the social consciousness as an element—cherished for some, vilified for others—of the culture of a community, city, or even nation, as Virginia Danielson has convincingly argued was the case for the Egyptian artist Umm Kulthūm, who for many was "The Voice of Egypt" (Danielson 1997).

By pointing out the presentational dimensions of *ṭarab*, I do not wish to deny that individuals who exhibit conventional *ṭarab* responses are "really" experiencing *ṭarab* or other emotions. Rather, since we cannot know what any given listener or performer is experiencing, my purpose is to call attention to the rhetorical and presentational aspects of these responses. When listeners rhetorically evoke the concept of *ṭarab* in their discourse about Arab music or about a given musical performance, they are not only describing a performance but also making claims to a wide range of metaphorical and metonymic associations between the music and emotional sincerity, cultural authenticity, the city of Aleppo, Syria, the Arab world, the so-called "Orient," and so forth. For example, my teacher's narratives of his musical experiences with great *ṭarab* artists helped to establish his claim to authenticity as a musician and as a true son of Aleppo in a city that celebrates its musical heritage. Similarly, by dismissing the contemporary Arab pop song as "inauthentic"—a common pastime for many of the artists and intellectuals with whom I worked—individuals promote their claims to emotional sincerity and authenticity. Indeed, discourses of authenticity tend to be negative, that is, made through assertions about the inauthenticity of certain other cultural practices and less often via assertions about any specific attributes of the so-called "authentic" practice; authenticity hence constitutes a negative or anti-discourse.[10]

Furthermore, by adopting a broad conception of performance to include a wide variety of events and situations in which such presentations are brought into play, we can understand listening to cassette tapes and other forms of mediated music (CDs and videos, for example) as "performance." Many of the dynamics of the *ṭarab* culture in the context of live performance also hold true for listening to mediated music, especially when people listen to music in groups.

Listeners often will respond to a tape player as they do in live concerts; this is certainly the case with Mr. Zakī's reactions in the opening to this chapter. I have even seen some listeners curse at their stereos with such phrases as "May God wreck your home! (*yikhrab baytak*!) to express delight at a performance (approbation is sometimes couched in negative evaluations); one man even slammed his fist down on a cassette player in consternation with a particular recorded performance, thereby enacting emotional presentations in the context of mediated music that might be more appropriate for "live" music.

In fact, the majority of *ṭarab* situations today are mediated by cassettes and other media; live performances of *ṭarab*-style music are relatively rare compared to other styles. It is well known that Umm Kulthūm's now-legendary Thursday evening performances drew together millions of listeners from across the Arab world into a sort of virtual *ṭarab* culture (Danielson 1997). The absence of the live artist in these contexts highlights the presentational aspects of the *ṭarab* culture, which (as numerous scholars of Arab music have noted) must be thought of as mediated by cultural conventions and expectations and not only by the musical details of performance (Danielson 1997; Lambert 1997; Racy 1991; Schuyler 1990/1991). In mediated contexts, listeners enact *ṭarab* cultures through their presentations of conventional *ṭarab* responses and the establishment of virtual connections with the performers.[11]

By displaying *ṭarab* responses, listeners demonstrate to others, and to themselves, that they are capable of being moved emotionally by music, which is a valued attribute of the self for many Aleppine artists and music lovers. These displays in the course of a performance are important presentational accompaniments to Aleppine rhetorics of the authentic self (Battaglia 1995) that, as I have argued, often center on music. Emotionality, as expressed by such qualities as *ṣidq,* is for many Aleppines an important if not defining component of their diverse self-conceptions. *Ṭarab* responses in a musical performance, and similar responses at poetry readings, the *dhikr,* and in the context of listening to recorded music, enact these deeply valued self characterizations.

Of course, self characterizations and their presentation and enactment in performance are never straightforward. Conceptions of the self are not so stable or fixed that they are immediately presentable and recognizable in performance situations. Rather, such conceptions are labile, situational, and multifaceted, and the presentation of "self" depends to a large extent on the precise performance situation—who is present, where the performance is held, the overall mood, and so on. Moreover, the presentation of self also is subject to plays of desire and power.[12] For example, the expectation of experiencing *ṭarab* and the willingness and desire to display *ṭarab* responses are as important as the music and *jaww* or atmosphere of the performance in determining whether listeners or artists experience *ṭarab*. The different presentations of self are not simple translations or reflections of the internal emotional states of the participants, nor are they fixed; one may wear different hats, as it were, at different times, or even during the course of the same performance. Furthermore, we should understand the emotions that these responses are thought to index as presentations of emotional states and not the emotional states themselves—"*ṭarab*," not *ṭarab*, "*salṭana*," not *salṭana*, "*ṣidq*," and not *ṣidq*, and so on (see Langer 1960).[13] In this regard, such qualities as *ṣidq* must be understood as presentational aspects of performance and not as essential attributes of a given performer; indeed, they are performative.

Music in the *ṭarab* culture may arouse emotional states in listeners, but it is important to remember that listeners present their responses to music through recourse to both aural and gestural economies. Following Langer, we can understand conventional *ṭarab* responses as iconic presentations of the emotions with which they are associated; the gesture or sigh or exclamation is identified as the emotion (though Langer would reject the suggestion that music expresses or communicates emotions through arousal of such states in listeners). Yet, my argument is that focusing on the music alone means missing the significant performative and presentational dimensions of the processes by which artists and audiences experience and communicate emotional states in the course of a performance.

The expectation and desire to experience *ṭarab*, the overall atmosphere, and the specific musical features of the performance provide the context in which artists and listeners may experience *ṭarab*. Performers, both artists and listeners, in fact make a number of important evaluative decisions during a performance. As Feld has argued (1994a: 85–89), performers make a series of "interpretive moves" or evaluations of certain qualities of the musical engagement by which they orient their experience of the music.[14] In the *ṭarab* culture, listeners make interpretive moves regarding the style of performance, the emotional sincerity of the artist, the authenticity of the musicians' renditions and treatment of modes, the overall atmosphere, and other aesthetic conventions of the *ṭarab* culture. Artists, for their part, make similar moves to assess the engagement of the audience, the quality of the music, the atmosphere, and so forth (see Racy 1991). These interpretive moves establish frames in which listeners and artists express and understand their experiences. With a shout, a sigh, or a movement of the arms, listeners create such frames and give symbolic expression to their having made certain interpretive moves regarding the performance's quality. With a cry in the voice or a rapid trill of the plectrum on the oud, a performer too may attempt to establish interpretive frames in performance.

These frames—and there will always be multiple, overlapping frames in any given musical performance—are contexts for the presentation of the self, understood performatively (Crapanzano 1992; Goffman 1959). Both artists and listeners make strategic choices in performance that frame what I call the conventional "performance personae" of the *ṭarab* culture. For example, through the manipulation of conventional musical idioms or through body movement and gesture, a performer might attempt pragmatically to establish his or her "self" as a "master performer" (*ustāz*) or as a "romantic lover" (*ʿāshiq*).[15] Because cultivated listeners may expect to hear conventional phrases that are known to produce *ṭarab* responses, artists often use these phrases at certain times to generate these responses or to reestablish a connection with an audience gone astray. Dalāl mentioned that when he feels that audience members are not following him or are somehow distant when he performs an instrumental improvisation, he will insert some conventional *ṭarab* phrases into his playing to get them excited. Doing so has the effect of re-centering the performance on the artist and the emotional relationship between him and the listener. By shouting, sighing, and gesturing, a listener might move to establish his or herself as a "skilled listener" (*sammīʿa*) or as a "connoisseur" (*dhawwāq*), in this manner playing off the artist's self presentation as a master performer. Hence the presentation of self—or the framing of conceptions of the self in performance—is a dialogical, intersubjective process in the *ṭarab* culture; the self is negotiated between the artist, the listener, and the culture's aesthetic conventions.[16]

Innovation, Authenticity, and *Ṭarab*

According to Dalal's narrative of *ṭarab* in Aleppo, an artist's ability to be creative (or be understood as being creative)—is one condition for producing *ṭarab* in listeners, and therefore of being considered by them to be an authentic performer. It does not suffice for an artist merely to follow musical conventions; he must be creative (*mubdiʿ*). The creative artist is another familiar performance persona in the Aleppine *ṭarab* culture, and it is also a standard term of praise for exceptional artists in all media. To be labeled "the great creative artist" is about the highest praise an artist can receive. Hence artists will strive to innovate or bring novelty to their works, and this is reinforced by art lovers who often express a desire to encounter something new—or their disdain when presented with the same old stuff. When I asked acquaintances what they thought of a certain performance, they often would reply critically, "there's nothing new" (*mā fī shī jadīd*). I heard the same pronouncements at fine arts exhibitions and poetry readings. These artists and intellectuals, many skilled in or knowledgeable about the classical musical repertoire or other heritage-related artistic styles, expressed a desire to engage with something new, with novelty in the context of tradition.

In Aleppo's *ṭarab* culture, authenticity, then, is linked closely to creativity and innovation. Perhaps it is more accurate to say that in the context of the *ṭarab* culture—at least in Aleppo—tradition and innovation are not mutually exclusive but *mutually implicated* domains. In contemporary Syria, the valuation of the old does not preclude innovation; in fact, there is often the expectation that a "genuine artist" will innovate within the parameters of tradition. For example, Ṣabāḥ Fakhrī may sing verses of well-known songs in his own manner, or improvise a *mawwāl* or *qaṣīda* in special and unexpected ways. The unexpected, if it falls within the realm of the possible and accepted, is valued and can elicit *ṭarab* responses. Something too far outside the realm of accepted practice (for example, an entirely unorthodox melodic modulation or change in tempo) would not produce *ṭarab* so much as ambivalence, possibly scorn. Artists therefore tread a fine line between innovation (*ibdāʿ*) and excess, on the one hand, and between innovation and the mere following of tradition (*ittibāʿ*), on the other.[17]

According to Dalal, innovation and creativity in music rely on two factors: the artist's internal harmony (*insijām*), and his storehouse of memorized musical material. As discussed above, the artist's internal harmony is a product of the intersubjective "mutual tuning-in process" of music making. It also reflects the artist's desire to experience and evoke *ṭarab* in performance as well as his or her self-characterization as a master artist. However, as Dalal and others related to me, innovation must be based on a firm understanding of tradition. A "genuine artist" will have learned and committed to memory a large storehouse of songs and styles upon which he or she can proceed to innovate and produce something new. Indeed, in the course of an improvisation, Arab musicians, like jazz artists, often incorporate phrases from instrumental and vocal "standards." For many, mastery of the various instrumental and vocal pre-composed genres is a prerequisite for improvisation.

To help me understand the relationship between learning pre-composed pieces and the ability to improvise, Dalal related the story of the youth who would be a poet. One day a young man went to the great poet Abū Nuwās (c. 760–815) and asked, "What do I have to do to become a great poet like you?" Abū Nuwās told him, "First you must memorize ten thousand lines of poetry." So the youth went off and spent several years roaming from town to town collecting and committing to memory as many poems as he could, until he had faithfully memorized some ten thousand lines. Returning to Abū Nuwās, the youth proudly declared, "I have memorized ten thousand lines. Am I now ready to become a poet?" "Now," said the great poet, "you must go and forget everything you memorized. Once you have forgotten them all, then you will be ready to write poetry!"

Like the would-be poet, the aspiring improviser, Dalal suggested, must first memorize hundreds of pre-composed pieces until they form a musical storehouse that can be accessed in performance.[18] Memorizing the "classical" repertoire "on the back of the heart" (*ʿan ẓahr al-qalb*) provides artists with the melodic tools from which to create their own melodies and truly improvise, that is, to create something new. Although no one suggested that I actually forget what I had learned, many argued that merely repeating what one has studied and memorized is not sufficient to be counted as a genuine artist. One must create novel forms from the storehouse of tradition. Hence development of the imagination (*khayāl*) is a critical component of musical and other artistic education, and, as mentioned above, astute audiences will expect a certain amount of imagination and novelty in performances. Ideally, following (*ittibāʿ*), should lead to innovation (*ibdāʿ*).

Ṭarab, Musical Performance Practice, and Temporality

I have been arguing that *ṭarab* should be thought of as an index of the social relations of musical performance—its production and reception; in other words, its aesthetics—and that often the specific features of the music being performed are less important than the desires of performers and audiences to experience and display *ṭarab*. However, as any Arab musician (and any cultivated listener) will tell you, this is only part of the story. Indeed, certain musical elements have come to be associated conventionally with the *ṭarab* culture, on which performers will draw strategically in order to produce *ṭarab* responses in audiences. Aficionados of "classical" Arab music will listen for and expect certain features in a musical performance, and their absence usually will be met with a lack of *ṭarab* responses. Although the overall atmosphere of a given performance is perhaps the most important factor in determining the extent to which audience members will experience *ṭarab*—that is, present *ṭarab* responses—musical properties usually are not unimportant, and some may be critical for the experience of *ṭarab*.

In this section, I move from a socially contextualized analysis of Aleppo's *ṭarab* culture—one based on the reported speech of "insiders" such as Dalal, as well as the responses of music lovers in Aleppo—to a somewhat more abstract analysis of some strategies used by Arab artists to produce *ṭarab* in performance. I draw on discussions of the responses of cultivated listeners to performances of *ṭarab*-style music by "insider" scholars such as Racy (1991), as well as on phenomenological and musicological studies of music, temporality, and emotion, to suggest that *ṭarab,* like similar states of heightened emotionality experienced in the course of performance, arise as a result of perceptions of transformations in time. In the final section of the chapter I return to a reading of the debates about *ṭarab* and emotion in contemporary Syria.

In terms of the musical correlates of *ṭarab,* an artist can induce *ṭarab* responses in audiences in a number of ways. A vocalist may trigger *ṭarab* responses through the interpretation and expression of the meanings of the lyrics (what is known as *taṣwīr al-maʿnā*): Umm Kulthūm, for example, was considered a master at this, and aficionados claim that she could sing a single verse twenty or more times, each time differently in order to bring out nuances of the text and produce characteristic *ṭarab* responses in her audiences (the majority of whom, as I have indicated, were virtual audiences experiencing her music through mass mediation). Ṣabāḥ Fakhrī is often praised for his *taṣwīr al-maʿnā,* though some critics claim that he always performs the same pieces in the same way, suggesting rote memorization and not the nuanced engagement with the song text that can produce aesthetic bliss or *ṭarab.*

In the absence of lyrics, extra-linguistic factors are responsible for these reactions. Therefore it is instructive to analyze *ṭarab* in the context of the genre of instrumental improvisation known as the *taqsīm.*[19] The *taqsīm,* derived from the verb *qassama-yuqassimu,* "to divide," implies both a division between the different genres of the *waṣla,* or musical suite, which are often marked by instrumental improvisations, and the divisions within the course of the improvisation itself. The conventional *taqsīm* generally consists of an opening section (*maṭlaʿ*) followed by sections of passing phrases (*murūr*) and modulation (*intiqāl*) to other modes, and a concluding section (*qafla*).[20] Each section and certain phrases within them also will conclude with a closing sequence, also called a *qafla,* as does the end of the *taqsīm* itself. A *taqsīm* usually begins and ends in the same melodic mode, though artists commonly explore a number of related modes in the course of a performance via modulation. A *taqsīm* may be either metrical or non-metrical, the non-metrical variety being most common in Aleppo and elsewhere in the Arab world today.[21]

Instrumentalists strive to elicit *ṭarab* responses through a variety of strategies, including the skillful use of melodic repetition (*tikrār*), modulation, and closing phrases, and by manipulating certain conventional musical phrases in the course of performance. Because cultivated listeners may expect to hear conventional phrases that are known to produce *ṭarab* responses, artists often use these phrases at certain times to generate these responses or to reestablish a connection with an audience gone astray. In the performance of a *taqsīm,* an artist can take the stock phrases of the *ṭarab* culture and combine them in novel ways, create unexpected modulations and rapid changes in tempo, or otherwise establish and modify a sense of musical flow or groove. My teacher mentioned that when he feels that audience members are not following him or are somehow distant when he performs a *taqsīm,* he will insert some conventional *ṭarab* phrases into his playing to get them excited. Doing so has the effect of re-centering the performance on the emotional relationship between him and his audience.

I would like to suggest that these strategies have the effect of altering the listener's experience of temporality. The experience of detemporalization and retemporalization, or of temporal transformation in general, may in fact be critical to the production of *ṭarab,* assuming the overall social atmosphere is appropriate. The best artists do this consistently, "[enlisting] the flux of time as a force to serve [their] ends," to borrow the words of Victor Zuckerkandl (1956: 181).[22] Although technical prowess, vocal range, and fast finger work may generate excitement among audiences, for listeners (both "astute" and "uncultivated"), an artist's ability to alter the experience of time is a primary indicator of his or her ability, creativity, and—ultimately—authenticity.

Repetition, Protension, Retension

Listening to a traditional, non-metrical *taqsīm* brings listeners out of the normal flow of time into a state of detemporalization as the performer creates intricate webs of interlocking melodic phrases. Melodic repetition and fluency of movement create this sense of suspended time, one which some performers and listeners described as a "soaring in Sufi airs" (*taḥlīq fī ajwāʾ ṣūfiyya*)—the same words were used by some participants of *dhikr* to narrate their experiences. Within this state of "soaring," the repetition of a musical phrase or motif simultaneously recalls those phrases that came before and anticipates those to come, thereby contributing to the establishment of a melodic-rhythmic groove. In this manner, the experience of the repetition of a musical phrase is never the same but rather cumulative and anticipatory. This contributes to a sense of suspended temporality as listeners hover between the "retentions" of the previously heard material and the "protensions" of material yet to come, to borrow the terminology of Husserlian phenomenology (Husserl 1990; Ricoeur 1984).

In the midst of this temporal suspension, skillful modulatory and closing phrases bring listeners back down from the rarefied heights of their auditory journey with the performer and effect a momentary retemporalization of their aesthetic experience. If executed with artistry, this retemporalization elicits the characteristic shouts, ahhs, and bodily movements of the *ṭarab* reaction. The *qafla* (literally meaning a lock or closure) is especially important in effecting this transformation; indeed, a skillful *qafla* can save an otherwise mediocre *taqsīm*, whereas a poor *qafla* can ruin a good one (S. Marcus 1993). In most *taqsīm* performances, *ṭarab* responses are strongest after these closing phrases. Listeners also may react during the playing and not only after a *qafla*, for example, by humming an accompanying tonic note, occasionally vocalized as "Allāh." This is a common response by the skilled listeners, the *sammīʿa*—or, importantly, those who would like to be thought of as skilled listeners (again, to emphasize the importance of self-characterization and presentation in Aleppo's *ṭarab* culture). That the strongest responses usually come after a *qafla* suggests the close relationship between Arab musical and verbal art forms. Similar responses are heard during the recitation of the Qurʾān, for example, but also in poetry recitals, storytelling, and, of course, vocal improvisations. Arab music also shares some aesthetic features with the visual arts, especially the arabesque, which I consider to be not merely an element of design but an aesthetic principle based on the processes of repetition and variation and the play between infinity and finitude, openness and closure, unity and diversity, circle and line (Behrens-Abouseif 1999; Kühnel 1976).

Studium and *Punctum* in the Experience of *Ṭarab*

Pursuing the arabesque metaphor suggests that music, like the visual arts, demands at least two varieties of aesthetic attention: first, to the overall design or flow of musical phrases and rhythms (even in non-metrical pieces, which exhibit internal if unfixed tempos and rhythms), and second, to the particular components of a performance that may strike listeners as noteworthy. Following Roland Barthes' examination of perception in the visual arts (1980), the first experience approximates what he terms the *studium* or contemplation of a work of art as a whole and the search for its meaning, while the latter corresponds roughly to what he terms the *punctum* of certain details forcing themselves upon beholders—"pricking them like arrows," as he puts it—and demanding an interpretation of the work's meaning.[23] Repetition of melodic phrases and the overall flow (*sayr*) of the performance establishes the temporal space of the *studium* or contemplation of the performance as a whole. It is associated with detemporalization, with a sort of suspension or removal from everyday temporalities. Modulatory phrases mark transitions and help to establish a change in the overall character of the performance, its overall temporal flow.

Novel modulations in particular will act as a type of *punctum* for the listener, retemporalizing the experience of listening in a new temporality separate from if linked to the temporality of the passing phrases. The *qafla*-s—both secondary ones that follow passing phrases and primary *qafla*-s that come at the end of distinct sections of the performance, including its conclusion—further reorient the listener in time. These strategic detemporalizations and retemporalizations—changes in the experience of the flow of time—can be occasions for the evocation of *ṭarab*, assuming all other conditions are appropriate.[24]

Detemporalization and *Ṭarab*

In the performance of a *taqsīm*, the experience of flow created in performance correlates with an experience of detemporalization, while the *qafla* engenders an experience of retemporalization, a recentering, and a simultaneous release of musical energies and tensions and the anticipation of the recreation of more. It is as if the skillful artist brings listeners on a journey to a different world where altered temporalities structure experiences and frame meanings. The French poet and critic Yves Bonnefoy (1972) describes this other world in the context of the perception of visual art as the *arrière pays* or "beyond" that provides a referent for the construction and interpretation of aesthetic experience and meaning.[25] Indeed, a number of Aleppine artists referred to the process of music making as a journey (*riḥla*) or traveling (*safar*), often, as mentioned above, framed metaphorically as a "soaring in Sufi airs." We can think of these "Sufi airs" as constituting a rhetorical frame for interpreting musical experience as transcendent or rather as transcending, processual. I would like to argue that in musical performance, and especially in the context of a *taqsīm*, artists bring listeners to a realm where they experience time as having been suspended or transformed. They are brought to a temporal margin—a *barzakh*, to use the Sufi terminology[26]—between the temporalities of everyday life and those of transcendent experience, for example the ecstatic states of *wajd* or *jadhba* experienced and evoked in the Sufi *dhikr*, or the musical rapture articulated as *ṭarab*. The repetition and fluency experienced in performance evoke this sense of transformation, if not transcendence, articulated rhetorically as a form of a "soaring." The closing phrases of a *taqsīm*, on the contrary, create the experience of being brought back from this beyond into the flow of everyday temporalities (which are themselves plural and conditioned by the context of performance). Like grammatical punctuation or the details in a work of visual art, the *qafla* frames the flow of time in the course of musical performance and delimits the listener's sentential and sensual awareness of musical phrases. It creates a disjuncture in the flow of performance, which itself marks a disjuncture from everyday time; thus we have the potential for a double-disjuncture in time, which, given the other contextual elements, may elicit *ṭarab*. In effect, the *qafla* gives shape to "shapeless time," to use Carol Greenhouse's term (1996:86), frames the process and experience of music making, and marks a temporary arresting of that process. As it closes, it also opens a time-space for further elaborations, further extensions, further repetitions.[27]

Thus, *ṭarab* may result both from the experience of being lifted from normal temporality, as when a performer executes especially fluent phrases, and from being brought back into it. Needless to say, unskillful performances or those that radically depart from the standard repertoire of performance practices cannot usually effect *ṭarab*, although certain individuals predisposed to experiencing *ṭarab* may do so even in poorly executed performances as a result of the social context and their personal motivations. In the end, a combination of musical, social, and personal factors interact in the experience of *ṭarab* and therefore in the construction of musical authenticity.

Music, Emotion, and Modernity: Syrian Contradictions

I now return to a reading of *ṭarab* and emotionality in Syrian music to explore how debates about music and emotion articulate with critical debates about Syrian and Arab society and culture. Specifically, *ṭarab* and *ṭarab* culture have come to serve as touchstones of critical discourses of modernity and modern subjectivity in contemporary Syria. As presented in the previous chapters, *ṭarab* has come to be the index of what many Syrian artists, critics, and music lovers understand as cultural "authenticity." Another important metonym of cultural authenticity is the concept of Oriental spirit (*rūḥ sharqiyya*). Yet, although *ṭarab* is an important component of conventional musical aesthetics in Syria and a central element in rhetorics of musical and cultural authenticity, not all Syrians experience, enjoy, or even approve of *ṭarab* and the *ṭarab* culture. Some intellectuals and artists despair about Arab emotionality, asserting that it is the cause of Arab "backwardness" (*takhalluf*), and they show little interest in authenticity—indeed, they consider authenticity to be an impediment to modernity. For them, *ṭarab* is no longer a positive aesthetic term; they prefer a more intellectual music that caters to the thinking listener and not the old-fashioned emotional *ṭarab* listener whose shouting and sighing to them seem "vulgar" (*hābiṭ*). In this view, *ṭarab* is non-modern, non-reflective, hopelessly repetitive and emotional.

A parody of *ṭarab?* Samīḥ Shuqair, Damascus, 1997.

Ṭarab versus Musical Expression

The disparagement of *ṭarab* and its implied emotionality by modernist critics relates to a wider and much older musical debate about the merits of emotionality versus musical expression in Arab music. In late nineteenth- and early twentieth-century Cairo, *ṭarab*-style music was not considered separate from voice. For example, in the songs of Salāma Ḥijāzī and ʿAbdū al-Ḥāmūlī the melodic line performed by instrumentalists tended to follow closely that of the vocalist. These older *ṭarab* songs were primarily about an idealized love expressed in classical Arabic, divorced from everyday reality. There was little relationship between song texts and the lived experience of the listeners. However, in the early twentieth century, at the same time that Arab and European musicians were debating the modernization of Arab music (such as at the Cairo Congress of 1932), new genres of light song arose associated with the musical theater and later the cinema. These genres were thematic, both in terms of the lyrics, which often dealt with contemporary social issues, and the music, which borrowed from European music the notion of expression (Lagrange 1996: 103–107, 109–41; Danielson 1997: 70–78). Composers and artists such as Sayyid Darwīsh, Muḥammad ʿAbd al-Wahhāb, and Muḥammad al-Qaṣabjī wrote songs that featured musical introductions (not a feature of the classical song), multiple melodic parts distinct from the vocal line, and some experiments with harmony. For these artists, the music could stand alone as an expressive medium—expressing not the vocalist's internal states, as in the past, so much as the composer's intention and interpretation of the meaning of the lyrics.[28] Contemporary Syrian artists similarly seek to advance modernist visions of Arab music that transcend *ṭarab,* or at least conventional understandings of *ṭarab* and *taṭrīb.* For example, the European-trained musician and composer Samīḥ Shuqair described *ṭarab* as follows:

> *Ṭarab* is a condition, one of repetition, like someone feeling [the beads of] a rosary: the same movements, over and over. It is a condition of forgetfulness, suspended time, whereas true musical expression (*taʿbīr*) requires the imagination. *Ṭarab* does not use the imagination; indeed, *ṭarab* is *against* the imagination. Western music is more expressive because it relies on more than one voice [and] requires the use of the imagination. Each voice provides a color. If you have many voices, you have many different colors. Just as in a painting, the more colors you have the better it will be, whereas a painting of only one color or line is not good.

That is, "classical" *ṭarab*-style music, being based on one voice, has only one color to "paint" with and therefore is limited in its ability to express ideas. Shuqair's music therefore uses more colors in order to express a wide range of ideas. He finds the *ṭarab* style to be limited and limiting. Interestingly, one feature of *ṭarab*-style music associated above with the production of emotional experience in music—namely, melodic repetition—for this artist serves as a sign of the music's backwardness, lack of imagination, and non-modernity. In fact, on a recent recording he parodies the *ṭarab* style through exaggerated expressions and excessive use of conventional *ṭarab* phrases.

In another effort to transcend *ṭarab* in Arab music, the Aleppine composer Nouri Iskandar began experiments in the 1970s and 1980s in what he terms "breaking the mode" (*kasr al-maqām*). Influenced by European atonal and twelve-tone music, Iskandar aims to reduce the *maqāmāt* into their constituent components in order to compose music that transcends the modal context of classical Arab music, which relies on a single family of related modes. His compositions recombine tetrachords into novel configurations or utilize a single segment of a mode to express distinct musical ideas. In particular, his works, which include string trios and quartets as well as works for oud and strings, aim to express the contradictions and violence of modern life through highly abstract and expressive uses of melodic segments, rapid changes in tempo, and dissonance.

Nouri Iskandar, Aleppo, 2004.

Similarly, Muḥammad Qadri Dalal, a colleague of Iskandar's, also experimented in the 1980s with what he calls "non-modal improvisations" (*taqāsīm lā maqāmiyya*).[29] Like Iskandar, Dalal takes the modal constituents and weaves them into improvisations that depart often radically from the conventional melodic structure of the *taqsīm*. For example, in a non-modal improvisation, Dalal will improvise on a single melodic segment and transpose it onto different tonic notes. He also may modulate to related tones and use variations of standard closing phrases as well. Yet his aim is not to produce *ṭarab* so much as to explore what he calls melodic ideas that engage the listener's mind and not just his heart—it is an intellectual enterprise related more to meditation (*ta'ammul*) than *ṭarab*.

Musician-scholars such as Dalal, Iskandar, and al-Qal'ah sometimes distinguish between *ṭarab*-style and meditative (*ta'ammul*) styles of improvisation, on the one hand, and between "real" *ṭarab* and "false" *ṭarab,* on the other. These artists associate the latter, "false" *ṭarab* with the performance of mechanical, clichéd phrases to elicit the conventional (and hence clichéd) *ṭarab* responses. In their view, the former, "real" or "true" *ṭarab* is something more "authentic" and sublime. Interestingly, they relate "true" *ṭarab* to Sufi notions of meditation so that *ṭarab* and meditation, instead of being opposed aesthetics, are synthesized at a higher level of understanding; for "true" artists, "true" *ṭarab* and musical meditation are, in the end, one and the same thing (al-Qalʿah 1997a). In their discourses, true *ṭarab* results when artists express their internal states and ideas through music. This requires a form of meditation and the creativity to formulate phrases capable of expressing internal states and ideas. Thus, *ṭarab* and musical expression become linked through the intermediate notion of meditation as a medium for the expression of creative musical ideas; this, in the end, is the meaning of "true" *ṭarab*. For these musical modernizers, conventional *ṭarab* is non-expressive, automatic, almost autonomic. "True" *ṭarab* is at once expressive and reflective; it expresses the artist's ideas and reflects higher emotional truths through meditation. In a sense, this understanding of "true" *ṭarab* combines mimetic and expressionist aesthetics (Abrams 1953; Dickie 1997).

An important dimension of the critique of *ṭarab* culture is socio-political as well as musical. Some intellectuals and artists, among them musicians, claim that *ṭarab* is a form of emotional escapism. For example, a leading Syrian artist, commenting on top Egyptian performers such as Umm Kulthūm, suggested that "Egyptian musicians are all 'hash heads' (they consume *ḥashīsh*). The music is a drug for them." In this view, *ṭarab*-style music offers an escape from reality and like a drug lulls listeners and performers into passive states. I also heard some Syrians claim that the Arabs lost the 1967 war with Israel because everyone was "high" (*maṭrūb*, experiencing *ṭarab*) on music, and that Israel took advantage of Arab emotionality by broadcasting Umm Kulthūm concerts at strategic times so that everyone would be listening to her when they attacked (it being a well-known fact that huge numbers of Arab listeners would tune in to Umm Kulthūm's concerts). According to them, when the Israelis attacked, there was no defense—everyone was listening to Umm Kulthūm. Hence, in these contexts music comes to play a role (decisive and negative) in narratives of national struggle; in particular, it is the emotional qualities of Arab music, what many consider to be the best part of the music, that also can become of the object of socio-political critique.

For their part, defenders of tradition assert that what passes today for *ṭarab* is in fact "false" as opposed to their more cultivated and hence "true" *ṭarab*. For these practitioners and critics, modern musical practices (and the "false" *ṭarab* they may induce) are hopelessly "vulgar" and "inauthentic." This was certainly the attitude of Zakī, Dalal, and the majority of artists and music lovers whom I knew in Syria, who would decry publicly the vulgarity of the modern pop songs (even if they consumed them in private). The European-trained composer, like others of his generation and background, finds the "false" versus "true" *ṭarab* debates meaningless: both are "vulgar" in his view, and he advocates a more intellectual music closer in form if not in spirit to European "classical" music.

Adorno (1976) suggests that every artistic genre expresses the contradictions of the society as a whole, and this is certainly the case with *ṭarab*-music and related concepts of emotional honesty, "Oriental spirit," and authenticity in Syria. Contradictions in attitudes toward *ṭarab* and emotionality articulate broader contradictions in Syria and the Arab world with the experience of modernity, as discussed in chapter 2.

Qafla

This chapter has investigated the cultural and musical phenomenon of *ṭarab*. *Ṭarab* must be understood not only as a socially constructed experience of musical rapture or ecstasy, as other models of Arab musical aesthetics have pointed out, but as a strategy for the presentation of conceptions of selfhood and the emotions that carry strong associations with constructions of authenticity in Aleppo. While the characteristics of the performer are important in the evocation of *ṭarab* and in evaluations of musical authenticity, it is the enactment of a strong relationship (*tawāṣul*) between artists and performers that provides the central arena for the presentation of *ṭarab* in performance. Another key factor in the evaluation of musical authenticity is the expectation of innovation (*ibdāʿ*) and not merely the following of tradition (*ittibāʿ*) in performance. Artists tread a fine line between "tradition" and "innovation," though I would argue that we need to understand innovation and musical "tradition" in Aleppo as mutually implicated and not exclusive domains.

Moreover, while the social context of performance is critical in both the experience of *ṭarab* and the construction of musical authenticity, certain musical properties also may be important in the Aleppine *ṭarab* culture. I suggest that the experience of transformations in the temporality of performance, as investigated in the context of instrumental improvisation, may elicit *ṭarab* responses when other factors of the musical engagement such as the overall atmosphere and connection between artists and listeners are appropriate. The experience of *ṭarab* and its association with authentic musical culture affirms the more general association examined in chapter 3 between authentic culture and detemporalized representations of historical experience.

Furthermore, examination of *ṭarab* in Aleppo reveals some of the important contradictions in contemporary Syrian musical aesthetics, especially regarding the role of emotions and emotionality in social and cultural life as well as music. While some artists argue for their construction of "true" *ṭarab,* others discount *ṭarab* altogether as an impediment to social modernization and cultural modernity in Syria. Just as different listeners may not necessarily agree on the quality of a given musical performance—the self-styled *sammīʿa* often have very different evaluations from those of less astute listeners—there is no consensus on the direction of music and the parameters of the diverse alternative modernities that are promoted by different constituencies in contemporary Syria.

Hence, debates about musical authenticity and the appropriateness of *ṭarab* express broader concerns among Syrian artists and intellectuals with the question of modernity and the future of the Syrian and Arab nation. Whether, in the end, eating more *samna* (the purified butter that serves as a powerful index of the local and the authentic around the Arab world) instead of Mazola will help revive a moribund *ṭarab* culture and at the same time contribute to the formation of a Syrian Arab modernity in which emotionality constitutes a primary index of cultural authenticity and modernity, remains to be seen.

SEVEN

Notes Toward Closure

Matlaʿ: Listening with the Heart

It is my last week in Aleppo before heading back to Damascus and then New York, and I pay a final visit to the vocalist and *munshid* Sabri Moudallal. Moudallal, a spry octogenarian and one of the few surviving students of ʿUmar al-Baṭsh, operates a small shop for household goods not far from his home in the Jālūm neighborhood of the Old City of Aleppo. I visit him there in the morning as he is getting ready to go to the Great Umayyad Mosque and deliver the noon call to prayer. He invites me to join him and, after he sets his trademark red tarboush on his head and grasps my arm, we set off through the old cobblestone streets. As we pass other shops, people shout out customary greetings of welcome and I feel proud to have the honor of walking with him, arm in arm, as I had done with Fateh Moudarres in Damascus on a number of occasions. For me, this walk through the streets of the Old City with the venerable ḥājj at my side is the picture of authenticity, one soon to be complemented, I imagine, by the sound of his voice when he calls the faithful to prayer.[1] As we pass through the streets, we talk about sundry things: how when he traveled to Europe he found it strange that people on buses there are so absorbed in reading newspapers and books that no one talks to anyone else; how the great ʿUmar al-Baṭsh used to charge his students half a lira for lessons but never charged him because he was his favorite; how he himself has composed over forty *muwashshaḥ*-s; and so on.[2]

As we near the mosque, I ask about the call to prayer (*adhān*) and how he chooses which melodic mode to present it in (like other forms of *inshād*, the *adhān* utilizes the Arab modes). He says that it depends on his mood, what he feels like; he'll start in one and then modulate to others, and then finish on the original one. I was told by others that Moudallal excels in the *adhān* and that

The Great Mosque, Aleppo, 1997.

his rendition in the mode *nahāwānd* is especially noteworthy, so I ask if he could present it in that mode for me to record. He says, "May your eyes be honored" (*tikram ʿuyūnak*). I had tried on other occasions to record him from outside the mosque, but my recorder had always failed me: usually the batteries were low or dead, or I had forgotten to bring a blank tape, or something had gone awry. However, today I am prepared, having that morning procured fresh batteries and a new cassette; I even tested them in the taxi on the way over to Moudallal's shop. This is, after all, my last chance to record him, and I don't want to blow it.

Sabri Moudallal (second from left) with Muḥammad Ḥamādiyeh (far left), ʿAdnān Abū al-Shāmāt (second from right), and the author (far right), Aleppo, 1996.

We remove our shoes and enter the great mosque. The faithful are beginning to stream in from the streets and head toward the main prayer room as the bright mid-morning sun glares from the marble floors of the courtyard. Some older men stoop before the central fountain to perform their ablutions, and children play hide and seek among the columns that form a portico around the courtyard. Hajj Sabri introduces me to the sheikh who coordinates the *adhān,* who warmly greets me and brings a chair for me to sit on. I get my recorder out and Moudallal, checking his watch and seeing that the time has come for him to begin, looks at me and asks, "Ready?" I nod and he walks into a small room off the main door of the mosque, opens a small metal cabinet on the wall that turns out to be the microphone for the mosque, and unceremoniously flips a switch. Taking a deep breath, he begins. I press the record button on my recorder and hold out the microphone.

Nothing happens. His voice begins to soar, *Allāhu akbar! Allāhu akbar*! (God is Most Great), but the recorder is lifeless, dead. How can this be?! Frantically I press buttons, shake the recorder, even smack it on the side in the way people superstitiously hit television sets and radios in the hope that it will fix them (even though it almost never does). I even take out the batteries to make sure that they are placed correctly, but to no avail: the recorder will not work. "Not again" I think, but Moudallal is in full force with the most beautiful *adhān* I have ever heard, so, resigned to the fact of yet another technological breakdown, I put the recorder down on the chair and stand and listen. "*Ashhadu ann lā ilāha illa allāh*!" (I witness that there is no deity but God) . . . he is in the mode *nahāwānd*, but then modulates to another. "*Ḥayya ʿalāʾl-ṣalāh*" (Come to prayer!), and then to another mode, "*Ḥayya ʿalā al-falāḥ*" (Come to salvation!), and so on through the course of the *adhān*. He prolongs each phrase, making dramatic melismatic runs up and down the modes, filling the words with passion, each phrase more beautiful than the one it follows. It is an incredible performance and I stand there spellbound.

Allāhu akbar! Allāhu akbar! Lā ilāha illa allāh! (*God is most Great! There is no deity but God!*)

Hājj Sabri finishes the *adhān*, flips off the switch, closes the metal cabinet, and looks over at me with a twinkle in his eye as if to say, "How was *that*?!" I say "*yā salām*!" (O peace!)—a common statement of wonder and approval—tell him it was fantastic, and ask which modes he used. He names about eight, then asks, seeing the recorder on the chair, "Didn't you record it?" When I tell him that the tape recorder failed, he smiles and says, "*maʿlish,* Oh well. Another time, God willing." Glancing out the door at the people heading into the main prayer hall, he puts his arm on my shoulder and says, "Time for prayer," and slowly moves out the door and across the courtyard. I stand for a moment watching him, then go to the door, put on my shoes, and head out to the streets.

The sound of the *adhān* is still in my ears and I feel not a little *mitsalṭan;* it really was beautiful. I think about the tape recorder and take it out to see what might be the matter. I press the record button and it jumps to life, whirring away as it records the street sounds outside the mosque. I am at a loss; five minutes earlier it was totally dead, but now it works fine! Why wouldn't it ever work when I wanted it to? I think back to Hajj Sabri in the simple little room of the mosque, to the beauty of his voice, and sense that his rendition of the call to prayer has engraved itself on my heart in a way that my tape recorder never could have registered anyway. Is this another sign, like finding the Most Beautiful Names of God inscribed in the *zāwiya*? The Qurʾān says: "We will show them our signs in the horizons and in themselves." Not knowing what to think, I throw the tape recorder back into my bag, take one last look around, and head to the bus station.

In some ways, my troubles with technology in the field—mute tape recorders, blind cameras, and amnesiac computers—led me time and again to conclude that the best way for me to understand the music and other aspects of the culture I was researching was direct experience and not that mediated through a recorder's ears or a camera's eyes, or even a notebook's memory. It was as if these moments of failure were trying to teach me a lesson: to listen more carefully, to observe both more acutely and more comprehensively, and above all to strive to remember "on the back of the heart," as so many Syrians put it, what I experienced and learned. Technology at best could assist me in this, but at worst it could distract me from what I was most intent on understanding: what my informants indicated was the heart (*qalb*) and spirit (*rūḥ*) of their music and culture.

My own ideas about the heart of the music and culture notwithstanding, many of the Syrian artists and intellectuals with whom I associated place great emphasis on the quality of "spirit" in what they deem to be authentic cultural practices. As I explored in chapter 6 and elsewhere in this work, spirit (*rūḥ*), and especially Oriental spirit (*rūḥ sharqiyya*), constitutes not only an important aesthetic term in the critical lexicon of contemporary Syrian art worlds and culture, but the defining characteristic of "authentic" culture. Regardless of the form of a given work of art (including, of course, musical performances), it is the amount of Oriental spirit that determines its authenticity (*aṣāla*) and aesthetic beauty; indeed, it was the coincidence of evaluations of authenticity and of aesthetic beauty in Syrian critical discourse that led me to focus my research on the aesthetics of authenticity in the first place.

While not all art works that critics consider to be aesthetically pleasing are necessarily authentic, yet for the group of artists and intellectuals about whom I have been writing, evaluations of authenticity and beauty often coincide, and moreover, each evaluation in turn implies a certain degree of Oriental spirit, often regardless of form. Thus, a realist or expressionist painting rendered in a demonstrably European style might be considered "authentic" if viewers felt it to exhibit sufficient Oriental spirit; this is certainly the case in the works of the Aleppine artist Lu'ay Kayālī, for example, and in the works of Fateh Moudarres.[3] Similarly, listeners might not consider a "traditional" song performed in a heartless and emotionless manner to be authentic or aesthetically pleasing; the form would be appropriate, but the rendition would lack emotional sincerity (*ṣidq*), and listeners likely would not experience *ṭarab*. Although Syrians usually do not associate contemporary pop songs with authentic culture—in fact, pop songs are often criticized by those who would preserve their visions of authenticity by banning them from the airwaves—some pop songs that listeners felt conveyed a sense of Oriental spirit might be classified as authentic.[4] For example, to my initial surprise, Fateh Moudarres, normally indifferent or even hostile to contemporary music, praised a contemporary popular singer whom he felt performed with sufficient spirit. The late Aleppine musician and teacher Nadīm al-Darwīsh, son of the master ʿAlī al-Darwīsh, experimented in creating novel genres for Arab music that preserved what he felt was the spirit of the music but in a non-traditional form (al-Darwīsh n.d.). Moreover, the Aleppine artists Muḥammad Qadri Dalal and Nouri Iskandar both strive to create "authentic" musical forms that break from traditional generic constraints, even from the modal structure itself. Thus, authenticity would seem to be more a matter of spirit than of form.

Whence the spirit? Fateh Moudarres urged me to find the spirit "among the jasmine trees," in the old cities of Aleppo and Damascus, in traditional locales; he suggested that I investigate folk culture as well, which for him, as for George in chapter 3 and many others, was a site of authenticity. Not any old city, not any countryside, but the imagined life ways of a pre-modern Syria, indeed a pre-"Syria" Syria, when the land was merely "*al-Shām*," what we refer to as the Levant but literally referring to "the North," that is, the northern regions of the Arab lands.[5] The image of pre-modern *al-Shām* incorporates those cultural practices that contemporary Syrians might label as heritage (*turāth*) as well as those that arose in the modern era but that are understood by Syrians to represent social contexts having a connection with heritage and laden with Oriental spirit, as in the famed musical soirées of Aleppo in the 1950s and 1960s.

Indeed, as I endeavored to show, Oriental spirit (*rūḥ sharqiyya*) and related terms such as sincerity (*ṣidq*) and musical rapture (*ṭarab*) are experienced in the *dhikr* and the *sahra* as a result not only of the musical and kinesthetic practices specific to these domains but as a result of the social relations that form the context of invocation and music making as well. "Oriental spirit," like other terms in the emotional-critical lexicon of Arab music, serves as a metaphor for the social relations and contexts for interaction in which these emotions are presented. A lack of spirit—or rather the rhetorical claim of such an absence in a given context—indicates an absence of or failing in the social relations of performance: television cameras at a *sahra*, for example, or a distant, unfamiliar audience or performer, often articulated as a lack of "atmosphere." Again, the form is less important than the social relations that structure the given performance or aesthetic experience.

Authenticity in Syrian music, painting, literature, and other domains of social and cultural life can be understood as a gloss of complex, situated practices that express and present (in Goffman's (1959) and Langer's (1960) different usages of the term) valued conceptions of selfhood and the emotions. Musicians and music lovers characterize and present their self characterizations through terms such as spirit and sincerity, through the narration of such nuanced varieties of emotional experience as *ṭarab,* and through the use of critical terms such as melody (*laḥn*), lyrics (*kalimāt*), and voice (*ṣawt*) that are thought to be vehicles for the expression of these sentiments. These aesthetic terms are performative in the sense that they both arise in specific performance situations (a *sahra, ḥafla,* round of *dhikr,* conversation, gesture, and so on) and perform or give form to what are labile and shifting conceptualizations of the self and society. Thus, authenticity and the aesthetics of authenticity through which conceptions of authenticity are brought into play in the arts express metaphorically and metonymically (as a part-for-whole relation) a series of complex and at times contradictory characterizations of self, the emotions, and social relations. In music, these conceptions find expression in evaluations of the authenticity of certain artists and songs, primarily through the use of a critical lexicon of terms that gloss intersubjective processes of self characterization, presentation, framing, interpretation, and—not to be forgotten—musical delectation. *Ṭarab* comes to serve as the primary musical metaphor of Oriental spirit, and hence of authenticity.

Musical Authenticity and the Affecting Presence

In a similar vein, the anthropologist of aesthetics Robert Plant Armstrong remarks that "the work of 'art' is a presence, and . . . it abides in power" (Armstrong 1981: xi). While Armstrong writes on the experience of "affecting presence" (1971) in African sculptures, I believe that if we extend the concept of the affecting presence to musical performance, we will discover that it is the social nexus of performance—the congeries of artists and listeners engaged in the mutual construction of musical experience—in which the "power" of the music abides. While a good, strong voice and compelling rhythm certainly contribute to the aesthetic experience of the music, it is the social context of performance that empowers a given musical event with its "power," its authenticity. *Ṭarab* as an affecting presence results from the collective engagement of artists and audiences in the construction of musical experience. To use Kantian terminology, there is no "free beauty," that is, no realm of autonomous aesthetic experience disengaged from the social and political context in which it is produced, indeed which produces it; as the art critics Becker and Danto note, it is the art world—the theories, histories, and institutions that are the context for aesthetic experience—that creates "art" (Becker 1982; Danto 1964; see also Marcus and Myers 1995: 28). In the art world of "classical" Arab music in Aleppo, the social contexts of performance form the most important institutional basis for musical aesthetic experience, more so than the music institutes and conservatories of today.

My failed recordings reminded me of the importance of the social context of music making, the intricate processes of establishing the "mutual tuning-in relationship" and the emotional closeness that is the heart of such domains as the *sahra* and the *dhikr*. Even my few moments with Hajj Sabri in the small antechamber of the mosque formed an occasion for such intersubjectivity; his call to prayer was as much addressed to me as to the faithful he was in fact calling to prayer, and my recorder was in a sense an intruder on this intimacy.[6] My attempt to document and record this performance, as so many others like it, betrayed the emotional immediacy of the experience. And so, the tape recorder's failure allowed me the opportunity to "listen with my heart," as some Aleppines urged me to do, to feel the power of aesthetic presence, in Armstrong's sense, as well as granting me a pretext to return in future times to reconstitute the social relations and networks that were the context for my activities in Aleppo, Damascus, and elsewhere. In fact, now a few years removed from the proverbial field, I have merely to look upon (let alone listen to) a cassette tape or CD from those days and a flood of sounds and images returns to me—not merely the sounds, but, importantly, feelings of closeness and intimacy with the artists. As Dalal said, the tape recorder cannot register the presence of the performance. That is a matter for an entirely different sort of instrument.

As I write these lines, I question to what extent my own desire for social intimacy and "authentic" social experience has colored my interpretation of discourses and aesthetics of authenticity in Syria. To some extent my life there was richer than elsewhere, and as with many anthropologists, my fieldwork experience was in many ways transformative. Life in America before and since has seemed to me "inauthentic"; that is, for me at least, American mass culture, including new internet cultures, and the hyper-driven forces of consumption and materialism have meant a severing of the social ties that I found so compelling in Syria. But am I imputing my own desires onto my interlocutors in the field? Many of them would share my criticisms of America and positive valuations of "Oriental" life, and like me their notions of authentic and inauthentic would be based as much on stereotypes as on personal experience. Moreover, social ties in Syria are not always as strong and harmonious as ideals of intimacy would imply.[7] Whatever elective affinities there may have been between my desire and that of my Syrian acquaintances for "authentic" experience, the large number of publications and panel discussions devoted to discussions of authenticity, heritage, and modernity in Syria suggests that these remain important and debated topics among Syrians and Arabs more generally.

The *Qafla* of the *Qafla*?

The *qafla* is the most important part of an instrumental improvisation, and hence the most difficult. Time and again in my lessons when I performed my own, Mr. Dalal would remark that while my melodic lines were acceptable (if uninspired), my *qafla*-s were not. They had to say something about what I had just been playing, he told me, and give the listener the impression that I had not merely been playing up and down the notes of a mode but rather allowing my imagination to work on some melodic ideas. Merely to end a performance was not the same thing as performing a *qafla,* he indicated; a *qafla* provides the finishing touch to a good improvisation. As I mentioned earlier, a poor *qafla* can ruin an otherwise acceptable performance, whereas a beautiful one might save an otherwise uninspired one.

Since in this work I have adopted the structure of the *taqsīm* as an implicit model for my writing—beginning each chapter with a *maṭlaʿ* or opening evocation and ending each with a short *qafla* or closing statement—I am faced now with the task of creating an appropriate *qafla* to what I have written. This is made especially daunting by the nature of the work itself, which has modulated through a variety of themes and issues related to the main problematic of authenticity and modernity in contemporary Syria. Through my evocations, I have striven to establish a sense of the time and place of my research and association with artists in Syria not only in the interests of advancing a variety of reflexive ethnography but in order to emphasize that the results I obtained—whatever "discoveries" I may have arrived at—are the product of my personal experience with the music and the people who perform and listen to it. Other scholars would necessarily have had different experiences and thus written different ethnographies. Moving beyond these evocations, I also have striven to set forth the main issues as I encountered them in the field: authenticity, modernity, and concern with heritage; the contradictions of a society in which the most popular cultural forms are often the most vehemently vilified; how individuals make sense of a changing world through artistic and intellectual activities. I do not pretend that my statements speak for the larger group of artists, intellectuals, musicians, critics, and music lovers with whom I associated during the time of my field research (1996–2000, 2004), and less so for "Syrian society and culture" in general. Nor do I hold that, even when my statements do describe accurately how some of my interlocutors felt some of the time, they necessarily represent perdurable sentiments and opinions. Rather, I hope to have captured a moment in the debate over alternative modernities in Syria, a moment understood, heard, and experienced through my work with musicians and conversations with other interested parties, one that was articulated in relation to concepts of authenticity and heritage through music and other domains of culture.

Toward Closure

This work has aimed to provide a number of evocative scenarios, hints at contradictions, and tentative interpretations concerning discourses about authenticity in Syrian music; yet, I defer the matter of closure, leaving it in a sense "open" for further resonances in the minds and ears of other scholars, performers, and listeners. No performance is ever self-sufficient or ever truly finished. As I noted earlier, every performance has, as Feld suggests (1994a: 89), a biography and a history, for listeners and performers bring to any given performance their accumulated experiences with past performances and attitudes toward artists, genres, styles, and venues. Moreover, no performance is ever truly concluded since, as the term *waṣla* suggests, each closing implies future performances, further openings. A given performance stands as a link to those that have come before it and those yet to come. In the same way, a performance is never finished, never truly concludes and achieves closure, but rather picks up in the next instance—and in the memory of those who have experienced it when they recall a performance or listen to a recording of one.

So this work closes with an opening to yet further elaborations on the construction of authenticity in contemporary Syria in the hope that by pointing in suggestive directions I and others who share these interests might enact future "performances." The above chapters articulate a certain vision—a highly personal and personalized one to be certain—of authentic musical culture in Aleppo during the time of my research, and at the same time suggest further and future articulations and elaborations, further evocations and partial closures. Just as the range of a given mode can never be exhausted in a single performance, so the complexities and contradictions inherent in the aesthetics of authenticity in contemporary Syria cannot be exhausted in a single work. The construction of musical authenticity articulates, as I suggest, with constructions of authenticity in literature, fine arts, architecture, and the diverse practices of daily life, all of which beg further exploration.

If there is to be a tentative closure to this work, it is that "authenticity" is a domain of debate and contradiction for a number of Syrian artists and intellectuals, one that they cannot abandon because it is related intimately to a wider debate over modernity—what is to be gained from it, what might be lost. I have attempted to show that these loosely affiliated practitioners and critics construct notions of modernity, authenticity, and selfhood in response to their diverse personal, social, and political motivations and interests. Authenticity, expressed through the language of sentiment ("Oriental spirit," emotional sincerity, musical rapture), articulates a drive for an alternative to both the perceived techno-rationality of Euro-American culture and to previous generations' attempts to assimilate or imitate a Western model of social modernization and cultural modernity, the Everything from the West is Best (*kull shī faranjī baranjī*) attitude. The rhetoric of the emotions, if not the "jargon" of authenticity, as Adorno termed it in a very different context (1973), is in many regards a response to the failure of Everything from the West is Best, especially in the post-1967 era. In this regard, the quest for authenticity articulates a search for a viable formula for the future course of Syrian culture and society. Yet, turning to "the past" in its many and contested forms is not so much an atavistic looking backward or escape from the realities of the present, as Syrian intellectuals as diverse as Adonis and Ṣādiq Jalāl al-ʿAẓm suggest, as it is an expression of a will to be modern, to address the present and prepare the road to the future.

In a similar vein, Bakhtin writes on what he terms the "historical inversion" in ancient Greek literature, that "a thing that could and in fact must only be realized exclusively in the future is here portrayed as something out of the past, a thing that is in no sense part of the past's reality, but a thing that is in its essence a purpose, an obligation" (1981: 147). That is, via a type of "mythological and artistic thinking [Greek novels locate] such categories as purpose, ideal, justice, perfection, the harmonious condition of man and society and the like in the past" (147). To what extent can we consider the concern of a set of Syrian artists and intellectuals with "the past," with heritage, tradition, and authenticity, to articulate a "purpose, an obligation" for their decadent present and uncertain future? Examining the discourses of authenticity has revealed that such characteristics as emotional sincerity, "Oriental spirit," and direct experience are thought to emanate from the past, from tradition, from heritage; in discourses of authenticity, the positive characteristics of Syrian society and culture are shifted to the past and located in particularly "authentic" sites, making these time-spaces seem more resonant and persuasive than present-day Syria, which is by extension a time-space of decline, lack, and inauthenticity.

Ṣādiq Jalāl al-ʿAẓm (2000: 11) claims that the Arabs are "the Hamlets of the twentieth century," living in the (imagined) glory of their past and waiting to revenge themselves on those (that is, Europe, the West) who have usurped what they rightly think belongs to them. In his critical view, the Arabs were dragged "kicking and screaming into modernity, on the one hand, and modernity was imposed on them by superior might, efficiency and performance, on the other." Making the claim that "Modern Europe got it all from us anyway," which al-

ʿAẓm rightly chastises, does little to advance the Arab cause in the present; indeed, in this view, the modern-day Arabs are putting their future at risk by adhering to such notions. Past-consciousness and concern with authenticity prevent them from taking the necessary steps toward responsibility for the present and future.

> In other words, either we [and with this "we" al-ʿAẓm implicates himself in these debates] come to terms critically with this deep-seated, ritualized and stratified complex of highly emotional beliefs, valuations and images that in their turn give the sanction of sacredness, taboo and immutability to inherited illusions, archaic institutions, dysfunctional attitudes and arrangements, anachronistic but cherished modes of living, thinking and governing, or, again, the Fortinbrases of this world will win the day and have the final say. (al-ʿAẓm 2000)

This returns us to Adonis's vision of dervishes spinning their blurring trousers into miracles, with which I opened this text. In my view, the concern with the past and the "complex of highly emotional beliefs, valuations and images" among the Syrian artists and intellectuals with whom I worked express not an abdication of responsibility for the present and future, nor a solipsistic, mystical escapism, but rather a more nuanced vision or rather set of visions for regaining a place in the present and future. These emotionally inflected orientations, I have been arguing, constitute the inchoate outlines for composing a modernity that finds resonance in the various art worlds of contemporary Syria. Nor is this alternative modernity separate or derivative from European modernities, as I have endeavored to show; the Arabs and other colonial subjects were not "dragged, kicking and screaming" into modernity so much as they helped to shape it both through their involvement in a European-dominated world economic system and through their influence on European political, social, moral, and artistic development. Whether, in the end, the Fortinbrases of the world will "have the final say," or whether the creative visions that I have delineated in this work will contribute to a less troubled future, remains to be seen. But I sense a degree of hope and not merely resignation or nostalgia in Fateh Moudarres's call to search for the spirit of the music, and possibly the germ of a new modern condition, among the jasmine trees.

Epilogue: 2000

On a return visit to Syria in the spring of 2000, in between my running around seeing friends and preparing a lecture I was to give at a local cultural center, I pay a final visit to Fateh Moudarres. He had died the year before, and though I knew he had been ill when I lived in Damascus, we never discussed his health and it came as somewhat of a shock to me. I suppose I had thought about his death, as I still reflect (morbidly, perhaps) on the impending loss of other elderly friends of mine in Syria and elsewhere, wishing to visit them one more time before they go. So I go to see Fateh, knowing that he is already gone.

I descend the familiar steps to his basement studio and find the familiar door; but now it has a large padlock on it. A piece of paper taped to the door says, in Fateh's unmistakable hand (I recall the numerous sayings—analects—that he had posted around his studio), "I'll be back soon. Please write your name and when you came by," in Arabic and English. This is placed under the old "Please knock" sign that he had posted years ago. Written on the paper are names of people who came to see Fateh while he was ill—leaving get well wishes or merely dates and times—as well as remarks by those who came once he had died: a lawyer wishing to discuss the rights to the studio, and a string of eulogies. On the wall to the left hangs a poster of one of Fateh's many exhibitions, "Steppes Syriennes," with his visage staring out mockingly, half self-consciously, or so it seems to me. To the other side of the door hangs a small name plate: "Fateh Moudarres." Overcome with emotion as I remember this fine character and wonderful artist—and friend—I take my pen and write at the bottom of the list, "We shall never forget you, Fateh. You will remain in our hearts forever."

I turn, ascend the stairs, and emerge into the midday Damascus sun, half blinded by the light. A largish Mercedes blares its horn as it attempts to maneuver

Fateh Moudarres's studio, Damascus, 2000.

through the street, no doubt coming from the swank "Orient Club" nearby. Some children run past in their school uniforms, a storefront shutter clatters closed for lunch. In the distance, Jabal Qāsiyūn looms over the city while the doves make their seemingly endless arcs, round and round, swooping and swirling through the afternoon sky . . .

NOTES

Preface (pp. xv–xxvi)

1. Adonis (ʿAli Ahmad Saʿid), "Elegy for the Time at Hand," from *The Pages of Day and Night,* trans. Samuel Hazo (Evanston, Ill.: Marlboro, 1994).
2. The *Maghreb* or *maghrib* (lit. where the sun sets) refers to the countries of North Africa, whereas the *mashriq* (lit. where the sun rises) refers to the countries of the Arab East, also known as the Levant.
3. Ibn Khaldūn, *The Muqaddima, An Introduction to History,* trans. Franz Rosenthal (Princeton, N.J.: Princeton University Press, 1967). See also Jacques Attali's pronouncement on the predictive powers of music (Attali 1985 [1977]).
4. See, among others, Appadurai 1996; Gaonkar 2001; Knauft 2002.
5. For recent studies of authenticity, music making and the construction of communal and national identities, see Askew 2002; Bigenho 2002; Erlmann 1996; Meintjes 2003; and Romero 2001, among others.
6. For more on the concept of *ṭarab,* see Racy 2003, Shannon 2003a, and chapter 5.
7. This is readily apparent on the websites for the Syrian Ministries of Culture and Tourism, which post information concerning Syria's pre-historic and historic heritage, including culinary, architectural, and musical dimensions. See, for example, the Ministry of Tourism's website: http://www.syriatourism.org/new/ (accessed February 8, 2005).
8. For an exploration of the dynamics of Syrian music in the global World Music market, see Shannon (2003b).
9. For a fascinating and deeply engaged study of the politics and aesthetics of painting in contemporary Egypt, see Winegar (2003).
10. The Andalusian heritage refers to the cultural and intellectual patrimony of medieval Muslim Spain (*al-Andalus*) and its many Mediterranean diasporas. While the Jewish elements of this patrimony have been studied under the rubric of Sephardic studies, few sources in Syria recognized the Jewish and in general non-Muslim aspects of "their" heritage. Yet, in private discussions, many Syrian musicians remembered fondly their Jewish co-performers and teachers as well as neighbors and friends.

11. The distinction between the "authentic" *waṣla* genre and "inauthentic" pop music is of course highly political and inconsistent with modern performance practices, where artists may cross over between these domains. Indeed, many of the most popular Arab artists have rigorous musical training either in conservatories or in religious cantillation, as Virginia Danielson argues (1990/1991, 1996).
12. For critiques of Kant's notions of free and dependent beauty, see Dickie (1997); Dutton (1994).
13. The Syrian Baʿth party is distinct from the erstwhile ruling Baʿth party in Iraq, which is an offshoot of the party founded in the 1940s by Michel Aflaq and Salah Bitar, both Syrian schoolteachers and promoters of pan-Arab unity and socialism (see Khoury 1987). Note that the word is commonly transliterated in English as "Baath."
14. Lisa Wedeen (1999: 45) argues that state rhetoric and public symbolism "orients" permissible speech and behavior for Syrians, at least in public domains, and provides guidelines for both compliance and resistance to this rhetoric and ideologies and symbols of state authority. One result, she asserts, is the "killing [of] politics" (Wedeen 1999: 33). Yet, at the same time, we need to acknowledge that the state's policies are not always successful and, while many Syrians will act publicly "as if" they believe the state-promoted ideologies (Wedeen 1998), there remain significant (and now growing) domains of resistance.
15. For example, see Blecher (2002); Heydemann 1999; Hinnebusch (1991, 2001); Lawson (1996); Thompson (2000); Van Dam (1996); Wedeen (1999). Notable exceptions to this trend include the work of Bennett (1999); Doerre (2004); Hood (2002); Lindisfarne (2000); Pinto (2002); Rugh (1997); Salamandra (2004); and Zenlund (1991).

Introduction (pp. 1–21)

1. "The Great Corrective Movement" is a translation of *al-ḥaraka al-taṣḥiḥiyya al-majīda.*
2. *Muṭriba* (masc. *muṭrib*) tends to be reserved for the most esteemed vocalists in the classical Arab tradition, those thought capable of producing *ṭarab* or musical rapture in listeners (and from which the term *muṭrib* is derived). A less esteemed vocalist or singer in an ensemble normally would be called a *mughaniyya* (masc. *mughannī*), from *ghinā'*, song. Today, most cabaret and night club vocalists have appropriated the term *muṭrib*/a for themselves.
3. *Baladī* is a simple 4/4 meter common in Levantine folk music that has become a staple of the Arab pop song, especially when played on the *ṭabla.*
4. Definitions of selected Arabic terms can be found in the glossary.
5. For a discussion of the relationships among gender, nationalism, and modernity in colonial Syria and Lebanon, see Thompson (2000). Abu-Lughod (1986) analyzes the complex interactions of gender ideologies and expressive culture among Egyptian

Bedouin. Rofel (1999) examines the gendered construction of modern subjectivities in China.

6. See Khoury (1983). For a recent study of notable families and kinship in Aleppo, see Meriwether (1999).
7. The ʿAlawite (*ʿalawī*) sect is an offshoot of Shiʿa Islam whose members are found primarily in the coastal and mountain regions of northwestern Syria and in Turkey. The late Syrian President Ḥāfiẓ al-Asad was an ʿAlawite, and he promoted the rise of many ʿAlawites to positions of authority in the Syrian military and government. See Wedeen (1999).
8. For a discussion of these terms in the context of criticism in and of the contemporary Arab world, see Armbrust (1996).
9. See Armbrust (1996), who discusses these terms in the context of criticism in and of the contemporary Arab World.
10. See Appadurai (1996); Gaonkar (2001); Knauft (2002); Mitchell (2000).
11. See Schade-Poulsen (1999) for an analysis of how masculinity is engendered in popular music performance in Algeria. See Koskoff (1989) and Magrini (2003) for discussions of women, gender, and music making. For analysis and reflections on some of the ambiguities and contradictions of gender in the modern Arab world and Middle East, see Shaaban (1988); Fernea (1998); Fernea and Bezirgan (1977); Abu-Lughod (1993, 1998); Kandiyoti (1996); and others.
12. For example, whereas contemporary Syrian film makers may produce a maximum of two or three films annually, Egyptian film makers today produce ten times as many, and this number is far down from the 1960s, when production was much higher (Armbrust 1996).
13. See Frishkopf (2004) for an analysis of how the Arabian Gulf has emerged as an important market in Arab music since the 1990s.
14. At the time of my research, North African music—both "classical" and "popular"—was not appreciated widely in Syria. For example, the genre of Algerian popular music known as *rai* (Schade-Poulsen 1999), which enjoys broad appeal in North Africa, the North African diaspora, and among World Music fans, is rarely appreciated in Damascus and Aleppo, where only a few of my acquaintances listened to such stars as Cheb Khaled and Cheb Mami. This can be attributed to language barriers (Moroccan colloquial Arabic is distinct from Levantine and Egyptian colloquial Arabic) and to the problems of the distribution and consumption of cultural and commercial materials from elsewhere in the Arab world within Syria. For the most part, World Music and World Beat selections were not consumed actively except by a very small fraction of Syrian music lovers.
15. When Syrians use the phrase "world music" (*al-mūsīqā al-ʿālamiyya*), they tend to refer to European classical or art music. The phrase might also be rendered as "transnational music."
16. The original Arabic reads *"min al-nawʿ al-rakhīṣ al-ladhī lā maʿnā lahu wa lā mafhūm wa-l ladhī tamajjuhu adhwāq al-muthaqqafīn lakin qadd taṭlubu lahu fīʾa*

kabīra min ʿāmat al-shʿab . . . wa aktharahu ʿibara ʿan kalām marsūf yughriqu fī al-ḥubb wa-l gharām wa-l ʿishq wa-l hiyām!" (al-Ḥuṣāmī 1954: 1). My translation.

17. The Arabic text reads "*hurāʾ ghayr maqbūl wa lā maʿqūl.*"
18. The late Iraqi oud master Munir Bashir studied with the Hungarian composer Kodaly, who encouraged him to modernize the performance practice of that instrument, leading to the rise of solo recitals as a staple of Arab concert music today. Prior to this, the oud was used primarily to complement the voice in smaller, more intimate performance situations.
19. See Crapanzano (2003) on the use of montage in ethnographic writing.
20. The word *iṣṣa,* from standard Arabic *qiṣṣa,* means a story or tale. In a similar manner, Stefania Pandolfo (1997) uses the Arabic *qila,* "it was said," to frame story telling in her ethnography of forms of memory in a southern Moroccan village.
21. Crapanzano (2000) explores the lack of such a humorous stance regarding language among fundamentalist Christians and literalist legal scholars in America.

1. Among the Jasmine Trees (pp. 22–51)

1. *Ustādh* (colloquial *ustāz*) literally means "master" or "teacher" but is an honorific of respect for older men, artists, musicians, and colleagues in a variety of fields.
2. Moudarres would have considered the revival of musical heritage and associated musical groups in contemporary Syria to be inauthentic and vulgar too, because of their situation in the context of a vulgar Syrian state.
3. Ensemble al-Kindi was established in 1983 by the French musician and convert to Islam Julien "Jalaleddine" Weiss, who resides part of the year in Aleppo. The ensemble consists of Weiss and Syrian and other Arab musicians (Ensemble al-Kindi 1998, 1999, 2001, 2003). For a discussion of Weiss's role as a performer and preserver of the Syrian Arab music traditions, see Shannon (2003b).
4. See, among others, Abu-Lughod (1986, 2004); Armbrust (1996, 2000); Danielson (1997); During (1994, 1997); Naef (1996); Plastino (2003); Salamandra (1998); Stokes (1992); Winegar (2003); and Zuhur (2001).
5. Recent interventions into postcolonial understandings of modern subjectivity include Bhabha (1994); Chakrabarty (2000); Chatterjee (1993); Mitchell (2003, 2000, 1991); Said (1978, 1994); and Viswanathan (1989), among others.
6. The advantages for the analysis of how cultures "hear" is explored at length in Erlmann (2004). See also Hirschkind (2001); Sterne (2003); and Thompson (2002).
7. I follow the ethnomusicological convention of using "Arabic" to refer to the language and literature of the Arabic speaking peoples, and "Arab" to refer to their music, while acknowledging that these are not unproblematic distinctions.
8. In the pre-colonial era, "Syria" referred to the lands of what was known as "Greater Syria," encompassing a geographical area from what is now southwestern Turkey and western Iraq to Lebanon, Syria, Palestine/Israel, and the Sinai. The Fertile Crescent is another common appellation for this region.

9. *Ṭarab* refers to the special emotional state experienced by listeners of this music and is translated variously as "musical rapture," "enchantment," and "ecstasy." A. J. Racy explores the concept and culture of *ṭarab* at great length in his important *Making Music in the Arab World: The Culture and Artistry of Ṭarab* (2003). This work constitutes the first lengthy discussion of *ṭarab*-style music from the perspectives of both performers and listeners, though, as Racy points out, listeners—especially the connoisseur listeners known as *sammīʿa*—are performers in their own right. See also Alfred Schutz's famous essay (1977) on music performance and the "mutual tuning-in relationship" between artists and what he termed "beholders."
10. Some Aleppines fancifully claim that he invented the *qānūn* (lap zither) there as well, though there is little evidence for the existence of the instrument prior to the nineteenth century (Poché 1984).
11. The *muwashshaḥ* (pl. *muwashshaḥāt*) is a genre of classical poetry of putative Andalusian origin set to music (al-Faruqi 1975). Aleppo became a center of the composition and performance of the *muwashshaḥ* in the eighteenth century (Touma 1996: 83). The *waṣla* is a suite of instrumental and vocal genres including the *muwashshaḥāt.*
12. Yet his major work, *al-Naẓariyyāt al-ḥaqīqiyya fī al-qirāʾah al-mūsīqiyya* (*The true theories about musical reading*), remains unpublished. Darwīsh's eldest son told me in an interview that he believes that the Egyptian authorities who acquired the rights to the manuscript over fifty years ago have yet to publish it because of a reluctance to publish the work of an important Syrian author (Ibrahim al-Darwīsh, personal communication, 1997).
13. Some Syrian scholars argue that Shambīr's compositions were attributed later to Darwīsh (Mahannā 1998: 149–51; Muḥammad Qadrī Dalāl, personal communication, 1997; Kamāl Sabbāgh, personal communication, 2000), an assertion that cannot be substantiated in available sources. It is important to note that in addition to Shambīr, the Damascene artist Aḥmad Abū Khalīl al-Qabbānī (1832/1835–1904) contributed significantly to the development of musical theater in Cairo in the 1880s; he also performed at Chicago's Columbian Exposition in 1893 (Mahannā 1998: 76; Bin Dhurayl 1989: 27–28).
14. Whether these sections actually were missing is less important than the idea that Aleppine composers serve as "completers" or fulfillers of a venerated tradition. Outside of Syria, most of these *muwashshaḥāt,* when performed at all, are performed without al-Baṭsh's additions. For example, al-Baṭsh added a *khāna* to the *muwashshah Yā ʿudhayba* (in *maqām sāz kār*), thought to have been composed by Sayyid Darwīsh, though *Min kunūzinā* attributes it to an anonymous composer and does not include al-Baṭsh's "missing" *khāna.*
15. See also Charles Hirschkind (2001) for a fascinating discussion of the aesthetics and ethics of listening to cassette-based religious sermons in Cairo and what this teaches us about the effects of mass media on aesthetics and spiritual discipline.
16. In modern Syrian constructions of cultural authenticity, Ottoman and Turkish cultural influences may be dismissed as inauthentic by those holding stronger Arab nationalist sentiments, while others may link their notions of authenticity not so

much to Arab versus non-Arab ethnicity but rather to political authority, Arab or otherwise.

17. The word *qadd* (pl. *qudūd*) is used in the sense of "the same as" or "equivalent to," *ʿalā qadd* (something). Musically it refers to a song in which the lyrics of one song, either secular or profane, are set to the melody of another song; for example, religious lyrics sung to a popular tune, or vice versa. The lyrics would thus be set to an equivalent melody, *ʿalā qadd al-laḥn*. See Shannon (2003c).
18. French occupation of Syria and Lebanon began in 1920 and ended in 1946. The League of Nations granted France a charter ("Mandate") over Syria-Lebanon in 1922. France ceded administrative government to a Syrian nationalist government in 1944.
19. Since 2003, Aleppo has seen an upsurge in development and restoration work in its Old City, both as part of its participation in UNESCO's World Heritage program and due to the Syrian government's commitment to the United Nation's "Agenda 21" sustainable development guidelines proposed by the UN Conference on Environment and Development (UNCED) held in Rio de Janerio, Brazil (1992), and affirmed at the UN World Summit on Sustainable Development (WSSD) held in Johannesburg, South Africa (2002). One aspect of this that may participate in the revival of aspects of the city's musical heritage is the renovation of historic sites and their dedication as spaces for musical performance.
20. The term *klāsīkī* has come in the modern period to be applied to the older urban music repertoire such as the *muwashshaḥāt* and *qudūd*. Precisely when *klāsīkī* came to refer to the older repertoire is not certain, though it is likely that it became common after 1908, when the same term began to be used in Turkish music (see O'Connell 1997; O'Connell personal communication, 2000).
21. See, for example, the serial *Khān al-ḥarīr* (The silk market; 2 parts, 1995 and 1997–1998), directed by Haytham Haqqī and written by Nihad Sirees.
22. On the concept of classicizing traditions, see Chatterjee, who writes on elite appropriations of folk culture in West Bengal (1993: 74). Similar processes of selection and appropriation are at work in the promotion of some varieties of Ottoman urban court musics as a classical "Arab" music. On Ottoman court music, see Feldman (1993, 1996).
23. The *dhikr* is a form of ritualized invocation of God accompanied by a repertoire of songs, chants, and bodily motions. See chapter 4, and Pinto (2002).
24. Wasoof makes claims to the Arab tradition by naming himself "The Sultan of *Ṭarab*" (*sulṭān al-ṭarab*) and even uses a well-known *qānūn* player in his orchestra. The *qānūn* is so closely associated with the "authentic" music that its placement in Wasoof's otherwise modern group adds a dimension of authenticity, even though the instrument cannot always be heard over the sounds of the violins, synthesizers, and drums. Wasoof had a "run in" with the Sultan of ʿOman, who refused to let the former perform there unless he changed his title to "King" of *ṭarab* since there can only one "Sultan" in the Sultanate! Wasoof did not change his name on the posters for the concert and hence did not perform.

25. Egyptians are well aware of this perception, as trumpeted in the brochures for the Cairo Conference on Arab Music in 1996, which featured numerous articles celebrating UNESCO's selection of Cairo as the Arab world's cultural capital for that year. As of 2005, Damascus and Aleppo had yet to be selected.
26. Syrians do so with respect to other media as well, for example through the identification of Egypt film as "Arab film" (*fīlm ʿarabī*).
27. This ministry administers *waqf* lands (pl. *awqāf*), that is, lands and properties whose usufruct rights have been granted to religious authorities for the promotion of good deeds.
28. These and similar remarks may indicate affiliation with or sympathy with ideologies of Islamic puritanism (*salafiyya*) associated with Syria's Muslim Brotherhood since the 1970s (ʿAbd-Allah 1983; Abu-Rabiʿ 1996).
29. For example, the song "*Min khamrat al-ḥubb*" [From the ferment of love] contains the verse "*in kāna lī dhanb, hāt al-sharḥ wa imlīlī*" [if I were at fault, hand me the goblet and fill it!].
30. Other pronouncements on *samāʿ* from the Sufi perspective include the great ninth-century Sufi Dhū al-Nūn, who writes: "*samāʿ* is a divine influence that moves the heart to see Allah, and those who listen with their souls pray to Allah, whereas those who listen with their senses and desires fall into sin" (cited in al-ʿAqīlī 1979: 259).
31. I have a strong background in music and have performed the saxophone on a semi-professional level for many years. I also have gained a modest facility on the *oud* and have performed publicly in Syria, the United States, and Morocco.
32. The question of emotional sincerity, usually linked strongly to the persona of Umm Kulthūm, is a theme I take up in chapter 6.
33. Like the English word "culture," *thaqāfa* implies cultivation in the educative and agricultural senses. In Syria, *thaqāfa* tends to refer to educational cultivation and sophistication and less often to either the arts (*funūn*) or what we would call "popular culture," *ʿadāt wa taqālīd* (lit. "customs and habits"). Syrians use the word *ḥaḍāra* (lit. "civilization") to refer to high culture. See Armbrust 1996.
34. "Jazz" assumes a somewhat wider range of styles and genres in Syria than in the United States, and often includes blues, rhythm and blues, and some pop in addition to what we normally might consider jazz (itself a flexible and ambiguous label even in the United States).
35. At the time of my research (1996 to 1998), US$1 was equivalent to approximately SYP 50 on the black market. The official exchange rate was about SYP44 to the dollar.
36. See Keil (1994c: 227–31), who argues against copyright laws, the commodification of music, and restrictions on the free exchange of music.
37. It is common practice in Islamic societies to give the Qurʾān pride of place in a home or shop, usually by displaying it on the highest shelf in a room.

2. Sentiment and Authentic Spirit (pp. 52–82)

1. By this formulation I do not wish to imply that "Syrian," "Arab," and "modern" are either mutually exclusive or well-defined essences. See below for a discussion of the concept of "alternative modernity" and my use of it in the context of this work.
2. Hourani (1983) classifies the "Liberal Age" of Arabic thought as extending from 1798 to 1939, approximately the first two periods of my classification. Barakat (1993: 242) divides modern Arab history and thought into three periods, roughly the same as my classification but combining the post-Independence and post-1967 eras. As will become clear below, a division between pre- and post-1967 Syrian thought is highly relevant for the purposes of this discussion.
3. The discourse of modernizing Syria assumes a central place in the ideology of the late Syrian President Ḥāfiẓ al-Asad as "The Builder of Modern Syria" (*bānī suriyya al-ḥadītha*).
4. See *The Oxford English-Arabic Dictionary of Current Usage* (1978), s.v. "authenticity."
5. The English word "authentic" derives from the Greek *authentikós,* meaning "original," "primary," and "at first hand."
6. In chapter 3, I explore how Syrians may locate "genuine" or "spurious" culture, to borrow Edward Sapir's terms, in both rural "folk" practices and in urban-based civilization (*ḥaḍāra*), depending on their particular interests, background, and understandings of history and the past.
7. The concept of an independent Arab musical tradition did not arise until the 1930s, especially after the first Congress on Arab Music held in Cairo in 1932. Operationally the distinctions between "Ottoman," "Persian," and "Arab" musical traditions were fluent prior to the modern period, and to a large extent they remain so today. Referring to the music as "Arab" reflected more nationalist than purely musical concerns (Danielson 1997: 77).
8. Ṭarābīshī uses the phrase *maf'ūl tanwīmī takhdīrī,* "an anaesthetized and narcotized object." I cannot find reference to the use of the term *ṣadma* or shock prior to 1967 and hence this model may reflect a reconstruction of the nature of the earlier (eighteenth- and nineteenth-century) engagement with Europe by Arab intellectuals coming to term with their society and culture in the aftermath of the defeat of 1967—intellectuals for whom, as I argue below, conceptions of authenticity and modernity would have been different from their nahḍawist counterparts. Indeed, available early texts that describe the interaction of Europeans and Arabs suggest less a state of shock than of fascination and curiosity mixed with abhorrence and disgust (for example, al-Jabarti 1993).
9. We might compare the concept of the *nahḍa* to that of the pre-Islamic *jāhiliyya* or Era of Ignorance in that both are ideological constructions of history and forms of self-constitution.
10. See Kuper (1988) and Stocking (1987) for similar discourses in Victorian-era anthropology.

11. Mitchell (1991: 122–23) indicates that the writings of Gustave Le Bon on comparative civilization, education, and crowd psychology were popular in early modern Egypt, as were the ideas of Durkheim.
12. On modernity in South Asia, see Chakrabarty (2001) and Chatterjee (1993); on Latin-America, see Canclini (1995) and Coronil (1997); on China, see Rofel (1999); on Africa, see Comaroff and Comaroff (1993), Piot (1999), and Spitulnik (2002), among others.
13. For the "development of underdevelopment" argument in the Middle East, Africa and Latin America, see Amin (1974); Escobar (1995); Frank (1969); and Rodney (1972), among others.
14. Palestine and portions of Iraq and the Arabian Gulf states fell under British rule. Egypt, though nominally a monarchy, had succumbed to British indirect colonial administration in 1882 (see Mitchell 1991).
15. These conceptions and ideologies arose in the context of French power and hegemony in Syria, and therefore it is important to understand how French and Syrian conceptions of culture and modernity interacted. Recent studies have shown how the colonial situation in Morocco and other French territories influenced conceptions of French modernity (Rabinow 1989), but few have investigated the reciprocal influences of French and Syrian conceptions of modernity during the Mandate (Burke 1973; Khoury 1987; Thompson 2000).
16. For example, the *maqām al-rāst* consists, in the tetrachord or "*ajnās*" theory, of two *ajnās: jins rāst* on C (C D E♭̸ F) and *jins rāst* on G (G A B♭̸ C). The symbol ♭̸ refers to a neutral interval or "half flat."
17. The *faṣila* of *rāst,* for example, would include all the *maqāmāt* that share the primary interval or tetrachord of *rāst: rāst, rāst kabīr, sūznāk, māhūr,* etc.
18. For example, the modes *māhūr* and *rast* share the same tetrachords but their treatment in performance is markedly different; performance of *māhūr* generally descends from the higher (secondary) tetrachord (*jins rāst* on the note *nawā,* G) to the lower (*rāst* on C), whereas performance of *rāst* always begins from the lower tetrachord (*rāst* on C) and notes below this (*rāst* on G, for example). Some modes having identical tetrachords transposed to different tonic notes may have very different treatments in performance, such as the modes *ḥijāz* on D and *ḥijāz kār* on C.
19. Sabbāgh adopted this title in competition with another prominent Aleppine violinist, Sāmī al-Shawwā, who claimed the title Prince of the Violin (*Amīr al-kamān*).
20. For example, articles published in the mid-1930s in the Syrian magazine *al-Thaqāfa* [*Culture*], edited by the leading intellectuals Khalīl Mardam Bāk, Jamīl Ṣalībā, Kāzim al-Daghastānī, and Kāmil ʿAyyād, dealt with such topics as French thought and literature, feminism, the merits of free verse versus classical prosody in Arabic literature, and reviews of scientific discoveries alongside articles about Islamic thought and Arabic culture.
21. Adonis (Adūnīs, né ʿAli Aḥmad Saʿīd) was born in Syria, assumed Lebanese citizenship (where he wrote and studied for many years), and carries a French passport

today. He generally is considered to be among the leading Arab poets of the modern era. In addition to his numerous poetic works, Adonis has published important volumes of literary and cultural criticism (1986). Ironically, Adonis himself illustrates this "double dependency" in his own life and work. He himself is deeply versed in the classical Arabic literary heritage and often alludes to this heritage in his poetry, and yet his work is decidedly modern in rejecting the traditional forms and genres in pursuit of a version of free verse based on modern European poetics; indeed, Adonis once wrote that it was through reading Baudelaire, Mallarmé, and Rimbaud that he discovered the importance of Arabic poetry. To what extent is double dependency a feature of modernity in all postcolonial societies?

22. This is Muḥammad Arkoun's definition of *turāth*, cited in Abu-Rabiʿ (1996: 21).
23. For a fascinating analysis of the modes of understanding inherent to conceptions of heritage in North American and European contexts, see Kirshenblatt-Gimblett (1998).
24. Of course, patronage by the cultural elite often goes hand in hand with patronage by the political establishment.
25. I have no independent verification of the figures, but they are less important than the idea that salaries are very low. Currency figures for the Syrian pound or *līra* (SYP) are translated into U.S. dollars according to the black market rate of approximately SYP50 per dollar in 1996 to 2000.
26. This has certainly been the case for the Ensemble al-Kindi.

3. Constructing Musical Authenticity (pp. 83–105)

1. Muslims refer to this as the "opening" (*fatḥ*) of Syria.
2. Examples of such include the 1996 and 1997 serials "*Khān al-ḥarīr*" I and II (*The Silk Market,* parts I and II), which dealt with aspects of the union with Egypt, and "*Ayyām al-ghaḍab*" (*Days of anger*), which dealt with rural resistance to the French Mandate. See also Salamandra (1998) for a discussion of the ways in which the television serial *Ayyām Shāmiyya* (*Damascene Days*), broadcast in the holy month of Ramadan, purvey notions of authenticity for nostalgic consumption by Damascene elites. By "Oriental" is not meant the Far East but rather some essential characteristics that many implied tie all "Easterners" or "Orientals"; the association of this commonly held sentiment with what Said describes as Orientalism in Western thought and artistic imagination is a striking example of auto- or self-Orientalism.
3. I explore the link between emotional honesty (*ṣidq*) and authenticity in Arab song in chapter 6 and chapter 7.
4. Clifford (1988: 236–37) suggests the utility of Bakhtin's notion of the "chronotope" (1981) for analyzing the spatial-temporal dimensions of culture. While Bakhtin's study focuses on literary chronotopes, it is clear that non-literary forms of discourse and narrative also are structured by specific chronotopes or chronotopic representations of time-space. In this work, I treat the more concrete condensations of

chronotopic understandings of cultural authenticity in contemporary Syria and not the more abstract notions of space and time that structure them. See also Holquist (1990).

5. Few Damascenes or Aleppines refer to the modern quarters of their cities as constituting the "new city," and unlike many North African cities, there is no Syrian concept of *la ville nouvelle*. The newer quarters are referred to simply by their names: such as Shahbā', Jamīliyya (in Aleppo), and Mazza, Mazraʿ, Abu Rumāneh, and Barzeh (in Damascus).
6. For example, the Aleppine author Nihad Sirees's *al-Kūmīdiyya al-fallāḥiyya* (*The peasant comedy*) (Sirees 1996) depicts the simplicity of the peasants and their corruption when they come in contact with modern urban life.
7. In 2002, Professor al-Qalʿah became the Syrian Minister of Tourism. His name often appears as al-Qalaa or al-Kalaah.
8. The word *nahj* (lit. course, method, or path) was used extensively in early Arabic and Islamic pedagogical texts, such as the famous *Nahj al-balāgha* (*Pathway to Eloquence*) of ʿAlī Ibn Abī Tālib, the son-in-law of the Prophet Muḥammad, which provides instruction and examples of proper living. Thus Dr. al-Qalʿah's program has classical associations.
9. However, medieval Arab theorists did not refer to the modes as *maqāmāt* but rather used diverse terms, among them the system of *asābiʿ* (fingers) and *majārī* (courses) said to have been developed by Isḥāq al-Mawṣilī (Sawa 1989: 73; Shiloah 1995: 14), the *dawāʾir* (sing. *dāʾira,* circle) outlined by the thirteenth-century writer al-Urmawī, and *ṭuruq* (ways, paths) mentioned in, among other sources, al-Ghazzali (1901–1902).
10. Syrian musicians often point to the fact of Darwīsh's visit(s) to Aleppo (which may have lasted for months or even years) as evidence that he got his musical materials from Aleppine artists. I have found no documentary evidence of the extent of Sayyid Darwīsh's visits to Aleppo.
11. ʿĀshūrāʾ is a Shiʿite festival commemorating the martyrdom of the Imam Husayn, grandson of the Prophet Muḥammad, who was murdered in the city of Karbalāʾ in 680 CE.
12. In a visit in spring 2004, I noted that the entrance and ground floor theater had received a much-needed renovation and cleaning, and I am happy to report that al-Maʿārī seems content on his perch today.
13. For the skeptical, let me add that a young hotel attendant in Aleppo could recite Hart Crane's ode to the Brooklyn Bridge and was familiar with William Carlos Williams; a fruit seller in southern Morocco recited Hamlet's famous soliloquy to me while he placed some oranges in a bag, and so on. How many Americans could recite any of these, let alone famous *Arabic* poems?
14. He is the publisher whom I cite in chapter 1 who referred to the modern Arab pop song as *qātila,* "killer."
15. Interestingly, in Syria the Arabic term for "world music" (*al-mūsīqā al-ʿālamiyya*) refers to European classical music and not what we in the West (that is, music production companies) term "World Music" or "World Beat."

16. The Aleppine *muwashshaḥ* differs from the Andalusian in that it is sung by a soloist with choral accompaniment, whereas the Andalusian *muwashshaḥ* is for a chorus of singers.
17. For example, the popular *qadd* (*al-qadd al-ḥalabī al-shaʿbī*), the *muwashshaḥ qadd* (*al-qadd al-muwashshaḥ*), and the *muwashshaḥ qadd* that uses the melody of a popular song (*al-qadd al-muwashshaḥ ʿala al-ughniya al-shaʿbiyya*).
18. These rural genres include the many varieties of the *mawwāl* such as *al-ʿatāba, al-nāyil, al-sawāḥilī,* and *al-sharqāwī.*
19. *Ghunna* also characterized aspects of Qurʾānic recitation, such as the rule of assimilation (*idghām*) with or without *ghunna*. See Nelson (1985). In Aleppo, "authentic" artists are those who follow closely the rules of Qurʾānic recitation in their singing; *ghunna* forms an essential component of Aleppine musical aesthetics (the same is not the case in Morocco's al-ʾĀla or Andalusian music, for example). I thank the Aleppine artist and teacher Muḥammad Qaṣṣāṣ for clarification of this important matter.
20. I am not advancing this claim but merely pointing out some assumptions.

4. Body Memory, Temporality, and Transformation in the *Dhikr* (pp. 106–129)

1. The Arabic plural of *dhikr* is *adhkār,* though for the sake of clarity I use *dhikr*-s. For other anthropological discussions of *dhikr,* see Frishkopf (1999) and Gilsenan (1973, 1982) on Egypt; Qureshi (1995) on India-Pakistan; and Doerre (2004), l'Hopital (1989), and Pinto (2002) on Syria.
2. The Arabic plural of *zāwiya is zawāyā.*
3. However, alternative explanations, while usually dismissed out of hand by Western commentators, are equally suggestive of the possible derivation of the term *al-taṣawwuf.* One informant in Aleppo, a local Sufi scholar, argued that the term derives from *al-ṣafā,* meaning "the stone" and referring to the sacred black stone in the Kaʿaba shrine in Mecca, the center of worship for Muslims. Hence, for this man, Sufism derives from the practices of those drawn to Mecca as a spiritual center and not from the wool garments they may have worn.
4. Some traditions state that al-Fārābī, though associated with rational philosophy, was a mystic and would wear the tattered garments of a Sufi mendicant (Netton 1992: 4).
5. Instead of *zāwiya,* some Aleppines use the word *takiya* (pl. *takāyā,* from the Turkish *tekke*) or, rarely, *khānah* (pl. *khānāt;* cf. Persian *khānah* and Turkish *hāne,* "house") to refer to the same place.
6. I follow the common practice of referring to the *wālī* as a saint, even though the term has heavy Christian connotations that are not found in the Muslim notion of *wālī.* A "saint's" tomb is generally known as a *maqām,* which is also the word for musical mode and station on the Sufi path.

7. Islamic tradition states that God has at least ninety-nine Names that refer to His Divine Attributes, though some refer to a secret one hundredth Name or even to higher numbers of Names. See Schimmel (1975, 1994) and Chittick (1989, 1998).
8. A similar statement is attributed to the great Egyptian composer and singer Dāwūd Ḥusnī, who was Jewish (Danielson 1997).
9. In this description I have consolidated the features of two different *zāwayā* and their *dhikr*-s in order to protect the anonymity of the participants and especially of the sheikh who so generously allowed me to attend and, in one instance, to record the *dhikr*. Audio and visual recording of the *dhikr* generally is prohibited even to Syrians who regularly attend *dhikr*. Though there are differences in the structure and repertory of the *dhikr*-s of the different orders in Aleppo, the two *zāwiya*-s on which I base my discussion belong to the Qādiriyya order and share a similar structure, physical features, and even participants. In addition to my own fieldwork in Aleppo and Damascus, discussions with *dhikr* participants and *munshid*-s, my analysis of the structure and dynamic of the *dhikr* is based as well on descriptions of the same *dhikr*-s by Paulo Pinto (2002) and on an unpublished manuscript on religious song in Aleppo presented by Muḥammad Qadrī Dalāl at the Third Annual Festival of Arab Music held in Cairo in 1993 (Dalāl n.d.). Mr. Dalāl was my guide to *dhikr*-s in Aleppo.
10. *Jalabiyya*-s are simple robes, usually white, that are popular throughout the region.
11. The writing of chronograms for pious scholars consisting of Qurʾānic verses whose numerical equivalents express the date of death is a common practice in the Islamic world (Schimmel 1994: 152).
12. *Thuluth* is a decorative calligraphic style commonly used to write Qurʾānic verses.
13. The phrases evoke the names The Merciful (*al-raḥmān*), The Compassionate (*al-raḥīm*), The Omniscient (*al-ʿalīm*), The Great (*al-ʿaẓīm*).
14. The Everlasting; the Sustainer.
15. They opened this particular section of the *dhikr* with the well-known *muwashshaḥ* "*kullama rumtu irtishāfan*" (Whenever I desire a sip), in the mode *rāst*. This is thought to have been composed by the fifteenth-century Turko-Persian composer ʿAbd al-Qādir al-Marāghī and refers to divine love. For text and notation, see Rajāʾī and al-Darwīsh (1956: 49).
16. See Nasr (1972); Schimmel (1994). I use the term "Sufi" advisedly since many Muslims who particpate in *dhikr* would not necessarily identify themselves as "Sufis," and also because the term has accumulated numerous associations in North American popular and academic discourses that do not necessarily coincide with (and indeed often contradict) beliefs and practices of Muslims in Syria among and with whom I conducted research.
17. It is important not to confuse the central Islamic tenet of *al-tawḥīd*, the Unity of God (as opposed to plurality), with the Sufi doctrine of *al-ittiḥād*, which refers to unity with the Divine Presence. The doctrine of *al-ittiḥād* is associated most closely with the works of al-Fārābī and the Ikhwān al-Ṣafā. Other Sufi schools of thought refer to this state as *ishrāq* (for example, Suhrawardī) and *wuṣūl* (for example, Ibn

Sīnā). For more information on these different conceptions, see the entry "Tasawwuf" in the *Shorter Encyclopedia of Islam* (*SEI*) 1995: 581.

18. Schimmel (1975; 1994) and other commentators make clear the distinction in Islam between human rational knowledge (*ʿilm*) and divine knowledge (*maʿrifa*). Practices such as the *dhikr* allow humans to witness the domain of *maʿrifa,* hence the term *mushāhada,* "witnessing," "viewing," or "seeing."
19. Remembering one's true, higher self-soul implies a transcendence of a fundamental forgetting or, to borrow from Lacan, the subject's "*méconnaissance*" of his own reality (Lacan 1991a: 167).
20. See Schimmel's discussion of the tenth-century Iranian Sufi Nifārrī's reference to *ḥijāb al-maʿrifa,* the veil of gnosis (Schimmel 1975: 46, 80–81, 192–93).
21. Some musicians indicated that in non-sacred musical realms this state is referred to as *ṭarab*. Whether *wajd* and *ṭarab* "actually" refer to the same or similar states in these diverse contexts cannot be assumed or determined through analysis. See chapter 7 for a discussion of *ṭarab*.
22. Paul Nwiya argues that this state be called "instasy" rather than ecstasy because the adept is brought into the depths of his self rather than outside of himself (Nwiya 1972: 276; cited in Schimmel 1975: 178).
23. I make no claims that this structure is fixed, perdurable, or comparable to *dhikr* elsewhere in Syria, or across the Islamic world generally. Indeed, descriptions of *ḥaḍra* and *dhikr* in Egypt and Morocco point to important differences. See, among others, Crapanzano (1973); Eickelman (1976); Frishkopf (1999); Gilsenan (1973); Lane (1973 [1836]); Waugh (1989).
24. The first prayer, called *istiʿwāẓ,* is: *aʿudhu bi-llāhi mina sh-shayṭāni l-rajīm* ("I seek refuge from the wicked Satan"). This prayer often is used outside formal religious contexts to express surprise, shock, or indignation. Muslims recite the *fātiḥa,* which means "The Opener," to commence and conclude a variety of formal religious affairs: sermons, lessons, engagements and marriage contracts, funerals, etc.
25. Eliade (1959), Smith (1982), and Turner (1975) all have written on the processes whereby ritual creates and delimits sacred or ritual spaces. See Bell (1992: 99).
26. In 8/4 time, having eight notes of quarter-note duration per measure, the rhythm is: ♩.♪♩♩♩♩𝅗𝅥. Initial tempo is approximately 100 beats per minute. Final tempo may exceed 240 bpm.
27. That is, I = beats 1 to 4 ("*lā ilāha*"); VI = beat 5 ("*il*"); VII = beat 6 ("*la*"); I = beats 7 and 8 ("*lāh*").
28. Left-handedness is suspicious in Islam and left-handed children are often forced to switch to using their right hands (Schimmel 1994: 61–62).
29. Some *muwashshaḥ*-s, such as *kullama rumtu irtishāfan,* are sung in both "sacred" and "profane" contexts.
30. *Tarqiyya* refers to both the elevation of musical pitch and a metaphorical spiritual elevation and refinement. The cognate *rāqī* means refined, civilized. Sometimes only one *muwashshaḥ* is sung on a given mode before moving to a new mode.
31. According to Dalal's study (n.d.: 8), the patterns are as follows (with the Arabic

pitch names in brackets): Pattern One (*Rāst*): opening in *rāst* on C [*rāst*], the progression of *tarqiyya* will be first to *bayyātī* on D [*dūkāh*], then to *jahārkāh* or *rāst* on F [*jahārkāh*], then to *bayyātī* on G [*nawā*], and finally to *huzām* on B♭ [*awj*]. Pattern Two (*Bayyātī*): opening in *bayyātī* on D [*dūkāh*], *tarqiyya* will be first to *jahārkāh* on F [*jahārkāh*] or *huzām* on F‡ [*nīm hijāz*], then to *bayyātī* on A [*ḥusainī*], then to *ʿajam* on C [*kirdān*], and finally to *muḥayyar* on D [*muḥayyar*]. Pattern Three (*Huzām*): opening with *huzām* on E♭ [*sīkāh*], *tarqiyya* will be to *bayyātī* or *ʿajam* on G [*nawā*], then to *awj ʿirāq* on B♭ [*awj*], then to *muḥayyar* on D [*muḥayyar*], and finally to *ʿajam* on F [*jawāb al-jahārkāh*]. In other words, each series of modulations follows a five-note tonic progression: (I) C–D–F–G–B♭; (II) D–F or F‡–A–C–D; and (III) E♭–G–B♭–D–F. The corresponding five-mode sequences draw predominantly from the following modes: *rāst, bayyātī, huzām-sīkāh, jahārkāh,* and *ʿajam*. Each five-note and five-mode progression is in effect a melodic extension of the potentialities inherent in the original mode of the series: *rāst* in the first, *bayyātī* in the second, and *huzām,* in the third. Taking the first pattern as an example, the modulations from *rāst* C to *bayyātī* D, then *rāst* or *jahārkāh* F, then *bayyātī* G, and finally *huzām* B♭ all fall within the normal melodic range of the mode *rāst*. We do not find, for example, modulation to *ḥijāz* F or *ḥijāz* A, or to other modes or tetrachords whose constituent intervals (*ʿuqūd/ajnās*) would fall outside the normal melodic range of *rāst* (though the final *huzām* B♭ does incorporate the tetrachord *ḥijāz* on D *muḥayyir*). In addition to these ascending patterns, it should be noted that certain descending melodic patterns sometimes are found in secondary sections of the *dhikr;* this process is known as *takhfīḍ* (lowering).

32. From *karata, yakrutu* = to accelerate. Forms of rhythmic modulation and indeed the phenomenon of rhythm in Arab music have not received much scholarly attention. See Sawa (2004, 2001, 1989).
33. Probably in reference to "Maulana" (Our Master) Jalāl al-Dīn Rūmī, founder of the *mawlawiyya* rite.
34. In the early stages of a section, the tempo tends to be slow, less than 100 bpm in 8/4 time. However, this tempo may increase to well over 240 bpm as participants approach the closure (*qafla*) of that section of the *dhikr*.
35. One such rhythm is:  for the phrase *lā ilāha ila allāh*.
36. The other principal sections are *muṣaddir* (introducer), *muṣaddir maqsūm* (divided introducer), *ṣāwī* (witherer, equivalent?), *khamārī* (intoxicator), and *damdama* or *dandana* (droning or humming). *Ṃusaddir* also may refer to the movement of the body from the chest (*ṣadr*), and *ṣāwī* may refer to a pious ancestor of that name. For alternative translations and explanations of these terms, see the liner notes to the recording *Sufi Chanting from Syria: Dhikr Qadiri Khalwati of the Zawiya Hilaliya, Aleppo* (2002). Tunisian *maʾlūf* music features a rhythm called *muṣaddir,* though to my knowledge no one has analyzed the possible relationships between the Tunisian and Syrian examples.
37. The *dhikr* that I recorded consists of the six primary sections: *jalāla, muṣaddir, muṣaddir maqsūm, khammārī,* and *damdama*.

38. Some secondary sections may include *takhfīḍ,* the sequential lowering of tonic pitches, in addition to *tarqiyya.*
39. This occurred in two different performances of *dhikr* that I attended, one in Aleppo, where an individual performed the dance, and one in Damascus, where a team of eight dancers performed it. For a brief description of the Turkish *mevlevi* dance, see Stokes (1992: 217–20).
40. *ʿAqīda* does not appear in the Qurʾān with this meaning. The word derives from the root *ʿ-q-d,* implying a binding together, a tying or linking, not dissimilar to the Latin *religare,* to tie back, to rebind, to yoke, from which "religion" derives.
41. See Hirschkind (2001) for an elaborate and ingenious discussion of what he terms the "ethics of listening" to cassette-based sermons among urban Muslims in Egypt. He argues that listening in these contexts must be understood as an embodied practice that conditions moral subjectivities.
42. Crapanzano (1992) advances a triadic conception of self characterization, which I explore in chapter 6. See also Goffman (1959).
43. For discussions of the concept of the *barzakh* or margin between the finite and Infinite worlds, see Chittick (1989: 117–18); Corbin (1998 [1958]); and Pandolfo (1997: 182–84).
44. See Pinto (2002: 199–204) for a discussion of the problems inherent in analyzing *dhikr* as ritual.
45. See the discussion of Muhamad Qadri Dalal's experiments in "non-modal" improvisations in chapter 6, and in his recent recording (Dalāl 2002).
46. This phrase also is used in aesthetic discourse to refer to the absence of qualities in an artistic work that might "*fishsh al-qalb.*" When asked about a concert or exhibition, one might respond, *ma fi shī bi-fishsh al-qalb* (lit. "there's nothing that releases the heart's tension"), in other words, "it was not very good."
47. What some participants identified as the dramatic structure and function of the *dhikr* recalls Victor Turner's (1968, 1974) discussion of the cathartic effect of ritual as "social drama" and Jane Harrison's (1912) examination of catharsis in the ancient Greek *dithyrambic* rites (yet, see Bell 1992, 1997, among others, for critiques of these models). Pinto (2002: 200) argues that the dramatic metaphor is not appropriate to the analysis of *dhikr* because it lacks a linear structure. I would argue that it does enact what we might term "serial liminality" that can be analyzed fruitfully as a variety of social (if not spiritual) drama in Turner's sense of the term. Moreover, an Aleppine playwright suggested that the *dhikr* is an intensely dramatic event and that he hoped one day to create a similar type of transformative drama for the stage.
48. Cf. Hugh of St. Victor's view that the Christian sacraments were instituted "on account of humiliation, on account instruction, and on account of exercise" (cited in Asad 1993: 78).
49. For some definitions of *baraka,* see Crapanzano (1973), Eickelman (1976), Geertz (1968), Schimmel (1994), among others.
50. See Doerre (2004) for a discussion of healing in a Damascene Sufi *ḥaḍra.*

51. See Asad (1993, 2003) for critiques of dominant Western ideologies of the religious and the secular. See Shannon (2003b) for a discussion of the close relationship between "sacred" and "profane" performance practice in Syria.
52. See Pinto (2002: 80–92) for debates about Sufism in Syria.

5. Authentic Performance and the Performance of Authenticity (pp. 130–157)

1. The English "youth" barely captures the connotations of the Arabic *shabāb,* which can include adolescents and unmarried men in their forties. It is also a common evocative, as in *Yā shabāb*!, meaning something more or less equivalent to "Hey guys!" Hence I use the Arabic term throughout this chapter.
2. The *riqq* is a type of tambourine, the *ṭabla* is a goblet-shaped drum, and the *daff* (or *diff*) is a frame drum.
3. These are both terms of endearment, equivalent to the English phrase "apple of my eye" or "my love."
4. The first line states, "*murr al-tajannī badīʿ al-muḥayyā/ḥilū al-tathannī ʾadr lī al-ḥumayyā*" (Bitter is the accusation, wonderful is the countenance/Sweet the swaying, the passion overflows me).
5. The *qaṣīda* often is interspersed with or at times introduced by a *layālī,* the singing of the words *Yā layl* and *Yā ʿayn* in an ad lib fashion meant to display the *mūṭrib*'s range and skill at modulation (*taṣwīr*). In this particular performance, Fakhri did not sing a *layālī.*
6. *Salṭana* (also *salṭanah*) derives from the verb *salṭana-yusalṭinu,* to rule or dominate. See Racy (2003: 120–46) for a detailed discussion of the dynamics of *salṭana.*
7. I have not verified this claim.
8. See Eickelman's (1976) discussion of the concept of *qarāba* or closeness in Morocco. I use the public-private distinction as a heuristic device while acknowledging its problems, especially with respect to the Arab world, for which we need to rethink our concepts of personal and non-personal spaces.
9. This is my term for a period that many Aleppines refer to as the most productive era of composition and performance of their music, and in a sense the period to which the term "*klāsikī*" refers.
10. These women's *sahra*-s are still held today, although I had no access to them during my research. For a brief description of some women's-only gatherings where singing is performed, see Mahannā (1998: 257–58). See also Turjumān 1998 [1990].
11. These include the caravanserais *Khān shūnah, Khān al-wazīr,* as well as the historic *Bimaristān* (hospital) *al-Kāmilī,* and a palace called *al-maṭbakh al-ʿajami.*
12. Literally meaning a suite, the *waṣla* in Syria comprises a number of *muwashshaḥ*-s, usually no more than four or five, as well as the *qaṣīda, mawwāl, dawr, taqsīm,* and light popular songs known collectively as *qudūd ḥalabiyya.* Usually the opening

muwashshaḥ is preceded by the performance of an introductory instrumental genre such as a *samāʿī* or *bashraf*. A *dūlāb* also may be used to introduce instrumental *taqāsīm* (improvisations) or changes in mode. Also referred to as *fāsil*, the Syrian *waṣla* differs from the Egyptian *waṣla* in terms of content and structure. For more on the Egyptian *waṣla*, see Racy 1983.

13. The *muwashshaḥ* consists of poetry in classical Arabic set to music and tends to follow set patterns. The most common structures correspond loosely to the European sonata and ternary rondo forms, that is, AABA and ABA (Apel 1944: 696, 451; al-Faruqi 1975; Shannon 2003c). Some are composed in colloquial Arabic, but the majority performed in Aleppo today are in the high or formal variety of Arabic, *al-fuṣḥā* (lit. the eloquent).
14. The structural similarities between the *dhikr* and the *waṣla* suggest that they share common roots. Indeed, there is some evidence that the present *waṣla* structure derives from earlier religious suites performed in Aleppine *zāwiya*-s. One such suite is the *faṣl* or *waṣla* "*Isq al-ʿiṭāsh*" (Quench the Thirsty), which is a suite of unknown but probable Aleppine or Egyptian provenance that consists of prayers of forgiveness and supplication for rain in a time of drought (al-ʿAqīlī 1979; Mahannā 1998).
15. Following Keil (1994a, 1994b) and Feld (1994b), we need to examine more closely the processes through which performers and audiences in different cultures and musics interact with themselves and with their sonic, natural, and social environments to create a sense of groove or flow.
16. The term "auditory vision" was used by the Aleppine vocalist Muḥammad Qaṣṣāṣ in a newspaper interview (cited in Racy 2003: 199).
17. Danielson (1997) and Racy (1998) discuss similar critical terms in their research on Arab musical aesthetics and aesthetic discourse in Egypt and Lebanon.
18. That is, "*laḥn*," "*kalimāt*," and "*ṣawt*" are in fact metapragmatic glosses expressed in referential or semantic terms of emotional characteristics that emerge through specific performance practices. See Crapanzano (1992); Silverstein (1976). Racy associates *ṭarab* with "Eastern soul."
19. Oddly, the ethnomusicological literature on Arab music is relatively silent on the issue of meter and rhythm despite its importance to Arab musicians and critics. For example, Scott Marcus's 800-page thesis on modern Arab music theory (1989) does not devote even a single paragraph to the topic, and Shiloah (1995) and Touma (1996) present only brief sections on meter and rhythm. Sawa (1989) discusses the theory of meter in al-Fārābī, and refers to contemporary performance practices that are similar to the tenth-century precursors. Yet the only recent and extended treatment of the role of meter (*īqāʿ*) in *ṭarab* music is found in Racy's comprehensive text (2003), in which he discusses the use of meter and rhythmic change as a "musical tool of ecstasy." The silence in the ethnomusicology of Arab music on meter might reflect what Chernoff (1979) and others (Keil 1979) have identified as a bias in favor of melodic rather than rhythmic analysis in Western musicology, as well as the notion commonly expressed by Arab musicians that their melodic modes are more complex than the meters and hence more worthy of study. Arab authors

also may be influenced by Western models of musical analysis and consider rhythm and meter to be less important than melody.

20. As I have indicated previously, some workers even impressed me with their knowledge of English poetry.
21. It is not uncommon for students to fail the Arabic examination because of its rigor and to repeat grades or, more commonly, to repeat the Baccalaureate exam, several times if necessary.
22. The enduring popularity of the *qudūd ḥalabiyya* among Syrian youth was demonstrated for me on a bus trip to Aleppo in early 2004. My assigned seat was in the back with a contingent of Aleppine *shabāb* going home for a weekend furlough from military service (there I was, stuck in the *shabāb* section again!). When the bus broke down for an hour or so, these young men broke out in song, but not the pop songs that fill taxis and public spaces in many Arab cities, but rather almost a complete *waṣla,* including *muwashshaḥāt* and *qudūd.* When I asked one of the young soldiers why they didn't sing some pop songs, he replied "This is our music."
23. This was an important theme of a number of episodes of al-Qalʿah's television program *Nahj al-aghānī* (1997b).
24. They may even result, as Touma suggests (1996: 45), from fluctuations in specific intervals in the non-tempered Arabic scale, especially the variable "medium second" interval that characterizes a number of common tetrachords such as *rāst, bayyātī, sīkāh,* and *ṣabā.*
25. For a similar discussion of vocal characteristics in Egypt, see Danielson (1997: 92–94).
26. Some Christian musicians emphasize what they claim are the Byzantine Christian roots of the Arabic modal system and hence their affiliation with an "authentic" Aleppine heritage.
27. My lessons in Arab voice and song with the performer and teacher Muḥammad Qaṣṣās began with the rules of Qurʾānic recitation, for he argued that they are the basis for singing all classical repertoire in Aleppo—that is, all songs in the formal variety of Arabic (*muwashshaḥ, qaṣīda,* etc.). When I undertook similar lessons in Fez, Morocco, to learn aspects of the Andalusian (*Āla*) tradition, these rules generally were not followed.
28. In *Sincerity and Authenticity* (1972), the literary critic Lionel Trilling advances a similar argument concerning the role of sincere behavior in Elizabethan England, a point also developed by Stephen Greenblatt (1980). Trilling opposes the Elizabethan concern with sincerity to the modern concept of authenticity. For the Elizabethans, sincere self-representation consisted in being true to one's self and at the same time being true to one's public personae. In the modern period, as revealed in the poetry of Yeats, for example, or in the novels of Joseph Conrad, sincerity was subordinated to a concern with authenticity, which meant being true to one's self with no consideration for public opinion; in fact, modern artists typically have avowed the inscrutability of the self, and its effacement in the interests of "art." Thus, according to Trilling, a gap between perception and reality characteristic of Elizabethan self-presentations was closed in the modern quest for authentic self-expression. In Syrian musical aesthetics, the concept of *ṣidq* assumes many of the characterizations of

the Eliabethan concept of sincerity, especially in that artists and audiences evaluate presentations of the self in musical performance in relation to public values and expectations. Authentic performances are those in which the participants are able to perform the roles of being themselves sincerely. The acknowledged gap between reality and performance is ameliorated in these cases.

29. His opinions about these Egyptian artists may relate to a wider understanding of Egyptian popular culture among Syrians as overly emotional or melodramatic, precisely qualities that Abu-Lughod (2000, 2004) claims are cultivated among Egyptian mass media producers and consumers.
30. According to Lorca, *duende* derives from the Spanish *duen de casa,* master of the house, and refers to a demonic earth spirit with whom artists as diverse as guitar players, dancers, and bullfighters must struggle and fight in their pathways to artistic excellence. Just as Arabs evaluate artistic authenticity based on the degree to which an artist or work of art displays Oriental spirit, Spanish enthusiasts of Flamenco argue that showing the influence of duende is a prerequisite for success (see García Lorca 1998: 48–62). For ethnomusicological and anthropological studies of flamenco and deep song, see Mitchell (1994); Washabaugh (1996). The idea of demonic possession is not commonly held among Syrian musicians, however.

6. *Ṭarab,* Sentiment, and Authenticity (pp. 158–187)

1. His calling me *ʿammū* (uncle) is one example of the Arab practice of referring to someone by the honorific that you would use in referring to him or her. For example, a father will call his young children, boys and girls, *bābā* (father), whereas a mother would refer to them as *māmā;* a grandfather would call his grandchildren *jiddū* (grandfather), and so on. Because I would refer to Mr. Zakī as *ʿammū* (metaphorically any older man who would warrant the respect of an uncle), he referred to me as "uncle" too.
2. On visits to his shop in 2000 and 2004, Zakī and his son Ayman were busy creating a CD-ROM archive of his collection and preparing a website—a far cry from the diverse notebooks in which he had scribbled information about each composer, singer, and song.
3. *Ḥilū* literally means "sweet," but serves as a general aesthetic term meaning "good" or "fine." My translations of other colloquial phrases are loose and attempt to capture the spirit of the words.
4. This style is sometimes called *taṭrīb* (causing *ṭarab*).
5. See Adonis (1992). For interesting discussions of the inter-relatedness of different domains of aesthetic experience in Arabic culture, see al-Faruqi (1978) and Boullata (1991). Of course, the Qurʾān is not a text of poetry, although it can be said to have its own poetics, which Muslims believe to be uniquely, indeed divinely, beautiful. On Qurʾānic recitation, see Nelson (1985).

6. Interestingly, this is connected in Dalal's narrative with the ability to be creative. *Ṭarab,* a chief index of authenticity, relies in part on innovation, on producing something new. While this might seem paradoxical, innovation and authenticity are not mutually exclusive domains and there is a close connection between authenticity and the expectation of innovation and originality in Aleppo, as in Syrian arts more generally.
7. These words are sung to an improvised melody in the vocal genre known as *layālī* (literally "nights").
8. The current *shaykh al-zāwiya* at the *dhikr* described in chapter 5 continues this tradition, dispensing 25 lira coins (approximately 50 cents) to the young boys at the *dhikr*.
9. Other terms in the Aleppine musical-aesthetic lexicon include *kayf* ("good feeling"), *basṭ* ("happiness"), and *tajallī* ("revelation, manifestation").
10. See Adorno (1973). See also Adorno (1997).
11. The extent to which *ṭarab* and other emotional experiences are not only mediated but in fact produced by technologies of recording, reproduction, and distribution has been little studied in the context of music in the Arab world. Recent work indicates that the modern mass media play a strong role in conditioning emotion and affect in Arab television dramas (Abu-Lughod 2000), and my research has shown that presentational and performative responses to music such as *ṭarab* are in many instances reinforced by mass media constructions of emotional reactions to listening.
12. See Crapanzano (1992).
13. My analysis borrows some terminology from Suzanne Langer's study of musical communication and symbolism, in particular her notion of "presentational" symbolism (Langer 1960). For Langer, music symbolizes *concepts* of feelings rather than the feelings themselves; that is, a particular musical passage, in her view, would not so much evoke emotions in listeners as present iconic concepts of the emotions in musical form. Unlike Langer, I focus on the reactions of listeners to music and argue that such responses as *ṭarab* present conceptions of emotions, but that the music itself does not present them; in fact, the music may have little to do with the emotional states that audiences claim to experience when listening to it.
14. According to Feld (1994a: 86–87), these include locational, categorical, associational, reflective, and evaluative "moves."
15. For explanations of the concept of the *ʿāshiq* (*ʿāsheq*) in Turkish and Persian musical cultures, see Erdener (1995) and Blum (1972).
16. In Crapanzano's terminology, the aesthetic conventions operate as a "Third" or "guarantor of meaning" in the triadic relationship of self, convention, and other (Crapanzano 1992: 72, 88–90).
17. In the context of Islamic jurisprudence, innovation or *bidʿa* may be viewed as an acceptable novelty or as heretical, depending on the school of thought (*Shorter Encyclopedia of Islam* (SEI) 1995: 62). Conservative theologians distinguish between

ittibāʿ, following—in other words, the *sunna*—and *ibtidāʿ*, unlawful innovation. However, few Aleppine musicians made a connection between musical or artistic innovation (*ibdāʿ*) and religious heresy (*bidʿa*) although the words derive from the same linguistic root.

18. Similarly, students of Persian music must master the *radīf*, a body of compositional materials and a type of musical "canon" from which they draw in improvisation (Nettl 1998), and jazz musicians master a large repertoire of songs and song forms that they use in the course of improvisation (Berliner 1994; Monson 1996). However, as Nettl suggests (1998: 16), we need to beware of making inferences about the similarities between diverse musical cultures (Arab, Persian, Indian, European, etc.) based on the use of the same word, "improvisation," to describe what might in fact be very different processes of musical composition in performance (see Blum 1998).
19. Artists sometimes refer to this practice in the plural, *taqāsīm*, but many of my teachers would also use the singular *taqsīm* or *taqsīma* to refer to one act of improvisation or to the genre of instrumental improvisation.
20. These terms are not standard or universally utilized in Aleppo. I use them as convenient heuristic devices for the purpose of discussing the structure and process of instrumental improvisation. Vocal improvisations such as the *mawwāl*, *qaṣīda*, and *layālī* follow similar patterns as the *taqsīm*, though no one in Aleppo refers to the vocal practices as forms of *taqsīm*, which is reserved for instrumental practice. Short solos on percussion instruments are common in contemporary practice, but I never heard anyone refer to them as *taqāsīm*.
21. Yet, even in a non-metrical *taqsīm*, a performer will establish a variety of internal tempos and rhythms.
22. While Zuckerkandl writes that the music itself "enlists the flux of time" for its own ends, I focus on the various strategies of performers to alter the experience of time to suit *their* goals, often the arousal of *ṭarab*.
23. Barthes also relates this to Lacan's notion of the *tuché*, an experience that transcends the ordinary and links the individual with the self and with history (Lacan 1977: 53–66).
24. Similarly, Langer (1953: 125) analyzes the production of artistic meaning as a result of the production in performance of a sense of "virtual time" distinct from "practical time." See Racy (2003: 201).
25. See Crapanzano (2003) for an elaboration of the idea of *arrière pays* or "imaginative horizon."
26. For more information on the concept of the *barzakh* in Sufi thought, see Chittick (1998, 1989); Corbin (1997); and Pandolfo (1997).
27. Kierkegaard writes, "when reality and ideality touch one another, repetition occurs" (Kierkegaard 1983: 186). The *qafla* in this sense marks the conclusion of a "touching" of the ideality of the melodic potential of the *maqām* and the reality of its actualization in performance.
28. *Nahj al-aghānī* (al-Qalaʿah 1997b) goes to some lengths to "prove" that Arab music is indeed expressive. His examples of musical *taʿbīr* come from the 1950s and 1960s,

such as the songs of ʿAbd al-Ḥalīm Ḥāfiẓ and Fairuz—precisely the period in which arguments against *ṭarab* were gaining popularity and well after expression became an important term of debate in musical circles.

29. See the composition entitled "Tarkīb Jadīd" [New Configuration] on his recent recording (Dalāl 2002).

7. Notes Toward Closure (pp. 188–199)

1. The honorific *ḥājj* (pl. *ḥujāj*, fem. *ḥājja*) refers to a someone who has completed the pilgrimage or *ḥajj* to Mecca, which is one of the "pillars" of Islam.
2. For a detailed biography of Moudallal and analysis and notation of his works, see Dalal (2005).
3. Luʾay Kayālī was a contemporary of Moudarres, with whom he represented Syria at the 1962 Venice Biennale. Kayālī specialized in portraiture, especially of the women of Syria's bourgeoisie. Although his canvases are influenced by styles of European portraiture, they capture sentiments that a number of viewers and collectors described to me as essentially Eastern or *sharqī*. Moudarres was influenced strongly by European modernism and his "expressionist" (*taʿbīriyya*) and "abstract expressionist" (*tajrīdiyya–taʿbīriyya;* the terms are used by Syrian critics) canvases are considered by critics to be authentically Syrian.
4. Sabah Fakhri suggested banning pop music in a conference on "The Role of the Arab Arts in the Present Condition" (*dawr al-fann al-ʿarabī ḥiyyāl al-waḍʿ al-rāhin*), held in Damascus in June 1997. Although no one seconded his recommendation, a large number of participants at the conference expressed their outrage at the contemporary popular song as if it alone were responsible for (and not only a product of) a perceived cultural decline across the Arab lands.
5. The phrase *shāman wa yamanan* means "northward and southward," with Syria (*al-shām*) at the northern and Yemen (*al-yaman*) at the southern extreme of the Arabian Peninsula.
6. In other contexts, it should be noted, my tape recorder played the role of mediator and often was addressed in the second person in interviews. People would ask it (rhetorically, of course), "Are you listening?" "Did you get that?" And, of course, such questions were also meta-commentaries on the process and context of my research addressed as much to me as to the recorder.
7. See Rugh (1997) for an exploration of the dynamics of Syrian family life and a comparison with aspects of American family life.

GLOSSARY OF SELECTED ARABIC TERMS

adhān Muslim call to prayer.

ʿaqd, ʿiqd (pl. *ʿuqūd*) Three-, four-, or five-note constituent unit of a *maqām* (melodic mode).

aṣāla Authenticity, rootedness; purity of descent.

aṣīl Authentic, pure.

aṣl (pl. *uṣūl*) Origin, root; lineage.

asmāʾ allāh al-ḥusnāʾ The Most Beautiful Names of God (also called the Ninety-Nine Names of God).

baqāʾ Remainder (of the higher soul in Sufi exegesis of the *dhikr*).

bashraf (pl. *bashārif*) Compositional form of Persian origin popular in Ottoman and Arab music but seldom performed in contemporary Syria.

basṭ Enjoyment, amusement.

daff (pl. *dufūf*) Small frame drum played with the hands.

dawr (pl. *adwār*) Complex, multi-part vocal form developed in Egypt in the nineteenth century and popular in Syria.

dhākir (pl. *dhākirūn*) Participant in the *dhikr* ritual.

dhākira Memory.

dhikr (pl. *adhkār*) Ritual invocation and remembrance of God.

dhikrā Remembrance, commemoration.

dhawq Taste, sensitivity, urbanity.

dūlāb (pl. *dawālīb*) Short instrumental piece that introduces vocal pieces, *taqasīm*, and modulations to another *maqām* in the performance of a *waṣla*.

fanāʾ Obliteration [of the lower soul in Sufi exegesis of the *dhikr*].

fann (pl. *funūn*) Art.

fannān Artist.

ghināʾ Song.

ḥadātha Modernity, newness.

ḥadīth New; prophetic tradition in Islam.

ḥafla (pl. *ḥaflāt*) Large concert (lit. "party").

ḥājj (pl. *ḥujjāj*) Honorific title of one who has made the pilgrimage (*hajj*) to Mecca.

ḥilū "Sweet," aesthetically pleasing.

inshād Varieties of religious song.

intiqāl Modulation from one *maqām* to another.

īqāʿ (pl. *īqāʿāt*) Meter.

irtijāl Improvisation, although this term is not used in medieval Arabic texts; see *taqsīm.*

jamāl Beauty.

jamāliyyāt Aesthetics (also *ʿilm al-jamāl*).

jināḥ (pl. *ajniḥa*) "Wing" or supporting *munshid* at a *dhikr.*

jins (pl. *ajnās*) Constituent melodic unit of a *maqām,* sometimes called a tetrachord.

kalimāt, kalām Lyrics.

kartah Gradual increase in the tempo of *inshād* in the *dhikr.*

kayf A state of pleasure, delight, and high spirits.

khayāl Imagination.

kull shī faranjī baranjī "Everything from the West is best." An expression of *tafarnuj.*

laḥn Melody.

layālī Solo singing of variations of the words *yā layl, yā ʿayn* (O night, O eye) to an improvised melody.

maqām (pl. *maqāmāt*) Musical mode based on a seven-note (heptatonic) scale; also, tomb of a Sufi "saint" (*wālī*).

maṭlaʿ (pl. *maṭāliʿ*) Opening, beginning; opening movement of a *taqsīm* or musical composition.

mawwāl (pl. *mawāwīl, mawāliyā*) Solo singing of colloquial poetry to an improvised melody that usually follows the *layālī.*

mihna (pl. *mihan*) Craft.

muftī Leading Islamic authority in a city or country.

mulaḥḥin Composer.

munshid (pl. *munshidūn, -īn;* fem. *munshida,* pl. *munshidāt*) Religious singer.

mūsīqā "Music," (Greek *mousiké*); refers in the modern period to instrumental music.

muthaqqaf "Cultured person," intellectual.

muṭrib (*muṭribūn, -īn;* fem. *muṭriba, pl. muṭribāt*) Vocalist.

muwashshaḥ (pl. *muwashshaḥāt*) Of probable Andalusian origin, the *muwashshaḥ* consists of classical Arabic poetry set to music and forms the staple of the Aleppine *waṣla.*

nafs (pl. *anfus*) Soul, self.

nāy (pl. *nayyāt*) Reed end-blown flute.

qafla (pl. *qaflāt*) Closing section or music phrase in instrumental and vocal improvisations and pre-composed genres.

qānūn (pl. *qawānīn*) Trapezoidal lap zither or psaltery.

qaṣīda (pl. *qaṣā'id*) Solo singing of classical Arabic poetry to an improvised melody.

qudūd ḥalabiyya (sing. *qadd halabī*) Light songs in the Aleppine and other colloquial Arabic dialects that are performed at the conclusion of the *waṣla*.

rayyis Lead *munshid* at a *dhikr*.

riqq (pl. *riqqāt, ruqūq*) Small tambourine.

rūḥ (pl. *arwāḥ*) Soul, spirit.

rūḥ sharqiyya "Oriental spirit," "Eastern Soul" (Racy 2003).

sahra (pl. *saharāt*) Small, intimate evenings of music, conversation, and food.

samāʿ Listening, audition; music and dance in Sufi exegesis.

samāʿī (pl. *samāʿiyyāt*) Instrumental introduction to the *waṣla*.

sammīʿ (pl. *sammīʿa*) Cultivated and skilled listeners.

samna (*samn*) Clarified butter, ghee.

ṣawt (pl. *aṣwāt*) Voice.

shahāda Muslim proclamation of faith.

al-shām Syria, the Levant; Damascus.

shaykh al-zāwiya The main sheikh of a *zāwiya* and leader of the *dhikr*.

ṣidq Emotional sincerity, honesty, truthfulness.

ta'ammul Meditation; meditative style of instrumental improvisational practice.

ṭabla (pl. *ṭablāt*) Goblet-shaped drum.

tadhawwuq Taste, appreciation, enjoyment.

tafarnuj Westernization, or the emulation of Westerness.

tajallī Manifestation, revelation, and a state of transcendence.

taqsīm (pl. *taqāsīm*) Instrumental improvisation.

ṭaqṭuqa (pl. *ṭaqāṭīq*) Variety of light song that arose in Egypt at the turn of the twentieth century and was also performed in Syria at this time.

ṭarab A state of musical rapture or ecstasy.

tarqiyya Gradual rise in the tonic pitch of *inshād* in the *dhikr*.

taṣwīr al-maʿnā "Depiction of the meaning," a vocalist's skill in interpreting the meaning of song lyrics.

ʿūd (*aʿwād, ʿīdān*) Oud; short-necked, fretless Arabian plucked lute having five or six courses of strings.

ughniya (pl. *aghānī*) Variety of light and popular song.

waṣla (pl. *waṣlāt*) Musical suite in Syria composed of an instrumental introduction followed by *muwashshaḥāt, qaṣīda, taqāsīm, layālī, mawwāl, dawr,* and *qudūd ḥalabiyya* sometimes referred to as fāṣil.

zāwiya (pl. *zawāyā*) A small mosque or section of a mosque where *dhikr* is performed.

For other musical terms, see the glossary in Touma (1996). For explanation of Islamic terms, see *The Shorter Encyclopedia of Islam* (1995).

SELECTED BIBLIOGRAPHY AND DISCOGRAPHY

Books and Periodicals

ʿAbd-Allah, Umar F. 1983. *The Islamic Struggle in Syria.* Berkeley: Mizan.

Abrams, M. H. 1953. *The Mirror and the Lamp: Romantic Theory and the Critical Tradition.* Oxford: Oxford University Press.

Abu-Lughod, Janet. 1989. *Before European Hegemony: The World System AD 1250–1350.* New York: Oxford University Press.

Abu-Lughod, Lila. 2004. *Dramas of Nationhood: The Politics of Television in Egypt.* Chicago: University of Chicago Press.

———. 2000. "Modern Subjects: Egyptian Melodrama and Postcolonial Difference." In *Questions of Modernity,* ed. Timothy Mitchell, pp. 87–114. Minneapolis: University of Minnesota Press.

———. 1998. *Remaking Women: Feminism and Modernity in the Middle East.* Princeton: Princeton University Press.

———. 1993. *Writing Women's Worlds: Bedouin Stories.* Berkeley: University of California Press.

———. 1986. *Veiled Sentiments: Honor and Poetry in a Bedouin Society.* Berkeley: University of California Press.

Abu-Rabiʿ, Ibrahim. 1996. *Intellectual Origins of Islamic Resurgence in the Modern Arab World.* Albany: State University of New York Press.

Abū al-Shāmāt, ʿAdnān. 1997. *al-Minhāj al-shāmil li-dirāsāt al-mūsiqā wa-l ghināʾ* [Comprehensive course for studying the music and song]. Damascus: Syrian Artists Syndicate.

Adonis (ʿAlī Aḥmad Saʿīd). 1994. "Elegy for the Time at Hand." In *The Pages of Day and Night,* trans. Samuel Hazo, p. 44: lines 17–29.Evanston, Ill.: Marlboro/Northwestern University Press.

———. 1992 [1985]. *An Introduction to Arab Poetics.* Catherine Cobham, trans. Cairo: The American University in Cairo Press.

———. 1986. *al-Thabit wa-l mutahawwil: Bahth fi-l ittibaʿ wa-l ibdaʿ ʿind al-ʿarab* [The Constant and the changing: Research into following and innovation among the Arabs]. Beirut: Dar al-Fikr.

Adorno, Theodor. 1997. *Aesthetic Theory*. G. Adorno and R. T. Tiedemann, eds., R. Hullot-Kentor, trans. *Theory and History of Literature*, vol. 88. Minneapolis: University of Minnesota Press.

———. 1976. *Introduction to the Sociology of Music*. New York: Continuum.

———. 1973. *The Jargon of Authenticity*. Evanston, Ill.: Northwestern University Press.

al-ʿAjjān, Maḥmūd. 1990. *Turāthunā al-mūsīqī* [Our musical heritage]. Damascus: Tallās l-l dirāsāt wa-l tarjama wa-l nashr.

Amin, Samīr. 1974. *Accumulation on a World Scale: A Critique of the Theory of Underdevelopment*. Brian Pearce, trans. New York: Monthly Review Press.

Anderson, Benedict. 1991. *Imagined Communities: Reflections on the Origin and Spread of Nationalism*, 2nd ed. London: Verso.

Apel, Willi. 1944. *Harvard Dictionary of Music*. Cambridge, Mass.: Harvard University Press.

Appadurai, Arjun. 1996. *Modernity at Large: Cultural Dimensions of Globalization*. Minneapolis: University of Minnesota Press.

———. 1990. "Disjuncture and Difference in the Global Cultural Economy." *Public Culture* 2(2): 1–24.

al-ʿAqīlī, Majdī. 1979. *al-Samāʿ ʿind al-ʿarab* [Listening among the Arabs]. 5 vols. Damascus, Syria.

Aristotle. 1962. *The Nicomachean Ethics*. trans. Martin Oswald. Indianapolis: Bobbs-Merrill/Library of Liberal Arts.

Armbrust, Walter, ed. 2000. *Mass Mediations: New Approaches to Popular Culture in the Middle East and Beyond*. Berkeley: University of California Press.

———. 1996. *Mass Culture and Modernism in Egypt*. Cambridge: Cambridge University Press.

Armstrong, Robert Plant. 1981. *The Power of Presence: Consciousness, Myth, and Affecting Presence*. Philadelphia: University of Pennsylvania Press.

———. 1971. *The Affecting Presence: An Essay in Humanistic Anthropology*. Urbana: University of Illinois Press.

Arnold, Matthew. 1994 [1869]. *Culture and Anarchy*. Samuel Lipman, ed. New Haven: Yale University Press.

Asad, Talal. 2003. *Formations of the Secular: Christianity, Islam, Modernity*. Stanford: Stanford University Press.

———. 1993. *Genealogies of Religion: Discipline and Reasons of Power in Christianity and Islam*. Baltimore: Johns Hopkins University Press.

Askew, Kelly M. 2002. *Performing the Nation: Swahili Music and Cultural Politics in Tanzania*. Chicago: University of Chicago Press.

Attali, Jacques. 1985 [1977]. *Noise: The Political Economy of Music*. Brian Massumi, trans. Minneapolis: University of Minnesota Press.

al-ʿAẓm, Ṣādiq Jalāl. 2000. "Owning the Future: Modern Arabs and Hamlet." *International Institute for the Study of Islam in the Modern World Newsletter* 5: 11.

———. 1969. *Naqd al-fikr al-dīnī* [Critique of religious thought]. Beirut: Dar al-Talīʿa.

———. 1968. *al-Naqd al-dhātī ba'd al-hazīma* [Self-criticism after the defeat]. Beirut: Dar al-Tali'a.
al-'Azmeh, 'Azīz. 1993. *Islams and Modernities*. London: Verso.
———. 1992. *al-Aṣāla aw siyāsat al-hurūb min al-wāqi'* [Authenticity or the politics of the flight from reality]. Beirut and London: Dar al-Saqi.
Bakhtin, Mikhail M. 1984. *Rabelais and His World*. Trans. Hélène Iswolsky. Bloomington: Indiana University Press.
———. 1981. *The Dialogic Imagination: Four Essays*. Michael Holquist, ed. Caryl Emerson and Michael Holquist, trans. Austin: University of Texas.
Baldick, Julian. 1989. *Mystical Islam*. New York: New York University Press.
Barakat, Halim. 1993. *The Arab World: Society, Culture, and State*. Berkeley and Los Angeles: University of California Press.
Barqāwī, Aḥmad. 1999. "*īdiyūlūjiyyat al-ḥadātha al-'arabiyya al-rāhina wa naqduhā*" [The Ideology of contemporary Arab modernity and its critique]. *al-Adab* 47 (1–2): 55.
Barthes, Roland. 1980. *La Chambre claire* [Camera lucida]. Paris: Gallimard.
Bateson, Gregory. 1972. *Steps to an Ecology of Mind*. New York: Ballantine.
Battaglia, Debbora, ed. 1995. *Rhetorics of Self-Making*. Berkeley: University of California Press.
Bauman, Richard. 1992. "Performance." In *Folklore, Cultural Performances, and Popular Entertainments: A Communications-Centered Handbook*, ed. Richard Bauman, pp. 41–49. New York and Oxford: Oxford University Press.
———. 1986. *Story, Performance, and Event: Contextual Studies of Oral Narrative*. Cambridge: Cambridge University Press.
———. 1977. *Verbal Art as Performance*. Prospect Heights, Ill.: Waveland Press.
Bauman, Richard, and Charles L. Briggs. 1990. "Poetics and Performance as Critical Perspectives on Language and Social Life." *Annual Review of Anthropology* 19: 59–88.
Becker, Howard. 1982. *Art Worlds*. Berkeley: University of California Press.
Behrens-Abouseif, Doris. 1999. *Beauty in Arabic Culture*. Princeton: Markus Wiener.
Bell, Catherine. 1997. *Ritual: Perspectives and Dimensions*. New York and Oxford: Oxford University Press.
———. 1992. *Ritual Theory, Ritual Practice*. New York and Oxford: Oxford University Press.
Belleface, Jean-Francois. 1992. "La Syrie, Complice Ou Comparse? (Quelques Notes Pour un Silence)." In *Musique Arabe. Le congrès du Caire de 1932*, ed. Sheherazade Qassim Hassan and Phillipe Vigreux, pp. 147–59. Cairo: CEDEJ.
Bennett, Marjorie Anne. 1999. "Reincarnation, Marriage, and Memory: Negotiating Sectarian Identity Among the Druze of Syria." Ph.D. dissertation, The University of Arizona.
Berliner, Paul F. 1994. *Thinking in Jazz: The Infinite Art of Improvisation*. Chicago: University of Chicago Press.
Berman, Marshall. 1982. *All That Is Solid Melts into Air: The Experience of Modernity*. New York: Penguin Books.

Berque, Jacques. 1974. *Cultural Expression in Arab Society Today*. Austin: University of Texas Press.

Bhabha, Homi K. 1994. *The Location of Culture*. London and New York: Routledge.

Bigenho, Michelle. 2002. *Sounding Indigenous: Authenticity in Bolivian Music Performance*. New York: Palgrave.

Bin Dhurayl, ʿAdnan. 1989. *al-Mūsīqā fī suriyya: al-Baḥth al-mūsīqī wa-l funūn al-mūsīqiyya*, 1887–1987 [Music in Syria: Musical research and the musical arts, 1887–1987]. Damascus: Dar Talass.

Blecher, Robert Ian. 2002. "The Medicalization of Sovereignty: Medicine, Public Health, and Political Authority in Syria, 1861–1936." Ph.D. dissertation, Stanford University.

Blum, Stephen. 1998. "Recognizing Improvisation." In *In the Course of Performance: Studies in the World of Improvisation*, ed. Bruno Nettl, with Melinda Russell, pp. 27–45. Chicago: University of Chicago Press.

———. 1990. "Commentary." *Ethnomusicology* 34 (3): 413–21.

———. 1972. "The Concept of the *ʿAsheq* in Northern Khorasan." *Asian Music* 4 (1): 27–47.

Bonebakker, S. A. 1988. "*Adab* and the Concept of *Belles-Lettres*." In *ʿAbbasid Belles-Lettres*. Cambridge History of Arabic Literature, ed. Julia Ashtiany et al., pp. 16–30. Cambridge: Cambridge University Press.

Bonnefoy, Yves. 1972. *L'Arrière-pays: Les sentiers de la création*. Geneva: Skira.

Boullata, Kamal. 1991. "La Pensée visuelle et la memoire semantique Arabe." *Peuples Méditerranéens*–*Mediterranean Peoples* 54–55: 93–110.

Bourdieu, Pierre. 1984. *Distinction: A Social Critique of the Judgment of Taste*. Chicago: University of Chicago Press.

———. 1977. *Outline of a Theory of Practice*. Richard Nice, trans. Cambridge: Cambridge University Press.

Burke, Edmund III. 1973. "A Comparative View of French Native Policy in Morocco and Syria, 1912–1925." *Middle Eastern Studies* 9 (2): 175–86.

Calhoun, Craig. 1993. "Habitus, Field, and Capital: The Question of Historical Specificity." In *Bourdieu: Critical Perspectives*, ed. Craig Calhoun, Edward LiPuma, and Moishe Postone, pp. 61–89. Chicago: University of Chicago Press.

Canclini, Néstor García. 1995. *Hybrid Cultures: Strategies for Entering and Leaving Modernity*. Christopher L. Chiappari and Silvia L. Lopez, trans. Minneapolis: University of Minnesota Press.

Casey, Edward. 2000. *Remembering, a Phenomenological Study*. 2nd ed. Bloomington: Indiana University Press.

Chakrabarty, Dipesh. 2001. "*Adda*, Calcutta: Dwelling in Modernity." In *Alternative Modernities*, ed. Dilip Parameshwar Gaonkar, pp. 123–64. Durham, N.C.: Duke University Press.

———. 2000. *Provincializing Europe: Postcolonial Thought and Historical Difference*. Princeton: Princeton University Press.

Chatterjee, Partha. 1993. *The Nation and Its Fragments: Colonial and Postcolonial Histories*. Princeton: Princeton University Press.

Chernoff, John M. 1979. *African Rhythm and African Sensibility: Aesthetics and Social Action in African Musical Idioms*. Chicago: University of Chicago Press.

Chittick, William C. 1998. *The Self-Disclosure of God: Principles of Ibn al-ʿArabī's Cosmology*. Albany: State University of New York Press.

———. 1989. *The Sufi Path of Knowledge: Ibn al-ʿArabī's Metaphysics of Imagination*. Albany: State University of New York Press.

Chodkiewicz, M. 1986. *Le Sceau des saints, prophétie et sainteté dans la doctrine d'Ibn Arabi*. Paris: Gallimard.

Clifford, James. 1988. *The Predicament of Culture*. Cambridge, Mass.: Harvard University Press.

Collelo, Thomas, ed. 1988. *Syria: A Country Study*. Washington, D.C.: Federal Research Division, Library of Congress.

Comaroff, Jean, and John L. Comaroff, eds. 1993. *Modernity and its Malcontents: Ritual and Power in Postcolonial Africa*. Chicago: University of Chicago Press.

Corbin, Henry. 1997 [1969]. *Alone with the Alone*. Bollingen Series XCI. Princeton: Princeton University Press.

Coronil, Fernando. 1997. *The Magical State: Nature, Money, and Modernity in Venezuela*. Chicago: University of Chicago Press.

Crapanzano, Vincent. 2003. *Imaginative Horizons: An Essay in Literary-Philosophical Anthropology*. Chicago: University of Chicago Press.

———. 2000. *Serving the Word: Literalism in America from the Pulpit to the Bench*. New York: The New Press.

———. 1992. *Hermes' Dilemma and Hamlet's Desire: On the Epistemology of Interpretation*. Cambridge, Mass.: Harvard University Press.

———. 1980. *Tuhami: Portrait of a Moroccan*. Chicago: University of Chicago Press.

———. 1973. *The Hamadsha: A Study in Moroccan Ethnopsychiatry*. Berkeley: University of California.

Csordas, Thomas, ed. 1994. *Embodiment and Experience: The Existential Ground of Culture and Self*. Cambridge: Cambridge University Press.

Cunningham, Robert B., and Yasin K. Sarayrah. 1993. *Wasta: The Hidden Force in Middle Eastern Society*. Westport, CT: Praeger.

Dalāl, Muḥammad Qadrī. 2005. *Shaykh al-Muṭribīn: Sabri Moudallal and the Influence of Aleppo in his Song and Compositions*. An Analytical and Musical Study of Aleppine Vocal Heritage. Damascus, Syria: Syrian Ministry of Culture.

———. n.d. "*Dirāsa wa taḥlīl al-inshād al-dīnī fi madīnat ḥalab suriyya*" [A study and analysis of religious song in the city of Aleppo, Syria]. Paper presented at the second annual Conference on Arab Music, Cairo, Egypt, November 1993.

Danielson, Virginia. 1999. "Moving into Public Space: Women and Music in 20th-Century Egypt." In *Hermeneutics and Honor: Negotiating Female "Public" Space in Islamic/ate Societies*, ed. Asma Afsaruddin. Cambridge, Mass.: Harvard University Press.

———. 1997. *The Voice of Egypt: Umm Kulthūm, Arabic Song, and Egyptian Society in the Twentieth Century*. Chicago: University of Chicago Press.

——. 1996. "New Nightingales of the Nile: Popular Music in Egypt since the 1970s." *Popular Music* 15 (3): 299–312

——. 1991. "Artists and Entrepreneurs: Female Singers in Cairo during the 1920s." In *Women in Middle Eastern History,* ed. N. Keddie and Beth Baron. New Haven: Yale University Press.

——. 1990/1991. "*Min al-Mashayikh:* A View of Egyptian Music Tradition." *Asian Music* 22 (1): 113–28

Danto, Arthur C. 1964. "The Artworld." *Journal of Philosophy* 61: 571–84.

al-Darwīsh, Nadīm. n.d. "*al-Qawālib al-ghinā' iyya wa al-mūsīqiyya fī al-mūsīqā al-sharqiyya*" [The vocal and instrumental genres in oriental music]. Interview on Syrian television. Video.

Davies, Stephen. 1994. *Musical Meaning and Expression.* Ithaca: Cornell University Press.

Derrida, Jacques. 1981. *Dissemination.* Barbara Johnson, trans. Chicago: University of Chicago Press.

——. 1978. *Writing and Difference.* Alan Bass, trans. Chicago: University of Chicago Press.

DeYoung, Terri. 1998. *Placing the Poet: Badr Shakir al-Sayyab and Postcolonial Iraq.* Albany: State University of New York Press.

Dickie, George. 1997. *Introduction to Aesthetics: An Analytic Approach.* New York and Oxford: Oxford University Press.

Doerre, Sharon L. 2004. "Children of the Zawiya: Narratives of Faith, Family, and Transformation among Sufi Communities in Modern Damascus." Ph.D. dissertation, University of Texas at Austin.

During, Jean. 1997. "Hearing and Understanding in Islamic Gnosis." *The World of Music* 39 (2): 127–37.

——. 1994. *Quelque chose se passe: le sens de la tradition dans l'Orient musical.* Lagrasse: Verdier.

Dutton, Denis. 1994. "Kant and the Conditions of Artistic Beauty." *British Journal of Aesthetics* 34 (3): 226–41.

Eagleton, Terry. 1990. *The Ideology of the Aesthetic.* Cambridge: Basil Blackwell.

Eickelman, Dale F. 1976. *Moroccan Islam: Tradition and Society in a Pilgrimage Center.* Austin: University of Texas Press.

Eliade, Mircea. 1959. *The Sacred and the Profane.* New York: Harcourt.

El-Shawan, Salwa. n.d. "al-Qadīm and al-Gadīd in al-Mūsīkā al-ʿArabiyya in Egypt." Lecture presented at the American Research Center in Egypt. Cairo, Egypt, October 1996.

——. 1980. "al-Mūsīkā al-ʿArabiyyah: A Category of Urban Music in Cairo, Egypt, 1927–1977." Ph.D. dissertation, Columbia University.

Elsner, Jurgen. 1997. "Listening to Arabic Music." *The World of Music* 39 (2): 111–26.

Erdener, Yildiray. 1995. *The Song Contests of Turkish Minstrels.* Milman Parry Collection of Oral Literature Series, Harvard University. New York: Garland Publishing.

d'Érlanger, Rodolfe. 1930–1959. *La musique arabe,* 6 vols. Paris: Paul Geuthner.

Erlmann, Veit, ed. 2004. *Hearing Cultures: Essays on Sound, Listening, and Modernity.* New York: Berg.

——. 1996. *Nightsong: Performance, Power, and Practice in South Africa.* Chicago: University of Chicago Press.

Escobar, Arturo. 1995. *Encountering Development: The Making and Unmaking of the Third World.* Princeton: Princeton University Press.

Fabian, Johannes. 1983. *Time and the Other: How Anthropology Makes Its Object.* New York: Columbia University Press.

Farmer, Henry George. 1929. *A History of Arabian Music to the Thirteenth Century.* London: Luzac & Co.

Faroqhi, Suraiya. 1987. "The Venetian Presence in the Ottoman Empire, 1600–1630." In *The Ottoman Empire and the World Economy,* ed. Huri Islamoglu-Inan, pp. 311–44. Cambridge: Cambridge University Press.

al-Faruqi, Lois Ibsen. 1985/1986. "Music, Musicians and Muslim Law." *Asian Music* 17 (1): 3–35.

——. 1978. "Ornamentation in Arabian Improvisational Music: A Study of Interrelatedness in the Arts." *The World of Music* 1 (1): 17–28.

——. 1975. "Muwashshah: A Vocal Form in Islamic Culture." *Ethnomusicology* 19 (1): 1–29.

Feld, Steven. 1996. "Waterfalls of Sound: An Acoustemology of Place Resounding in Bosavi, Papua New Guinea. In *Senses of Place,* ed. Steven Feld and Keith Basso, pp. 91–136. Santa Fe, N.M.: School of American Research.

——. 1994a [1984]. "Communication, Music, and Speech About Music." In *Music Grooves.* ed. Charles Keil and Steven Feld, pp. 77–95. Chicago: University of Chicago Press.

——. 1994b [1988]. "Aesthetics as Iconicity of Style (Uptown Title); or (Downtown Title), 'Lift-Up-Over Sounding': Getting into the Kaluli Groove." In *Music Grooves,* ed. Charles Keil and Steven Feld, pp. 109–50. Chicago: University of Chicago Press.

——. 1990 *Sound and Sentiment: Birds, Weeping, Poetics, and Song in Kaluli Expression.* Philadelphia: University of Pennsylvania Press.

Feldman, Walter. 1996. *Music of the Ottoman Court. Makam, Composition and the Early Ottoman Instrumental Repertoire.* Berlin: VWB-Verlag für Wissenschaft und Bildung.

——. 1993. "Ottoman Sources on the Development of the Taksim." *Yearbook for Traditional Music* 25: 1–28.

Fernea, Elizabeth Warnock. 1998. *In Search of Islamic Feminism: One Woman's Global Journey.* New York: Doubleday.

Fernea, Elizabeth Warnock, and Basima Qattan Bezirgan, eds. 1977. *Middle Eastern Muslim Women Speak.* Austin: University of Texas Press.

Frank, Andre Gunder. 1998. *ReOrient: Global Economy in the Asian Age.* Berkeley: University of California Press.

——. 1969. *Capitalism and Underdevelopment in Latin America.* New York: Monthly Review Press.

Frishkopf, Michael A. 2004. "Arab Music across Boundaries." Presentation, Annual Meeting of the Society for Ethnomusicology, Tucson, Arizona, November 7, 2004.

——. 2003. "Some Meanings of the Spanish Tinge in Contemporary Egyptian Music." In *Mediterranean Mosaic: Popular Music and Global Sounds,* ed. Goffredo Plastino, pp. 143–78. New York: Routledge.

——. 1999. "Sufism, Ritual, and Modernity in Egypt: Language Performance as an Adaptive Strategy." Ph.D. dissertation, University of California at Los Angeles.

Gaonkar, Dilp Parameshwar, ed. 2001. *Alternative Modernities*. Durham, N.C.: Duke University Press.

——. 1999. "On Alternative Modernities." *Public Culture* 11 (1): 1–18.

García Lorca, Federico. 1998. *In Search of Duende*. Christopher Maurer, trans. New York: New Directions.

Geertz, Clifford. 1973 [1966]. "Religion as a Cultural System." In *The Interpretation of Cultures*, pp. 87–126. New York: Basic Books.

——. 1968. *Islam Observed: Religious Development in Morocco and Indonesia*. Chicago: University of Chicago Press.

Geurts, Kathryn Linn. 2002. *Culture and the Senses Embodiment, Identity and Well-Being in an African Community*. Berkeley: University of California Press.

al-Ghazzālī, Abū Ḥamid Muḥammad b. Muḥammad [1058–1111]. 1991. "Concerning Music and Dancing as Aids to the Religious Life." In *The Alchemy of Happiness*, pp. 64–74. London: John Murray.

——. 1901–1902. "Emotional Religion in Islam as Affected by Music and Singing." Duncan Macdonald, trans. *Journal of the Royal Asiatic Society* 22: 195–252, 705–47; 23: 1–28.

Gholmieh, Walīd, and Tawfīq Kurbāj. 1996. *Nazariyyāt al-mūsīqā al-sharq ʿarabiyya* [Theories of Arab-Oriental music]. Beirut: The National Conservatory.

Ghuṣūb, Māī. 1992. *Ma baʿd al-ḥadātha: al-ʿArab fī laqtat fīdiū* [Postmodernism: The Arabs in a video clip]. Beirut: Al-Saqi.

Giddens, Anthony. 1991. *The Consequences of Modernity*. Stanford: Stanford University Press.

Gilsenan, Michael. 1982. *Recognizing Islam: Religion and Society in the Modern Arab World*. New York: Pantheon.

——. 1973. *Saint and Sufi in Modern Egypt: An Essay in the Sociology of Religion*. Oxford: Clarendon Press.

Goffman, Erving. 1959. *The Presentation of Self in Everyday Life*. Garden City: Doubleday.

Göle, Nilüfer. 2002. "Islam in Public: New Visibilities and New Imaginaries." *Public Culture* 14 (1): 173–90.

Greenblatt, Stephen. 1980. *Renaissance Self-Fashioning: From More to Shakespeare*. Chicago: University of Chicago Press.

Greenhouse, Carol J. 1996. *A Moment's Notice: Time Politics across Cultures*. Ithaca: Cornell University Press.

Guettat, Mahmoud. 2000. *La musique arabo-andalouse: l'empreinte du Maghreb*. Paris: Éditions El-Ouns.

Habermas, Jurgen. 1987. *The Philosophical Discourse of Modernity: Twelve Lectures*. Frederick Lawrence, trans. Cambridge, Mass.: MIT Press.

Harrison, Jane. 1912. *Themis: A Study of the Social Origins of Greek Religion*. Cambridge: Cambridge University Press.

Hassan, Sheherazade Qassim, and Phillipe Vigreux, eds. 1992. *Musique Arabe. Le congrès du Caire de* 1932. Cairo: CEDEJ.
Helmreich, Stephan. 2003. "Trees and Seas of Information: Alien Kinship and the Biopolitics of Gene Transfer in Marine Biology and Biotechnology." *American Ethnologist* 30 (3): 340–58.
Heydemann, Steve. 1999. *Authoritarianism in Syria : Institutions and Social Conflict, 1946–1970*. Ithaca: Cornell University Press.
al-Ḥilū, Salīm. 1961. *al-Mūsīqā al-nazzariyya* [Theoretical music]. Beirut: Dar Maktabat al-Hayat.
al-Ḥimsi, ʿUmar ʿAbd al-Raḥmān. 1994. *al-Mūsīqā al-ʿarabiyya: Tarīkhuhā ʿulūmuhā funūnuhā wa anwāʿuhā* [Arab music: Its history, science, art, and genres]. Damascus: al-Barq.
Hinnebusch, Raymond A. 2001. *Syria: Revolution from Above*. London: Routledge.
———. 1991. "Class and State in Baʿthist Syria." In *Syria: Society, Culture, and Polity*, ed. Richard T. Antoun and Donald Quataert, pp. 29–48. Albany: State University of New York Press.
Hirschkind, Charles. 2004. "Hearing Modernity: Egypt, Islam, and the Pious Ear." In *Hearing Cultures: Essays on Sound, Listening and Modernity*, ed. Veit Erlmann, pp. 131–52. New York: Berg.
———. 2001. "The Ethics of Listening: Cassette-Sermon Audition in Contemporary Cairo." *American Ethnologist* 28 (3): 623–49.
Holquist, Michael. 1990. *Dialogism: Bakhtin and His World*. New York and London: Routledge.
Hood, Kathleen. 2002. "Music and Memory in a Global Age: Wedding Songs of the Syrian Druzes." Ph.D. dissertation, University of California at Los Angeles.
l'Hopital, Jean-Yves. 1989. "Le desire fou de la passion nous enivre." *Bulletin d'Études Orientales* 39–40: 67–96.
Hourani, Albert. 1983 [1962]. *Arabic Thought in the Liberal Age, 1798–1939*. Cambridge: Cambridge University Press.
al-Ḥuṣāmī, Ratib. 1954. "*al-Aghānī al-rakhīṣa*" [The cheap songs]. *Majallat al-idhaʿa al-suriyya* 21: 1.
Husserl, Edmund. 1990 [1907]. *The Idea of Phenomenology*. Boston: Kluwer Academic.
Hymes, Dell. 1975. "Breakthrough into Performance." In *Folklore: Performance and Communication*, ed. Dan Ben-Amos and Kenneth S. Goldstein, 11–74. The Hague and Paris: Mouton.
Ibn Khaldūn, ʿAbd al-Raḥmān. 1967. *The Muqaddima: An Introduction to History*. Franz Rosenthal. trans. 3 vols. Princeton: Princeton University Press.
Inalçik, Halil. 1997. *An Economic and Social History of the Ottoman Empire, 1300–1914*. Cambridge: Cambridge University Press.
———. 1987. "When and How British Cotton Goods Invaded the Levant Markets." In *The Ottoman Empire and the World Economy*, ed. Huri Islamoglu-Inan, pp. 374–83. New York: Cambridge University Press.

al-Jabartī, ʿAbd al-Raḥmān. 1993. *Napoleon in Egypt: Al-Jabarti's Chronicle of the French Occupation, 1798.* Shmuel Moreh, trans. Princeton and New York: Markus Wiener.

al-Jābrī, Muḥammad ʿĀbid. 1999 [1994] *Arab-Islamic Philosophy: A Contemporary Critique.* Aziz Abbassi, trans. Austin: University of Texas Press.

———. 1991. *al-Turāth wa-l ḥadātha* [Heritage and modernity]. Beirut: Center for the Study of Arab Unity.

———. 1986. *Bunyat al-ʿaql al-ʿarabī* [The structure of the Arab mind]. Beirut: Center for the Study of Arab Unity.

———. 1984. *Takwīn al-ʿaql al ʿarabī* [The formation of the Arab mind]. Beirut: Center for the Study of Arab Unity.

Kandiyoti, Deniz. 1996. *Gendering the Middle East: Emerging Perspectives.* Syracuse: Syracuse University Press.

Kant, Immanuel. 1952 [1790]. *Critique of Judgment.* James Creed Meredith, trans. Oxford: Clarendon Press.

Kapchan, Deborah A. 1995. "Performance." *Journal of American Folklore* 108 (430): 479–508.

Keil, Charles. 1994a [1966]. "Motion and Feeling through Music." In *Music Grooves,* ed. Charles Keil and Steven Feld, pp. 53–76. Chicago: University of Chicago Press.

———. 1994b [1987]. "Participatory Discrepancies and the Power of Music." In *Music Grooves,* ed. Charles Keil and Steven Feld, pp. 96–108. Chicago: University of Chicago Press.

———. 1994c. "On Civilization, Cultural Studies, and Copyright." In *Music Grooves,* ed. Charles Keil and Steven Feld, pp. 227–31. Chicago: University of Chicago Press.

———. 1979. *Tiv Song.* Chicago: University of Chicago Press.

Khoury, Philip S. 1987. *Syria and the French Mandate: The Politics of Arab Nationalism, 1920–1945.* Princeton: Princeton University Press.

———. 1983. *Urban Notables and Arab Nationalism: The Politics of Damascus, 1860–1920.* Cambridge: Cambridge University Press.

al-Khulaʿī, Muḥammad Kāmil. 1993 [1904]. *Kitāb al-mūsīqā al-sharqī* [The book of oriental music]. Cairo: Dār al-ʿarabiyya lil-kitāb.

Kierkegaard, Soren. 1983 [1843]. *Fear and Trembling/Repetition.* Howard V. and Edna H. Hong, eds. and trans. Princeton: Princeton University Press.

Kirshenblatt-Gimblett, Barbara. 1998. *Destination Culture: Tourism, Museums, and Heritage.* Berkeley: University of California Press.

———. 1995. "Theorizing Heritage," *Ethnomusicology* 39 (3): 367–80.

Kitāb muʾtamar al-mūsīqā al-ʿarabiyya [The book of the Congress on Arab music] 1933. Cairo: al-Matbaʿa al-Amiriyya.

Kivy, Peter. 1989. *Sound Sentiment: An Essay on the Musical Emotions.* Philadelphia: Temple University Press.

Knauft, Bruce M., ed. 2002. *Critically Modern: Alternatives, Alterities, Anthropologies.* Bloomington: Indiana University Press.

Koran, The. 1990. N. J. Dawood, trans. London and New York: Penguin.

Koskoff, Ellen, ed. 1989. *Women and Music in Cross Cultural Perspective.* Urbana: University of Illinois Press.

Kühnel, Ernst. 1976 [1949]. *The Arabesque: Meaning and Transformation of an Ornament.* Graz: Verlag Fur Sammler.
Kuper, Adam. 1988. *The Invention of Primitive Society: Transformations of an Illusion.* London: Routledge.
Lacan, Jacques. 1991a. *The Seminar of Jacques Lacan. Book I: Freud's Papers on Technique 1953–1954.* Jacques-Alain Miller, ed. John Forrester, trans. New York and London: W. W. Norton & Co.
———. 1991b. *The Seminar of Jacques Lacan. Book II: The Ego in Freud's Theory and in the Technique of Psychoanalysis, 1954–1955.* Jacques-Alain Miller, ed. Sylvana Tomaselli, trans. New York and London: W. W. Norton and Co.
———. 1977 [1964]. *The Seminar. Book XI. The Four Fundamental Concepts of Psycho-analysis.* John Forrester, trans. London: Hogarth Press and the Institute of Psycho-analysis.
Lagrange, Frédéric. 1996. *Musiques d'Egypte.* Paris: Cité de la Musique/Actes Sud.
Lambert, Jean. 1997. *La médicine de l'ame: Le chant de Sanaa dans la société yéménite.* Nanterre: Société d'ethnologie.
Lane, Edward William. 1978 [1863] *Arabic-English Lexicon,* 8 vols. Lahore, Pakistan: Islamic Book Centre.
———. 1973 [1836]. *An Account of the Manners and Customs of the Modern Egyptians.* Stanley Lane Poole, ed. New York: Dover.
Langer, Suzanne. 1960 [1942]. *Philosophy in a New Key.* Cambridge, Mass.: Harvard University Press.
———. 1953. *Feeling and Form.* New York: Scribner.
Laroui, Abdallah. 1976. *The Crisis of the Arab Intellectual: Traditionalism or Historicism.* Diarmid Commel, trans. Berkeley: University of California Press.
Lawson, Fred. 1996. *Why Syria Goes to War.* Ithaca: Cornell University Press.
Lindisfarne, Nancy. 2000. *Dancing in Damascus.* Albany: State University of New York Press.
Lord, Albert B. 1965. *The Singer of Tales.* New York: Atheneum Press.
MacIntyre, Alasdair. 1984 [1981]. *After Virtue,* 2nd edition. Notre Dame, Ind.: Notre Dame University Press.
Magrini, Tulia, ed. 2003. *Music and Gender: Perspectives from the Mediterranean.* Chicago: University of Chicago Press.
Mahannā, Nūr. 1998. *Ahl al-ṭarab fi ḥalab wa bilād al-ʿarab* [The followers of tarab in Aleppo and the Arab lands]. Aleppo: Dar Sahara.
al-Mahdī, Sālaḥ. 1993. *al-mūsīqā al-ʿarabiyya.* Beirut: Dār al-gharb al-islāmī.
Mahmood, Saba. 2004. *Politics of Piety: The Islamic Revival and the Feminist Subject.* Princeton: Princeton University Press.
———. 2001. "Feminist Theory, Embodiment, and the Docile Agent: Some Reflections on the Egyptian Islamic Revival." *Cultural Anthropology* 16 (2).
Manuel, Peter. 1993. *Cassette Culture: Popular Music and Technology in North India.* Chicago: University of Chicago Press.
Marcus, Abraham. 1989. *The Middle East on the Eve of Modernity: Aleppo in the Eighteenth Century.* New York: Columbia University Press.

Marcus, George E., and Fred R. Myers. 1995. "The Traffic in Art and Culture: An Introduction." In *The Traffic in Culture: Refiguring Art and Anthropology,* ed. George E. Marcus and Fred R. Myers, pp. 1–54. Berkeley: University of California Press.

Marcus, Scott. 1993. "Solo Instrumental Improvisation (*Taqāsīm*) in Arab Music." *Middle Eastern Studies Association Bulletin* 27: 108–11.

———. 1992. "Modulation in Arab Music: Documenting Oral Concepts, Performance rules and Strategies." *Ethnomusicology* 36 (2): 171–95.

———. 1989. "Arab Music Theory in the Modern Period." Ph.D. dissertation, University of California at Los Angeles.

Mason, Robert Scott. 1988. "The Society and its Environment." In *Syria: A Country Study,* ed. Thomas Collelo, pp. 49–105. Washington, D.C.: Federal Research Division, Library of Congress.

Mauss, Marcel. 1979 [1936]. "Body Techniques." In *Sociology and Psychology: Essays,* ed. and trans. B. Brewster. London: Routledge and Kegan Paul.

Mbembe, Achille. 2001. *On the Postcolony.* Berkeley: University of California Press.

———. 1992. "The Banality of Power and the Aesthetics of Vulgarity in the Postcolony." *Public Culture* 4 (2): 1–30.

McGowan, Afaf Sabeh. 1988. "Historical Setting." In *Syria: A Country Study,* ed. Thomas Collelo, pp. 3–48. Washington, D.C.: Federal Research Division, Library of Congress.

Menocal, María Rosa. 2002. *Ornament of the World: How Muslims, Jews, and Christians Created a Culture of Tolerance in Medieval Spain.* Boston and New York: Back Bay Books.

Meintjes, Louise. 2003. *Sounds of Africa! Making Music Zulu in a South African Studio.* Durham, N.C.: Duke University Press.

Meriwether, Margaret L. 1999. *The Kin Who Count: Family and Society in Ottoman Aleppo, 1770–1840.* Austin: University of Texas Press.

Merleau-Ponty, Maurice. 1962. *Phenomenology of Perception.* Colin Smith, trans. London: Routledge.

Mitchell, Timothy. 2003. *Rule of Experts: Egypt, Techno-Politics, Modernity.* Berkeley: University of California Press.

———. 2000. "Introduction." In *Questions of Modernity,* ed. Timothy Mitchell, pp. xi–xxvii. Minneapolis: University of Minnesota Press.

———. 1991 [1988]. *Colonising Egypt.* Berkeley: University of California Press.

Mitchell, Timothy J. 1994. *Flamenco Deep Song.* New Haven: Yale University Press.

Monson, Ingrid. 1996. *Saying Something: Jazz Improvisation and Interaction.* Chicago: University of Chicago Press.

Moroccan Ministry for Cultural and Educational Affairs. 1969. *Kitāb al-mu'tamar al-thānī lil-mūsīqā al-'arabiyya* [The book of the second congress on Arab music]. Fez, Morocco: Moroccan Ministry for Cultural and Educational Affairs.

Murtaḍā al-Zabīdī, Muḥammad ibn Muḥammad [1732/1733–1791]. 1966. *Tāj al-'arūs min jawāhir al-qāmūs. al-Kuwait: Matba'at ḥukūmat al-kuwait.*

Naef, Silvia. 1996. *A la reserche d'une modernité arabe.* Geneva: Slatkine.

Nasr, Seyyed Hossein. 1972. *Sufi Essays.* London: G. Allen and Unwin.

Needham, Rodney. 1975. "Polythetic Classification: Convergence and Consequences." *Man* 10: 349–69.
Nelson, Kristina. 1985. *The Art of Reciting the Qur'an*. Austin: University of Texas Press.
Nettl, Bruno. 1998. "Introduction: An Art Neglected in Scholarship." In *In the Course of Performance: Studies in the World of Musical Improvisation*, ed. Bruno Nettl, with Melinda Russell, pp. 1–23. Chicago: University of Chicago Press.
Netton, Ian Richard. 1992. *Al-Farabi and His School*. London and New York: Routledge.
Nwiya, Paul. 1972. *Ibn ʿataʾ allah et la naissance de la confrérie shadilite*. Beirut: Dar el-Machreq.
O'Connell, John. 1997. "Alaturka Revisited: Style as History in Turkish Vocal Performance." Ph.D. dissertation, University of California at Los Angeles.
Oxford English-Arabic Dictionary of Current Usage, The. 1978. N. S. Doniach, ed. Oxford: Clarendon Press.
Pandolfo, Stephania. 1997. *Impasse of the Angels: Scenes from a Moroccan Space of Memory*. Chicago: University of Chicago Press.
Peristiany, John G. 1966. *Honour and Shame: The Values of Mediterranean Society*. Chicago: University of Chicago Press.
Pickthall, Muḥammad Marmaduke. 1981. *The Meaning of the Glorious Qur'an*. New York: Penguin.
Pinto, Paulo. 2002. "Mystical Bodies: Ritual, Experience and the Embodiment of Sufism in Syria." Ph.D. dissertation, Boston University.
Piot, Charles. 1999. *Remotely Global: Village Modernity in West Africa*. Chicago: University of Chicago Press.
Plastino, Goffredo, ed. 2003. *Mediterranean Mosaic: Popular Music and Global Sounds*. New York: Routledge.
Poché, Christian. 1984. "*Qanun*." In *Grove Dictionary of Musical Instruments*, vol. 3. p. 169–71.
Qabbānī, Nizār. 1992. *Lā Ghāliba ilā Allāh* [There is no victor save God]. Beirut: Nizar Qabbani Publications.
Qalʿajī, ʿAbd al-Fattāḥ Rawwās. 1988. *Min shiʿr amīn al-jundī* [From the poetry of Amīn al-Jundī]. Damascus: Syrian Ministry of Culture.
al-Qalʿah, Saad Allah Agha. 1997a. "*Ayy taṭawwur aw ibdāʿ lāhiq yajibu an yakuna murtabintan bi-judhūrihi*" [Any forthcoming development must be linked to its roots]. Interview by ʿAli al-Ahmad, July 9, 1997. *al-Thawra al-thaqafiyya* [Damascus, Syria] 77: 4.
———. 1997b. *Nahj al-aghānī* [The course of songs]. Television. Damascus: al-ʿAwj. 13 episodes.
Qaṣṣāb Ḥasan, Najat. 1988. *Ḥadīth dimashqī 1884–1973* [Damascene tales 1884–1973]. Damascus: Alif Baʾ al-Adib.
Qureshi, Regula Burkhardt. 1995. *Sufi Music of India and Pakistan: Sounds, Context and Meaning in Qawwali*. Chicago: University of Chicago Press.
Rabinow, Paul. 1989. *French Modern: Norms and Forms of the Social Environment*. Cambridge, Mass.: MIT Press.

Racy, ʿAli Jihad. 2003. *Making Music in the Arab World: The Culture and Artistry of Ṭarab.* New York: Cambridge University Press.
———. 1998. "Improvisation, Ecstasy, and Performance Dynamics in Arabic Music." In *In the Course of Performance: Studies in the World of Musical Improvisation,* ed. Bruno Nettl, with Melinda Russell, pp. 95–112. Chicago: University of Chicago Press.
———. 1991. "Creativity and Ambience: An Ecstatic Feedback Model from Arab Music." *The World of Music* 33 (3): 7–28.
———. 1986. "Words and Music in Beirut: A Study of Attitudes." *Ethnomusicology* 30 (3): 391–496.
———. 1983. "The *Waslah:* A Compound-Form Principle in Egyptian Music." *Arab Studies Quarterly* 5 (4): 396–403.
———. 1977. "Musical Change and Commercial Recording in Egypt, 1904–1932." Ph.D. dissertation, University of Illinois.
Rajā,ʾī, Fuʾād, and Nadīm al-Darwīsh. 1956. *Min kunūzinā* [From our treasures]. Aleppo.
Rasmussen, Anne K. 1996. "Theory and Practice at the 'Arabic org': Digital Technology in Contemporary Arab Music Performance." *Popular Music* 15 (3): 345–65.
Reddy, William. 2001. *The Navigation of Feeling: A Framework for the History of Emotions.* New York: Cambridge University Press.
Reynolds, Dwight F. 1995. *Heroic Poets and Poetic Heroes: The Ethnography of Performance in an Arabic Oral Epic Tradition.* Ithaca: Cornell University Press.
Rice, Timothy. 1993. *May It Fill Your Soul: Experiencing Bulgarian Music.* Chicago: University of Chicago Press.
Ricoeur, Paul. 1984. *Time and Narrative.* Chicago: University of Chicago Press.
Rodney, Walter. 1972. *How Europe Underdeveloped Africa.* London: Bogle-L'Ouverture Publications.
Rofel, Lisa. 1999. *Other Modernities: Gendered Yearnings in China after Socialism.* Berkeley: University of California Press.
Romero, Raúl R. 2001. *Debating the Past: Music, Memory, and Identity in the Andes.* New York: Oxford University Press.
Rugh, Andrea B. 1997. *Within the Circle: Parents and Children in an Arab Village.* New York: Columbia University Press.
Russell, Alex. 1756. *The Natural History of Aleppo and Parts Adjacent. Containing a Description of the City, and the Principle Natural Productions in Its Neighborhoods; Together with an Account of the Climate, Inhabitants, and Diseases; Particularly the PLAGUE, with the Methods Used by the Europeans for Their Preservation.* London: A. Miller.
Saadé, Gabriel. 1993. "L'Histoire de la musique arabe." *Bulletin d'etudes orientales* 45: 201–20.
Sabbāgh, Tawfiq. 1950. *al-Dalīl al-mūsīqī al-ʿamm fi atrab al-angham* [The general musical guide to the most pleasing modes]. Aleppo: Matbaʿat al-Ihsan.
Said, Edward. 1994. *Culture and Imperialism.* New York: Vintage.
———. 1978. *Orientalism.* New York: Pantheon.
Salamandra, Christa. 2004. *A New Old Damascus: Authenticity and Distinction in Urban Syria.* Urbana: Indiana University Press.

——. 2000. "Consuming Damascus." In *Mass Mediations: New Approaches to Popular Culture in the Middle East and Beyond,* ed. Walter Armbrust, pp. 182–202. Berkeley: University of California Press.
——. 1998. "Moustache Hairs Lost: Ramadan Television Serials and the Construction of Identity in Damascus, Syria." *Visual Anthropology* 10: 227–46.
Sawa, George Dmitri. 2004. "Baghdadi Rhythmic Theories and Practices in 12th-century Andalusia." In *Music and Medieval Manuscripts: Paleography and Performance. Essays dedicated to Andrew Hughes,* ed. J. Haines and R. Rosenfeld. Burlington, Vt.: Ashgate.
——. 2001. "Theories of Rhythm and Meter in the Medieval Middle East." In *The Garland Encyclopedia of World Music,* vol. 6: *The Middle East,* ed. Virginia Danielson, Scott Marcus, and Dwight Reynolds, pp. 387–94. New York and London: Garland.
——. 1989. *Music Performance Practice in the Early ʿAbbasid Era 132–320 AH/750–932 AD.* Toronto: Pontifical Institute of Medieval Studies.
Schade-Poulsen, Marc. 1999. *Men and Popular Music in Algeria: The Social Significance of Raï.* Austin: University of Texas Press.
Schechner, Richard. 1985. *Performance Theory.* New York: Routledge.
Schimmel, Annemarie. 1994. *Deciphering the Signs of God: A Phenomenological Approach to Islam.* Albany: State University of New York Press.
——. 1975. *The Mystical Dimensions of Islam.* Chapel Hill: University of North Carolina Press.
Schutz, Alfred. 1977 [1951]. "Making Music Together: A Study in Social Relationship." In *Symbolic Anthropology,* ed. J. Dolgin, pp. 106–19. New York: Columbia University Press.
Schuyler, Philip. 1990/1991. "Music and Tradition in Yemen." *Asian Music* 22 (1): 51–72
Seale, Patrick. 1986 [1965]. *The Struggle for Syria: A Study of Post-War Arab Politics 1945–1958.* New Haven and London: Yale University Press.
Shaaban, Buthaina. 1988. *Both Right and Left Handed: Arab Women Talk about Their Lives.* London: The Women's Press
Shannon, Jonathan H. 2003a. "Intersubjectivity, Temporal Change, and Emotional Experience in Arab Music: Reflections on *Tarab.*" *Cultural Anthropology* 18 (1): 72–98.
——. 2003b. "Sultans of Spin: Syrian Sacred Music on the World Stage." *American Anthropologist* 105 (3): 266–77.
——. 2003c. "*al-Muwashshahāt* and *al-Qudūd al-Halabiyya:* Two Genres in the Aleppine *Wasla.*" *MESA Bulletin* 37 (1): 82–101.
al-Sharīf, Ṣamīm. 1991. *al-Mūsīqā fī sūriyya aʿlam wa tarīkh* [Music in Syria: history and masters]. Damascus: Syrian Ministry of Culture.
Shiloah, Amnon. 1995. *Music in the World of Islam, a Socio-Cultural Study.* Detroit: Wayne State University Press.
——. 1979. *The Theory of Music in Arabic Writings (Ca 900 to Ca 1900).* Munich: RISM.
Shorter Encyclopedia of Islam (SEI). 1995 [1953]. H. A. R. Gibb and J. H. Kramers, eds. Leiden: Brill.

Silverstein, Michael. 1976. "Shifters, Linguistic Categories, and Cultural Description." In *Meaning in Anthropology,* ed. K. Basso and H. Selby, pp. 11–55. Albuquerque: University of New Mexico Press.

Sirees, Nihad. 1996. *al-Kūmīdiyyā al-fallāḥiyya* [The peasant comedy]. Aleppo.

Small, Christopher. 1998. *Musicking: The Meanings of Performing and Listening.* Middletown, Conn.: Wesleyan University Press.

Smith, Jane I., and Yvonne Y. Haddad. 1981. *Death and Time in Islam.* Albany: State University of New York Press.

Smith, Jonathan Z. 1982. *Imagining Religion: From Babylon to Jonestown.* Chicago: University of Chicago Press.

Spitulnik, Debra. 2002. "Accessing 'Local' Modernities: Reflections on the Place of Linguistic Evidence in Ethnography." In *Critically Modern: Alternatives, Alterities, Anthropologies,* ed. Bruce M. Knauft, pp. 194–219. Bloomington and Indianapolis: Indiana University Press.

Stallybrass, Peter, and Allon White. 1986. *The Politics and Poetics of Transgression.* Ithaca: Cornell University Press.

Sterne, Jonathan. 2003. *The Audible Past: Cultural Origins of Sound Reproduction.* Durham, N.C: Duke University Press.

Stocking, George W. 1987. *Victorian Anthropology.* New York: Free Press.

Stokes, Martin, ed. 1994. *Ethnicity, Identity and Music: The Musical Construction of Place.* Oxford: Berg.

———. 1992. *The Arabesk Debate: Music and Musicians in Modern Turkey.* New York: Oxford University Press.

Stoller, Paul. 1997. *Sensuous Scholarship.* Philadelphia: University of Pennsylvania Press.

Ṭarābīshī, George. 1991. *al-Muthaqqafūn al-ʿarab wa al-turāth* [Arab intellectuals and their heritage]. London: Riad Rayyes Books.

Taylor, Charles. 1999. "Two Theories of Modernity." *Public Culture* 11 (1): 153–74.

———. 1989. *Sources of the Self: The Making of Modern Identity.* Cambridge, Mass.: Harvard University Press.

Thompson, Elizabeth. 2000. *Colonial Citizens: Republican Rights, Paternal Privilege, and Gender in French Syria and Lebanon.* New York: Columbia University Press.

Thompson, Emily. 2002. *The Soundscape of Modernity: Architectural Acoustics and the Culture of Listening in America, 1900–1933.* Cambridge, Mass.: MIT Press.

Touma, Hassan Habib. 1996. *The Music of the Arabs.* Laurie Schwartz, trans. Portland: Amadeus Press.

Trilling, Lionel. 1972. *Sincerity and Authenticity.* Cambridge, Mass.: Harvard University Press.

Turino, Thomas. 1990. "Structure, Context, and Strategy in Musical Ethnography." *Ethnomusicology* 34 (3): 399–412.

Turjumān, Sihām. 1998 [1990]. *Yā māl al-shām* [O the wealth of Damascus]. Damascus: Alif-Baʾ al-Adib. [trans. 1994, Andrea Rugh, as *Daughter of Damascus: Taken from Ya Mal al-Sham.* Austin: University of Texas Press].

Turner, Victor. 1987. "Carnival, Ritual, and Play in Rio de Janeiro." In *Time Out of Time: Essays on the Festival,* ed. Alessandro Falassi, pp. 74–92. Albuquerque: University of New Mexico Press.

———. 1975. "Ritual as Communication and Potency: an Ndembu Case Study." In *Symbols and Society: Essays on Belief Systems in Action,* ed. Carole E. Hill, pp. 58–81. Athens: University of Georgia Press.

———. 1974. *Drama, Fields, and Metaphors.* Ithaca: Cornell University Press.

———. 1968. *The Drums of Affliction.* Oxford: Oxford University Press.

United National Development Program (UNDP). 2002. *Arab Human Development Report* 2002. New York: United Nations Publications.

Van Dam, Nikolaos. 1996. *The Struggle for Power in Syria: Politics and Society under Asad and the Baʿth Party.* London and New York: I. B. Tauris.

Van Nieuwkerk, Karin. 1995. *"A Trade Like Any Other:" Female Singers and Dancers in Egypt.* Austin: University of Texas Press.

Viswanathan, Gauri. 1989. *Masks of Conquest: Literary Study and British Rule in India.* New York: Columbia University Press.

Wallerstein, Immanuel, ed. 1975. *World Inequality: Origins and Perspectives on the World System.* Montréal: Black Rose Books.

Washabaugh, William. 1996. *Flamenco: Passion, Politics, and Popular Culture.* New York: Berg.

Watenpaugh, Keith. 1999. "Bourgeois Modernity, Historical Memory, and Imperialism: The Emergence of an Urban Middle Class in the Late Ottoman and Inter-War Middle East, Aleppo, 1908–1939." Ph.D. dissertation, University of California at Los Angeles.

Waugh, Earl H. 1989. *The Munshidiin of Egypt: Their World and Their Song.* Columbia: University of South Carolina Press.

Wedeen, Lisa. 1999. *Ambiguities of Domination: Politics, Rhetoric, and Symbols in Contemporary Syria.* Chicago: University of Chicago Press.

———. 1998. "Acting 'As If': Symbolic Politics and Social Control in Syria." *Case Studies in Society and History* 40 (3): 503–23.

Wehr, Hans. 1994. *Arabic-English Dictionary.* J. M. Cowan, ed. Ithaca, N.Y.: Spoken Language Services.

Williams, Raymond. 1977. *Marxism and Literature.* New York: Oxford University Press.

———. 1973. *The Country and the City.* New York: Oxford University Press.

Winegar, Jessica. 2003. *Claiming Egypt: The Cultural Politics of Artistic Practice in a Postcolonial Society.* Ph.D. dissertation, New York University.

Wirdī, Mīkhāʾīl Khalīl Allāh. 1948. *Falsafat al-mūsīqā al-sharqiyya* [The philosophy of Oriental music]. Damascus: Ibn Zaydun.

Wittgenstein, Ludwig. 1953. *Philosophical Investigations.* Oxford: Oxford University Press.

Wolf, Eric R. 1982. *Europe and the Peoples without History.* Berkeley and Los Angeles: University of California Press.

Yapp, Malcolm. 1987. *The Making of the Modern Near East, 1792–1923.* New York: Longman.

Zenlund, Darrow. 1991. "Post-Colonial Aleppo, Syria: Struggles in Representation and Identity." Ph.D. dissertation, University of Texas at Austin.

Zuckerkandl, Victor. 1956. *Sound and Symbol: Music and the External World.* Princeton: Princeton University Press.

Zuhur, Sherifa. 2001. *Colors of Enchantment: Theater, Music, Dance and the Visual Arts of the Middle East.* Cairo: American University Press.

Discography

Dalāl, Muḥammad Qadrī. 2002. *Unwonted [sic] maqāmāt.* INEDITW 260105.

Ensemble al-Kindi. 2003. *Aleppian Sufi Trance.* With Sheikh Habboush. Le Chant du Monde CMT 5741251.52.

———. 2001. *The Crusades Seen Through the Eyes of the Orient.* With Omar Sarmini. Le Chant du Monde CMT 574 1118.

———. 1999. *The Whirling Dervishes of Damascus.* With Sheikh Hamza Shakkur. Le Chant du Monde CMT 574 1123.24.

———. 1998. *The Aleppian Music Room.* With Sabri Moudallal and Omar Sarmini. Le Chant du Monde CML 574 1108.09.

Sabri Moudallal Ensemble. 1993. *Chants Sacrés et Profanes de Syrie.* Blue Silver 303

———. 1988. *Wasla d'Alep.* Maison des Cultures du Monde W 260007.

Shuqair, Samih. 1998. *Zamani.* Damascus, Syria. Rec. 1998.

Sufi Chanting from Syria: Dhikr Qadiri Khalwati of the Zawiya Hilaliya, Aleppo. 2002. INEDITW 260109.

Syrie: Muezzins d'*Alep/Chants Religieux de l'Islam.* 1992. Ocora/Radio France C 580038.

al-Turath Ensemble. 1994. *The Music of Spanish al-Andalus.* Almaviva DS-0123.

Selected Arabic Newspapers, Magazines, and Journals

al-Ayyām (Damascus). 1931–1935.

al-Baʿth (Damascus). 1996–1998.

al-Funūn (Damascus). 1996–1998.

al-Ḥayāt (London). 1996–2000.

al-Ḥayāt al-mūsīqiyya (Damascus). 1993–1998.

al-Madā (Damascus). 1993–1998.

Majallat al-idhāʿa al-sūriyya (Damascus). 1953–1967.

al-Tāj (Aleppo). 1928.

al-Thaqāfa (Damascus). 1933–1934.

al-Thaqāfa al-mūsīqiyya (Damascus). 1935.

al-Thawra (Damascus). 1996–1998.

al-Thawra al-thaqāfiyya (Damascus). 1996–1998.

Tishrīn (Damascus). 1996–1998.

INDEX

'Abd al-Wahhāb, Muḥammad, 14, 27–28, 303–32, 42, 47–48, 50, 93, 95, 101–102, 158, 182
Abu-Lughod, Lila, 205n11, 22 n11
adhān, 188–191, 227. *See also* call to prayer
Adonis ('Alī Aḥmad Sa'īd), xv, 54, 59, 61, 77, 80, 198, 211–212n21
Adorno, Theodor, 15, 53, 54, 186, 198
Aesthetics, xvi, xix, xxii, xxiii; and authenticity, 6, 25; and emotion, 9; and modernity xvi; and music, 53, 156; and politics, 15. *See also* Adorno; Kant
alternative modernities. *See* modernity, alternative
Andalusian music, 144, 162, 203n10, 214n16
Arab music: genres, xxi, 29, 36, 101, 145, 149, 221n27, 224n20; instruments, 36, 40, 132; origins of, 92–104; pedagogy, 24, 44, 45, 103, 148; performance contexts, 35–36, 42, 87, 119, 140–142, 163, 166 (see also *sahra*); theory of, 72–73, 83
Aristotle, 127
Arkoun, Mohammed, 212n12
Armstrong, Robert Plant, xxiii, 194
art world, 26, 194. *See also* Danto, Arthur C.
Asad, Talal, 64, 119, 121, 219n51
aṣāla. *See* authenticity
Asmahān, 48, 93, 95
al-Aṭrash, Farīd, 93
authenticity (*aṣāla*), xviii, 6–7, 17, 20, 24–26, 54, 57–58, 66, 82, 84, 87–92, 140, 144, 186, 192–195, 198, 203n5, 227; and aesthetics, xvi, 6, 25; and innovation 174, 175, 193, 223n6; and music, 12, 24, 203n5
al-'Aẓm, Ṣādiq Jalāl, 81, 195, 198–199

Bakhtin, Mikhail M., 98, 212n4
Barthes, Roland, 179, 224n3
al-Baṭsh, 'Umar, 8, 29, 32, 37, 99
Bell, Catherine, 199, 121
Bonnefoy, Yves, 180

Congress on Arab Music, 28, 70–71, 147, 210n7
Chatterjee, Partha, 10, 67
Christianity, and music in Syria, 37–38, 95–96, 100, 153
class, and music 35, 40, 91
colonialism, 34, 84–85, 211n15. *See also* French mandate; Ottoman Empire
Crapanzano, Vincent, 206n19, 206n21, 218n42, 218n49, 223n16, 224n25

Dalāl, Muḥammad Qadrī, 30, 38, 45, 108–109; on *ṭarab* 164–170, 184–185
Danielson, Virginia, xviii, 154, 171–172, 204n11
Danto, Arthur C., 26, 194. *See also* art world

modernity, xix, 55, 63, 67, 210n1, 211n12; and colonialism, 204n5; crisis of, xv–xvi; emotion and, 198; improvising, 66–67; shock of, 58–61, 78, 210n8
musical modes (*maqāmāt*), 71–73, 94, 144–145, 151, 228
Moudallal, Ṣabri, 29, 153, 167, 188–191
Moudarres, Fateh, 22–24, 86, 90, 188, 199–201
music and emotion. *See* emotion and music
musical expression, 150–151, 182–186. *See also* emotion and music
muwashshaḥ, 28–29, 32, 36, 101, 117–118, 132–134, 136, 149, 164, 207n11, 208n20, 229. *See also* Arab music, genres

nahḍa (Arab Renaissance), 58–60, 78, 210n9
nationalism, and music, 16, 150
Needham, Rodney, 68
North Africa, music of, xxii, 39, 94, 144, 205n14

Oriental spirit (*rūḥ sharqiyya*), xix, 6, 9, 21, 85, 140, 147, 156–157, 186, 192–194, 198, 229
Ottoman empire, 32–34, 36, 55, 58, 65, 84; and influences on Arab music, 36–37, 94, 102

Palestine, xvi, 76
popular music, xviii, 14–15, 39, 48, 101

al-Qabbānī, Abu Khalil, 139, 207n13
qaṣīda, 101, 118, 136, 144, 149, 165, 175, 229. *See also* Arab music, genres
al-Qal'ah, Saad Allah, 30, 93–94, 102–103, 184–185
qudūd ḥalabiyya, 34, 36, 101, 149, 150, 208n17, 208n20, 229. *See also* Arab music, genres

Racy, Ali Jihad, xviii, 30, 140, 146, 151, 160–162, 167, 169–170, 203n6, 207n9, 219n6
rai. *See* North Africa, music of
religion and music, 37–38, 95–96, 100, 102, 153, 188–191. See also *inshād; adhān;* Islam and music; Christian music
rhythm, 220n19. *See also* Arab music
rūḥ sharqiyya. *See* Oriental spirit
Rūmi, Jalāl al-Dīn, 4, 107. See also, *mawlawiyya* rite; Sufism

al-Ṣabbāgh, Tawfiq, 74–76
sahra, 35–36, 87, 119, 140–142, 163, 166, 229. *See also,* Arab music, performance contexts
Said, Edward, xvi, 62
salṭana, 136, 138, 162, 165–167, 173, 219n6. *See also* emotion and music
samā', 44, 112–113, 148, 229. See also *dhikr;* Sufism
sammī'a, 30–32, 132, 147, 163–166, 169, 174, 179, 229
self and personhood. See *ṭarab,* and presentation of self
ṣidq. *See* emotional sincerity
Sufism, 5, 29, 37, 44, 106, 113–115, 123, 178, 209n30, 214n16, 214n17
Sukkar, 'Abd al-Fattāḥ, 155

taqsīm, 177–178, 229. *See also* improvisation
ṭarab, xix, 6, 9, 20, 27, 204n2, 207n9, 223n6, 229; and authenticity, 170, *passim;* and mass media, 171; and presentation of self, 169–174; techniques of, 177–178; and temporality, 176–181. *See also* emotion and music
Ṭarābishi, George, 60–61
tarqiyya, 117, 127, 145, 216n30, 229
temporality. See under *ṭarab*
Trilling, Lionel, 221–222n28
turāth. *See* heritage
Turner, Victor, 218n47

Umm Kulthūm, xviii, 8, 14, 27–28, 30, 101–102; religious training of, 42; and musical authenticity, 48–49, 95, 156–158; and *ṭarab* 162, 171–172, 185
UNESCO, 89, 208n19, 209n25

voice (*ṣawt*), 20, 45, 146, 151–152, 157, 194, 229

waṣla, 36, 100–101, 138, 141, 144–145, 230. *See also* Arab music, genres
Wedeen, Lisa, 204n14
Westernization and music, 74–76
Williams, Raymond, 12, 92
Wittgenstein, Ludwig, 18, 68
world music, 203n8, 205n14, 205n15, 213n15

youth culture, xxii, 131, 146

al-Zakī, ʿĀdil, 158–160, 185
Zuckerkandl, Victor, 178, 224n22

MUSIC/CULTURE

A series from Wesleyan University Press

Edited by Harris M. Berger and Annie J. Randall

Originating editors, George Lipsitz, Susan McClary, and Robert Walser

Listening to Salsa:
Gender, Latin Popular Music, and Puerto Rican Cultures
by Frances Aparicio

Jazz Consciousness:
Music, Race, and Humanity
by Paul Austerlitz

Metal, Rock, and Jazz:
Perception and the Phenomenology of Musical Experience
by Harris M. Berger

Identity and Everyday Life:
Essays in the Study of Folklore, Music, and Popular Culture
by Harris M. Berger and Giovanna P. Del Negro

Bright Balkan Morning:
Romani Lives and the Power of Music in Greek Macedonia
by Dick Blau and Charles and Angeliki Keil

Musical Childhoods and the Cultures of Youth
edited by Susan Boynton and Roe-Min Kok

Music and Cinema
edited by James Buhler, Caryl Flinn, and David Neumeyer

My Music
by Susan D. Crafts, Daniel Cavicchi, Charles Keil, and the Music in Daily Life Project

Born in the USA:
Bruce Springsteen and the American Tradition
by Jim Cullen

Presence and Pleasure:
The Funk Grooves of James Brown and Parliament
by Anne Danielsen

Echo and Reverb:
Fabricating Space in Popular Music 1900–1960
by Peter Doyle

Recollecting from the Past:
Musical Practice and Spirit Possession on the East Coast of Madagascar
by Ron Emoff

Locating East Asia in Western Art Music
edited by Yayoi Uno Everett and Frederick Lau

Black Rhythms of Peru:
Reviving African Musical Heritage in the Black Pacific
by Heidi Feldman

"You Better Work!":
Underground Dance Music in New York City
by Kai Fikentscher

The Hidden Musicians
Music-Making in an English Town
by Ruth Finnegan

The Other Side of Nowhere:
Jazz, Improvisation, and Communities in Dialogue
edited by Daniel Fischlin and Ajay Heble

Empire of Dirt:
The Aesthetics and Rituals of British "Indie" Music
by Wendy Fonarow

The 'Hood Comes First:
Race, Space, and Place in Rap and Hip-Hop
by Murray Forman

Wired for Sound:
Engineering and Technologies in Sonic Cultures
edited by Paul D. Greene and Thomas Porcello

Sensational Knowledge:
Embodying Culture Through Japanese Dance
by Tomie Hahn

Voices in Bali:
Energies and Perceptions in Vocal Music and Dance Theater
by Edward Herbst

Traveling Spirit Masters:
Moroccan Gnawa Trance and Music in the Global Marketplace
by Deborah Kapchan

Symphonic Metamorphoses:
Subjectivity and Alienation in Mahler's Re-Cycled Songs
by Raymond Knapp

Music and Technoculture
edited by René T. A. Lysloff and Leslie C. Gay, Jr.

A Thousand Honey Creeks Later:
My Life in Music from Basie to Motown—and Beyond
by Preston Love

Songs, Dreamings, and Ghosts:
The Wangga of North Australia
by Allan Marett

Phat Beats, Dope Rhymes:
Hip Hop Down Under Comin' Upper
by Ian Maxwell

Some Liked it Hot:
Jazz Women in Film and Television, 1928–1959
by Kristin A. McGee

Carriacou String Band Serenade:
Performing Identity in the Eastern Caribbean
by Rebecca S. Miller

Global Noise:
Rap and Hip-Hop outside the USA
edited by Tony Mitchell

Popular Music in Theory:
An Introduction
by Keith Negus

Upside Your Head!
Rhythm and Blues on
Central Avenue
by Johnny Otis

Coming to You Wherever You Are:
MuchMusic, MTV, and Youth Identities
by Kip Pegley

Singing Archaeology:
Philip Glass's Akhnaten
by John Richardson

Black Noise:
Rap Music and Black Culture
in Contemporary America
by Tricia Rose

The Book of Music and Nature:
An Anthology of Sounds, Words,
Thoughts
edited by David Rothenberg
and Marta Ulvaeus

Angora Matta:
Fatal Acts of North-South Translation
by Marta Elena Savigliano

Making Beats:
The Art of Sample-Based Hip-Hop
by Joseph G. Schloss

Dissonant Identities:
The Rock 'n' Roll Scene in Austin, Texas
by Barry Shank

Among the Jasmine Trees:
Music and Modernity in
Contemporary Syria
by Jonathan Holt Shannon

Banda:
Mexican Musical Life across Borders
by Helena Simonett

Global Soundtracks:
Worlds of Film Music
edited by Mark Slobin

Subcultural Sounds:
Micromusics of the West
by Mark Slobin

Music, Society, Education
by Christopher Small

Musicking:
The Meanings of Performing
and Listening
by Christopher Small

Music of the Common Tongue:
Survival and Celebration in
African American Music
by Christopher Small

Singing Our Way to Victory:
French Cultural Politics and Music
During the Great War
by Regina M. Sweeney

Setting the Record Straight:
A Material History of
Classical Recording
by Colin Symes

False Prophet:
Fieldnotes from the Punk Underground
by Steven Taylor

Any Sound You Can Imagine:
Making Music/Consuming Technology
by Paul Théberge

Club Cultures:
Music, Media, and Subcultural Capital
by Sarah Thornton

Dub:
Songscape and Shattered Songs in Jamaican Reggae
by Michael E. Veal

Running with the Devil:
Power, Gender, and Madness in Heavy Metal Music
by Robert Walser

Manufacturing the Muse:
Estey Organs and Consumer Culture in Victorian America
by Dennis Waring

The City of Musical Memory:
Salsa, Record Grooves, and Popular Culture in Cali, Colombia
by Lise A. Waxer